Greek Settlements in the Eastern Mediterranean and the Black Sea

Edited by

G. R. Tsetskhladze
A. M. Snodgrass

BAR International Series 1062
2002

Published in 2016 by
BAR Publishing, Oxford

BAR International Series 1062

Greek Settlements in the Eastern Mediterranean and the Black Sea

ISBN 978 1 84171 442 4

© The editors and contributors severally and the Publisher 2002

The authors' moral rights under the 1988 UK Copyright,
Designs and Patents Act are hereby expressly asserted.

All rights reserved. No part of this work may be copied, reproduced, stored,
sold, distributed, scanned, saved in any form of digital format or transmitted
in any form digitally, without the written permission of the Publisher.

BAR Publishing is the trading name of British Archaeological Reports (Oxford) Ltd.
British Archaeological Reports was first incorporated in 1974 to publish the BAR
Series, International and British. In 1992 Hadrian Books Ltd became part of the BAR
group. This volume was originally published by Archaeopress in conjunction with
British Archaeological Reports (Oxford) Ltd / Hadrian Books Ltd, the Series principal
publisher, in 2002. This present volume is published by BAR Publishing, 2016.

Printed in England

BAR titles are available from:

BAR Publishing
122 Banbury Rd, Oxford, OX2 7BP, UK
EMAIL info@barpublishing.com
PHONE +44 (0)1865 310431
FAX   +44 (0)1865 316916
       www.barpublishing.com

Contents

Preface..iii
G.R. Tsetskhladze (London) and A.M. Snodgrass (Cambridge)

Greeks and Syria: Pots and People..1
John Boardman (Oxford)

**Greek Contact with the Levant and Mesopotamia in the First Half of the
First Millennium BC: A View from the East**..17
Amélie Kuhrt (London)

**The *Poleis* of the Southern Anatolian Coast (Lycia, Pamphylia, Pesidia) and their Civic
Identity: the "Interface" between the Hellenic and the Barbarian *Polis***...................................27
Antony G. Keen (East Grinstead, UK)

**Herodotus on the Black Sea Coastline and Greek Settlements:
Some Modern Misconceptions**..41
John Hind (Leeds)

**The Shape of the New Commonwealth: Aspects of the Pontic and Eastern
Mediterranean Regions in the Hellenistic Age**...49
Zofia Halina Archibald (Liverpool)

**The Myths of Panticapaeum: Construction of Colonial Origins in the
Black Sea Region**..73
David Braund (Exeter)

Ionians Abroad...81
Gocha R. Tsetskhladze (London)

Archaische attische Keramik in Ionien..97
Yasemin Tuna-Nörling (Heidelberg)

Preface

This volume publishes revised versions of papers originally given at a joint seminar of the Faculty of Classics, University of Cambridge and the Department of Classics, Royal Holloway and Bedford New College, University of London, held in Cambridge in the autumn of 1996. The main aim of the seminar was to give as clear a picture as possible of the Greeks settled in the Eastern Mediterranean and the Pontus. It is a matter of regret that the paper given by A.J. Graham on the colonisation of Samothrace is not included here. The author felt that his conclusions were too provisional to warrant it, and that the preparation of a definitive version would require a long gestation period. We have included a paper by Yasemin Tuna-Nörling which was not delivered during the seminar. It suits our theme very well and extends the picture of the Eastern Mediterranean.

The papers presented here focus on Greek colonisation and on the manifold aspects of Graeco-native relations - cultural, political, economic, etc. - not simply from a Hellenic point of view but also from that of the locals. Some authors concentrate on literary or archaeological evidence; others seek to combine them in various ways. It would be redundant to summarise the papers. Their titles indicate clearly what they are about, and all are written by well-known specialists, who 'need no introduction'.

Since the seminar took place, the subject of the Greek presence in the areas under discussion has witnessed a considerable burgeoning of scholarly interest. Several important and interesting volumes have appeared (AWE; Antonetti 1997; Archibald *et al.* 2001, 245-70; Boardman 1999, 267-82; Boardman, Solovyov and Tsetskhladze 2001; Bouzek 1997; Brock and Hodkinson 2000, 365-402; Brunet 1999, 245-356; Gorman 2001; Graham 2001, 365-402; Greek Archaeology 2002; Karageorghis and Stampolidis 1998; Krinzinger 2000; Lordkipanidzé and Lévêque 1999a; 1999b; Nawotka 1997; Oliver *et al.* 2000, 25-74, 133-50; Podossinov 1999; Tsetskhladze 1998; 1999; 2001; Tsetskhladze and de Boer 2000-01; etc.), as have many articles. One fact should be emphasised, that whereas these two regions, the Eastern Mediterranean and the Black Sea, had in the past been studied largely in isolation from each other, now there is increased dialogue between scholars. This has been demonstrated by the large attendance of Black Sea specialists at the international conference 'Early Ionia: the State of Research' (Güzelçamli, Turkey, Sept.-Oct. 1999), and by experts on the Eastern Mediterranean at the Taman Conference 'Greeks and Natives in the Cimmerian Bosporus, 7th-1st Centuries BC' (Oct. 2000).

We would like to thank, first of all, the authors for their contributions and patience. Without the generous financial and practical assistance of the Faculty of Classics of the University of Cambridge, the seminar would never have taken place. We are most grateful to those who attended and questioned and discussed the papers. Especial thanks go to Dr David Davison and his staff at Archaeopress.

G.R. Tsetskhladze and A.M. Snodgrass

Bibliography

AWE - *Ancient West & East* 1.1 (2002) (Leiden/Boston/Cologne; new periodical)

Antonetti, A. (ed.) 1997: *Il dinamismo della colonizzazione greca*, Naples.

Archibald, Z.H., Davies, J., Gabrielsen, V. and Oliver, G.J. (eds.) 2001: *Hellenistic Economies*, London/New York.

Boardman, J. 1999: *The Greeks Overseas. Their Early Colonies and Trade* (4th Edition), London.

Boardman, J., Solovyov, S.L. and Tsetskhladze, G.R. (eds.) 2001: *Northern Pontic Antiquities in the State Hermitage Museum*, Leiden/Boston/Cologne.

Bouzek, J. 1997: *Greece, Anatolia and Europe: Cultural Interrelations during the Early Iron Age*, Jonsered.

Brock, R. and S. Hodkinson (eds.) 2000: *Alternatives to Athens. Varieties of Political Organization and Community in Ancient Greece*, Oxford.

Brunet M. (ed.) 1999: *Territoires des cités grecques*, Paris.

Gorman, V. B. 2001: *Miletos, the Ornament of Ionia. A History of the City to 400 B.C.E.*, Ann Arbor.

Graham A.J. 2001: *Collected Papers on Greek Colonization*, Leiden/Boston/Cologne.

Greek Archaeology 2002: *Greek Archaeology without Frontiers*, Athens.

Karageorghis, V. and Stampolidis, N. (eds.) 1998: *Eastern Mediterranean: Cyprus-Dodecanese-Crete, 16th-6th cent. BC*, Athens.

Krinzinger, F. (ed.) 2000: *Die Ägäis und das westliche Mittelmeer. Beziehungen und Wechselwirkungen 8. bis 5. Jh. v. Chr.*, Vienna.

Lordkipanidzé, D. and Lévêque, P. (eds.) 1999a: *La mer Noire zone de contacts*, Paris.

Lordkipanidzé, D. and Lévêque, P. (eds.) 1999b: *Religions du Pont-Euxin*, Paris.

Nawotka, N. 1997: *The Western Pontic Cities. History and Political Organization*, Amsterdam.

Oliver, G.J., Brock, R., Cornell, T.J. and Hodkinson, S. (eds.) 2000: *The Sea in Antiquity*, BAR Int. Ser. 899, Oxford.

Podossinov, A.V. (ed.) 1999: *Northern Black Sea Littoral in Antiquity: Source Criticism*, Moscow (in Russian).

Tsetskhladze, G.R. (ed.) 1998: *The Greek Colonisation of the Black Sea Area. Historical Interpretation of Archaeology*, Stuttgart.

Tsetskhladze, G.R. (ed.) 1999: *Ancient Greeks West and East*, Leiden/Boston/Cologne.

Tsetskhladze, G.R. (ed.) 2001: *North Pontic Archaeology. Recent Discoveries and Studies*, Leiden/Boston/Cologne.

Tsetskhladze, G.R. and de Boer, J.G. (eds.) 2000-01: *The Black Sea Region in the Greek, Roman and Byzantine Periods* (*Talanta* XXXII-XXXIII), Amsterdam (2002).

Greeks and Syria: Pots and People

John Boardman

My initial subject is the relationship between Greeks and Syria from the reign of the Assyrian king Shalmaneser IV to that of Sennacherib, in what we believe to be the years between the early 8th and early 7th centuries BC. The evidence is partly textual - Assyrian documents and Greek historians - neither of them wholly reliable because they are so incomplete or remote, but at least the eastern texts are mainly contemporary. Other evidence is archaeological, and I do not mean simply what has been found in Syria since there are far broader archaeological and cultural considerations which are most relevant. It will lead into speculation about the interpretation of pottery of these years and later, about comparisons between Greek and eastern pottery use, about attitudes to Phoenicians, and eventually into reflections on the attitudes and motivation of those of us who deal with such subjects, since I believe that scholars are today no less subject to prejudice, even those properly inveighing against it, than at any time in the past.[1]

Greeks and Syria

This is a subject that is too easily dealt with piecemeal and has suffered no little pro- and anti-Greek prejudice. The physical evidence from excavation in Syria needs attention at the start. In the 1930s American archaeologists dug several sites in the Amq plain behind the lower Orontes valley. At what seems to have become later a provincial Assyrian capital, Tell Tainat, and at Çatal Hüyük and Judeideh, they found Greek pottery. Unfortunately it has never been published and it was only a few years ago that it became clear that the Greek pottery was found in quantity, hundreds of sherds, all mainly 8th-century.[2] We still do not know how these finds relate to the whole assemblages but they are impressive in such a concentration of important sites on or near the route inland. In 1936-7 Sir Leonard Woolley dug at the mouth of the Orontes, at Al Mina, which must be judged an entry port or stop-off for traffic up the Orontes. He too found much Greek pottery although again it has only become clear recently that it is also to be measured in hundreds.[3] It was prominent enough when first found for the orientalists to talk of Al Mina as a Greek colony. No classical archaeologist who has thought about it has been so incautious. Dunbabin, writing in the 1950s,[4] went no further than to say that in the alleged presence of Greek pottery *on its own* in the earliest levels "there is nothing to differentiate the place from one of the many Greek colonies in" the west. Study of the finds shows that he was doing no more than follow the report of the excavator, with whom he had corresponded, and the observation is not meaningless since it is not possible to identify any pre-Greek history at Al Mina, and the diagnostic pottery from the earliest levels can now be seen to include virtually nothing but Greek-related material. Calling Al Mina a typical Greek colony, in the same terms as the colonies in the west, along with its mis-identification, also first proposed by the excavators, with Posideion, which is at Bassit to the south, are by now long out of all serious discussion, though requiring closer inspection.[5] It should be easy to be objective. Although a classicist, I have long been convinced by the proposition that much of what is important in Greece from the 9th to the 6th century was the gift of the east. The question is whether it was a solicited gift or one thrust upon Greeks by easterners, and if either, by whom, when and why. Part of the problem comes from regarding the Aegean as a different cultural sphere from the Levant, as indeed it became in the 5th century, and as in some way a cultural district of Europe; better to regard Greece as the western extremity of the Levant in the years that concern us.

I start in the Bronze Age and at the other end of the Mediterranean, since we have to lay the ghost of the so-called Dark Ages, at least as a period of alleged non-communication. I have elsewhere commented on the way the pattern of eastern and Greek interest in the west in the Late Bronze Age seems closely mirrored by that of the 8th century.[6] In the Bronze Age there is a strong Cypriot interest in Sardinia, and a yet earlier strong Greek interest in south Italy and Sicily, also overlapping into Sardinia. In the 8th century comparable people are occupied in the same areas, but now it is Phoenicians in Sardinia, and mainly Euboean and Corinthian Greeks in south Italy and Sicily. Communications east-west were surely not interrupted in the

---

[1] I am indebted to the editors for allowing me to expand on the matter of my lecture in Cambridge into areas only sketched there, and to add the final section. This paper was written in 1998 and has been only modestly updated.
[2] The evidence assembled in Saltz 1978, which is an unpublished thesis, whence the brief account in Boardman 1990, 169-75. Chicago has announced a return to fieldwork in North Syria; one wonders about academic priorities.
[3] Initially, Boardman 1990, 171-2. Kearsley (1995) published a detailed account of much of the Greek pottery from Levels 10-8, which is invaluable. There is more material available now for study, and it needs consideration beside the non-Greek material and other finds, as well as with closer attention to the excavation evidence; this I have attempted (1999a).

[4] Dunbabin 1957, 25.
[5] Bronze Age connections may have been effected farther upstream (Mycenaean pottery at Sabouni three miles away), while the Iron Age Greeks were kept at arm's length at the river mouth. The topography of the delta will be the subject of an article by H. Pamir and S. Nishiyama in *Ancient West and East* 1.2 (20020. Much depends on what is meant by 'colony': I use it in its modern restricted sense as a permanent settlement overseas established for the benefit of trade or subsistence or both. I have more on Al Mina in an article in *Ancient West and East* 1.2 (2002).
[6] In *La colonisation grecque en méditerranée occidentale* (Hommage à G. Vallet, Rome, 1999) 39-50; cf. Boardman 1999b, 268-9.

intervening years; it is just that they were at a low level and did not affect the cultural record. Nor is it credible that the Greeks needed to be led by Phoenicians into waters that they had been exploring long before any easterners, and which were in their own backyard, across from the Corinthian Gulf or around the Peloponnese, via Greek islands, yet this has been argued by some.

If we now look east, at the end of the Bronze Age there were strong Greek associations, whether or not settlement, on the Levant coast. There is much at Atchana, which is the Bronze Age equivalent to Tell Tainat in Syria, and there is Ugarit down the coast, as well as whatever one chooses to make of any Greek role with the Sea Peoples.[7] Add speculation about Danaos and the Danunim of Cilicia, or Mopsos and Muksas, and Greek post-Trojan War settlements or myths associated with the Cilicia/Syria area, let alone Cyprus, and we may suspect something of importance happening at a time when Greece as such had nothing much to offer the east, while many Greeks had good reason to want to go east. Much depends on which philologist you believe, and no answers are offered here, but I simply observe the phenomena west and east, and conclude that there were continuing even if intermittent associations between the Greek world and the north Levant coast over many centuries, just as there had been between both Greeks and easterners and discrete areas in the west Mediterranean.

In Syria we deal with an area where a neo-Hittite culture of a very distinctive type archaeologically was flourishing, though probably already under the domination of Assyria. Aramaeans had also arrived from middle Mesopotamia around 1000 BC, and became dominant in various cities, but culturally, it seems, absorbed in Syria. But it was for *their* language that Phoenician script was adapted and was to provide the, as it were, *scripta franca* of the east. Cilicia constitutes a rich plain approached readily from the Anatolian hinterland and, by sea, via the Gulf of Alexandretta. It has neo-Hittite sites like Kara Tepe and Tarsus, and there are some Phoenician traits - the language and script were already being used in places as an official alternative to Luvian and hieroglyphs, without adjustment of the script, as in Syria.[8] Then there is Syria proper which is the Orontes valley and the plain beyond, to the Euphrates and the dominant Assyrians, with sea access west via the Orontes. It is divided from Cilicia by the Amanus mountains which are not negligible. Alexander's and Darius' armies managed to miss each other completely by marching up and down either side of the range years later. The Syrian territory, including Aramaean cities such as Hama and Damascus, runs on south with the Orontes to border the lands of Israel and Judah, but the coastal strip, behind and to the west of the mountains, is the home of the great Phoenician city-ports. So far as traffic is concerned the route between Syria and the Aegean via the Orontes, Cyprus and Rhodes was a relatively easy one, though subject to seasonal weather problems. It need not have been an important one for Phoenician shipping west, since this could travel more directly via Cyprus and south Crete or the Greek islands; not much, I think, along the north African coast.[9] There were good direct routes from Egypt, not coastwise, to Cyprus, Rhodes and Crete.[10]

Finally, Cyprus itself. Connections are similar to those with the coast to the east, with the difference that the evidence for Greek settlement at and after the end of the Bronze Age is stronger. More important for us perhaps is the discovery, still barely digested by scholars, that the so-called Classical Cypriot syllabary had been devised by around 1000 BC, apparently to write a Greek dialect (Arcado-Cypriot), for which it continued to be used for centuries.[11] The Greeks may have become absorbed by the dominant local physical culture but their language and identity as Greek-speakers were not, and suddenly Cyprus emerges as a far more Greek island at a far earlier date than had been imagined, provided one does not regard pottery as the *only* signifier of a culture. A prism of Esarhaddon of 673/2 BC lists ten kings of Cyprus, and eight seem to have Greek names.[12] All this may be relevant to Greek associations with Syria. Al Mina is but 80 miles from the coast of Cyprus and there is an abundant presence of Cypriot and Cypriot-type pottery, and very probably Cypriots, in Syria. So long as the identity and activity of the Eteocypriots remains shadowy, we are entitled to surmise that much Cypriot that travelled outside Cyprus could have been in the hands of Greek-speakers. One notes the Cypriot trademark appearing on Greek pottery of about 700 BC in two Greek areas, in Chalcidice and south Italy.[13]

---

[7] I note a 7th-century Philistine king of Ekron called Akhayus: S. Gitin *et al.*, *IEJ* 47 (1997), 11.

[8] Bilinguals: Lemaire 1991, 133-46; R. Tekoglu and A. Lemaire, *CRAI* 2000, 961-1006. I. Winter gives an archaeological assessment of Phoenician influence in Cilicia in *Anatolian Studies* 29 (1979) 115-51, contrasting it with the situation in Syria; also, *eadem* 1995, 248-71; but I cannot take the Lyre Player seals as Phoenician (*OJA* 15 (1996) 338) and there is better evidence for them being of Syrian than Cilician manufacture. G. Kestemont in *Studia Phoenicia* I/II (1983) 53-78, and III (1985) 135-61 argues that Myriandros on the Gulf of Alexandretta was Phoenician at an early date, but the testimonia for this are classical, when it was a port for the Persian Mediterranean fleet.

[9] The identification of a Phoenician amphora at Tocra (P. Bartolini, *Rivista di Studi Fenici* 23 (1995) 191-8), even if early, is no more evidence for early Phoenician trade along the coast than the Middle Geometric pot in Spain is for Athenian trade in Iberia. On the absence of ports along this coast see now D. and A.P. White, *Journal of the American Research Centre in Egypt* 33 (1996) 11-30.

[10] This paragraph summarizes a fuller account written for forthcoming volumes on Greek colonization, edited by G.R. Tsetskhladze (Brill). The relevant chapters in *CAH* III.2 (1991) and III.3 (1982) present most of the data and testimonia.

[11] T.B. Mitford and O. Masson in *CAH* III.3 (1982) 74-5. See also relevant articles by C. Baurain, A.-M. Collombier and T. Palaima in Baurain *et al.* 1991, 389-472.

[12] E. Lipinski in *Ah, Assyria* (Studies...H. Tadmor, 1991, eds. M. Cogan, I, Eph'al), 58-64.

[13] I. Vokotopoulou and A.-P. Christidis, *Kadmos* 34 (1995) 5-12.

We come to texts, which I summarize. Eastern texts can be taken seriously where they are contemporary or seem to derive from contemporary records. There is always the danger of propaganda, but propaganda does not need to tell lies, merely to exaggerate, and even where a defeat or unresolved contest can be made to look like a victory, at least we can be sure that something had happened. Omission is a more serious matter. Greek texts have to be judged in terms of the motivation of the writer and the motivation of his sources. We usually need some external criteria for important matters but unbiased trivia are often revealing. Both east and west suffer from self-advertisement and bragadoccio, in the east from king-emperors, in Greece mainly from late writers and modern commentators.

We sadly lack helpful texts from the most crucial areas - Syria, Cilicia and Phoenicia. Assyrian interest was very distant and references are too sparse to give anything like a coherent account rather than allusion to isolated episodes. The Assyrians knew the Greeks as Ionians, whom they accordingly called Yawan, pronounced and sometimes written, Yamana.[14] In our period Ionians include Euboeans and some islanders, who seem to have been the principal sea-goers east and west, as well as the Ionians of western Anatolia who seem somewhat less prominent internationally until the 7th century. Cyprus is partly Greek-speaking but not Ionian, and it is Yatnana, not Yamana. The mere fact that the Assyrians had a name for Ionians suggests close contact. Later the term might have been applied loosely to all westerners, rather like the later term Franks, and thus in the 6th century the Babylonians may have used it of other Anatolians,[15] but we should remember that the Persians could distinguish Ionians from Carians from Lydians. There were many bearing Anatolian names, themselves probably of mixed parentage, totally Hellenized and speaking/writing Greek (e.g. Carian authors Panyassis, Skylax).

Around 725 BC we have from Assyrian sources record under Tiglath-Pileser III of Ionian raids: "The Ionians have come. They have fought in the cities of Sams[imuruna], Harisu and..." (the towns are not located). Then there is Sargon's success over Ionians "caught in the midst of the sea as a fowler does fish", and in one text "and [dep]orted (?) them". For some reason or other an Ionian is mentioned in an account of silver payments as a member of the household of the Assyrian Queen Mother;[16] and for the earlier 7th century record in the work of a far later Babylonian priest, who may have had a good source, about Sennacherib winning a battle after the Greeks had entered Cilicia to make war, and defeating Ionian warships off the Cilician coast. The overall picture is of an Ionian sea presence, which would have little point if it was not involved with the land, and indeed seems to have attacked it, in our period. The record is of Ionian failures but we would not expect any successes they may have had to be recorded by easterners, and they fall in a period for which Greeks themselves had no serious recorded or remembered history. But the Ionians seem to have been persistent. Recall the Late Bronze Age and subsequent Greek associations with this general area, especially the north, and with Cyprus, and there can be no good reason to doubt that there was renewed activity along old routes which had never quite been abandoned; we *know* that between Greece and Cyprus they were active through much or all of the alleged Dark Ages, and that there were Greek-speakers living in Cyprus.

Down to towards the end of the 8th century virtually all the Greek pottery found in the east comes from the island of Euboea; this is clear on grounds of style and clay analysis; some may be from Cycladic islands under Euboean control, there is a very little Attic (as also in Euboea itself) and only a little more Corinthian and East Greek, mainly from North Ionia (especially Samos). The Euboean starts to arrive as early as the 10th century and is scattered all along the Levant coast, and a little inland, from Cilicia to Askalon, with an isolated find as far away as Nineveh.[17] The main period of arrival is the 8th century, but everywhere except in Syria it comprises an extremely small proportion of the pottery found, and how it arrived is a matter for pure speculation. Since proportions are more important than sheer numbers in these matters I tried to work this out, but there was little to go on except to see that at Al Mina it was proportionately up to 50 times more in evidence than elsewhere. Another attempt to measure it was by frequency per square metre excavated, producing virtually the same result, which is reassuring for the method.[18] In terms of absolute numbers there now seem to be some 2000 Greek pieces of 8th-century date from Syria which is around five times as much as all the other Greek finds in the east put together. At Al Mina the concentration is from about the second quarter of the 8th century to its end or just after. Both common sense and the distribution pattern suggest that this concentration indicates the main region of interest, not any region(s) farther off. At this point it is necessary to reflect upon the interpretation of such pottery finds, in general and with specific reference to the Greek finds in Syria.

Pottery and History

There is no reason to believe that a pot found on a site other than that in which it was made must indicate that it arrived in

---

[14] Brinkman (1989) collects the texts; and *cf.* T.F.R.G. Braun, *CAH* III.3 (1982), 14-19, which needs correction at some points.
[15] Brinkman 1989, 58-9. That the Yawan should come to include the part-hellenized neighbours of the Ionians is not surprising.
[16] *State Archives of Assyria* VII (1992) 56, no. 48; not in Brinkman 1989. Dr Dalley tells me this is probably Esarhaddon's mother, so early 7th-century. The texts are discussed by Amélie Kuhrt elsewhere in this volume.

[17] Summarised in Boardman 1990, 169-75; 1999b, 38-46. For the Nineveh sherd, *idem*, *OJA* 16 (1997) 375.
[18] Boardman 1990, 171-5. Considerably updated in Boardman 1999a, giving much the same proportion of Greek to non-Greek at Al Mina, but greater for the first generation there, and more plentiful and so more concentrated in the excavation area with a higher yield per sq.m.

the hands of, or in the ship of, a fellow-countryman of its maker. This refrain is a common one in many recent articles, and Jim Muhly[19] has elevated David Harvey's remark (no doubt to his surprise), made *à propos* of Sostratos' dedication of an anchor at Graviscae, to the status of Harvey's Thesis: "the presence of any pottery of any given state at any given site is no evidence for the activity of traders (or indeed settlers) from that state at that site". The words "not necessarily evidence on its own for" would have been more just, and a distinction needs to be drawn between treatment of single or sparse finds and the plentiful. No one imagines that a 7th-century Ionian vase found near Kiev got there in Greek hands or ship, but equally no one doubts that plentiful Corinthian vases in the early years of a Corinthian colony attest and confirm the presence there of Corinthians, and at least lend colour to the idea that Corinthians sent them there, whether on their own ships or on the ships of others. On the other hand the hundreds of Athenian vases in Etruria did not require the presence of an Athenian. Different sites and different circumstances call for different explanations, and we cannot assume that what was probably true of some trade in the time of Sostratos (around 500 BC) was equally or at all true two or three hundred years before.

It is time to pay more attention again to the pots themselves. When Robert Benchley was asked to report on the 'Cod War' on the Great Banks studied from the point of view of (a) the USA, and (b) Canada, he replied - "I have no knowledge of either (a) or (b). Accordingly I propose to approach this question from the point of view of the cod."

There seems in some recent work to be a readiness to discount all prejudicial pottery evidence in the interests of other prejudices, to the point even of denying any credit for trade and enterprise to those producing the objects of trade. What applies to Greek pottery must apply to non-Greek pottery, and to other objects. We need evidence beyond simply identity of finds to demonstrate origins or presence of people, but plentiful pottery is an important indicator. Pots are for use, generally by the people most accustomed to using them; finer objects more readily pass from hand to hand, soon leaving the possession of those who made them, or are acquired for their status value. Real trade in manufactured luxuries, as opposed to gift-exchange of varying degrees of regulation, is not a phenomenon to be much expected at an early date. Pots may be less spectacular but more eloquent, especially in the early period before they acquire some degree of status as 'art', although, I suppose, a few Greek vases may have travelled before the 7th century BC for their perceived quality or novelty. Although the presence of a state's pottery is not always an indication of the presence of its people or direct commercial interests, good reasons need to be apparent for it *not* to be. There is, indeed, in any dismissive attitude to pottery, a certain danger of throwing out the baby with the bathwater, or of getting close to arguing that because there are some black swans there are no white swans.

Much of course depends on *how* pots moved around the Mediterranean, about which distribution maps tell little. The matter has been much explored but most evidence is late. In Homer Phoenicians bring their goods and then loiter for a year to pick up a return cargo (*Od.* 15. 455-456). We assume but cannot be sure that the ship-owner/captain is the prime mover, like the alleged Taphian king looking for copper and carrying iron in *Od.* 1. 180-184. There seem to be several traders on the ship conjured in *Od.* 8. 161-164. Hesiod's ship-owner peddles his own wares (*Op.* 678-694). Of the cast of merchants presented to us by Herodotos Korobios is simply described as *porphyrios*, a purple man, presumably a dealer in purple dye, probably a Levantine *emporos* and perhaps not a shipowner, since although he knows what to find on the African coast he is carried to Thera and then to Libya on the ships of others (4. 151-153). Kolaios (4. 152) is called a *naukleros*, which can only mean shipowner who managed his own cargo. Sostratos of Aegina is not described (*ibid.*), except as a most successful trader, but since he dedicated an anchor at Graviscae on the coast of Etruria he is more likely to have been a shipowner than an *emporos*, and he may have done his own buying in Athens for shipment to Italy. And there is Charaxos, Sappho's brother, who traded Lesbian wine to Naukratis. Herodotus (2. 135) does not describe his trade but Strabo (17. 1. 33) said he 'brought down' (*katagein*) wine to Egypt *kat'emporian*, and he was surely an *emporos*. Sostratos demonstrates that in a state like Aegina, which has no notable products for export but a strong reputation for sea-faring and trade (which is why the Aeginetans are the only homeland Greeks with a formal stake in Naukratis), there is no necessary identity between producer and trader. I doubt whether this was altogether normal, and trade (in varied commodities like pottery, rather than raw materials and bulk foodstuffs, if any at this date), was as readily conducted by *emporoi* (essentially 'passengers') who negotiated a place for themselves and their cargo on a ship. That ship is on the whole more likely to be owned by a fellow-citizen with whom a regular schedule could be arranged than with another Greek or a foreigner, although it need not be, and could not be if home did not breed seafarers. The idea of a merchant standing on the quayside at Piraeus beside his crates waiting for the next ship to Italy, whatever its flag, does not appeal. But even if the ship was not Athenian it would be foolish to dissociate the producer altogether from responsibility or credit for the trade. It was he, after all, who produced the surplus for trade and often (as with Athens' potters) carefully observed market preferences. For all we know, potters and their families did not work all year at the wheel or brush but were their own *emporoi*, and thus in a good position to observe and meet market demands and even manipulate them. This cannot be pressed, and from the merchant marks it seems that many of the marketing agents may not have been Athenian; but then,

---

[19] J.D. Muhly in *The Crisis Years; the 12th century B.C.* (eds. W.A. Ward and M.S. Joukowsky, 1992) 13.

neither, probably, were all the potters, the metic class being prominent in such activities as is also indicated by their names.[20]

If an Aeginetan or Phoenician ship carries Athenian pottery to Italy or Morocco, is this more Aeginetan/Phoenician trade than Athenian? It could not have happened without Athenian production of what was to be traded, and undoubtedly to the profit of the producer as well as the agents or carriers; and especially to the profit of the producer if he or his agent were the *emporos*. The pottery remains no absolute indicator of presence, only of an interest of varying degrees of directness, especially where we can see that the preferences of the customer seem to be observed by the producers, and this *can* be observed to some extent from the 8th century on.

The distinction between gift-exchange and trade is a fine one for the early period. Where a pattern of giving develops with clear expectations of the nature and value of the return gifts we are dealing with no more than elegant barter. And if precious metals become one side of the equation it is already virtually buying and selling. Many gifts must have carried an implicit price-tag with expectations of a return; they still do - vide the 'free lunch'. When, in the *Iliad*, Glaukos foolishly exchanged gold for brass, the unequal gift-exchange is explained by Zeus taking away his wits (6. 234); only the modern commentator tries to make of it gift-value graduated according to rank. When I, if not others, speak of Greek, Phoenician or Cypriot shipping and trade in the early period, I assume that it was principally a matter of folk carrying their own products/materials, in search of products/materials which they needed or valued. They might also, clearly, acquire products/materials from other sources to trade, en route or through lack of their own resources, but I doubt whether this was very common for major cargoes before the 7th century. They might well accept on board an *emporos* with his goods, and in this case again, the source of the *emporos*' stock is more significant than the nationality of the ship or its owner or even the *emporos*. A city with a merchant fleet would stand to profit also from such activity, which would certainly be true of the Phoenician cities and Aegina, but the former were also producers of note (mainly textiles and timber to judge from texts). It is easy and probably wrong to read back into the early period many of the normal procedures of later, organized trade, and its financing, by state or individual.

Merchant marks, well explored by Alan Johnston (1979), should be a valuable source for the pottery trade from the mid-6th century on, and they seem to indicate that in Athens *emporoi* were involved, whether or not all of Athenian birth (see above); the earlier Corinthian merchant marks suggest Corinthians only.[21] The Athenian *emporoi* were not necessarily the potters, but there is still considerable correspondence between potter-workshops and merchant marks for export, as though the potter was more intimately involved in the trade than many would admit. Elsewhere there may be evidence for the *emporoi* in 'foreign inscriptions'.[22] But the Athenian pottery trade, to which I shall revert, belongs to a more sophisticated and later period than that with which we are immediately concerned, down to the 7th century.

If the point is taken that the presence of pots is not altogether to be ignored as evidence for some sort of involvement with those who made them, then absence of a particular class from any otherwise prolific site might also be significant. It would be difficult to argue for any role for a trading and pot-producing state on a site which yielded little or none of that state's pottery; provided, of course, that it produced any of significance and whether or not it was a major item of trade. This needs to be observed in terms of proportion rather than quantity.[23] It is why we have no reason to suspect any real Greek presence at Tyre because the Greek pottery there, from the 10th to 8th century, represents a minute proportion of all found,[24] however interesting it may be as evidence for early and possibly indirect involvement with its source (mainly Euboea) but via intermediaries who might or might not be Greek. It is why the extreme paucity of any Levantine pottery at Lefkandi argues against any substantial eastern presence there, the few fine eastern objects falling into the category of gifts that might as readily be carried by recipients as donors. And the possible practice there of eastern jewellery techniques requiring some degree of personal contact, might have been effected by no more than one craftsman, whose skills might even have been observed in the east rather than the west.[25] It is why the proportionately little Phoenician pottery at Kommos in Crete should make us hesitant about arguing for any sustained presence there rather than regular visits, which were more probably east-to-west than west-to-east (where Cretan pottery is conspicuously absent). At Kommos the argument for presence has to depend on an explanation for the strange shrine which can find some but mainly later Phoenician/Punic parallels. These probably mean something, but just possibly not that much in an island where tri-columnar shrines were old news, and when the bronze disc/shield behind the pillars remains a distinct oddity in a shrine that ought to have some fertility function if the eastern parallels are real.[26] Kommos surely,

---

[20] More on this in J. Boardman, *The History of Greek Pottery* (London 2001) ch. 4.
[21] A.W. Johnston, *BSA* 70 (1975) 148-9.

[22] A.W. Johnston, *Kokalos* 39/40 (1993/4) 155-69.
[23] This is a basic principle that vitiates much of R. Osborne's data to support his arguments in *Antiquity* 70 (1996) 31-44. It is idle to compare sheer numbers from different sites and contexts, rather than proportional representation between reasonably prolific sites. His conclusion in favour of early 'directional exchange' need not be wholly rejected, however.
[24] Boardman 1990, 173.
[25] For the orientalia at Lefkandig see Popham 1994.
[26] For Kommos, J.T. Shaw, *AJA* 93 (1989) 165-83. The finds attest the earliest deliberate Phoenician moves west, and the shrine, if Phoenician, may mean no more than the influential presence for some years of an immigrant priest who persuaded the folk into new ritual practices. He or she

though, indicates early Phoenician moves west along an alternative route to that through central Greek islands. There are, of course, wider implications. If people are to be identified by objects at all, surely common pottery ('for people') is more reliable than luxury goods (gifts or souvenirs), especially if the former is plentiful, the latter scattered and diverse in character. Yet it is the latter that prompt the image of "overwhelming archaeological evidence for a Phoenician presence in Geometric and even Proto-Geometric Greece", while Greek pottery at foreign sites is 'intrusion'.[27]

Another aspect of the same problem is the interpretation of imitations of pottery styles made away from their homes. This is far more complex and yields no simple pattern. In Greek colonies there is no question that the imitations are the products of immigrant craftsmen or their pupils, and they match closely the wares at home, but of course it need not always be so, and where there is no evidence about identity other criteria have to be applied. Pots are for people, so imitations are made for people who are used to or who value the models, and who might buy them or even trade them competitively against 'originals'. Here an appeal to style, not altogether subjectively interpreted, might be made. It is not difficult to identify Etruscan hands imitating Attic black- or red-figure, but South Italian red-figure is no less surely from the hands of Greeks (at first Athenians, no doubt) imitating Attic. In the Greek colonial world where identities are not controversial examples can easily be multiplied. Mycenaean-style pottery in the Levant is mainly identified now from analysis, since stylistically it is indistinguishable from the home Mycenaean tradition. It is, therefore, hard to see it as initiated by non-Mycenaeans. Local taste might, however, change, and local craftsmen might become trained in the new styles and not be too readily identified, and the products come to admit many local features. The same is true of Greek pottery made in Greek western colonies, although the 'local' is not generally non-Greek. On the other hand the Mycenaean Greeks' own imitation of Minoan pottery is relatively easy to make out.

A question has to be asked whether, where imitations of a ware are produced in a foreign context, they should be regarded as the work of others. When imitations of Greek Geometric skyphoi are made on west Phoenician sites, and the cup type (as we shall see below) is not one natural to the behaviour of an eastern population, we are bound to wonder by and for whom they could have been made; and why, if not either for visiting or even resident Greeks, rather than for easterners who had uncharacteristically picked up Greek, or at least western, drinking-cup habits. Their quality is good if not of the highest. Yet the assumption is that they are Phoenician products.[28] In the east there are what I would call

Euboeo-Levantine cups, plentiful at Al Mina, surely the products of, and mainly for, Greeks heavily influenced by the eastern environment in which they lived, probably in Cyprus or beside Cypriots or in Syria.[29] On Ischia there are poor imitations of eastern Red Slip bowls, and the shape is also employed for purely Greek Geometric decoration which was certainly applied by Greeks.[30] The imitation Red Slip was presumably for people who were used to it and made after models which were not necessarily Phoenician since the ware is a Levantine *koine*. The Greek-decorated versions of these shapes were surely for Greeks.[31] The assumption seems to be that the former were made by immigrant Phoenicians which sits oddly with the common view about the producers of Greek-style cups in west Phoenician sites!

We should distinguish pottery types and functions; some pots are produced for commercial purposes. Obvious examples are the KW flasks made on Rhodes in imitation of Cypriot flasks in the later 8th and 7th centuries.[32] These soon entered the flow of trade west and could better be regarded as a case of local commercial opportunism than evidence for the presence of eastern perfumiers. And at the Phoenician site of Kition on Cyprus the deposit below the floor of Temple 2, so of around 800 BC, contains many Cypriot Black-on-Red flasks and a small group of plain grey burnished pots of Phoenician character (several conical-topped oinochoai), and one in the shape of a Greek skyphos.[33] So the type of vase and its function and likely market must also influence our judgement about the information it might offer about the involvement of its maker in its presence away from home.

These are generalities, with select examples, to demonstrate the need for caution in either using or ignoring pottery sources to identify makers or users or traders. In what follows I investigate the case of the Greek pottery in Syria.

Pots and People

There is a great deal of Greek, mainly Euboean 8th-century pottery in Syria, as we have seen. The material is somewhat better known than, and the proportion of Greek is very considerably in excess of, that in any other eastern area including Cyprus. Moreover, at Al Mina, the earliest levels have virtually nothing but Greek pottery. I, with others, had

---

was not from Cyprus, it seems.
[27] H.G. Niemeyer in *Biblical Archaeology Today* 1990 (1993) 342.
[28] C. Briese and R. Docter, *Madrider Mitteilungen* 33 (1992) 25-69. Most

are subgeometric, 7th-century, but derive mainly from LG Euboean and Thapsos Class skyphoi. I discuss the question of imitations in a forthcoming paper for a volume dedicated to Brian Shefton.
[29] I had thought (1959) these could have been made in Al Mina until I submitted some for analysis: also Jones (1986, 694-6). They are Kearsley's group 15 (1995, 77-8, with nos. 233-4). I discuss these further in 1999a, 148.
[30] G. Buchner in Niemeyer 1982, 283-90.
[31] For a cautious approach to the identification of easterners on Ischia see Boardman 1994a, 95-100.
[32] See Boardman 1994a, 97 for references, pointing out that the imitations are of Cypriot not Phoenician models.
[33] V. Karageorghis, *Kition* (1976) 108, pls. XVII, XVIII, 84; *idem et al.*, *Excavations at Kition* IV (1981) 27, no. 68.

thought it enough to argue a Greek presence, presumably for commercial purposes since the products of the hinterland were responsible for the whole Orientalizing Revolution in the Greek homeland, and the distribution of Syrian goods corresponded closely with the Greek sphere of influence (and not with the far wider Phoenician one).[34] We can hardly tell whether the presence was regular or seasonal, nor how numerous it was, though the evidence of the earliest levels tells for dominant Greek interest. There is, however, a strong view now that it was not Greeks who brought the pots there, but 'Phoenicians' who had brought them back with them. No satisfactory explanation is offered for why the Phoenicians were so selective, since they were ranging most Mediterranean shores, nor why they left them in Syria and took so few back home, but a Greek presence in the east is no longer considered desirable or Correct, and the evidence of the distribution of Syrian goods and of texts recording a Greek presence, and plentiful finds coming from a Cyprus where Greek was spoken by established inhabitants, is ignored.

This is a question that cannot be judged from too narrow a viewpoint. Thus, it is generally agreed that relations between Cyprus, Syria and Phoenicia on the one hand, and Crete on the other, were maintained throughout much of the 'Dark Ages', and there is more of eastern (mainly Syrian and Cypriot, except for the Phoenician at Kommos) origin and inspiration in Crete than in any other part of Greece in the 9th to 7th centuries. Yet not one Cretan pot or other artefact has been certainly identified in the east to match the hundreds (originally thousands) of Euboean. That the latter were brought home by easterners who had an inexplicable but deep-seated aversion to all Cretan pottery is inconceivable, but it is easy to understand Cretans playing a relatively passive role, except perhaps with Cyprus, and not themselves going farther east.

If, however, it is still held that the pots could not be brought to Syria by Greeks, then they came, and in numbers, for a purpose. The old view that the easterners of this period were not much interested in Greek painted pottery for its own sake - which is certainly the impression one gets from early finds in the rest of the east - has then to be revised in favour of a great interest in it on the part of Syrians who went to some trouble, or put others to some trouble, to acquire it.

Here we need to recall that pots are for people, and usually particular classes of pottery are for people who are accustomed to them. Most of the pots are cups, with some larger vases and some flattish dishes (with pendent semicircles) which seem to be an early example of an export model made in Euboea for Cyprus, where the shape is at home.[35] In Al Mina the pots seem not to have been found in clusters, as if for onward trade, which was later true of classical Athenian export wares found there. Indeed their presence beside Cypriot and eastern pottery on a single floor has been used to identify a Greek dwelling.[36] If the obvious explanation, that they were there primarily for Greeks, is for whatever reason inadmissible, we have to think of them as being attractive, almost luxury goods that the (As)syrians (though not others in the east) wished to acquire in quantity. The concentration of finds is on or near the coast, not farther off.

At this point some simple archaeological observation is called for in support of the 'pots are for people' principle. Since the Bronze Age the Greek world preferred to drink out of cups that had two handles and a base, sometimes even a high stem. The preference remained strong for centuries to come and it was largely shared by Cyprus where there had been a Greek-speaking and Greek-writing population of unknown size but persistent presence and presumably growth since at least the 12th/11th century. Moving east from Cyprus the preference stops dead. From the Bronze Age on, for centuries, indeed millennia, the preferred drinking cup in the east was relatively small, often roughly hemispherical, without handles and usually without any flat base. These are the rule in early Iron Age Syria. Some Assyrian are deeper but with a pointed base, or with a modelled lion head, the latter being smaller versions of the lion-head situlae.[37] Others are slightly broader, versions of the commoner later phialai.[38] They were handled on fingertips.[39] Finds in metal and pottery as well as many representations of cups in use demonstrate all this quite clearly. The difference is virtually that between the cups used for the English and Japanese tea ceremonies, or between a beer tankard and a wine glass. Can we really suppose that for a short period the (As)syrian élite, sought after handled, footed Greek cups, and of mere clay and not metal?[40] - a shape which found no echo in scenes or local production then or at any time later, until classical Greek behaviour became more pervasive in the nearer east.

Apparent exceptions prove the rule. The most prominent

---

[34] See the maps in Boardman 1990, 180-1; 1999b, fig. 319. Obvious examples are the Syrian Lyre Player seals and glass eye-beads. For the former see above, n. 8; for the latter M. Martelli, *Atti VII Giornata archeologica* (Genoa, 1995) 18, n. 11. There used to be a gap in distribution maps for these, with no finds of the beads in Greece, which was used to argue for a different route or carriers west, but this gap is now filled: Martelli points out that Perachora had been missed, and Attica (Mounichia) can now be added. But the distribution hardly supports her claim for the role of Rhodes, at least as regards the glass and seals.

[35] Coldstream 1994, 47-8; and Popham 1994, 27; A. Nitsche, *Hamburger Beiträge zur Archäologie* 13/1 (1986/7) 31-44. P. Courbin publishes Euboean oil amphorae of the 10th/9th century from Bassit, but inevitably believes them carried by Phoenicians: *Hesperia* 62 (1993) 95-113.
[36] Kearsley 1995, 75-6; room 8 of Level 8; on this see Boardman 1999a, 141.
[37] J. Edgeworth Reade, The Symposium in Ancient Mesopotamia, in Murray 1995, 45-6, figs. 11-13.
[38] B. Hrouda, *Die Kulturgeschichte des assyrischen Flachbildes* (1965) 78.
[39] *Cf.* R.W. Hamilton, *Iraq* 28 (1966) 3-6, on the handling of such bowls (*à propos* of a silver bowl in Oxford, now seen to be false).
[40] Anyone who incurred the Persian king's displeasure was obliged to use clay drinking cups: Ctesias (*ca.* 400 BC) in Athenaeus 464b.

copies of Greek cups in the Phoenician world are in the west, where Greeks as well as their cups were constant visitors, and where handled cups were the norm, if not for easterners. For these, see above. At Al Mina there is evidence from the earliest levels of the Euboeo-Levantine cups, made by Greeks, for Greeks, with some Cypriot traits in the decoration; and beside them, it seems, much Cypro-Levantine, made somewhere off the island and well distributed in Syria and Cilicia. The appearance of stray Greek cups from the 10th century on in many eastern sites, in Cilicia, Phoenicia and to the south, shows merely that these were arriving sparsely and casually in the area. Their very strong presence in Syria means something else and to describe Al Mina as "simply a Syrian port with imported Cypriot and Greek pottery" betrays a strange unwillingness to face the evidence in all its volume and complexity.[41] Remembering too the Greek presence in Cyprus, I repeat the query whether we can be sure that the considerable import of Cypriot pots into Syria in these years has nothing to do with Greek-speakers in the island, quite apart from the production of Cypro-Levantine vessels, just mentioned? The matter is made clearer by closer inspection of the Al Mina finds, which is reported elsewhere.[42]

The clear division in cup preferences east and west must reflect drinking habits: the Greeks went for draughts of diluted wine, returning often to the cup which betweenwhiles they put down;[43] the Easterners went for the quick gulp from a generally smaller cup which was constantly being replenished by the attendant always shown in drinking scenes.[44] If it is set down, a separate ring base would need to be supplied. These are by no means conspicuous in the published archaeological record though I understand that stand-rings of ivory and other materials were common finds at Nimrud. The difference has some interesting repercussions in later Greek copying of eastern shapes, to which I return in the next section.

Feet and Handles

Greek obsession with having a cup that will stand on its own and which can be lifted by its handles has some interesting consequences. For one thing it enabled the Greeks to anthropomorphize their cups as they did other vase shapes. This seems an appropriately Greek interest. The cups can be made to look like heads or masks, with eyes, mouths, feet and handle-ears. Though figure vases are known in the east this metaphorical use of standard vase shapes seems uncommon at least.

From time to time Greek potters were moved to copy foreign shapes and their treatment of some eastern shapes is revealing. The drinking horn has to be slung and has no foot. It appears in 6th-century Greek art mainly in the hands of ribald revellers (the *komastai*) and is a normal rustic vessel, not for house use. The eastern form of horn rhyton, with animal head spout, is copied in 6th-century Smyrna, footless.[45] But in the 5th century the horn-shaped cups (not, of course, necessarily copying the eastern vessels, though probably so since they often carry eastern or foreign subjects, perhaps for export) are invariably given figure groups to support them on a flat base: negroes with crocodiles, camels, etc., notably those from Sotades' workshop, but they are very few.[46] The eastern rhyton with an animal forepart and a spout for pouring has a long history and there is a rich Achaemenid Persian series. For some the forepart is so arranged that the creature sits flat, supporting the cup, but for most the horn stands free and could only be suspended or lain down when not in use. When Greeks made one in the 5th century for a customer east of the Black Sea, they provided it with an incongruous flaring foot.[47] Otherwise the Greeks only copy the type late in the Persian period and thereafter, and it acquires particular importance seen in the hands of the heroised dead; an importance not matched by any numerous finds of Greek rhyta of the type *in corpore*, although the protomes of the eastern rhyta soon assume realistic Greek

---

[41] A. Sherratt, *Cambridge Archaeological Journal* 5 (1995) 147, n. 18. Also no little geographical naivety is involved. Thus the Sherratts (1993) place Al Mina in the Gulf of Alexandretta (p. 365), to the north of its true location and in the approach to Cilicia and the routes into Anatolia, not recognizing, it seems, the main route to (As)syria along the Orontes and past Al Mina and Tell Tainat. Moreover, for most of their article they seem to have forgotten Egypt completely, and they force early Phoenician exploration in Greek waters up the Euboean creek, to the unexplained exclusion of other Aegean shores, to judge from what they regard as Phoenician acquisitions in Greece (Euboean pots). Their minimalist attitude to early trade I would otherwise approve, though how then can they explain the many Euboean pots in Syria, except in the terms I have suggested, i.e., in the hands of Greeks?

[42] Boardman 1999a.

[43] It is not clear whether the remark of Sophocles (fr. 611) that a cup without a bottom should not be put on the table (which became a proverb) is relevant here; the word is *apyndakotos*.

[44] The distinction is almost that between wine and spirits, a distinction observed by British excavators, at least a generation or two ago, digging at either Greek or eastern sites: S. Lloyd, *The Interval* (1986) 122. The Greek idea that barbarian cups were larger than Greek ones, recorded in Athenaeus 497a, quoting Chamaileon (*ca.* 300 BC), is in reference to rhyta only and prompted by thoughts of barbarian drunkenness; *cf.* H. Hoffmann, *Getty Vases* 4 (1989) 134.

[45] J.M. Cook, *BSA* 60 (1965) pl. 39.

[46] J. Boardman, *Athenian Red Figure Vases. The Classical Period* (London 1989) figs. 101, 104, 106. H. Hoffmann, *Sotades* (1998) illustrates all and interprets them idiosyncratically.

[47] A. Leskov, *Grabschätze der Adygeen* (1990); Boardman 1994b, 207, fig. 6.30; I. V. Ksenofontova and N. G. Zaitseva, *Ancient Civilizations from Scythia to Siberia* 4 (1997) 265-293. It may be noted that its silver foot seems solid, not hammered, and that the profile of the cavity is cylindrical (from personal observation, thanks to Dr Mkrtychev of the State Museum of Oriental Art, Moscow). This is the shape for clay cups in Greece no later than the early 5th century, which must be the date of creation of this foot. If it was made for the rhyton, the rhyton itself should be as early, as the horse head and mane might indicate, and the gigantomachy frieze added, not necessarily any later than the mid-5th century. S. Ebbinghaus is preparing a detailed study of decorated horn-rhyta and I am indebted to her for discussion of relevant matters.

Figure 1.

animal forms in place of the hieratic and stylized eastern, and the threatening lions become little more than playful pussies. The only other comparable eastern type, the animal head cup, acquires an upright handle in Greece, but cannot stand unaided if full, although some *are* given flaring feet; most others must have been used as were drinking horns (or stirrup cups), and put down empty, upside down or hung up.[48] Human-head cups can stand on their neck cut-offs. Otherwise the only Greek cup shape which is footless is the *mastos*, explained by its suggestive name. Even clay cauldrons (*lebetes, dinoi*) which are essentially shapes to be supported over a fire on tripod stands, are often supplied with ring bases, or, as in *lebetes gamikoi*, get high stands attached in place of the separate tripods or stands, and handles.

One eastern shape known in Greece since the early Iron Age could usually sit still without a foot or handle - the phiale. It is not too clear whether it was normally used as a drinking cup in the east. This shape too is copied in Greece in clay, but it may be significant that it has no real role as part of symposion equipment,[49] rather than as a cult instrument, into which a libation is poured, to be spilled on to the ground. It is not normal dining-room furniture, but for a special purpose and commonly used by the libator standing. Exceptions are few and many carry a cult or heroic connotation. Even then some Greeks can add a handle.[50]

There are other types of shallow dish current in the east, their bottoms either flat or lightly convex. There are, for example, the eastern Red Slip dishes with straight rims, slightly angled out, and there are eastern types with vertical concave rims. It is unlikely that these were all used for drinking. It remains something of a mystery why the Greeks were prepared to use open, shallow cups (what we call *kylikes*) from the mid-6th century on, since they must spill very easily and their use for playing *kottabos* can hardly have been an essential one. Take the eastern dishes just described; add handles and a high stem, and you have the Greek Little Master cups of the mid-6th century on, which develop into the classical *kylix*, a shape that remains popular until the late 4th century, when it begins to decline in favour of more practical deep cups. If this derivation of the shape is correct - an adaptation of eastern dishes for Greek symposiac purposes - then it is more likely to have happened in the East Greek world than in Athens, where it is best attested. There are few, but early Little Master shapes in Ionia, notably Samos, and that the shapes spread thence to Athens at a time of other Ionian influence, both in the arts and behaviour, is quite plausible. The Greeks would have been predisposed to such shapes by the broader but deep skyphoi of Late Corinthian and the Athenian Siana cups, both far easier to manage than the new open *kylix* bowls since they are inturned below the rim, which counters spilling. The eye-cup shape is essentially a handled, footed

---

[48] H. Hoffmann, *Attic Red-figured Rhyta* (1962).
[49] F. Lissarrague in Murray 1995, 126-44; on the changing use of the word in Greek from Homer to Pindar, N.V. Mele, *Scienza dell'Antichità* 5 (1991) 381-95.
[50] E.g., *Münchener Jahrbuch der bildenden Kunst* 1992, 188-9. Syrian lotus-handled bowls and those with swing handles (and their Phrygian derivatives) are larger and not for drinking, though perhaps for libation; *cf.*

Boardman 1999b, 89. The phiale may be a very rare occurrence in Greek symposion scenes, but has an interesting career, apart from libating, as a container for Aphrodite's love charms: to cast in the eyes of Menelaos (*LIMC* IV, Helene nos. 272, 279bis) and perhaps Paris (Sarajevo fr., *Pandora* (ed. N. Reeder, 1995) 65, fig.4); and for Medea's poisons (*LIMC* VII, Theseus nos. 203-7). The smaller Persian bowls may have been for perfumed oil, and *cf.* Athenaeus 462d (perfume).

phiale. Fig. 1 is designed to show how eastern bowls with additions resemble Greek cups. I would not suggest that this is the direct derivation but the eastern forms were surely influential in what is generally regarded as a purely Greek development. The same phenomenon is as clear in the 5th century when the source of inspiration for closely comparable shapes (notably the Acrocup) is Persian loot.[51]

Non-Greek Western Asia Minor seems to have been neutral in terms of the preferences for cups with feet and handles in the early period. They are generally absent in Hittite and Phrygian pottery. In Archaic Lydia there was a close cultural symbiosis with neighbouring Ionia from the late 7th century on. Both behaviour and art seem shared in a common Lydo-Ionian style which mingles some eastern pattern-formality with Greek novelty, and may have helped contribute to the Greek adoption of stemmed cups, explored in the last paragraph. Medes threatened in the early 6th century, and in the mid-century, successfully, the Persians. Sardis became a Persian capital and mainland Ionia with some of the islands was subjected. Eastern forms were already known before the Persians arrived but soon become yet more familiar, especially in metalware in which a distinctive Perso-Lydo-Ionian style may be recognised. The komasts shown on some East Greek vases carry eastern-type small handleless cups.[52]

The commonest Lydian cup type is generally called a skyphos and superficially resembles the Corinthian skyphos (which started life in archaeological parlance as a *kotyle*). It is roughly the same shape, with ring base and loop handles, but much more rounded in profile, often closing perceptibly towards the lip. This is not a characteristic of Greek skyphoi/kotylai of the period, where a degree of narrowing at the lip only starts in the 5th century, and on slimmer shapes. Surely the Lydian cup is simply a version of the eastern hemispherical, given handles and foot in the western manner (Fig. 2). Sometimes its foot is conical. Another eastern cup or small bowl shape, especially common in the Persian period and probably deriving from Assyrian cups, has a rounded bowl with a vertical concave lip. Add a conical foot and we have something very like the Lydian vessel generally known as a *lydion* and thought to be a container for perfumed oil, which might have been one of the functions of its model. It is not given handles.[53]

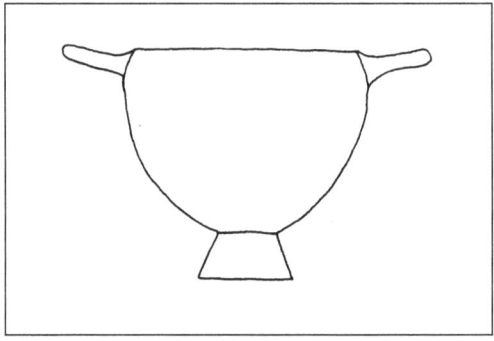

Figure 2.

Finally, to pursue elsewhere the Greek preference, consider their practice with oil or perfume containers, whose shapes derive from small skin flasks. These were generally carried slung from the wrist, or hung up. Even the early ovoid and piriform aryballoi of Protocorinthian have such narrow feet that they cannot stand, though they may derive from eastern globular flasks which *do* have feet, but in the east the preference for the handleless was exercised wholly on drinking vessels, not other shapes. The Greeks come to use two types of what we call *alabastra*: one (the 'Corinthian') is simply an elongated *aryballos* of pear shape - both shapes deriving from leather vessels. The other copies the Egyptian stone alabastron, again with a rounded bottom. In time the Greeks gave this a base too, in 4th-century South Italy,[54] while in Macedonia there is a silver version supplied with both base and two handles.[55] Even the Corinthian alabastron can be persuaded to stand by cutting off its lower part and creating the so-called Columbus alabastron, a shape that starts in Greece but was most popular in Italy. When the aryballos is made large it too may be given a ring base, in Corinth and Athens. And in Athens small flasks are given a monumental, footed apparel in the tall cylindrical lekythoi many of which effectively disguise the relatively small capacity of their bag-like interiors. The yet larger Greek version of the sagging-shaped oil container, the *pelike*, always has a flat base and handles. Egyptian bronze situlae are round-based with swing handles; the closest Greek version is the Archaic Rhodian clay 'situla', which is, inevitably, given a base and side handles. In the many studies devoted in recent years to the Greek copying of foreign shapes, or of shapes in other materials, too little attention may have been paid to quite different cultural preferences which dictated how such translation or copying was conducted and the appearance of the end product. It is a socio-cultural factor of some importance.

People, Ancient and Modern

The 'people' of my title was intended to embrace not only ancient cup-users but modern scholars. In a recent article

---

[51] See Margaret Miller's account (*Archäologische Mitteilungen aus Iran* 26 (1993) 109-46) of Greek copying of Persian shapes and motifs in 5th-century black gloss: "The additions of handles and base served to 'Hellenize' oriental forms - or we might say 'tame', or even 'democratize' oriental forms" (p.141, *cf.* 122); and now in *Athens and Persia in the Fifth Century* (Cambridge 1997) 145.

[52] Handleless cups in the hands of komasts appear on Milesian (Fikellura) vases and some Laconian (M. Pipili, *Laconian Iconography* (1987) figs. 106-7; there were strong Spartan-Ionian connections); but komasts are rough fellows who may also dance holding plain drinking horns.

[53] For the shape see C.H. Greenewalt, *Lydian Pottery of the 6th century BC. The Lydion and marbled ware* (Microfilms 1979). The Egyptian parallels for the shape are telling but far too early to be influential (*ibid.*, 83); there are some roughly similar Assyrian clay examples. The presence of the Persian footless cup of 'lydion' proportions in both clay and silver at Gordion is instructive: *AJA* 66 (1962) pl. 41.1.

[54] E.g., *JdI* 87 (1972) 258-98, the shape studied by K. Schauenburg.

[55] M. Andronikos, *Vergina* (1984) 154, figs. 117-8.

which convincingly modifies without dispelling theories about a major Euboean role in Early Iron Age settlement in the north Aegean, John Papadopoulos remarks on the role of "particularly those associated with excavations in Euboia" (named Britons and a Greek) who "have tended to exaggerate Euboian participation in early Greek maritime enterprise" (1996). Later he refers to other scholars as 'a Euboian man' and 'another Euboian man'. Whether these scholars' alleged exaggeration is the result of bias or of a better knowledge than most of the relevant evidence is not easy to judge. The latter must count for something, but we all are well aware of the tendency of any excavator to magnify the importance of his/her own site; or should we say 'draw attention to the importance of', which is no more than his/her duty? There are national preferences to be observed too, both for sites and subjects, preferences fostered by teachers, universities, colleagues, life in general (more on this below). Papadopoulos, an excavator at north Greek Torone, might be judged by the same criteria either to have better knowledge of north Greek archaeology (which he well displays), or himself to be exaggerating through prejudice; possibly both.[56]

The archaeology of colonies has became very fashionable again. In keeping with other issues of the day, not all of them scholarly, it has led to speculation about the degree to which former studies have been influenced by more recent practices of colonialism. Before World War II this could be regarded by westerners and even many colonies, as mainly beneficent, at least in the long run. In the last 50 years the aspirations of former colonies and dominions of European countries have meant that the European-based empires have gradually disappeared (while the American has grown; there were only 48 states when I was a boy). Moreover, there is growing resentment of the colonizers by the colonized, as well as guilt over long-past treatment by colonists of indigenous peoples in America, Africa and Australasia, which has, with certain events of the last war, conspired to throw disapproval on the west's cultural ancestor (Greece rather than Rome, it seems).[57] This has now led, not to the exploration in more detail of the role, achievement and influence of ancient non-Greek cultures, since these studies have long flourished in the west, but to award them a more conspicuous and sometimes dominant place in the history of western man and to demote the colonizers. The Greeks, of course, have a lot to answer for. They were responsible for 'the first significant contraction' that the great Persian Empire suffered (an observation, incidentally, made by an orientalist),[58] and eventually contributed to its overthrow, and they unwittingly provided the intellectual basis for subsequent western, now almost global, culture. Their own earlier debt to the east and Egypt has been well explored and acknowledged, but this is not enough and a degree of 'affirmative action' is required. Unfortunately, scholarly exploration of these aspects of antiquity have not been immune to modes of Political Correctness which have no roots at all in accurate scholarship or observation, yet seek to impose rules of conduct and censorship in many walks of life, including the academic. In this sphere it is resisted with varying success and conviction. Sometimes it seems to have become motivated by self-preservation (in the academic community) or self-assertion.

We are wise enough to realise that every generation, and therefore every scholar, has a view of the past coloured by its/his/her own education, experience and environment. There is no reason why we should not consciously try to avoid doing the same by exploring and admitting such prejudices as we may be exercising. I do not say 'try to avoid the mistake', since it is arguable that since the past is in the main unknowable, it is not by any means a mistake to explain it in the light of whatever we currently believe to be a proper view of history, past or present, although it is obviously (to my mind) a mistake to apply criteria which derive from studies of totally alien periods and cultures. Take colonialism.

What follows tries to be a dispassionate assessment of attitudes and will not, I hope, give offence. It explores areas which are familiar to all scholars but usually never laid out in print. Papadopoulos (Greek/Australian, now resident in the USA) has expressed critical comments on European 'Euboean men', as we have seen. He has himself excavated in what antiquity regarded as the Euboean colony of Torone, and worked on Zagora on Andros, which a colleague of his (then Swiss in Australia, but a 'Euboean man' through excavating at Eretria) had described as an Eretrian colony.[59] One might understand the feeling of being beleaguered by Euboeans, mainly championed by native Europeans. R.A. Kearsley (Australia) had cut the Euboean pendent-semicircle-cup culture down to size by down-dating its appearance at Al Mina in the east (with some justification), but also prolonging its life unduly and suggesting that much was made in Cyprus or Syria.[60] But she is not essentially anti-Euboean at all. A more determined anti-Euboean scholar, J.Y. Perreault, is French/Canadian.[61] A former Oxford doctoral student, Franco De Angelis (Canadian), has pointed out what might be evidence of a colonial approach to archaeological evidence on the part of T.J. Dunbabin

---

[56] S. Hornblower, *OJA* 16 (1997) 177-186 shows that antiquity thought Torone was a colony from Chalcis, whence the name Chal*ci*dice. The 'Eretrian' colony at Mende has now produced purely Eretrian subgeometric amphorae (*BSA* 91 (1996) 323, fig. 2).
[57] An interesting reflection on Antipodean attitudes and European man in R Hughes, *The Culture of Complaint* (1993) lecture 2.
[58] T. Cuyler Young in *CAH* IV (1988) 76.

[59] J.-P. Descoeudres, *Antike Kunst* 16 (1973) 87-8.
[60] *The Pendent Semi-Circle Skyphos* (1989); 1995, 7-81; and in *Classical Art in the Nicholson Museum* (eds. A. Cambitoglou and E. Robinson, 1995) 17-28.
[61] In *Prakt. A' diethnous arch. synedriou, Delphoi 1986* (1991) 393-406, and *L'Emporion* (eds. A Bresson and P. Rouillard, 1993) 59-83. *Cf.* Boardman (1994, 96, n. 4; 99, n. 20).

(Australia) in *The Western Greeks*.[62] When this was being worked on, pre-World War II, colonialism was viewed with less passion than it is today, when it is judged unfair to compare the colonial and post-colonial conditions of some countries, and any non-dominant partner must always be on the side of the angels. (Dominant peoples are racist; non-dominant are at worst prejudiced.) I notice that serious study of South Italian (colonial Greek) red figure pottery has become an Australian virtue, for which we are all deeply grateful. A major conference whose papers are entitled *Greek Colonies and Native Populations* was held in Australia in 1985, very conscious of the possible special contribution to such studies of Australia, 'both a colonized and colonizing power'. I hope is is not churlish to voice the suspicion that such a background might prove as distorting as illuminating when antiquity is under review, but could hardly insist that a European one might be any better. A scholar ought to be affected by neither.

I have confined observations, selectively, to east/west, colony/mother-city relations in the Greek period. It could no doubt be extended. Not all biases need be misleading nor prejudices wrong, but the mere mention of modern colonialism in the same breath as ancient should invite caution, and the assumption that all attitudes of earlier scholarship are wrong is uncritical. Some colonies were cast-offs, others a successful venture for a mother-city with need for land or aspirations to wealth; some colonists' new neighbours enjoyed an enhanced culture through their presence, others were utterly blighted. But it is not for scholars to exercise old or new resentments. Serious scholarly interest in such matters in antiquity has been generated in the last 50 years not by modern experience but by new excavations and by the fact that these are excellent subjects which respond well to that marriage of archaeology and socio-economic history to which all archaeologists and some historians aspire. It need not have been, nor continue to be a matter of taking sides, whether Marxist, Structuralist, Imperialist or Correct.

Reformed attitudes to colonialism in antiquity are not confined to the Greek world or period. In a recent paper on the Kushite kingdom the tendency to regard it as dependent on Egypt is criticised, but without dispelling the fact that its real contribution depended mainly on Egypt, whatever its independence of attitude from time to time.[63] Whole volumes have been devoted to studies of nationalism in scholarship,[64] without, so far as I can see, pointing out that it is up to authors to self-regulate in this respect if they wish to be taken seriously. For a different classical period, the Roman, Ronald Syme (New Zealand) vigorously argued in *The Colonial Élites, Rome, Spain, the Americas* (1958) - lectures delivered in Canada - the debt that Imperial Rome owed to its colonials: 'Energy, ambition and opportunism brought the provincial élite to the conquest of the metropolis.'.[65] It is the choice of subject rather than its correctness that is interesting, the vigour with which it is argued, and the assumption that modern experience can help explain antiquity rather than simply mould expectations. Thus, I have heard it questioned whether students of Rome in the East have been ready enough to acknowledge the importance of Arab presence, until, with Mohammed, it becomes unignorable.

On a narrower front, Classical scholars have long been trying to be less Atheno-centric in their approach, difficult for most who have been brought up on Athenian art because it is the most prominent and demonstrably influential, becoming easier for those who have also worked seriously outside Athens and Athenian art. All are now enjoined also to be less Helleno-centric. This need not lead scholars to adopt the Mis-hellenism which some non-Classical scholars, and those Classical who have been swept along by Correct approaches, now exercise. It has some unusual effects. One of the oddest is the presentation of the great Dipylon amphora as 'Phoenicianizing'.[66] Latent anti-semitism is sometimes invoked, though carefully projected onto past generations. The allowable ancient champions of the non-Greek world have been chosen: Egyptians and Phoenicians, the former for their assumed dependence on Black Africa, the latter because they are thought (equally wrongly) to have been given a bad time by Greeks (ancient, and modern scholars), and deserve better. It was M. Fredericksen (Australia, an expert on colonial and native Campania), who remarked some years back that 'the Phoenicians are on the way back'. In near eastern studies (As)syria, which was the really influential Semitic area, is brushed aside. So far as can be judged from texts, most ancient Greeks would have agreed about their foreign mentors, though Herodotus' obsessive interest in making assimilations with Greek deities north, east and south, has not helped to a balanced view of this; and Classical scholars of the last hundred years may have lauded Hellenism but have generally not been at all dismissive of non-Greeks, although they can be made to appear so through selective quotation and abridged bibliographies. It is as though F. Poulsen's *Der Orient und die frühgriechische Kunst* (1912) has been forgotten, as well as many a 19th-century dictionary article. Such evenhandedness cannot now

---

[62] *Antiquity* 72 (1998) 539-49.
[63] L. Török, Kush: an African state in the first millennium B.C., *Proceedings of the British Academy* 87 (1995) 1-38.
[64] E.g., P.L. Kohl and C. Fawcett eds., *Nationalism, Politics and Archaeology* (Cambridge 1995); *cf.* E. Gabba, Colonie antiche e moderne, *Scienze d'Antichità* 5 (1991) 601-14.

[65] In the introduction G.P. Gilmour remarks that Syme 'addressed an audience whose thought and ways have been strongly influenced, whether by way of reaction or imitation, by the theories and practices of the strong men who led in settlement and exploitation distantly or immediately south of the Canadian border in the sixteenth to eighteenth centuries'.
[66] G. Kopcke (German, now USA) in Kopcke and Tokumaru 1992, 108, 112, frontispiece. The two subsidiary friezes of animals may have been introduced to Attica from the east, but not exclusively if at all from Phoenicia, and not directly into the Dipylon Painter's work, and they are turned to geometric pattern by the Greek. 'The rhythmization of the human figure' (*ibid.*, p. 108) is attributed to Phoenician renderings unknown to me.

be admitted. I take one or two recent cases to illustrate the point.

Nicolas Coldstream, in more complete control than most if not all scholars of the evidence for Geometric Greece, observed imitation of eastern pottery in Rhodes. He cited many parallels from Cyprus and Syria, few in Phoenicia. The most conspicuous class of pottery in question (KW flasks) copied Cypriot. He proposed that there was an eastern presence in Rhodes. This was not an altogether necessary deduction, and decidedly not to the extent that it relied on identity of people from pottery being copied rather than imported, especially when the motive seems to have been commercial rather than local use. Moreover, he identified the immigrants as Phoenicians, in line with common archaeological bias in their favour (which I find I exercised to some degree in *The Greeks Overseas*).[67]

For the second case, Papadopoulos identifies Phoenician presence at Lefkandi and the grave of a resident alien there, on the strength of the Egyptian, Cypriot, Syrian and dubiously Phoenician objects found in it.[68] If similar evidence had been Greek on a foreign shore, even from a single source, he would probably have been reluctant to explain it as evidence for Greek presence, but such double standards are sadly rife in these areas of study, so deep-rooted is commitment to the Correct solution. His views on these matters echo those of Sarah Morris, whose *Daidalos* is a singularly brilliant if sometimes prejudiced attempt to define and explain the eastern in Greece. Thus, she writes of the exaggeration of the Euboean role "largely by European excavators of Al Mina, Lefkandi and Pithekoussai",[69] and that to "identify 'Euboians' in Syria, Cyprus, Crete, Ischia, and even Euboia itself may be a mistake"![70] The 'European' tag is interesting in the light of what I have already written about colonialism.

Whether hobbies affect attitudes or are determined by them I do not know, but I remarked some time ago that in *Who's Who* the hobbies of a scholar dedicated to survey and decrying excavation were 'mountaineering and skiing', and of a devoted excavator 'gardening'.[71] I have mentioned national preferences already. These are quite apparent throughout the world of classical scholarship, from Britain to Greece. I have not detected the same tendencies in the near east, no particularly chauvinistic Lebanese/Phoenician views opposed to Israeli/Israel-Judah, or Egyptian; the prejudices are more readily exercised by foreigners to these areas or perhaps expatriates. In the United States I suspect that scholars who are first- or second-generation Americans are most likely to champion the colony or non-Greek than the longer established, who have forgiven the 'poverty, oppression and persecution' (*sic*; I quote from the film *Independence Day*) suffered under the British, and have come to adopt a colonizer's viewpoint. No one seems to reflect that Britain has been more colonized, from Romans to French, than most European countries.

There are many other less academic motives which might induce some to adopt unusual attitudes, especially the revisionist: disappointment in jobs, in an unfinished or unpublishable thesis, the publicity value of saying something apparently outrageous or revolutionary (academic hooliganism), fear of not keeping pace with new ideas in other disciplines, discovering that the best way to deal with the complicated structure of a subject may be to deny its validity, envy, showing-off, unwillingness or inability to face the rigours of some traditional approaches, ill health, delusions of inferiority/superiority, pique at being left out of something. The rarity is passion for the truth and readiness to admit either failure or the impossibility of finding a solution.

The Phoenician question has assumed an important role in determining scholarly allegiances, and requires some comment in the context of this article. Our evidence for the importance of the Phoenicians depends in part on eastern texts, in which they generally play the role of traders, often tributaries of the Great Powers, or craftsmen-patrons of the kings of Israel, and Greek texts, where they are often merchant adventurers, allegedly treated rather on a par with latterday car-salesmen and estate agents. In fact Greeks and Phoenicians got on with one another better than many might admit.[72] No one doubts the Phoenicians' eventual role in the west Mediterranean, but we are invited to believe that they led the Greeks there, despite the Greeks' far longer involvement in the west and closer proximity. But this is another story. Except in the west, the Phoenicians' archaeological identity remains elusive. The excuse that their main cities have never been properly excavated is a thin one, and has given some *carte blanche* to declare Phoenician what they will. There is a mass of material from Phoenicia, and if its precise provenance and context is commonly unknown this is hardly a worse case than that in many other eastern areas. At any rate, the well-documented finds in areas south are regularly recruited to fill the gap, possibly correctly, although in a craft which we can judge - scarab-making, identified as Phoenician or other by inscription - there are very marked regional differences away from

---

[67] J.N. Coldstream, The Phoenicians of Ialysos, *BICS* 16 (1969) 3-8; *cf.* Boardman 1994a, 97. A result is such incautious remarks as 'there is now clear evidence that Phoenicians were manufacturing perfumes on Rhodes before 700' (W. Burkert, *The Orientalizing Revolution* (1992) 17).

[68] Papadopoulos 1996, 159. The occupant must be identified by the type of burial and furniture (Greek pots and weapons), not exotica acquired in life and included. And see now *idem*, 'Phantom Euboians' in *Journal of Mediterranean Archaeology* 10.2 (1997) 191-219.

[69] In Kopcke and Tokumaru 1992, xiv.

[70] *Daidalos* (1992) 141. Phoenician pots and objects at Ischia, Knossos, Kommos, anywhere in the Mediterranean, seem to be taken unhesitatingly by some as evidence for Phoenician presence; the return courtesy for Greek goods is disallowed except in an avowed Greek colony; the rest must be carried by Phoenicians.

[71] *Antiquity* 62 (1988) 796.

[72] Boardman 1994b, 49-50.

Phoenicia.⁷³ Pottery helps hardly at all since most major eastern classes are proving from analysis to have been made in many different centres, from Cyprus and all along the Levant coast: this applies from Red Slip to the so-called Canaanite amphorae. Thus, the difference between the Red Slip at Al Mina and in Palestine is shown by analysis, and Joan du Plat Taylor long ago observed that the former was unlike the classic 'Samaria ware'.⁷⁴ So whence is the Red Slip on Ischia, for example, and by/for whom was it ever copied (see above)?

Coldstream gave a good account of Phoenicians in the Aegean long ago, in 1982, and there have been several since, more partisan.⁷⁵ Phoenician identity is simply assumed and in many cases is demonstrably wrong, as some of even Coldstream's own observations and parallels show, but he has the advantage of a mainly archaeological rather than ideological approach. The tendency to declare Phoenician anything that looks Egyptian in the Mediterranean is uncritical and does less than justice to the Phoenician achievement. The Phoenicians' egyptianizing is highly competent; we can judge that from the inscribed scarabs (see above), metalwork and ivories.⁷⁶ Garbled versions of Egyptian style are generally Greek - certainly in Naukratis and almost certainly earlier in Rhodes.⁷⁷ To call the egyptianizing work of Cyprus (an island often close to Egypt politically and with direct sea access) Phoenician cannot be the whole truth and disregards the remarkable record of continuity, identity and prosperity in the island. Moreover, we now know that both Greek and probably Phoenician were being spoken and written in the island from about 1000 BC. There is no convincing archaeological support for thinking that the Greek Orientalizing Revolution was a product of Phoenician influence rather than Syrian/Assyrian; it is not an either/or question and generally the customer can be shown to have called the tune. The wrong Semites are being privileged. The Greek Classical Revolution of the 5th century depended, in arts and crafts, on the way Greek art had developed in the preceding Archaic period of the 6th century, and this in turn depended wholly on the preceding Orientalising period. Any independence still enjoyed by the Syrian states disappeared under the blows of Assyria by the early 7th century, but their legacy was the Orientalising culture of Greece. The phenomenon was due to a combination of Syrian skills and Greek enterprise. Both deserve their share of the credit, without belittling Phoenician enterprise in the west Mediterranean and parts of Italy, or the quality of Phoenician art.

The Greeks used the term 'Phoenician' rather loosely, while for Herodotus much from the Black Sea to Egypt was 'Syria'. From Homer on Phoenicia was Sidon rather than Tyre. We would naturally have taken the women who painted the ivory cheekpieces in Homer (*Il.* 4. 141-142) for Phoenician, but for the fact that he calls them Lydian and Carian. Helen's 'Cypro-Phoenician' silver workbasket on wheels was in fact a gift from Egypt (*Od.* 4. 128-132). Most modern accounts of Phoenicians in Homer make him appear critical of them, yet the attitude is no different to that applied in his poems to all seafarers, who are regularly asked whether they are merchants or pirates (*Od.* 3. 71-74), while all merchants are despised by landowners (*Od.* 8. 161-164). And when Odysseus does speak well of a Phoenician (*Od.* 13. 276-277) this has now to be dismissed as a deliberate indication of uncharacteristic behaviour.⁷⁸ There is far more complexity in these matters than many make appear, and we would do well to use no ethnic epithet for people or objects without circumspection.

Neglect of Egypt is no less reprehensible, and comes easily to those who apply the label 'Phoenician' indiscriminately. A recent review of the Mediterranean economy in the early first millennium manages to ignore it almost entirely.⁷⁹ A champion of Egypt has been Martin Bernal, with whom we return to the 'people' and modern intellectual aspects of this subject, and leave antiquity behind. So far Bernal's detailed arguments have concerned the Bronze Age and we have yet to see what he makes of the Iron Age though there are many hints in Volume I of *Black Athena* (1987). He has been much misquoted but his heavily partisan approach must leave him open to the suspicion that at least in part there is a response to western guilt over Black Africa, and he is open in his belief that anti-semitism has been a major factor in western scholarly attitudes. But even casual reading in 19th-century literature suggests that the record is more evenly balanced, or at least no more unbalanced than it is today. He came to the subject from an already distinguished career in the study of east Asian languages. What he calls the 'scattered Jewish components of my ancestry' played, he writes, no obvious part in his decision to turn to Hebrew studies, though then to be convinced by the historical conclusions of the linguists Gordon and his pupil Astour is even less obviously explicable, unless he was more heavily predisposed to be

---

⁷³ *Studies in the Iconography of Northwest Semitic Inscribed Seals* (eds. B. Sass and C. Uehlinger, 1993) usefully collects and illustrates seals with Aramaic, Phoenician, Ammonite, Moabite and Hebrew inscriptions. The illustrations show the many differences between each group in terms of iconography and are an invaluable guide to identifying the many non-inscribed. The Phoenician have a rather limited range of Egyptian subjects, single figures rather than hieroglyphs, which appear more often from Egypt itself and on egyptianizing work from Greek (Rhodes and Naukratis) or Cypriot workshops: Gorton 1996.
⁷⁴ *Iraq* 21 (1959) 79. W. Culican makes a distinction between 'metropolitan' Red Slip of Phoenicia and the 'other contemporary tradition of red-slipped ware in the early Iron Age of the Levant': *CAH* III.2 (1991) 475. For analyses of Red Slip, D.J. Liddy in J.N. Coldstream and H.W. Catling (eds.) *Knossos, the North Cemetery* II (1996) 481-94. *Cf.* Boardman 1999a, 149-50.
⁷⁵ In Niemeyer 1982, 261-75. But *cf.* O. Negbi, *AJA* 96 (1992) 599-615.
⁷⁶ G. Hölbl, *Orientalia* 58 (1989) 318-25; G. Markoe, *BASOR* 279 (1990) 13-26 for a good assessment.
⁷⁷ Gorton 1996.

⁷⁸ Winter 1995, 248, citing Rhys Carpenter. A more sympathetic assessment of Homer and Phoenicians by Sherratt 1996, 91-2.
⁷⁹ Sherratts 1993.

convinced than many scholars, including orientalists.[80] He has attempted the impossible but totally desirable task, to move from linguistic studies to a comprehensive view of the history and archaeology of the Bronze and Iron Ages of the Middle East (which may be allowed to include Greece and Egypt). The impossibility has led him to be rather highly selective of evidence from the work of scholars whose own motivations are not readily judged by an outsider, let alone by many insiders. It also encouraged a very single-minded approach which brooks no challenge or willingness to accept either evidence for broader issues or more detailed objections, a style of reasoning that is met in several of the wilder extremes of Politically Correct thought (Animal Rights, etc.) where what might be a laudable intention becomes a passionate obsession.

Bernal's grandfather was a distinguished Egyptologist, Sir Alan Gardiner, whom I had the privilege of knowing. Bernal is able to quote his apparent, but not passionately felt, resentment of Greek attitudes to Egypt.[81] Bernal's father to whom he dedicates *Black Athena*, 'who taught me that things fit together, interestingly', was a polymath and brilliant physicist and geneticist; also possibly a model for single-minded devotion to a defective cause.[82]

An influential work of recent years on related matters is E. Saïd's *Orientalism* (1978). He paints a vivid picture of the partly imaginary 'orient', its eccentricity and shortcomings conjured by the scholarship and prejudice of the west, from its partial, though often profound, experience of 'the east'. He quotes his sources generously so that it is possible to see where his commentary on them may sometimes seem strained. In these matters whatever you seek you can find. Criticism led to his polite retraction of some misapprehensions of his intentions in his appendix to a later edition (1995). He has a short, perhaps revealing explanation of what led him to the work, and comments 'The life of an Arab Palestinian in the West, particularly in America, is disheartening'. He had been brought up in colonial (*sic*) Palestine and Egypt, and the USA. One cannot help wondering what he would have written had he spent his adult working life, not in the USA, but in Britain, which has been traditionally more sympathetic to the Arab world.

And then there is Boardman (1927-). Perhaps this will set a fashion for declaration of interests by scholars dealing with special issues where other and prejudicial factors might be thought to operate.[83] I have no colonial affiliations but one grandmother was Irish (Dublin). I was educated at a Public School ('Private' to Americans) but did not 'live in', and all my education and early research were paid for by the state or scholarships from school and college, a product of the 'pre-Welfare-State'. This is one reason why I feel that scholars who can should repay their debt by making their subjects accessible to the wider public that has supported them. A significant part of World War II was spent in London air-raid shelters - which might account for a certain realist or even fatalist approach to the world, but also a touch of chauvinism and deafness. My father had been a devout but not obsessive Christian, my mother the daughter of a village carpenter. My father came from what seems to be a long line of City clerks which might explain my (and my brother's) aptitudes for mathematics rather than languages. My education was heavily linguistic in classics until I attended a lecture by Charles Seltman at Cambridge and realised what more there was. Post-war I was as leftist as most of my age, and subsequently rather a-political. My army service was spent mainly teaching map-reading in Sussex. I became 'a Euboean man' by accident. Any pupil of Robert Cook naturally looked for an Archaic Greek ware to study, but in 1948 none was accessible in Athens except for Eretrian, which was suggested to me by Semni Karouzou, while Dr Threpsiades let me loose in the Eretria *apotheke*. I recall sitting out the effects of a hangover on the hill overlooking the Stadion in Athens in 1949 with a philosopher friend (Renford Bambrough) who asked why on earth I was studying such dull pottery. I said, with no conviction whatever, that it might prove to have some historical significance. My job in Oxford enabled me to identify a few pieces of Euboean pottery in the Al Mina material, and I speculated that there might be much more, a view that was vindicated by the finds at Lefkandi and clay analysis. I have not dug in Euboea and visited Al Mina for the first time in 2001. I was more 'an Ionian man' after Old Smyrna (Bayrakli) and the Chios excavations; or 'a Cretan man' after the Knossos tablets and the Oxford Cretan Collection. I wrote *The Greeks Overseas* not because I was interested in colonies, which was what Max Mallowan, the editor, asked for, but because he allowed me to include east and south, for which the Al Mina material, editing Dunbabin's last book, and the Chios-Naukratis connection had supplied an interest. Some of my friends thought I had defected to the oriental. I recognize the book as old-fashioned but it seemed worth updating modestly after 20 years, and several recent translations suggest that old-fashioned approaches have a significant survival value. I distrust work in which theory drives the evidence rather than emerges from it. Excavating a colony, at Tocra, was the result of sheer cupidity in the face of the promise of so much fine Archaic pottery. Gem studies resulted from idle moments in Athens fascinated by Furtwängler's great volumes, and from the arrival in Oxford of R.M. Dawkins' brother with an old sock full of Island Gems. I was not a pupil of Beazley and learnt to trust his method by practising it. Iconographic interest stemmed from casual observations about specific scenes, not a deliberate

---

[80] Reviews of M. Astour's *Hellenosemitica* (1965) by what might seem to be a dedicated classicist (me) and a dedicated orientalist (Richard Barnett) were remarkably similar: *Classical Review* 1966, 86-8; *Journal of Semitic Studies* 13 (1968) 256-8.
[81] *Black Athena* I (1987) 265-6.
[82] *Dictionary of National Biography 1971-80* (1986) 54.
[83] *Compromising Tradition; the personal voice in classical scholarship* (eds. S.P. Hallett and T. Van Nortwick 1997) strikes warning notes, and is itself a warning.

search for political symbolism or any other -ism, although they came to serve such subjects; and from involvement in *LIMC*. I am neither a gardener nor physically assertive, only sporadically energetic in early years; I value comfort but distrust luxury. I find I have a growing affection for the post-antique east. And so on. My resentment at being thought prejudiced may be misguided, and I am sure I cannot detect all influences, but I am far more conscious of the effects of assisted serendipity and joy in the subject than of any programme or attitudes induced by education or politics or persons; I hate being misquoted or misrepresented but am well used to it by now; and I can do little about my instinctive intolerance of the intolerant, or desire to ridicule the ridiculous.

Bibliography

Baurain *et al.* (eds.) 1991: *Phoinikeia Grammata*, Namur.

Boardman, J. 1959: Greek Potters at Al Mina?. *Anatolian Studies* 9, 163-9.

Boardman, J. 1990: Al Mina and History. *OJA* 9, 169-90.

Boardman, J. 1994a: Orientalia and Orientals on Ischia. *AION* N.S. 1, 95-100.

Boardman, J. 1994b: *The Diffusion of Classical Art in Antiquity*, London.

Boardman, J. 1999a: The Excavated History of Al Mina. In G.R. Tstetskhladze (ed.) *Ancient Greeks West and East*, Leiden, 135-62.

Boardman, J. 1999b: *The Greeks Overseas*, London.

Brinkman, J.A. 1989: The Akkadian words for 'Ionia' and 'Ionian'. In R.F. Sutton (ed.), *Daidalikon*, Wauconda, 53-71.

Carter, J.B. and Morris, S.P. (eds.) 1995: *The Ages of Homer*, Austin.

Coldstream, J.N. 1994: Prospectors and Pioneers: Pithekoussai, Kyme and Central Italy. In Tsetskhladze and De Angelis (1994) 47-60.

Dunbabin, T.J. 1957: *The Greeks and their Eastern Neighbours*. London.

Evely, D. *et al.* (eds.) 1996: *Minotaur and Centaur*, Oxford.

Gorton, A.F. 1996: *Egyptian and Egyptianizing Scarabs*, Oxford.

Johnston, A.W. 1979: *Trademarks on Greek Vases*, Warminster.

Jones, R.E. 1986: *Greek and Cypriot Pottery*, Athens.

Kearsley, R.A. 1995: The Greek Geometric Wares from Al Mina Levels 10-8 and associated pottery. *Mediterranean Archaeology* 8, 7-81.

Kopcke, G. and Tokumaru, I. 1992: *Greece between East and West: 10th - 8th Centuries BC*, Mainz.

Lemaire, A. 1991: L'écriture phénicienne en Cilicie. In Baurain *et al.* 1991, 133-46.

Murray, O. (ed.) 1995: *In vino veritas*, London.

Niemeyer, H.G. (ed.) 1982: *Phönizier im Westen*, Madrider Beiträge 5, Mainz

Papadopoulos, J.K. 1996: Euboians in Macedonia? A Closer Look. *OJA* 15, 151-82.

Popham, M.R. 1994: Precolonisation: early Greek contact with the East. In Tsetskhladze and De Angelis 1994, 11-34.

Reyes, A.T. 1994: *Archaic Cyprus*, Oxford.

Saltz, D. 1978: *Greek Geometric Pottery in the East* (Harvard diss.).

Sherratt, S. and A. 1993: The Growth of the Mediterranean Economy in the early first millennium BC. *World Archaeology* 24, 361-78.

Sherratt, S. 1996: With us but not of us: the role of Crete in Homeric epic. In Evely *et al.* 1996, 87-99.

Tsetskhladze, G. and De Angelis, F. (eds.) 1994: *The Archaeology of Greek Colonisation*, Oxford.

Winter, I.J. 1995: Homer's Phoenicians. In Carter and Morris 1995, 248-71.

Greek Contact with the Levant and Mesopotamia in the First Half of the First Millennium BC: A View from the East

Amélie Kuhrt

Introduction

The aim of a series of seminars held in Cambridge was to gain a clearer grasp of Greek interaction with areas to the north and the Near East. I shall concentrate in this paper on the period from the 8th to the 6th centuries. The conventional periodisations of Greek history that parallel this are not especially meaningful in the context of the *longue durée* of Near Eastern history, where we are dealing with a great spectrum of diverse and highly developed cities and states (see, most recently, Sasson *et al.* 1995; Kuhrt 1995). This is a feature that I may seem to be overemphasising at times, but should be constantly kept before us. Between *ca.* 900 and 500 BC Greek communities were, by comparison with the Near East, poor, and their socio-political structures relatively underdeveloped (see Osborne 1996). Momentous changes were, of course, taking place and accelerating late in the period, but if we look at some of the contemporary large states and rich cities of the Near East, such as the Neo-Assyrian and Babylonian empires, Egypt, Urartu, the Phoenician cities, the small Syro-Palestinian kingdoms, the comparative backwardness and poverty of Greece is obvious. In many respects it might be fair to regard developments in Greece as dependent on what was happening in the Near East, and in that sense it could even be helpful to regard it as a marginal, or frontier, zone. First and foremost, the large states of the Near East offered a living to Greeks, primarily and most importantly through their need for manpower, especially in the military sphere - this could take the form of a limited period of service or the incorporation of recruits into Near Eastern armies together with grants of heritable land plots sufficient to support a family (see Lloyd 1983, 279-348; Wallinga 1991, 179-97; 1993, 89-92). In this respect, the Near East was a crucially important source of employment for members of Greek communities. There were also other ways in which Greek-Near Eastern relations could be formulated: eastern kings occasionally extend their patronage to Greek craftsmen, their courts attract Greek philosophers, learned men and experts of various kinds, such as doctors.[1] Greek interaction with the Near East is further signalled by stories about 'Phoenician' merchants in the Aegean,[2] the finds of Near Eastern artefacts in Greek territory (for recent surveys, see Curtis 1996; Hoffman 1997), the 'orientalising' phase in Greek art,[3] the influence of Near Eastern literary types on aspects of Greek writing and, of course, the adoption of the Phoenician alphabet.[4] What is unclear and continues to be debated is precisely how these relations are to be visualised, how intense they were and where exactly contact took place.

When searching for answers to these questions, two further points need to be kept in mind. First, the term 'the ancient Near East' does not refer to a single, monolithic entity. It embraces a region that is marked by immense variety in terms of cultures, physical environments, languages, writing systems, religious, social and political structures, historical, literary and artistic traditions. To speak about Greece and the Near East as two contrasting units confronting each other is a nonsense, certainly in the period before the development of the Achaemenid empire. Therefore, contacts between Greek communities and various parts of this enormously variegated region are likely to have taken a mass of different forms. The second point is the span of time involved: several groups in the ancient Near East could, at the beginning of the first millennium, look back on a traceable, *memorialized* history that stretched back over 2000 years. Within that long period immense transformations had taken place; they may not always be clear to us but are, nevertheless, a fact. Further, in the period with which I am concerned here (i.e. the time between 1000 and 500 BC), we can identify a number of critical changes:

a) **Egypt** underwent a whole series of profound political upheavals from a country consisting of largely Libyan-dominated principalities to subjection by Nubia, Assyrian domination and finally independence and reunification under another Libyan dynasty (dynasty 26, the Saites) (Kitchen 1986; Lloyd 1983; Kuhrt 1995, ch. 12).

b) **Assyria** in the same period expanded, in a series of conquests, from a small kingdom confined to North Iraq to become an empire embracing the whole of the Fertile Crescent from *ca.* 700 BC until its final collapse in *ca.* 610 (*CAH* III parts 1 and 2, chs. 6-7, 21-25; Kuhrt 1995, cap. 9).

c) The **Babylonian state** experienced periods of

---

[1] The main attestations are, in Herodotus, for Lydia; Greek doctors are, as far as I am aware, only attested at the Persian court (the best-known being Democedes of Croton (Hdt. 3. 129-137, to be read in conjunction with Griffiths 1987, 37-51) and, of course, Ctesias of Knidos), see the list in Miller 1997, 100; for the long history of foreign artisans, scholars and doctors residing at courts in the ancient Near East, see Zaccagnini 1983, 245.

[2] See, for example, Carpenter 1958, 35-53 (a conspectus on classical sources relating to Phoenician expansion); also Bunnens 1979; Latacz 1990 (Homer); Powell 1938, *s.v. Phoinix* (Herodotus).

[3] For a broad assessment, see Gunter 1990; and see the stimulating study by Morris 1992.

[4] The classic study is Burkert 1992; see now the detailed analysis by West 1997.

extreme political turmoil, generated by difficult internal conditions and exacerbated by incorporation into the Assyrian empire, whence it emerged between 626 and 605 BC as the successor state to the Assyrians (Brinkman 1968; 1984; Frame 1992; Kuhrt 1995, ch. 11).

These examples are used simply to illustrate how important it is to be aware of change over time within Near Eastern lands; it does not even touch on the complexities of developments in Anatolia, among the small polities of the Levant and western Iran, which all formed part of this political and cultural mosaic. But the implications of the point I am making should be obvious: any Greek contacts within this period will have been affected and modified by these upheavals - just as they will also have differed from region to region.

After these preliminaries, I shall now focus on two particular points in order to clarify the picture of Greek contacts with 'the east', which may serve as an example of the kinds of problems of understanding and shifts in the dynamics of relationship of which we need to be aware. Because of the particular rôle in the debate that has been played by possible Greek settlements in the Levant, at sites such as Al Mina, Ras-el-Basit and Tell Sukas, I shall ignore Egypt and concentrate on Assyria and Babylonia as the two largest Near Eastern empires preceding the Achaemenid realm. I shall discuss, first, the textual evidence for Greek contacts with them,[5] how precise it is and what the implications are. Secondly, since the picture of Greek interaction with the Near East is dominated by the image of mercantile links and settlements, I shall consider briefly the trading mechanisms of the successive states of Assyria and Babylonia to provide a clearer idea of what kind of commercial patterns Greeks might have encountered and to which they had to accommodate themselves.

Assyrian sources

The Neo-Assyrian evidence is not extensive, but has at times been made much of, particularly by Braun (1982); it requires correction and clarification before conclusions can be drawn.

a) Tiglath-pileser III (744-727 BC)
1. NL 69 (H.W.F. Saggs, *Iraq* 25 (1963)) 1.3
This is a letter from Qurdi-Aššur-lamur, active in the region of Tyre, Mount Lebanon, Sidon and Kašpuna (identified as Al Mina by Parpola),[6] after the expansion of Assyrian power there between 735 and 727 BC, to the Assyrian king. It is occasionally dated to the reign of Sargon II, but is more likely to date to the reign of Tiglath-pileser III:

> The 'Ionians' (kur *ia-u-na-a-a*) have come. They have fought in the cities of Sams[imuruna], Harisu and [...]

The points to note are:
(i) there is no earlier reference to Ionians in the Assyrian texts;
(ii) contra Braun (1982, 15), this passage tells us nothing more than that the 'Ionians' are a hostile force, active along the Lebanese coast;
(iii) the references to 'in his ships' and 'in the midst of the sea' which occur 5 lines further on in a broken context cannot be linked directly to the Ionians, nor are we told what exactly the Ionians were doing here. Braun's recreation of piratical Greeks from Cilicia Aspera is pure speculation; it is certainly possible, but not testified to by this text.

2. It has been suggested by Parpola (1970, 186-7) that NL 12 (H.W.F. Sagga, *Iraq* 17 (1955)), 11.40-44, an important letter to which I return below, contains a reference to Ionians. It, too, was written by Qurdi-Aššur-lamur:

> I appointed a eunuch as fortcommander over them, and sent in 30 [...] *ia-na-a-a* (Parpola emends: [KUR *i]a-ú-na-a-a*) troops to keep guard, (and) 30 (other) troops willl relieve them. With regard to the king's instruction, that I should send 10 KUR *ia-su-ba-a-a* (Parpola emends: KUR *ia-ú-na-a-a*) into Kašpuna ...

As Brinkman (1989, 55) has pointed out, Parpola's proposed emendations do not fit the traces as preserved in the original publication. Moreover, Postgate in his treatment of this text (Postgate 1974, 392) restored and read it quite differently. According to him, the reference at the relevant points is to troops from Shianaia, a place in the area of the Levant and member of the coalition formed against Shalmaneser III in 853 BC (Grayson 1996, Shalmaneser III A.O. 102.2 ii94). Yasuba, troops of which are referred to in the last line, is north-east of Babylonia; but this need not be an objection to Postagte's interpretation as the reference here could well be to deported families from there settled in the vicinity of Tyre.

The results from this are meagre: there is one reference to an Ionian raid on western coastal centres; but the Ionians are not otherwise located (even vaguely), so their base of operations is unknown. The aim, size and nature of the attack remains unclear; there is no hint of any kind of commercial relationship between Ionians and the Levant.

---

[5] For a collection of the relevant passages and discussion on philological problems, see Brinkman 1989.
[6] See the map at the end of Parpola 1987.

b) Sargon II (721-705 BC):

3. H. Winckler, *Die Keilschrifttexte Sargons* 1889, I 148: 34-5:

> (Sargon) ... who caught 'Ionians' (kur *ia-am-na-a-a*) of the midst of the sea like fish

4. F.H. Weissbach, *ZDMG* 72 (1918) 178: 15-6:

> I ... caught 'Ionians] of the midst of the sea of the setting sun like fish and [dep]orted (?) them

5. C.J. Gadd, *Iraq* 16 (1954) 199: 1.19:

> (Sargon) ... who in the midst of the sea caught 'Ionians' as a fowler does fish

6. D.G. Lyon, *Keilschrifttexte Sargons, Königs von Assyrien (722-705 v.Chr.)* 1883, 4: 21:

> (Sargon) ... who in the midst of the sea caught 'Ionians' as a fowler does fish

All four passages are in the nature of summary statements linked to sweeping surveys of the empire and the king's achievements in the later part of Sargon's reign. In all cases the Ionians are associated with the Mediterranean, but any further precision is lacking: they appear as a distant and hostile group, used to define the most distant western lands of Assyrian power.

c) Directly comparable to the Sargon passages is a solitary one by Esarhaddon (680-669 BC), which is also the latest Neo-Assyrian reference to Ionians:

7. R. Borger, *Die Inschriften Asarhaddons, Königs von Assyrien* 1956, 86/AsBbE: 10-11:

> All kings from the midst of the sea, from the land of Cyprus (kur *ia-da-na-na*), the land of 'Ionia' (kur *ia-man*) to the land of Tarsisi, bowed at my feet. I received their heavy tribute.

This again gives us a bird's eye view of the Assyrian empire, casting the net as wide as possible in the direction of all the points of the compass. Again, any direct contact, war or conquest of any kind is not indicated, aside from the generalized statement of gifts acknowledging the Assyrian king's power. If, as often argued, Tarsisi here really does mean Tartessos (Braun 1982, 20; Lipinski 1992, 440-2, *s.v.* Tarshish) that point is obvious. Localisation and identity, aside from the Mediterranean, remain vague in the extreme - perhaps an east to west sweep of Phoenician trade contacts is being envisaged, *i.e.* Cyprus-Aegean-Spain.

d) One reference, adduced by Braun (1982, 19), which must be separated from Assyrian mentions of Ionians, occurs in Sennacherib's *Annals* (**8** below), recording an Assyrian river and sea-borne attack on Elam in 694 BC:

8. D.D. Luckenbill, *The Annals of Sennacherib* 1924, 73: 58-61:

> Mighty ships, the workmanship of their land, they built dexterously. Tyrian, Sidonian (and) Cypriot (kur *ia-ad-na-na-a-a*) sailors, prisoners of my hand, I ordered (to descend) the Tigris with them ...

The word which Braun has interpreted as a reference to Ionians/Greeks, is in fact well attested by other Assyrian references to Cyprus = *Yadnana*. It is definitively identified as such on Sargon's Cyprus stele and the word is quite distinct from the Akkadian rendering of 'Ionian' = *Yam/wan*.[7] What Braun suggested was that this reference to supposed Ionian sailors being set to work in the Assyrian heartland and sent through Babylonia to the Persian Gulf in 694 BC should be connected to a campaign fought by Sennacherib's generals in Cilicia in 698 (Luckenbill 1924, 61-2). Unfortunately, as he admits, the Assyrian account of the campaign makes no reference to any encounter with Greeks/Ionians; but because, as he would argue, Greeks were settled in Cilicia, they must have been involved in the revolt put down by Sennacherib's commanders. So, after the Assyrian victory, they would have been deported and, as expert sailors, used to build and man the Assyrian fleet constructed a few years later for the war in the Gulf. To underpin this argument, he points to two passages preserved in the very much later Armenian version of Eusebius' *Chronicon*:

9.
a) Berossus ap. Eusebius *Arm. Chron.* (*FGrH* 680 F7):

> When report came to him (Sennacherib) that Greeks had entered the land of the Cilicians to make war, he hastened against them. He set up front against front. After many of his own troops had been cut down by the enemy he won the battle. As a memorial of victory, he left his image erected on the spot ...

b) Abydenus ap. Eusebius *Arm.Chron.* (*FGrH* 685 F5):

> ... Sennacherib ... on the seacoast of the Cilician land defeated the warships of the Ionians and drove them to flight. And he also built the temple of the Athenians, erected bronze pillars, and in inscriptions indeed, so he says, he had engraved his great deeds.

These two passages are not, in fact, separate accounts of the same event, but (as many have argued) the Abydenus passage is dependent on Berossus, itself preserved only at third hand through Alexander Polyhistor. In other words, we have only one account of this particular event taken by

---

[7] For the details, see Brinkman 1989, 54; for a translation of the Cyprus stele, see Luckenbill 1927, paras. 180-189.

Eusebius from different excerptors of Berossus.[8] Precisely how we are to understand the appearance of Ionians/Greeks here is uncertain. One thing that will become clear a little later, is that the term 'Ionian' before the Achaemenid period did not necessarily always designate 'Greek'. It is, therefore, possible that Berossus could have interpreted the 'Ionians' of his sources as 'Greeks' in this instance because the word had acquired that meaning *by the time he was writing* (early 3rd century BC) (Helm 1980, 194). It is also conceivable, as Momigliano (1934, 412-6) suggested long ago, that the inclusion of Greeks in this battle was an addition by Berossus to make his history more interesting to his intended audience. These are both, of course, only hypotheses and must, in the nature of things, remain so. However, what is certain is:

(i) Sennacherib made no mention, in his fairly detailed account of the campaign, of an Ionian presence in Cilicia;

(ii) *if* Berossus had access to another account that *did* mention Ionians here, it would imply that Ionians should be placed in Cilicia by 698 BC; but the equation 'Ionian' = 'Greek' in the early 7th century is uncertain;

(iii) the preserved Berossus passage is very late and has gone through a highly complex process of transmission; its reliability and original purpose remains opaque.

Finally, there is one broader observation to be made about the Neo-Assyrian attestations of Ionians: in the reign of Sargon II, we hear of a ruler of Ashdod called Yamani, and there are occasional references in legal documents found in the Assyrian heartland during the 7th century to individuals called Yamanu. It has been argued from time to time that this is a personal name derived from an ethnic label and denotes Ionians/Greeks,[9] who would thus be participating in the day-to-day life of the Assyrian empire. However, as Brinkman has shown (for example, Braun 1982, 16-7, 21), philologically 'Yamanu' is incompatible with the clear adjectival designation 'Yamnaya', i.e. 'Yawnaya', which definitely does mean Ionian. The two terms need to be carefully separated - the surface similarity should not mislead. Braun's assumption that Yamani/u indicates Greeks, however much he tries to hedge it, cannot stand.

To sum up the deductions to be drawn from this survey of the very restricted Neo-Assyrian textual material:

1) Beyond a general association of Ionians with the Mediterranean, the references do not tell us where Ionia is nor where Ionians were located.

2) Assyrian contact with the country and people is indirect and distant; in this respect, Ionia is perceived as a place that is more remote to the Assyrians than Bahrain or Cyprus.

3) The one exception to this is the mention of Ionians raiding the Levant coast.

I am not a specialist on the archaeological evidence and I know that people hold divergent views about the intensity and date of a Greek presence at sites such as Al Mina, Tell Sukas and Ras-el-Basit. My own impression, working from the Neo-Assyrian written sources, is that the minimalist view,[10] according to which there was no significant Greek settlement or trading presence in the Levant before the late 7th/early 6th century BC, and that these sites fit into a common Cypro-Levantine cultural domain, accords well with the vague and slender Assyrian evidence, which suggests that direct Greek links with this great empire were slight.

The Neo-Babylonian evidence

I shall now look at the Assyrian successor state, Babylonia (626-539 BC), with respect to Ionia and the Ionians:

a) 10. YOS 17, 253: 1-6; dated 29.4.601:
    4.5 minas of purple wool of 'Ionia' (KUR *ia-a-ma-nu*) for [making x garments], at the disposal of Kudurru, son of Be-nasir, and Nanaya-iddin, son of Nabu-ušallim, the weavers

The text dates to 601 BC, and specifies a coloured wool connected with Ionia and being used in Uruk. In itself it is unclear what this means: it could simply describe a type of fabric or yarn equivalent to terms in use now, such as 'tweed', rather than indicating that the wool was imported from Ionia. If the wool actually came from Ionia, it still does not divulge anything about what trading mechanism was in operation, nor what routes were being used: e.g., the wool could have come via Cyprus or been imported by Phoenicians. Greek traders bringing the wool to Babylonia, or even to the Levant, do not have to be assumed.

b) Quite different are the ration texts from Nebuchadnezzar's citadel in Babylon, dating to 592/1 BC, because they certainly refer to groups of Ionians among the palace workforce:

11. E.F. Weidner, *Mélanges Dussaud* 2, 1939: 923-35:
i) 8 'I[onian]' (lú *i[a-man-na-a-a]*) carpenters

ii) LABBunu, the LÚ.EDIN-*ú* of the land of the 'Ionians' (kur *ia-man-na-a-a*)

iii) Kunzumpiya the LÚ.EDIN-[*ú*] of the land of 'Ionia'

---

[8] Burstein 1978, 24; Kuhrt 1987; Verbrugghe and Wickersham 1996 omit this fragment altogether.
[9] For example, *ADD* 76 1.11; 233 11.29, 32; 214 11.4, 10.

[10] Represented, for example, by Graham 1986; Helm 1980.

(kur *ia-man-na*)

iv) 8 'I<o>nian carpenters (lú *ia-<man>-na-a-a*)

v) Aziyak the 'Ionian' carpenter (lú *ia-man-na-a-a*)

vi) 8 of the same (sc. carpenters), 'Ionians' (lú *ia-a-man-a-[a]*)

vii) 7 of the same (sc. carpenters), 'Ionians' (*ia-man-a-a*)

viii) [x] 'Ionian' carpenters (lú *ia-man-a-a*)

Two of the professional terms here (ii and iii) are unclear: the possible emendations, yielding the sense of 'smith' or 'potter' have been suggested, but remain uncertain. The most frequent professional designation is that of carpenter. Two other points are worth noting:

i) The Ionians appear scattered through a long list of people, several of whom are also carpenters; they include Jews, Phoenicians, Philistines, Elamites, Medes, Persians, Egyptians and Lydians. In other words, we get a picture of the Babylonian court employing a great number of artisans, coming both from subject territories and from neighbouring states; Ionians form only a part of this workforce.

ii) In the two cases where personal names are fully preserved and can be linguistically analysed (Kunzumpiya, Aziyak - iii and v), they are certainly not Greek, although the individuals are described as Ionian.

c) That fairly strong links with the region called Ionia by the Babylonians existed in this period is shown by the massive quantities of bronze[11] and iron that were imported into Uruk between 552 and 550 BC, as shown by the next two texts (**12** and **13**). As with **10**, the organisers of this trade are unknown. Given the source of other items, such as Egypt and Lebanon, Phoenician/Levantine merchants seem likely, especially if it is remembered that the name of the chief official in charge of mercantile activities at Nebuchadnezzar's court had a Phoenician name.[12]

12. *TCL* 12: 84; dated 14.10.551 (*cf.* A.L. Oppenheim *JCS* 21 (1967))

    295 minas of bronze from Iamana
    55 minas of lapis lazuli
    153 minas of *tumanu*-fibres
    233 minas of alum from Egypt with their containers
    130 minas of iron from Iamana
    257 minas of iron from Lebanon

---

[11] The problems of distinguishing 'copper' and 'bronze' in Akkadian are treated by Brinkman 1988.
[12] Hanunu, chief of the king's merchants, Unger 1931, 285, 290 col. IV 19.

    37 minas of tin
    8 boxes (?) of bronze, whose contents have not been established
    11 minas 20 shekels of blue-purple wool together with two dyed fabrics
    3 jars with *huratu*-dye
    126 minas of [...]
    2 *šamallu*-jars with *inzahuretu*-dye

The two linen fabrics dyed blue-purple are the income of Nadin-ahi. All this is the consignment of Nadin-ahi, son of Innin-aha-usur. VII/5/5, Nabonidus, king of Babylon.

13. *YOS* 6: 168; dated 15.10.550 (*cf.* A.L. Oppenheim *JCS* 21 (1967))

600 minas of bronze from Iamana .... at 3 minas 20 shekels of silver
80 minas 20 shekels of *i*-dye .... at 2 minas 2 shekels
37 minas of tin .... at 55.5 shekels of silver
16 minas 15 shekels of blue-purple wool .... at 2 minas 40 shekels
all this: (blank) of Samaš-zera-ibni son of Nana-iddin

---

295 minas of bronze from Iamana ... at 1 mina 38.3 shekels
55 minas of lapis lazuli .... at 36.6. shekels
153 minas of *tumanu*-fibres .... at 1 mina 42 shekels
233 minas of alum from Egypt .... at 1 mina 17.6 shekels
32 minas 20 shekels of *i*-dye................... at 48.5 shekels
130 minas of iron from Iamana .... at 32.5 shekels
257 minas of iron from Lebanon .... at 42.6 shekels
132 litres of assorted honey .... at 26 shekels
20 jars of white wine .... at 1 mina
120 minas of *huratu*-dye .... at 30 shekels
40 minas of *hashaltu*-spice (?) .... at 2 shekels
1 *kurru*-measure of *taturru*-spice (?) .... at 10 shekels
1 *kurru*-measure of juniper resin .... at 3 shekels
all this: (blank) of Nadin-ahi.

Date. VII/7/6, Nabonidus, king of Babylon. 3 minas 10 shekels of the blue-purple wool are the tithe of Nadin-ahi; 5 minas of the blue-purple wool and 40 minas of the iron are the tithe of Samaš-zera-ibni.

The conclusions to be drawn from this material are, first, that the tentacles of the Neo-Babylonian trade network certainly reached as far as Ionia and, secondly, that Ionians formed part of the skilled workforce of the Babylonian kings. Relations between Ionia and Babylonia thus seem more intimate and direct than in the preceding Neo-Assyrian period. However, there is still no clear indication of precisely what is meant by Ionia/Ionians - the onomastic evidence suggests Anatolia generally; nor is there any suggestion that Ionians themselves were actively engaged in organising the trade between Babylonia and the Aegean.

d) One thing we do know for certain is that the Babylonian rulers employed Greek soldiers - Alkaios' poem welcoming his brother home is definitive proof of this (Diehl 1924-25). When this Babylonian recruitment began and under what circumstances is unknown. It is quite possible that, as in Egypt, it was first mediated through the Lydian kings, with whom (judging by the story of the Battle on the Halys in 585 BC, Hdt. 1. 74), relations were good. Certainly, Babylonian territory in the north-west abutted Lydian controlled land. But, direct links with Greek communities, such as are known to have existed between Greek cities and Egypt, are not attested. Nor is there any hint in the Babylonian material of an awareness of Ionia in particular as a source for soldiers, against Braun's assertion (Braun 1982, 23), based on text **14**.

14. BM 33041 obv.13-rev.3:
obv.
[...] MU 37 KAM *Nabu-kudurri-uṣur* LUGAL KÁ.DINGIR [......]
[......] *mi-ṣir a-na e-peš* MÈ *il-[lik* ....]
rev.
[...]*a-su* LUGAL KUR *mi-ṣir um*[.........]
[...]*ku-úša* URU *pu-tu-ia-a-man [*......]
[...]*na-gi-i ni-su-tú ša qe-reb tam-tim*[......]

translation:
obv.
[...] Year 37, Nebuchadnezzar, King of Babyl[on ......] (*i.e.* 568 BC)
[......] Egypt to do battle ca[me ....]
rev.
[..Am]asis, King of Egypt, ar[my ......]
[...] ? of/from 'Libya of the Ionians' [......]
[...] distant regions of/from the midst of the sea [......]

As Edel (1978, 13-20) argued, very convincingly, 'Libya of the Ionians' almost certainly describes the Greek colony of Cyrene with whom Amasis made an alliance (cemented by a dynastic marriage) in order to strengthen his hand against Nebuchadnezzar's attempt to reinstate the deposed Egyptian ruler, Apries. So this particular text has to be taken out of the discussion for Babylonian-Greek, as well as Egyptian-Greek relations - it makes no reference to mercenaries from the Aegean area: its focus is Cyrene.

In terms of the archaeological evidence from this period, the picture is unclear: a site such as Mesad Hashavyahu, generally accepted to have been a Greek settlement, must (certainly by the 580s BC) have come under Babylonian control. Tell Sukas, too, will have formed part of Babylonian territory, so that any Greeks living in this Phoenician town will have been subject to the king of Babylon. Al Mina seems to have been abandoned for about 80 years at the end of the 7th century; it looks as though this break coincided with the collapse of Assyria and the whole period of Babylonian power. Ras-el-Basit shows no signs of Greek settlement, although Attic pottery increases substantially and dominates the ceramic assemblage in the 6th century. Hints in the archaeological picture, which suggests an intensification of Levant-Aegean links in the Neo-Babylonian period, match the image derived from textual sources, although we are far from grasping the details of that interaction with clarity.

Trade and empires

To gain understanding of how Greeks might have been drawn into commercial dealings in the Near East, we need to look more closely at how mercantile centres of the Levant, especially the Phoenicians, were affected by successive Neo-Assyrian and Neo-Babylonian control (recent discussion by Elat 1992, 21-35; Diakonoff 1992, 168-93).[13]

The Neo-Assyrian empire did not penetrate the world of the Levant profoundly until the middle of the 8th century BC, when Tiglath-pileser III began his great wars of expansion, many of which were directed at securing and widening the Assyrian hold on the west. This process, begun in 738, was completed by 705 by Sargon II. In the space of just over 30 years, the Assyrian kings established their dominance, directly and indirectly, over the entire Mediterranean coast, Cilicia and southern Anatolia. Trading and diplomatic agreements were set up regulating communications with Egypt, Phrygia and Urartu;[14] commercial and political links with small adjacent kingdoms such as Bahrain and those in Cyprus had been formed;[15] similar links with the small but prosperous trading centres of Western Iran and the caravan cities of the Arabian desert, whose existence and wealth depended on being able to operate within, and in relation to, the Assyrian empire, were in force.[16] Into this network we need to slot the Phoenician cities, who were certainly subject to the Assyrians, but whose expertise in bulk transport and the acquisition of metals was also needed by their political masters (Frankenstein 1978, 263-94). The care with which the Assyrians controlled and harnessed their activities emerges from two well-known documents:

15. NL 12 (*Iraq* 17 (1955)); between 735 and 727 BC:
With regard to the ruler of Tyre, of whom the king said that I was to speak kindly to him - all the quays are open to him, (and) his subjects enter and leave the quay-houses (*bit-karani*) as they wish,

---

[13] The basic article on overland trade is Oppenhein 1967.
[14] Sargon II opened the 'sealed harbour' of Egypt 'to make Egyptians and Assyrians trade with each other', Tadmor 1958, 34. Assyrian-Phrygian links, Parpola 1987, no. 1 (Sargon II). Urartian-Assyrian relations, Borger 1956, para. 68 (Esarhaddon).
[15] Cyprus and Bahrain: Luckenbill 1927, para 70 (Sargon II); for Assyria's links with the Gulf, see Potts 1990, 333-38.
[16] Assyria and West Iran: Brown 1986. Arabs and Assyria: Eph'al 1982, chs. IV and V.

(and) sell and buy. Mount Lebanon is at his disposal, and they go up and down as they wish, and bring down the wood.

I levy taxes (*mikse*) on anyone who brings down wood, and I have appointed tax-collectors over the quays (*karani*) of all Mount Lebanon, and they keep a watch on ...

I appointed a tax-collector (lú *makisu*) over those who come down to the quays which are in Sidon, but the Sidonians chased him off. Then I sent the Itu'aeans into Mount Lebanon, and they made the people grovel. Afterwards, they sent to me, and they brought the tax-collector (back) into Sidon.

I made a statement to them, that they might bring down the wood and do their work with it (but) that they were not to sell it to the Egyptians or to the Palestinians, or I would not allow them to go up to the mountains.

What we see here of how the Assyrians managed their relations with the Phoenicians is fairly clear: every aspect of commerce, especially the timber trade, while being encouraged, is closely overseen and taxed by Assyrian officials in Tyre and Sidon; selling the valuable wood straight to the Egyptians and Palestinians (not under Assyrian control at this point, at least, not directly) is completely prohibited, because the Assyrians want the trade to move through the centres and along the routes they have established further south, presumably in order to cream off more dues.

Continued very close Assyrian supervision and intervention in the mercantile activities of the Phoenician cities is attested about 60 years later by the treaty between Esarhaddon and the ruler of Tyre:

16. R. Borger, *Die Inschriften Asarhaddons, Königs von Assyrien*, 107ff. (*cf. SAA* II, no. 5):

> [The treat]y (*adê*) of Esarhad[don, king] of Assyria, son of [Sennacherib, likewise king of Assyria, with Baa]l, king of Tyre, with [... *his son, and his other sons and grandsons,* with a]ll [Tyrians], young and old [..]
>
> ———
>
> (Several very broken sections)
> [If the royal deputy (*qepu*) whom] I have appointed over you [...] anything in [......] the elders (lú *paršamute*) of your country [*convene to take*] council (*milku*) the royal deputy [will] with them   [......] of the ships [...]
> BREAK
> [You may not ... any ship ...] which comes to you; [if ...], do not listen to him, [do not ...] without the royal deputy; nor must you open a letter which I send you without the royal deputy. If the royal deputy is absent, wait for him and then open it, or [...] the messenger.
>
> ———
>
> If there is a ship of Baal or the people of Tyre that is shipwrecked off the land of the Philistines or within Assyrian territory, everything that is on the ship belongs to Esarhaddon, king of Assyria; however, one must not do any harm to any person on board the ship but one must return them all to their country.
>
> ———
>
> These are the ports of trade (*karanu*) and the trade routes (*hulu*) which Esarhaddon, king of Assyria, [entrusted] to his servant Baal: to Akko, Dor, to the entire district of the Philistines, and to all the cities within Assyrian territory on the seacoast, and to Byblos, the Lebanon, all the cities in the mountains, all (these) being cities of Esarhaddon, king of Assyria.
> (Followed by regulations about the levying of tolls 'as in the past').

The occasion for the treaty was probably the devastation of Sidon in 676 BC and the building of a new Assyrian trading post on the coast opposite the old Phoenician city. As a result the commercial circuits were affected: Tyre's territory was augmented at the expense of Sidon, while additional payments to the Assyrian king were imposed on the Tyrian king. All this necessitated a redefining of the Assyrian-Phoenician relationship. While the Tyrian ruler was permitted access to the network of trade-routes and trade-centres within Assyrian territory, the continued levying of dues was affirmed, his contacts and communications with outsiders were overseen by an Assyrian inspector resident at his court, and the goods of any Tyrian shipwrecks outside the immediate territory of Tyre were claimed as the property of the Assyrian king.

It is probably these increasingly strict regulations, coupled with Assyrian demands for metals and tax payments, which stimulated Phoenician commercial and colonial activities in the western Mediterranean, as so well argued by Frankenstein (1978). In all of this, any direct Greek participation is unlikely and certainly not documented. And this is the pattern which then dominated the eastern Mediterranean littoral until the 630s when, with the crumbling of Assyrian power, the picture changed. At this point the Levant came under repeated pressure from Egyptians and Babylonians for whom this was an area of imperial competition. Disruption (political, economic and social) was extensive and affected a place such as Tyre profoundly, as it lost out to its neighbour and rival Sidon. The situation of armed conflict fought out between the two powers on the soil of the Levant was not resolved until after 570 BC when Babylonia and Egypt reached a concordat, with the Levant passing effectively into Babylonian hands. From this point on, increasing numbers of documents in Babylonia show active trade between individual merchants,[17] acting privately and on behalf of temples and importing bulk quantities of materials from the west. The agents acquiring goods for the Babylonians from abroad (places such as Cyprus, Lebanon, Egypt and Ionia) are almost certainly Phoenicians. This pattern seems, as far as we can tell, to persist and develop, with relatively little disruption, into the Persian period.[18]

Conclusions

What conclusions can be drawn from this rather sceptical look at the evidence between *ca.* 750 and 500 BC?

a) Ionia/Ionians is, in the Neo-Assyrian and Neo-Babylonian periods, an imprecise geographical term - not a clear ethnic label denoting Greeks. While it is pretty certain that 'Ionian' was used to designate Greeks in the Achaemenid period, this is not necessarily always the meaning it had earlier.

b) As far as the evidence goes, Ionians scarcely figure in the Near East before the Neo-Babylonian period, and even then their number is limited. A reason why they became more prominent in the late 7th and 6th centuries may be connected with imperial manpower needs in the changed circumstances of the post-Assyrian period: Media, then Persia, Lydia, Babylonia and Egypt were linked in territorial rivalry and an armed uneasy balance of power. This was very different from the situation of the Assyrian empire which had effectively been the militarily dominant force until the 630s.

c) All the evidence at our disposal suggests that, at all times, it was the 'Phoenicians' who were the prime organisers of trade for the empires.

d) Some fluctuations in commercial patterns can be charted in this period: there was an open trade network in the Levant, in which the Phoenicians were prominent, until about 730 BC. Then we find the Phoenicians having to accept a steady tightening of, and impositions of controls on, their trading mechanisms from the Assyrians, which led to an intensification of their mercantile activities in the west between 730 and 630 BC. That pattern was disrupted between 630 and 570 BC as Babylonia and Egypt struggled for control of the Levant. The situation then stabilized and commerce became again more active from the 560s on, as shown by Babylonian documents and reflected, perhaps in settlements such as al-Mina and Tell Sukas.

e) As John Curtis has shown (1996; also Hoffman 1997), Mesopotamian objects found in the Aegean are few; they probably reflect occasional dedications by Greeks (such as Antimenidas) returning home from Babylonia with the odd precious prize for a military exploit. It is also possible that another reason for the scantiness of Mesopotamian material was that Lydia acted as the mediating agency supplying Babylonia with soldiers, so that there was perhaps no direct contact between the Babylonian kings and Greek tyrants on the model of Amasis and Polycrates.

In other words, direct contact between Greece and the Mesopotamian empires was slight in this period. Greek trade goods for most of the period were probably largely imported by Phoenicians who dominated commerce. The main attested Mesopotamian-Greek links date to the Neo-Babylonian period only and appear to be at the level of supplying manpower needs in the realms of palace production and the army.

Bibliography

(Abbreviations can be found in Kuhrt 1995).

Borger, R. 1956: *Die Inschriften Asarhaddons, Königs von Assyrien*, Graz.

Braun, T.F.R.G. 1982: The Greeks in the Near East. *CAH* III.3, 1-31.

Brinkman, J.A. 1968: *A History of Postkassite Babylonia (1158-722)*, Rome.

Brinkman, J.A. 1984: *Prelude to Empire: Babylonian Society and Politics, 747-626 BC*, Philadelphia.

Brinkman, J.A. 1988: Textual Evidence for Bronze in Babylonia in the Early Iron Age, 1000-539 BC. In J. Curtis (ed.), *Bronzeworking Centres of Western Asia c.1000-539 BC*, London, 135-68.

Brinkman, J.A. 1989: The Akkadian Words for 'Ionia' and 'Ionian'. In *Daidalikon: Studies in Honor of Raymond V. Schoder, S.J.*, Waucoda, Ill., 53-71.

Brown, S.C. 1986: Media and Secondary State Formation in the Neo-Assyrian Zagros: an Anthropological Approach to an Assyriological Problem. *JCS* 38, 107-19.

Bunnens, G. 1979: *L'expansion phénicienne en Méditerranée: essai d'interprétation fondé sur un analyse des traditions littéraires*, Brussels.

Burkert, W. 1992: *The Orientalizing Revolution: Near Eastern Influence on Greek Culture in the Early Archaic Age*, Cambridge, Mass.

Burstein, S.M. 1978: *The Babyloniaca of Berossus*, Malibu, Ca.

Carpenter, R. 1958: Phoenicians in the West. *AJA* 62, 35-53.

Curtis, J. 1996: Mesopotamian Bronzes from Greek Sites: the Workshops of Origins. *Iraq* 56, 1-25.

---

[17] See texts **12** and **13**, and the important discussion by Oppenheim 1967.
[18] For a discussion of shifts in the main trade circuits in the eastern Mediterranean, see Salles 1991; 1994.

Diakonoff, I.M. 1992: The Naval Power and Trade of Tyre. *IEJ* 42, 168-93.

Diehl, E. 1924-25: *Anthologia Lyrica Graeca*, Leipzig.

Edel, E. 1978: Amasis und Nebukadrezar II. *Göttinger Miszellen* 29, 13-20.

Elat, M. 1992: Phoenician Overland Trade within the Mesopotamian Empires. In *Ah, Assyria ...: Studies in Assyrian History and Ancient Near Eastern Historiography Presented to Hayim Tadmor*, Jerusalem, 21-35.

Eph'al, I. 1982: *The Ancient Arabs: Nomads on the Borders of the Fertile Crescent. 9th to 5th Centuries BC*, Jerusalem.

Frame, G. 1992: *Babylonia 689-627 BC: a Political History*, Leiden.

Frankenstein, S. 1978: The Phoenicians in the Far West: a Function of Neo-Assyrian Imperialism. In M.T. Larsen (ed.), *Power and Propaganda*, Copenhagen, 263-94.

Graham, A.J. 1986: The Historical Interpretation of Al Mina. *DHA* 12, 51-65.

Grayson, A.K. 1996: *Assyrian Rulers of the Early First Millennium BC II (858-745 BC)*, Toronto.

Griffiths, A. 1987: Democedes of Croton: a Greek Doctor at Darius' Court. *AchHist* II, 37-51.

Gunter, A. 1990: Models of the Orient in the Art History of the Orientalizing Period. *AchHist* V, 131-47.

Helm, P. 1980: *"Greeks" in the Neo-Assyrian Levant and "Assyria" in Early Greek Writers* (diss. University of Pennsylvania).

Hoffman, G.L. 1997: *Imports and Immigrants: Near Eastern Contacts with Iron Age Crete*, Ann Arbor.

Kitchen, K. 1986: *The Third Intermediate Period in Egypt (1100-650 BC)* (2nd ed.), Warminster.

Kuhrt, A. 1987: Berossus, *Babyloniaka* and Seleucid Rule in Babylonia. In A. Kuhrt and S. Sherwin-White (eds.), *Hellenism in the East: the Interaction of Greek and non-Greek Civilizations from Syria to Central Asia after Alexander*, London, 32-56.

Kuhrt, A. 1995: *The Ancient Near East c.3000-330 BC* (2 vols.), London.

Latacz, J. 1990: Die Phönizier bei Homer. In U. Gehrig and H.G. Niemeyer (eds.) *Die Phönizier im Zeitalter Homers*, Mainz, 11-21.

Lipinski, E. 1992: *Dictionnaire de la civilisation phénicienne et punique*, Turnhout.

Lloyd, A. 1983: The Late Period, 664-323 BC. In B.G. Trigger *et al.*, *Ancient Egypt: a Social History*, Cambridge, 279-348.

Luckenbill, D.D. 1924: *The Annals of Sennacherib*, Chicago.

Luckenbill, D.D. 1927: *Ancient Records of Assyria and Babylonia*, Chicago.

Miller, M. 1997: *Athens and Persia in the Fifth Century BC: a Study in Cultural Receptivity*, Cambridge.

Momigliano, A.D. 1934: Su una battaglia tra Assiri e Greci. *Athenaeum* 12, 412-16.

Morris, S.P. 1992: *Daidalos and the Origins of Greek Art*, Princeton.

Oppenheim, A.L. 1967: An Essay on Overland Trade in the Early First Millennium BC. *JCS* 21, 236-54.

Osborne, R. 1996: *Greece in the Making 1200-479 BC*, London.

Parpola, S. 1970: *Neo-Assyrian Toponyms*, Neukirchen.

Parpola, S. 1987: *The Correspondence of Sargon II, Part 1*, Helsinki.

Postgate, J.N. 1974: *Taxation and Conscription in the Assyrian Empire*, Rome.

Potts, D.T. 1990: *The Arabian Gulf in Antiquity* vol. I, Oxford.

Powell, J.E. 1938: *A Lexicon to Herodotus*, Cambridge.

Salles, J.-F. 1991: Du blé, de l'huile et du vin ... notes sur les échanges commerciaux en Méditerranée orientale vers la milieu du 1er millénaire av. J.C. *AchHist* VI, 207-36.

Salles, J.-F. 1994: Du blé, de l'huile et du vin ... notes sur les échanges commerciaux en Méditerranée orientale vers la milieu du 1er millénaire av. J.C. *AchHist* VIII, 191-215.

Sasson, J. et al. (eds.) 1995: *Civilizations of the Ancient Near East*, New York.

Tadmor, H. 1958: The Campaigns of Sargon II of Assyria. *JCS* 12, 22-40, 77-100.

Unger, E. 1931: *Babylon die heilige Stadt nach der Beschreibung der Babylonier*, Berlin (repr. 1970).

Verbrugghe, G.P. and Wickersham, J.M. 1996: *Berossus and Manetho, Introduced and Translated: Native Traditions in Ancient Mesopotamia and Egypt*, Ann Arbor.

Wallinga, H.T. 1991: Polycrates and Egypt: the testimony of the *samaina*. *AchHist* IV, 179-97.

Wallinga, H.T. 1993: *Ships and Sea-power before the Great Persian War*, Leiden.

West, M.L. 1997: *The East Face of Helicon: West Asiatic Elements in Greek Poetry and Myth*, Oxford.

Zaccagnini, C. 1983: Patterns of Mobility among Near Eastern Craftsmen. *JNES* 42, 245-55.

The *Poleis* of the Southern Anatolian Coast (Lycia, Pamphylia, Pisidia) and their Civic Identity: The "Interface" Between the Hellenic and the Barbarian Polis[1]

Antony G. Keen

Introduction

This paper looks not so much at Greek settlements, but settlements that wanted to become Greek. It examines the urban communities of the southern Anatolian coast, in Lycia, Pamphylia, and Cilicia, in the period before Alexander the Great's conquests. These communities had their origins in differing circumstances. Some of them were native communities of *barbaroi*, becoming progressively Hellenized; this is largely true of the urban settlements in Lycia. Others were Greek colonies sent out in the great age of colonization; Phaselis and the other Rhodian settlements in eastern Lycia and perhaps Soli in Cilicia fall into this category. Others still seem to have murky Greek origins in post-Mycenaean settlements, but acquired a great number of more local features over the Greek Dark Ages; the cities of Pamphylia perhaps fall into this category.

To a Greek of the Classical period, all these places were *poleis*. Stephanus of Byzantium cites the 6th-century geographer Hecataeus of Miletus (*FGrH* 1) as applying the term *polis* to many of these sites (e.g. Lyrnatia in Pamphylia, F 261, or Patara in Lycia, F 256).[2] There is, however, some question about whether Stephanus is citing Hecataeus' terminology accurately (see Whitehead 1994b, esp. 119). Although in the case of geographers, such as Hecataeus, he seems more often accurate than not, as has been pointed out by others (Chaniotis 1997, 732; Hansen 1997b, 18), this does not warrant the assumption that every citation of Hecataeus is accurate. By the time of the *Periplous*, the 4th-century geographic work attributed to Scylax of Caryanda, no such questions arise; a whole series of settlements along the Anatolian coast are described as *poleis* (100-102), many of them very minor locations.

A Greek would expect all these places to have all the trappings he would associate with a *polis* (whatever those were; this is not the subject for this paper). They might not necessarily be, in Ps.-Scylax's phrase, *poleis Hellenides*,[3] Greek *poleis*, but all *barbaroi* were thought to live in *poleis*, like the Greeks. To quote Hansen (1994, 15), considering the proposition that "[t]he *polis* was a typically Greek form of society and is often opposed to barbarian peoples and nations (called *ethne*)":

> Apart from Aristotle, most Greeks believed that many of their neighbours lived in *poleis* more or less as they did themselves [e.g. Hdt. 1. 76. 2; Thuc. 6. 88. 6; Xen. *HG* 4. 1. 1; [Scylax] 21]. Admittedly the barbarian *poleis* were not considered autonomous, but that applied to many Greek *poleis* as well. The evidence for barbarian *poleis* has been almost completely neglected. (Hansen, 1994, 16)

The question that this paper is attempting to examine is: how far was such a view shared by the inhabitants of these cities themselves? To what extent did the inhabitants of Xanthus in Lycia or Perge in Pamphylia or Soli conceive of themselves as inhabitants of Greek-style *poleis*, i.e. as members of, to use Aristotle's phrase, a *koinonia politon politeias* (Arist. *Pol.* 1276 b 1-2)?

This is not a question that is easy to answer, and this paper will produce no real answers, other than very vague ones. All that can be done in this preliminary treatment is highlight some of the important aspects that need to be considered.[4]

The reason for the impossibility of giving an answer lies in the state of the evidence. There is little from writers of Greek origins concerning the southern Anatolian coast. What there is deals largely with those occasions on which these cities intersected with the histories of the great Greek powers, Athens (in particular) and Sparta. Little of the Greek evidence deals directly with the civic identity of these locations, and when it does it is always through a framework of Greek ideas of their own civic self-identity. The literary evidence is not concerned with what the inhabitants of Lycian or Pamphylian cities themselves thought. As a result, the fully barbarian *polis* is a difficult notion to describe, as what can be said about such settlements largely represents Greek preconceptions about nucleated urban settlements they might encounter. Sometimes, it is not even that; the Persian empire, for instance, could be conceived of as a *polis* (Xen. *Cyr.* 1. 3. 18; 4. 25; 5. 7, and *cf.* Aesch. *Pers.* 682, 715; see Hansen 1993, 20 and no. 142).

---

[1] I should like to thank Dr G. Tsetskhladze and Prof. A. Snodgrass for their kind invitation to contribute to this seminar series and volume. I should also like to thank Dr M. Herman Hansen for inviting me to participate in the work of the Copenhagen Polis Centre, from which much of the following derives.

[2] The relevant entries from Stephanus are *FGrH* 1 F 255-268.

[3] On πόλεις Ἑλληνίδες, see Flensted-Jensen, Hansen 1996.

[4] The evidence for *polis* identity will be presented at greater length in Keen forthcoming a and b. Some of the aspects of this paper relating to Lycia are also dealt with in Keen 1998, 53-6.

To get at an internal view, one has to consult epigraphic evidence, specifically decrees and the like issued by the relevant cities, and here the scholar runs into a blank wall. It is not a blank wall without a few chinks in it — some decrees issued by southern Anatolian cities before Alexander are preserved — but they are rare.[5] It is not until the Hellenistic period that there is a reasonable body of material to work with concerning the political institutions within individual *poleis*. The question then becomes, what use can legitimately be made of this Hellenistic evidence to reconstruct the situation as it stood in the 5th and 4th centuries BC?

The answer seems to be very little. The conquest of Alexander brought, as all schoolchildren and undergraduates are told, a significant change to the Asian world. Recent studies have tended to suggest that the Hellenization of Asia Minor, in all aspects of life, was a process underway before Alexander (see particularly Hornblower 1982), and there is much truth in that. Yet there seems also much truth in the contention that the most significant period for the evolution of civic identity within these particular Anatolian cities began sometime after *ca.* 300 BC, and that matters were in a state of flux until about 250 BC, after which they became more stable and developed less rapidly. This change is particularly dramatic in Lycia; it is rather less so in the more Hellenized Pamphylian cities, but nonetheless does seem to be taking place.

Some of the factors that drove this 3rd-century evolution certainly were in play before 300 BC, or even before 334 BC. However, one cannot reconstruct from the overall shape of Anatolian civic identity in the Hellenistic period the form in which the individual elements of that identity had been assembled in the Classical period, or even how many of them were present. Hellenistic evidence is useful for demonstrating continuity from existing Classical evidence, but it is not often a useful way of illuminating ignorance. So, for instance, numerous recent studies have been made on the *chorai* of Lycian cities, such as the work of Zimmermann and Schweyer (e.g. Zimmermann 1992a; Schweyer 1993, 1996). Both these scholars are concerned with the *chorai* over a wide time scale, and so adduce Hellenistic and Roman evidence.[6] However, this may not be useful for the Classical period, when the citizens of urban settlements in Lycia may not have even considered that land was controlled by their cities, rather than by individual members of local élites.

There are other, non-epigraphic, sources that relate to civic identity; coinage and public building. There is certainly coinage in Classical southern Anatolia. Public building is a rather different question. There was certainly some; there are excavated temples at Xanthus in Lycia (Metzger 1963, 29-36, 40-2), and a temple of Artemis Pergaia at Perge must have existed (it is referred to by [Scylax] 100), even if nobody has ever been able to find it (Brandt 1992). However, not much survives from the Classical period (as in most of the Greek world outside Athens). Hellenistic building seems to have swept away the vast majority of what was there previously, if there was much in the first place, before being itself largely swept aside by Roman construction; almost all the buildings at Perge or Aspendus are Roman in date (Bean 1979, 9-38, 49-55). These later constructions reveal little of the pre-Alexandrian condition of the area. Moreover, temples are the only type of public building traceable; there is no evidence of pre-Hellenistic *bouleuteria* or suchlike[7] (but there is little evidence of these elsewhere before *ca.* 300 BC; see Hansen and Fischer-Hansen 1994).

A final class of evidence one might consider are mythographic traditions. These, of course, are fraught with danger for the unwary scholar (whose traditions are they representing? when did they arise? what is their point?) and little use shall be made of them here.

Having made these *caveats*, then, one can proceed to what use can be made of the evidence that *does* survive.

Lycia

In her recent study of the Lycian cities, Schweyer (1996, 66) writes:

> Il ressort de cette étude topographique que la Lycia présente un quadrillage cohérent de πόλεις. Chaque πόλις possède son terretoire, avec ses villages, κῶμαι. Les habitants de χώρα doivent être des citoyens au même titre que ceux de la πόλις, et on peut ainsi considérer que la notion de communauté humaine prime sur la notion restrictive de « lieu habité » comme celle, trop élitiste, d' « organisation politique » de cette communauté.

Schweyer's study, however, is of the Classical and Hellenistic periods. As she herself is aware, much changes over the two epochs, and one may not be able to apply her conclusions so clearly to the Classical period.

Lycia was settled from early on in its history in urban communities. The earliest archaeological evidence comes from the 8th century BC, from Xanthus (see Metzger

---

[5] When I began preparing this paper, I thought that I would discover that the evidence from Pamphylia and Cilicia was better than that from Lycia with which I was familiar; it appears that the truth is that the Pamphylian/Cilician evidence is worse.

[6] The problem of *chorai* developing over the time scale studied is acknowledged by Schweyer 1996, e.g. at 58.

[7] See below on the supposed 4th-century *prytaneion* at Tlos.

1972). By the end of the Classical period there are more than 80 settlements of various sizes identifiable (Keen forthcoming a). Other settlements known of in later times may also have been inhabited in this time, but it is impossible to trace their existence, and most significant settlements of the later period have produced Archaic or Classical-period evidence.[8] At some settlements (e.g. Limyra, Arycanda, Cyaneae), remains of Classical-period housing have been found near the city.[9]

Given that Lycia, like Greece, was settled by numerous cities, it was natural for Greek writers to see those cities as *poleis*. The Lycians, however, were not Greeks, but *barbaroi*, described by Ps.-Scylax as an *ethnos*. Greek mythography gave them a Cretan origin, but when Herodotus in the mid-5th century BC recounted this tale (1. 173. 1) he was careful to point out that Crete at the time was settled by *barbaroi*:

> οἱ δὲ Λύκιοι ἐκ Κρήτης τὠρχαῖον γεγόνασι (τὴν γὰρ Κρήτην εἶχον τὸ παλαιὸν πᾶσαν βάρβαροι).

> The Lycians originated in ancient times from Crete (for *barbaroi* formerly possessed all of Crete).[10]

This myth probably has no factual basis, as the evidence of the Lycian language, which survives on inscriptions and coins, suggests that the Lycians entered Asia Minor from the north-west along with the Hittites, to whom they seem to have been related.[11] Another foundation myth, that presented in Panyassis (F 18 K), gives the eponymous founder of the Termilae (the Lycian name for themselves; see below), Tremiles, an autochthonous origin.[12] In any case, the Lycians continued to be perceived as *barbaroi* into the 4th century BC (compare Ephorus *FGrH* 70 F 162 and Men. *Aspis* 25)

The earliest Greek use of *polis* to refer to Lycian settlements is in the fragments of Hecataeus,[13] but there is, as already noted, some question over how accurately he is reported. Herodotus, for his part, never calls a Lycian settlement a *polis*,[14] and the earliest unequivocal description of Lycian urban settlements as *poleis* is, surprisingly, not found until Ps.-Scylax (100), probably, in this section, describing the situation in the 330s BC,[15] though he describes Lycia as an *ethnos*.

> ἀπὸ δὲ Καρίας Λυκία ἐστὶν ἔθνος· καὶ πόλεις Λυκίοις αἵδε Τελμισσὸς καὶ λιμὴν, καὶ ποταμὸς Ξάνθος, δι' οὗ ἀνάπλους εἰς [Ξάνθον πόλιν,] Πάταρα πόλις [ἣ] καὶ λιμένα ἔχει· Φελλὸς πόλις καὶ λιμὴν ... Λίμυρα πόλις ... εἶτα Γαγαία πόλις ... ἔστι Φασηλὶς πόλις λαὶ λιμὴν ...

> After Caria is the Lycian *ethnos*. And the Lycian *poleis* are these: Telmessus, and a harbour, the river Xanthus, by which one sails to [the *polis* of Xanthus], and the *polis* of Patara, which has a harbour; the *polis* and harbour of Phellus ... the *polis* of Limyra ... then the *polis* of Gagae ... there is a *polis* and harbour at Phaselis ...

Of later authors, Diodorus, probably very closely drawing upon Ephorus,[16] calls the Lycian settlements *poleis* (11. 60. 4), whilst Arrian (*Anab.* 1. 24. 4) uses the term *polisma* for many of those in western Lycia, and *polis* for others, especially those *kato* (1. 24. 5-6), whatever that may mean (see Keen 1996, 115-116). *Polisma* appears to be a term that denotes the physical reality of a *polis* but not its political existence (Flensted-Jensen 1995, 129-131), yet Arrian seems to be drawing a distinction between the two types of settlement; in any case, it is uncertain whether this terminology can be traced back to Arrian's source.

Long before Ps.-Scylax, however, one can see in other Greek sources evidence that Lycian settlements were seen as being *poleis*. Herodotus (1. 176) speaks of Xanthus in terms that suggest that he thought of it as a *polis*, even if he never actually uses the term, to the point of mentioning an *akropolis* of Xanthus in the centre of the *asty*.

> Λύκιοι ..., ὡς ἐς τὸ Ξάνθιον πεδίον ἤλασε ὁ Ἅρπαγος τὸν στρατόν, ἐπεξιόντες καὶ μαχόμενοι ὀλίγοι πρὸς πολλοὺς ἀρετὰς ἀπεδείκνυντο, ἑσσωθέντες δὲ καὶ κατειληθέντες ἐς τὸ ἄστυ συνήλισαν ἐς τὴν ἀκρόπολιν τάς τε γυναῖκας καὶ τὰ τέκνα καὶ τὰ χρήματα καὶ τοὺς οἰκέτας καὶ ἔπειτα ὑπῆψαν τὴν ἀκρόπολιν πᾶσαν ταύτην καίεσθαι· ταῦτα δὲ ποιήσαντες καὶ

---

[8] The only major exceptions are Olympus, probably a Hellenistic settlement (Ruge 1939, 317), and the *tripolis* of Acalissus, Idebessus and Cormus.

[9] Limyra: Seyer 1991-1992; 1993; Borchhardt 1993, 33-6. For Cyaneae, see in Kolb 1995.

[10] Compare Hdt. 1. 173. 4: "they have some Cretan customs, and some Carian".

[11] For the language, see Neumann 1990. On the Anatolian origins of the Lycians, see Keen 1998, 26.

[12] I overlooked this passage at Keen 1998, 68. The aetiological myth of Lycia's name told by Antoninus Liberalis, which he traces back to Menecrates of Xanthus (*Met.* 35 = *FGrH* 769 F 2), does not necessarily deny any later Hellenic settlement.

[13] F 246, 255-259; he names Corydalla, Xanthus, Patara, Isinda, Phellus and Melanippe, though he thinks the last two are in Pamphylia. The general formula is πόλις Λυκίας. Ἑκαταῖος.

[14] Except for Phaselis (Hdt. 2. 178. 2), which, as noted below, is a rather different matter.

[15] For the reasons for this date, see Keen 1996, 117 no. 50; Flensted-Jensen and Hansen 1996, 137-8.

[16] Compare Diod. 11. 60 with Ephorus *FGrH* 70 F 191.

συνομόσαντες ὅρκους δεινούς, ἐπεξελθόντες ἀπέθανον πάντες Ξάνθιοι μαχόμενοι. τῶν δὲ νῦν Λυκίων φαμένων Ξανθίων εἶναι οἱ πολλοί, πλὴν ὀγδώκοντα ἱστιέων, εἰσὶ ἐπήλυδες αἱ δὲ ὀγδώκοντα ἱστίαι αὗται ἔτυχον τηνικαῦτα ἐκδημέουσαι καὶ οὕτω περιεγένοντο. τὴν ... δὴ Ξάνθον οὕτως ἔσχε ὁ Ἅρπαγος.

The Lycians, when Harpagus led his army onto the Xanthian plain, came out and fought, although they were few against many, and displayed much bravery. Beaten and forced back to the *asty*, they brought their wives, children, possessions and slaves together on the *akropolis*, and then set fire to and razed the entire *akropolis*. When the Xanthians had done this, they swore terrible oaths, came out against [the enemy], and all died in battle. Of those Lycians who now say that they are Xanthians, the majority, save for 80 families, are immigrants. The eighty families themselves happened to be away from the city at this time and so survived. Thus Harpagus took Xanthus.

Herodotus' account is a classic example of seeing a Lycian city through a Greek framework. He speaks of communal actions by 'the Xanthians' in their resistance to Persia. Internal evidence from Lycia, in contrast, suggests that Xanthus was ruled by a monarch at this time, and may have been the centre of a 'feudal' system that spread throughout Lycia.[17]

There is also evidence suggesting that the communities of Lycia could be viewed as somewhat less than full *poleis*. As well as Arrian's remark about *polismata*, Ps.-Scylax's near-contemporary, Menander, when he wrote of the Lycian communities in his play the *Aspis* (30-2), described them as *komai*. This term is very rarely used of south Anatolian communities; the only other references are to *komai* associated with Telmessus in the 3rd century BC (*SEG* 28 1224. 25-9, 279 BC), and the *Kardakon kome* (Maier 1959, No. 71, 181 BC), also associated with Telmessus (Wörrle 1991, 229-30 cites some examples from Caria).

One indication of possible *polis* status used by the Copenhagen Polis Centre is an appearance on the Athenian Tribute Lists (see Schuller 1995). Some Lycian communities, mainly on the western fringes of the peninsula, do appear on the Tribute Lists, but the core Lycian communities do not. Instead, the Lycians are listed in a single entry:

Λύκιοι καὶ συν[τελ(εῖς)]

The Lycians and their dependencies.[18]

(*IG* I³ 266. III. 34 [Athens, 446/5 BC]; *cf.* 261. I. 30, 262. V. 33)

All this evidence suggests a somewhat ambivalent Greek attitude towards the '*polis*-ness' of Lycian communities.

What of the perception held by the Lycians themselves? It is, to a degree, possible to trace through internal inscriptions the growing use by Lycian communities of the term *polis* and the associated concepts. The earliest use in an internal Greek-language inscription from Lycia of the term (after a fashion) is on the twelve-line epigram from the so-called 'Inscribed Pillar' or 'Xanthus Stele' (*SEG* 42 1245 = Meiggs-Lewis 93), which dates to the end of the 5th century BC or the beginning of the 4th. On this (ll. 7-8) the term *akropolis* is used:

[πο]λλὰς δὲ ἀκροπόλεις σὺν Ἀθηναίαι πτολιπόρθωι | [π]έρσας συνγενέσιν δῶκε μέρος βασιλέας·

Having stormed many *akropoleis* with the aid of Athena Ptoliporthos, he gave a share in his kingdom to his relatives.

What are the political connotations of this term? In the mind of a Greek, an *akropolis* would probably mean the presence of an associated *polis*, and a *polis* was both a topographic and a political designation (Hansen has shown repeatedly that where there was a physical Greek *polis*, so that physical location was almost without exception the centre of a *koinonia politon politeias*; see Hansen 1996b, 33; 1998). It is rather less certain that one can expect a Lycian, expressing a foreign idea in a language that was not his own, to automatically have similar associations in his mind. In any case, it is not even known where these *akropoleis* were; it is possible that they were beyond the frontiers of Lycia.[19]

The next inscription in date that survives definitely relates to Lycian settlements.

[εἰν ἑ]νὶ μηνὶ πόλις τρεῖ[ς --- ἔπερσεν, | Ξάνθ]ον καὶ Τελεμεσσὸν [--- ἡδὲ Πίναρα·]

In one month he stormed three *poleis* ... Xanthus and Telmessus [... and Pinara.]

---

[17] For a full discussion of the Lycian 'nobility' and the system of rule there, see Keen 1998, 38-60; forthcoming c.

[18] On the *synteleis*, see Keen 1998, 41-2.

[19] De Ste. Croix (1972, 38) thinks the reference specifically to Greek cities, but this is unprovable.

(SEG 39 1414. 24-5 [Letoön, ca. 390–380 BC])

This inscription is perhaps very nearly contemporary with the Inscribed Pillar, in honour of the Xanthian dynast Erbbina (or Arbinas). As can be seen, he speaks of having taken in one month three *poleis*, Xanthus, Telmessus and Pinara. Again, it is not clear that anything more is meant by the term than a topographic description. Supporting such an interpretation is that elsewhere on the document the same three locations are referred to as *aste* (ll. 5-6: *tria as[te],/Xanthon te ede Pinara kai eulimenon Tel[emesson]*), a term also used elsewhere in the document for the conquests Erbbina has made (l. 12: *polla ... astea eperse ...*), in lines which are almost identical in their meaning to those where *polis* is being used. The suspicion is that *polis* and *asty* may be being used indiscriminately as alternatives.

To confuse the issue still further, part of this inscription, including the lines referring to *aste*, was written by Symmachus, who was probably a Greek. How much was he expressing concepts understood by the Lycians who commissioned him? Is the situation possibly that Symmachus wrote his lines correctly referring to *aste*, but a Lycian writer responsible for the rest of the inscription demonstrated no knowledge of the correct distinction between the terms *polis* and *asty*?

So, by the end of the 5th and beginning of the 4th century BC, the Lycians had begun to adopt Greek political terminology, but were not really using it in a political way.

The first completely unequivocal use of *polis* in a political sense in a Lycian inscription does not come until the famous trilingual (Lycian, Greek and Aramaic) inscription (Neumann 1979, No. 320 = SEG 27 942) from the Letoön, a sanctuary associated with Xanthus, which is securely dated to 337/6 BC (so Badian 1977).

> ... ἔδοξε δὴ Ξανθίοι|ς καὶ τοῖς περιοίκοις ἱδρύσασθα|ι βωμὸν Βασιλεῖ Καυνίωι καὶ Ἀρ|κεσιμαι...

The Xanthians and the *perioikoi* decided to dedicate an altar to the Basileus Caunius and Arcesimas ...

> ... καὶ ἔδωκαν[20] ἡ πόλις ἀγρὸ|ν ὂγ Κεσινδηλις καὶ Πιγρης κατη|ργήσατο καὶ ὅσον πρὸς τῶι ἀργῶι | καὶ τὰ οἰκήματα εἶναι Βασιλέως | Καυνίου καὶ Ἀρκεσιμα, καὶ δίδοτ|αι κατ' ἔκαστον ἐνιαυτὸν τρία ἡμ|ιμναῖα παρὰ τῆς πόλεως ...

... and the *polis* gave the land which Cesindelis and Pigres worked and whatever was [needed] for the field and buildings of Basileus Caunius and Arcesimas, and gives each year three half minas from the *polis* ...

> ... καὶ ἐποιή|σαντο ὅρκους Ξάνθιοι καὶ οἱ περ|ίοικοι ὅσα ἐν τῆι στήληι ἐγγέγρ|απται ποιήσειν ἐντελῆ τοῖς θεο|ῖς τούτοις καὶ τῶι ἱερεῖ ...

... and the Xanthians and the *perioikoi* swore oaths to do completely for these gods and the priest whatever has been written on the stele ...

(Neumann 1979, No. 320. b. 5-8, 12-18, 26-30)

At the beginning of the document the decree is identified as a decision of the Xanthians (ll. 5-6); but as it progresses, the *polis* (of the Xanthians) is found giving out grants of land (ll. 12-13), and cash allowances are given out *para tes poleos* (ll. 16-18). Here the term *polis* is being used to refer to a political entity. This, however, is a very late document for the Classical period, and one drawn up at a time when Lycia was under Carian domination and influence. It seems that during this period the Hecatomnid dynasts were using a number of methods to justify their rule and break down any sense of Lycian nationalism (for which see below) that might be a challenge to that. One method of doing this was to promote a *polis* identity as an alternative.

A final document (SEG 36 1216 = TAM I 46), from approximately the same period (ca. 340–334 BC), exempts Xanthus, Tlos, Pinara and Cadyanda from payment of commercial taxes.

> ἔδωκεν Πιξώδαρος Ἑκατόμ[νου Ξα]|νθίοις, Τλωίτοις, Πιναρέοι[ς, Κανδα]|ϋδέοις δεκάτην τῆς ἐμπο[ρίας τῆς] | οὔσης [ἐ]ν τῆι π[ό]λ]ει ...

Pixodarus, son of Hecatomnus, gave the tithe from the *emporia* in the *poleis* to the Xanthians, Tloans, Pinarans and Cadyandans ...

(SEG 36 1216. 1-4)

This indicates the presence in these cities of *emporia*, and suggests some form of communal responsibility for taxation. Moreover, the use of city-ethnics may have some significance. The use of city-ethnics in the Greek world is taken by the Copenhagen Polis Centre as an important signifier for *polis* identity (Hansen 1996c). Here four are being used, in itself a development from most of the Classical period (see the discussion of Lycian ethnics below). Again, however, it comes from the period of Carian rule, when things were different from the way they

---

[20] SEG 27 prints ἔδωκεν to agree with πόλις, but this may misunderstand the Lycian concept of the *polis*; see below.

had been in the 5th and early 4th centuries BC.

Another political term found in the Trilingual is the term *perioikoi*. This is a term duplicated in later inscriptions, from Telmessus and Limyra (in this last case, a grant of citizenship to two Caunians):[21]

> ἐπ' ἀρχνότων Ἰάσον[ος, τοῦ δεῖνος,] | Ἀπολλοδώρου· ἐκλ[ησίας κυρίας] | γενομένης· ἔδοξε [Τελμεσσέων] | τῆι πόλει καὶ τοῖς π[εριοίκοις·]

> In the archonships of Jason, x, and Apollodorus; the *ekklesia kyria* took place; the *polis* and the *perioikoi* of the Telmessians decided: ...

(Robert 1966, 55 ll. 5-9 with Wörrle 1978, 237 no. 189 [Telmessus])

> ... δεδόχθαι Τελμησ[σ]έων τῆι πόλει καὶ τοῖς περιοίκοις ...

> ... to have been decided by the *polis* and the *perioikoi* of the Telmessians ...

(*SEG* 28 1224. 21-2 [Telmessus, 279 BC])

> Λυμυρέων τῆι πόλει καὶ τοῖς | [π]εριοίκοις ...

> ... by the *polis* and the *perioikoi* of the Limyrans
> ...
> ... εἴς τε τὴν πόλιν τὴν Λιμυρέων κα[ὶ] | τοὺς περιοίκους καὶ εἰς τοὺς ἄλλους Λυκίους[22]

> ... towards the *polis* and the *perioikoi* of the Limyrans and towards the other Lycians ...

(*SEG* 27 929. 2-3, 6-7 [Limyra, 279 BC])

Hahn (1981, 54) also cites as a reference to Lycian *perioikoi OGIS* 55. 28-9 (= *TAM* II 1, Telmessus, 240 BC):[23]

> ... ςυμπορεύεσθαι δὲ πάντας τοὺς π[ολί]τας καὶ τοὺς παροίκους ἐπὶ τὴν Θυσίαν.

> ... all the citizens and *paroikoi* to go together to the sacrifice.

In the Trilingual, the *periokoi* appear as partners of the *polis* of Xanthus, in the formulation 'the Xanthians and the *perioikoi*'. This is reinforced by the fact that *he polis* takes a plural verb, *edokan*, which may suggest that the *polis* was conceived of as a union of the Xanthians and the *perioikoi*.[24] In the Hellenistic examples the formulation has changed to 'the *polis* of the Telmessians/Limyrans and the *perioikoi*'. Even by the period of these inscriptions, an alternative formulation of 'the *polis* and its *archontes*' is found in the second inscription from Telmessus mentioned, and in another inscription from Xanthus:

> ... βασιλεύοντος Πτολεμαίου τοῦ Πτλεμαίου ἔτους | τετάρτου μηνὸς Δίου ἐκκλησί[ας κυρίας γενομένης καὶ τῆς πα[ρα τοῦ βασιλέως ἐπιστολῆς ἀνα[γ]νωσωείσης ἐν ἧι ἐγέγραπτο· Βασιλεὺς Πτολεμαῖος Τελμησσέων | τῆι πόλει καὶ τοῖς ἄρξουσι χαίρειν.

> In the fourth year of the reign of Ptolemy son of Ptolemy, in the month of Dios, the *ekklesia kyria* took place and the letter from the king was read, in which he wrote: King Ptolemy to the *polis* and *archontes* of the Telmessians, greetings.

(*SEG* 28 1224. 2-8 [Telmessus, 279 BC])

> ... μηνὸς Περ[ιτίου] | ἐκκλησίας κυρίας γενομένης· ἔδοξεν Ξανθίων τῆ[ι] πόλε[ι] | καὶ τοῖς ἄρχουσιν·...

> ... in the month of Peritios the *ekklesia kyria* took place; the *polis* and *archontes* of the Xanthians decided: ...

(*SEG* 33 1183. 2-4 [Xanthus, 260/59 BC])

By the 2nd century BC, decisions in Lycian cities are made not by the *polis* at all, but by the *demos* and their leaders (see Rhodes with Lewis 1997, 444-6),[25] as in this example from Araxa:

> ... ἔδοξεν Ἀραξέων τῷ δήμωι καὶ τοῖς ἄρ|χουσιν· ...

> ... the *demos* and the *archontes* of Araxa decided: ...

(*SEG* 18 570. 3-4 [Araxa, *ca.* 150 BC?])

A community called Pernis, found in the 4th century dealing with Pericles of Limyra, has been suggested as a

---

[21] Herodotus' reference to the *perioikoi* of the Lycians at 1. 173. 3, is, however, clearly a reference to people outside, rather than within, Lycia.
[22] The question of who these 'other Lycians' are and what they have to do with a decision of Limyra is obscure.
[23] Hahn also cites *OGIS* 219, but this in not an inscription from within Lycia.

[24] As argued by Wörrle 1978, 238. Hahn 1981, 53-4, argues that the singular subject with plural noun implies that a second part of the subject, καὶ οἱ περίοικοι, should be understood; but this inscription never uses 'the *polis* and the *perioikoi*', only 'the Xanthians and ...'
[25] The Cytenians write to the *boule* and *demos* of Xanthus (*SEG* 38 1476. 80-1, 89-90).

perioecic settlement of Limyra, with its own local assembly (see Wörrle 1991, 228-31; *SEG* 41 1379-80; but *contra* [though overstated], Keen 1998, 160-1). *Peripolia* have been found in a 2nd-century inscription from the Letoön (Bousquet and Gauthier 1994, 339-43), where they are distinct from the *polis*, and in a Hellenistic inscription from near Cyaneae (Davies 1895, 109 no. 19, where the community is named). It may even be that the large number of tombs at Limyra shows *perioikoi* being buried in the central settlement (Borchhardt 1993, 36).

There has been much discussion of these *perioikoi* (see now Hahn 1981; Borchhardt 1990, 133-5; Gygax 1991, reported by *SEG* 41 1337). Are they perhaps a second tier of citizenry within Lycian political communities, inhabitants of outlying settlements, with lesser status than those in the cities themselves? This is the view held by Hahn (1981, 55-6) and Bryce (1986, 170).[26] Most recently, Rhodes writes (Rhodes with Lewis 1997, 444):

> [W]e do find the remarkable phenomenon of *perioikoi*, who are not citizens but who share in decision-making rights with citizens.

Such an interpretation is not impossible, but it seems to the current author that Rhodes reads too much into the division between *perioikoi* and *polis*, interpreting it in terms of mainland Greek use of the terminology; as Wörrle notes (1981, 229), it is not really known how the Greek and Lycian understanding of the city-state (*Stadtgemeinde*) related.

In the Xanthian inscription, the formula 'Xanthians and *perioikoi*' is used as an alternative to *polis*.[27] Only in the later inscriptions is the *polis* distinguished from the *perioikoi* and even there the *perioikoi* appear as equal partners with the *polis*; the two together make up the Telmessians or the Limyrans, and at least at Limyra the *perioikoi* are consulted about grants of citizenship. Moreover, in the Telmessus inscription of 279 BC, the decision-making body can be either 'the *polis* and the *perioikoi*' or 'the *polis* and its *archontes*'. We have already seen the Lycians use *polis* and *asty* as if they were synonyms. Here is a further blurring of the distinction between the two, with *polis* being used to denote the political community, but only that part of the political community domiciled in the urban centre.[28] From that it is a small step to referring to the inhabitants of the urban centre as *politai* without necessarily suggesting that those outside the urban centre were not citizens; this seems to be the usage in *OGIS* 55.

The interpretation of Wörrle (1978, 236-46) seems correct.[29] *Perioikoi* here simply means, as it usually does in e.g. Herodotus (see Shipley 1997, 196-8, 217-23), those living around the *polis*, i.e. citizens of the *polis* not domiciled in the nucleated urban settlement (their communities perhaps represented by the references to *peripolia*). These citizens may well have had their own local assemblies, but they probably held an equal share in the citizenship with people living in the *polis* itself. The model for these should be the relationship between the demes of Attica and Athens, rather than that between Sparta and her perioecic *poleis*. The abandonment of this terminology after the mid-3rd century BC, in favour of a distinction between *asty* and *chora*, with inhabitants of both as *politai* (see *SEG* 40 1380), perhaps represents a recognition that the term *perioikoi* could imply a lower status of citizenship, a status that the Lycians, as they became more sophisticated in their understanding of Greek political terminology, wished to make clear did not exist (*cf.* Wörrle 1991, 231).

There are other considerations to take into account. One is the evidence for Lycian self-identity as Lycians. It is very rare for a Greek or Roman literary source to identify a Lycian as anything other than a Lycian. Herodotus (1. 176) speaks of Xanthians and Lycians as if the terms were interchangeable (see Keen 1998, 58 and No. 183 and refs. therein), and, as already noted, the Lycians appear *en masse* in the Athenian Tribute Lists as *Lykioi*, in contrast to other areas of Asia Minor, where settlements tend to be named individually. These Greek sources seem to be representing something internal to Lycia, which 5th and 4th-century documents written in the Lycian language further illustrate. In those texts, the use of the Lycians' name for themselves, *Trm̃mili*,[30] outweighs other uses of ethnics. Excluding coin inscriptions, the ethnic of a Lycian city appears in only 14 instances in the known Lycian inscriptions. *Trm̃mili* is used 21 times (of course not every occasion may refer to an individual), and is a well-enough known term that Herodotus mentions it (1. 173. 3). This trend seems to continue into the Hellenistic period. An Olympic victor from 256 BC, Tlepolemus, is identified by Pausanias (5. 8. 11) simply as a Lycian. There is an early 3rd-century epitaph from Citium for 'Smyrnus the Xanthian from Lycia' (*SEG* 40 1355). In an Athenian inscription from after *ca.* 180 BC is the pancratiast

---

[26] Hahn further suggests that the non-urban *perioikoi* were non-Hellenized, as opposed to the heavily Hellenized inhabitants of the *polis*. Whilst it is likely that country-dwellers would be less culturally sophisticated than their urban fellows, Hahn lays too much stress on this point.

[27] This interpretation is supported by the fact that the Lycian version of this inscription (Neumann 1979, No. 320*a*) the same phrase, *teteri seyepewẽtlm̃mẽi*, translates both 'the Xanthians and the *perioikoi*' (*a*.31-2 = *b*.27-8) and *polis* (*a*.13-14 = *b*.11).

[28] This is a slightly different use of *polis* to any of the four meanings of the term (1: = *akropolis*; 2: = urban centre; 3 = territory; 4 = political community) discussed in Hansen 1996b, 25-8.

[29] As followed by Schweyer 1996, 68. I may have slightly misrepresented Wörrle's views in Keen 1998, 55-6.

[30] For all references to *Trm̃mili* and other words derived from it, such as *Trm̃mis*, the name for Lycia itself, see Melchert 1993, 78-9.

Menander, a 'Lycian from Gagae' (*IG* II² 2315. 10).³¹ It appears that a Lycian thought of himself as a Lycian first, and as an inhabitant of his city second, in the same way that an Athenian was an Athenian first and an Acharnian second.³² This probably reflects a political unity in Classical Lycia (Keen 1998, 40-2).

Coinage should be mentioned, as this is often used as a test of civic identity.³³ In the case of Lycia, this can be a trap. Though their coins borrow many artistic motifs from Greek coinage, the actual idea probably came not from the Greeks, but from the Lydians. Lycian coinage falls into two types, that minted in western Lycia, and that minted in central and eastern Lycia. The western is no guide for civic identity, because almost all the coinage that carries the name of a city also carries the name of a dynast (Keen 1998, 54); the place-name is simply a means of locating where these coins were minted, and does not really say anything about the site's inhabitants and their self-identity. The only real exception is a series of coins with the head of Athena on the obverse and various city-names on the reverse; but there the head of Athena is probably acting as a dynastic emblem instead of a dynast's name (Keen 1998, 54, 146-7).

In central and eastern Lycia, things were a little different (see Keen 1998, 54-5). In that region there does seem to be a tradition of cities striking coinage in their own right. This at the very least is a proclamation of self-determination. The difference between the two areas probably has its roots in geography and politics. Western Lycia, those communities lining the valley of the river Xanthus, seems to have been politically united from a very early time (Keen 1998, 39-40). Eastern Lycia, where the high mountains and valleys hinder communications from one city to the next, encouraged communities that were more self-sufficient, and distrustful of the growing power of western Lycia (it is interesting to note that Hecataeus, to judge from F 258, seems to have placed the communities of what is generally called central and eastern Lycia in Pamphylia; see Keen 1998, 18; forthcoming a). Their coinage was perhaps a reaction to western Lycia's encroachment upon their independence.

Public building is rare,³⁴ though there are a few temples in some of the cities.³⁵ There is also one supposedly 4th-century reference to a *prytaneion* from Tlos (Miller 1978, 214 No. 445):

ἐν πρυτανείωι ἄνδρα ἀγαθὸν γεγονότα καὶ διὰ προγόνων εὐεργέτην τοῦ δήμου

In the *prytaneion*, being a good man and, through his ancestors, a benefactor of the *demos*.

(*TAM* II 582. 1-3 = *CIG* 4239).

Kalinka in the *TAM* publication (of which Miller seems unaware) dates this inscription to the 1st, rather than the 4th, century BC. This is surely correct, as the formulation resembles decrees of the Hellenistic and Roman periods rather than those of Classical Lycia. There is no other reference to a Lycian *prytaneion*, and the earliest evidence of a *bouleuterion* does not come until the 1st century BC (at Antiphellus: Gneisz 1990, 304, no. 60).

At the eastern side of the Lycian peninsula, there were a small number of Rhodian colonies, of which the most important is Phaselis. These cities are rather different from the other Lycian cities; they have traditions of Greek foundation, sometimes in the time of Mopsus (e.g. Rhodiapolis, according to Theopompus, *FGrH* 115 F 103. 15), sometimes in the early 7th century BC (e.g. Phaselis, according to Hieronymus).

Phaselis seems to have had many of the features that expected in a Greek *polis*: it minted coins, issued with a magistrate's name (Head 1911, 696); there was an *agora* (attested in Plut. *Alex*. 18. 4); a cult of Athena Polias was established by the 5th century BC at the latest (*TAM* II 1184); it made treaties with Athens (*IG* I³ 10) and with Mausolus of Caria (*TAM* II 1183). The citizens of Phaselis presumably thought of themselves as Greek *politai*.

The other cities are less well-known, but they may have been similar to Phaselis when first settled. Phaselis, however, was protected from the encroaching political power of the Lycian kingdom by the Lycian Mt. Olympus, and is often considered not Lycian, but Pamphylian (Aristodemus, *FGrH* 104 F 1. 45; *Suda s.v.* Κίων). The other settlements, further west, did not have such protection, and seem to have become 'Lycianized' in the 5th century BC. At Rhodiapolis the Classical inscriptions are not in Greek, but in Lycian (*cf.* Arrian's comments on Side; see below).

---

³¹ Larsen 1945, 72-3 uses some of these examples as evidence for an early existence of the Lycian League. Gagae originally was a Rhodian settlement (for which see below) but by the end of the Classical period had become 'Lycianized'.

³² For the ethnics of Lycians outside Lycia, see Zimmermann 1992b, 211-212 no. 55.

³³ On Lycian coinage, see Keen 1998, 11, and refs. therein.

³⁴ The impressive 5th- and 4th-century funerary monuments to be found in Lycia, the Nereid Monument, the Harpy Tomb, etc., are monuments for public display, but *not* expressions of a community's self-perception. Rather they are statements made by ruling dynastic individuals; see Keen 1998, 36, 183-4.

³⁵ Xanthus: Metzger 1963, 29-36, 40-2. A Classical period temple discovered in the territory of Cyaneae is mentioned in Kolb and Kupke 1992.

Pamphylia

Pamphylia presents a rather different aspect from Lycia. There are fewer cities whose existence can be demonstrated than are found in Lycia. This does not necessarily mean that there were in actuality fewer (though it may be the case),[36] and Ps.-Scylax devotes the same amount of space to Pamphylia as to Lycia (once account is taken of his including half of Pamphylia under Lycia); it merely means that the evidence, besides Ps.-Scylax and a series of settlements known to have been mentioned by Hecataeus (F 261-4), largely fails. Of many of the cities that are identifiable, almost nothing at all can be said for this period, save that they warrant a notice in Ps.-Scylax or Hecataeus. If one wishes to discuss at all the civic identity of Pamphylian cities, one has to turn to the 'Big Four'; Perge, Aspendus, Sillyum and Side.

One must also note a strong sense amongst the Pamphylian cities that they were, to one degree or another, Greek. Aspendus was supposedly settled by Argives (Strabo 14. 4. 2), Side supposedly from Cyme ([Scylax] 101), though according to Arrian (*Anab.* 1. 26. 4) the settlers intermingled with the natives to such an extent that they gave up speaking Greek and spoke a 'barbaric' tongue.

Closely tied in with the mythography of these cities is the legendary seer Mopsus. He gave his name to the sites of Mopsouestia and Mopsoucrene in Cilicia; there are Roman-period statue-bases from Perge identifying Mopsus and Calchas amongst the city's founders (Merkelbach and Şahin 1988, nos. 24, 27); a similar statue base is found at Sillyum (Hereward 1958, 57-8). Some Greek sources also make him the *oecist* of Aspendus (and for that matter Phaselis and Rhodiapolis in Lycia in some accounts). How far back such mythography goes is unknown; internal claims to Mopsus are all post-Hellenistic, but the legend of Greek foundation of Pamphylia is in Herodotus (7. 91), and Mopsus' involvement is in Theopompus (F 103. 15). Some archaeologists and historians believe that these tales do reflect a degree of truth; the cities of Pamphylia (with the exception of Side) are cautiously said to have been foundations of the Late or post-Mycenaean period, which subsequently developed in isolation from the rest of Greece (Olshausen 1972, 442-3).[37]

One should mention the various languages of the cities. Inscriptions from Perge, Aspendus, Sillyum and Selge are in what appears to be a heavy dialect form of Greek (one might compare the Arcado-Cypriot dialect), strongly influenced by native forms (Brixhe 1979; 1991). This would tie in with Arrian's story of Greek-speakers turning to a barbarian tongue, had Arrian not applied that story to Side; but there inscriptions are found in a different script and language, probably the native Pamphylian language (see most recently Nollé 1988). So the Cymaean settlers at Side, if they ever existed, must have been swiftly absorbed into the native population.

What is particularly interesting about these languages is their survival. Both Graeco-Pamphylian and Sidetan continued to be used as epigraphic languages into the Hellenistic period, certainly into the 3rd century BC and possibly into the 2nd, before finally being wiped out by the spread of *koine*. This contrasts with the situation in Lycia, where their language has gone from epigraphy by 300 BC (Bryce 1986, 50). There is not yet a good explanation for this.

What can be said about the civic identity of these places? The first thing to note is that it appears that in Pamphylia one was a citizen of Perge or Aspendus first, and a Pamphylian second, if at all. The impression given by an investigation of the sources is that *Pamphylos* has simply geographic connotations, indicating which part of the world certain people originated from, most often in army lists or arrangements of provinces. So Herodotus speaks of the contribution made to Xerxes' army by 'the Pamphylians' (7. 91); but there is no Pamphylian leader named as there is a Lycian (7. 98). The ethnic does not appear to be applied to any individuals, as *Lykios* certainly is.

Instead of the Pamphylians taking action, usually the Aspendians or Pergeans are heard of; worth noting here is Arrian's account of Alexander's movements through Pamphylia.[38] Even more important for this is the evidence from the Athenian Tribute Lists. The Lycians, as already noted, appear on the inscriptions as a single mass; but when Pamphylian communities appear, as Aspendus, Perge and Sillyum do on the Assessment Decree for 425/4 BC,[39] they are listed as individual contributors in their own right.

Side and Aspendus were early issuers of coinage, both beginning minting in the early 5th century BC (Aspendus: Hill 1897, 93-4; Side: Hill 1897, 143-4). Olbia also minted at the same time (Hill 1897, 118), but no later coinage is known. This is likely to be an expression of civic identity, although some of the coinage clearly was minted by Persian officials for their own purposes.[40]

Perge provides a good example of an important cult in action. The cult of Artemis Pergaia is known from a 5th-

---

[36] Only 46 sites can be demonstrated in Pamphylia and Cilicia combined; Keen forthcoming b.
[37] But Cook 1975, 795-6 doubts any settlement on the southern coast of Asia Minor in the immediate post-Mycenaean period.

[38] It is noteworthy that Arrian's sources seem rather better informed about Alexander's movements through Pamphylia than those through Lycia.
[39] Aspendus: *IG* I³ 71. II. 156-7; Perge: II. 113; Sillyum: II. 114.
[40] Note the coin issued at Side by the Persian (or Lycian) Artembares: Atlan 1958.

century Graeco-Pamphylian inscription:

> To the Mistress of Perge, Clemytas, son of Lvaramus, *varisvotas*, has dedicated the setting-up [of this monument].
>
> (Merkelbach and Şahin 1988, No. 1)[41]

Though the deity is termed there 'mistress of Perge' it can hardly be other than an early description of the cult of Artemis (*cf.* the description of Leto at the Letoön [*TAM* I 56. 4; Neumann 1979, No. 320. *a*. 38] as 'mother of this Sanctuary'). Ps.-Scylax (100) may mention the associated temple (depending on an emendation of his text). Strabo (14. 4. 2) certainly mentions the temple, as outside the boundaries of the city itself. The probable conclusion is that the Pergeans felt strongly about the importance of this cult, and promoted it sufficiently that it became known outside Perge.

The city best-known of these 'Big Four', is Aspendus, because this city intersects most with the history of Greece, largely due to of its strategic importance on the river Eurymedon and its regular use by the Persians as a naval base for their actions against the Aegean. Thucydides, Xenophon and Diodorus all have something to say about the history of Aspendus in the 5th and 4th centuries BC (Thuc. 8. 81. 3, 87-8, 108; Xen. *HG* 4. 8. 30; Diod. 14. 99. 4-5); Arrian's portrait of Aspendus, as a high peak, difficult to scale peak (described by Bean 1968, 72, as 'in general precipitous') on which lay the city's *akropolis*, surrounded by houses on the lower slopes enclosed by a low wall, is one of the better-realized of his descriptions. Xenophon calls Aspendus a *polis* (*HG* 4. 8. 30; also Diod. 14. 99. 5), and if he had not actually been there in person, he had at least been in the general region.

The Aspendians act *en masse*, negotiating with Thrasybulus in 388 BC (Xen. *HG* 4. 8. 30), and with Alexander in 333 BC (Arr. *Anab.* 1. 26. 2), and contributing troops to a Persian army (Nep. *Dat.* 8. 2). But how can it be known that this represents any sort of feeling of communal citizenship amongst the inhabitants, and not simply the same sort of misrepresentation that Herodotus applied to Xanthus?

This question can be answered by an inscription from Aspendus, the best piece of internal evidence for the city's civic identity (*SEG* 17 639).

> ἐπὶ δημιουργοῦ Ἀπολλωνίου τοῦ
> Δημοχάριος, ἐκκλησίας κυρίας
> γενομένης, ἔδοξε τῶι δήμωι τῶι
> Ἀσπενδίων· ὅσοι μετὰ [Φι]λοκλέους κ[αὶ]
> 5 Λεωνίδου παραγενόμενοι ἐβοή[θη]σαν
>   τῆι πόλει τῆι Ἀσπενδίων [Πάμφ]υλοι,
>   Λύκιοι, Κρῆτες, Ἕλληνες, Πισίδαι,
>   ἐπειδὴ, ἄνδρες ἀγαθοὶ γεγ[ένη]νται
>   καὶ χρήσιμοι τῶι τε βασιλ[εῖ
> 10 Π]τολεμαίωι καὶ τῆι πόλει, εἶναι
>   [αὐτο]ὺς πολίτας καὶ εὐεργέτας το[ῦ]
>   [πλήθ]ους καὶ ἐκγόνους· στήλην δε
>   σ[τησ]άτωσαν ἐν τῶν [ἱερῶι τ]ῆς Ἀρτέ[μι]δος
>   καὶ ἀναγραψά[τωσα]ν τὰ ὀνόματα
> 15 αὐτῶν καὶ π[ατέρω]ν· ἐὰν δε
>   [τι]ς αὐτῶν βούληται [κατ]αχωρ[ισθῆ]ναι
>   εἰς φυλήν, [τελείτω ἀργ]υριον [ὅσον]
>   ἡ πόλις βου[λεύσηται].

In the *demiourgeia* of Apollonius son of Democharius, at the principal assembly, the *demos* of the Aspendians decided: whoever came with Philocles and Leonidas and helped the *polis* of the Aspendians, Pamphylians, Lycians, Cretans, Greeks, and Pisidians, since they are good men and useful to King Ptolemy and the *polis*, they will be citizens and benefactors of the masses and sons [of the *polis*]; they shall set up a stele in the temple of Artemis and write their names and those of their fathers; if any of them wishes to take up a place in a *phyle*, he should pay the price the *polis* decides.

This is an honorary inscription that dates to 301/298 BC. Here already are many of the features expected in a typical Greek *polis* of the Hellenistic period. The *polis*, as a political entity, is making decisions (l. 18) and (ll. 9-10) being assisted by foreigners; public decrees are inscribed and displayed in the temple of Artemis (ll. 12-14); decrees are dated by the holders of offices of the *demos* (ll. 1-2). There is (l. 2) an *ekklesia kyria*, a principal assembly of the people. This is a feature that does not seem to be found in Lycian cities until *ca.* 280 BC when it appears definitely at Telmessus (*SEG* 28 1224. 2-3; Robert 1966, 56 ll. 6-7), and possibly at Araxa (*ASAA* 8-9 [1925–6] 313-15 No. 1, either 278/7 BC or 240/39 BC), and soon after at Xanthus (*SEG* 33 1183. 2-4; *TAM* II 262 [256 BC]).[42] Ultimate power within the *polis* is vested in the *demos* (ll. 3-4); there is a concept of citizenship, that can be given to honoured foreigners (ll. 10-11); there is even evidence for the city's population being subdivided into *phylai* (l. 17). The Trilingual of Xanthus shows that particular Lycian community having developed some of the same practices, but Aspendus seems much more sophisticated. Is this simply a result of the Aspendian decree being nearly forty years later that the Xanthian? (After all, Lycian cities themselves had some of these features, e.g. the *ekklesia kyria*, in only another 20 years.) Or is it an indication that

---

[41] Translation adapted from Brixhe 1976, 236.

[42] I exclude the inscriptions from Lissa, dated 275-245 BC, cited by Wörrle 1991, 229, as Lissa lies outside Classical and Hellenistic Lycia (see Keen 1998, 17-18).

Aspendus had got slightly further than Xanthus in developing a sense of itself as a *polis* in the sense of a *koinonia politon politeias*?

This is the best piece of internal evidence from the Pamphylian cities; none of the other cities seem to have left similar decrees to posterity. Is it then legitimate to speculate on the basis of the Aspendian decree that a similar stage had been reached at the end of the 4th century BC at Side, Sillyum and Perge?

The answer is probably, yes. There is as yet nothing quite as spectacular as the Aspendian inscription, but what there is (the cult of Artemis Pergaia, the Sidetan coinage) suggests developments in those cities roughly parallel to those found in Aspendus (though Aspendus' situation might have been affected by its role as a military port and the consequent passage through of a considerable number of people from different backgrounds). Sillyum, on the other hand, may be a slightly different case. As far as Arrian is concerned (*Anab.* 1. 26. 5) it was no more than a fortified location, staffed by mercenaries and *barbaroi*. There may, however, be some significance to the fact that the *barbaroi* are *epichorioi*, locals; and Sillyum featured as a political community on the Athenian Assessment Decree and is unequivocally described as a *polis* by Ps.-Scylax (101). It is probably legitimate to treat Sillyum as similar to Aspendus, Perge and Side.

Cilicia

If anything, the evidence for Cilicia is even more impenetrable than Lycia and Pamphylia. Like Pamphylia, it was supposedly settled by Greeks led by Mopsus and Calchas, or Calchas and Amphilochus, or other combinations of the three (Strabo 14. 4. 3, 14. 5. 16). In Cilicia, however, clearly any Hellenic settlement in the late Bronze Age that there might have been (and the archaeological evidence at Tarsus suggests that there may have been some) left far less mark than in Pamphylia. Bing (1969, 114) draws attention to the fact that neither Xenophon (*An.* 1. 2. 20-3. 1, 1. 4. 1-4) nor Arrian (*Anab.* 1. 26. 1-28. 1, 2. 4. 4-7. 2) note Cilicia as a strong area of Greek settlement. Bing suggests that the Greek colonists there possessed remarkably short memories; but it may be more likely that the development of myths of Greek origins belongs to the post-Alexander period, and Graham (1982, 93) is right to stress the dangers of postulating Archaic colonies from such late evidence.

An exception to this is Mallus, where tales of Argive origin were maintained, and which possessed a cult of Amphilochus important enough to merit a visit from Alexander (Arr. *Anab.* 2. 5. 9).[43] Gradually the Greeks came back, but largely as traders within native cities rather than founders of their own colonies. The main exception to this is Soli, discussed below; the idea that Tarsus and other Cilician cities were resettled as Greek colonies the early 7th century BC seems implausible.[44] By the 5th century BC, Cilicia was ruled by kings called Syennesis, who were subservient to the Persian empire (Duchesne-Guillemin 1975, 440). It was a *barbaros* monarchy, similar to that which existed in Lydia before Cyrus the Great's conquests, and which probably also existed in Lycia (Keen 1998, 45-53).

As with Pamphylia, the picture of the spread of settlements in the Classical period is mainly based upon Ps.-Scylax, who lists a series of place-names, some of which certainly and others of which may not even have been what he thought of as *poleis*, and a series of places mentioned by Hecataeus (F 265-8). Some of these, such as Adana and Anemurium, would become of considerable importance in later years; but for this period next to nothing is know about them beyond the snippets found in the *Periplous* and Hecataeus.

A few do slip into the sources elsewhere. Issus, of course, was the site of Alexander's defeat of Darius III, but Xenophon had already noted it in his *Anabasis* (1. 4. 1), as a *polis* that was *megale kai eudaimonia* ('great and prosperous').[45] One suspects, however, that in this case Xenophon calls Issus (or Issoi, as he has it) a *polis* simply because it was an urban settlement, and all urban settlements were in his mind *poleis*.

Two Cilician settlements however, do provide evidence from which some conclusions concerning their civic identity can be drawn. One is the rather minor site of Celenderis, supposedly settled from Samos (Pomponius Mela 1.77). This appears on the Athenian Assessment Decree of 425/4 BC (*IG* I³ 71. II. 146), as a community expected to contribute to the Athenian war-coffers. Little else is known about Celenderis, although Ps.-Scylax did consider it worth clearly identifying the site as a *polis*.[46]

The other location is Soli. Alexander fined this community for supporting Persia (Arr. *Anab.* 2. 5. 5), a sign of the existence of some political entity that could act on behalf of the inhabitants. However, this might be expected. Soli was supposedly a Greek settlement,[47] founded by Rhodes and Achaea in collaboration (so Strabo 14. 5. 8), perhaps in the early 7th century BC (so Boardman 1980, 50); Ps.-Scylax emphatically calls it a *polis Hellenis*. So, like

---

[43] Triedler 1969 suggests a Phoenician foundation, from the name.

[44] Bing 1969, 104-8; Bing 1971, 103; against the idea, see Erzem 1940, 74-5; Goldman 1963, 142, 159-60; Boardman 1980, 46 no. 37.

[45] μεγάλη καὶ εὐδαίμονια. On this phrase, see Dillery 1995, 95-8.

[46] Nagidus was also supposedly founded from Samos, and is accepted by Graham 1982, 93 as a genuine Archaic colony.

[47] But clearly not accepted as such by Graham 1982, 93, who omits it from the list of Greek colonies on the south Anatolian coast. The language spoken at Soli was non-Greek.

Phaselis, the inhabitants of Soli should perhaps be expected to think of themselves as inhabitants of Greek-style *poleis*.[48]

Beyond these examples, knowledge of the civic identity of Cilician cities lies beyond our ability to interpret the evidence.

Conclusions

Having looked at the evidence relating to individual settlements, can any general conclusions be reached for the study of the southern Anatolian coast as a whole? Any conclusions must, through the nature of the evidence, be very speculative and tentative, but perhaps a few can be drawn.

In those places where Greek colonial settlements had been made as part of the colonizing movement of the 8th and 7th centuries (*e.g.* Phaselis, and perhaps Soli), the inhabitants seem to have conceived of themselves as *politai* of *poleis* from the moment they arrived, though in some cases (e.g. Rhodiapolis) they were unable to maintain their Greek identity in the face of the native culture. In the other urban settlements in southern Anatolia a sense of '*polis*-identity' seems to have progressively emerged over the 6th, 5th and 4th centuries BC. It was probably largely absent in the 6th century BC (though there is little or no evidence for that period), but had reached a significant point of development by Alexander's conquests. The communities were naturally open to such evolution, as they were already nucleated urban settlements.

This development (which was not unique to Anatolia; similar processes were at work in e.g. Aetolia and Acarnania, though these communities had a different starting-point) took place at different rates in the different regions. In Lycia the process ran fairly slowly, even though they were in the forefront of the general Hellenization of Asia Minor, using Greek or Greek-inspired artists as early as the mid-6th century BC (Keen 1998, 66 and refs.). It looks as if, although the Lycians adopted the term *polis* by the end of the 5th century BC, *poleis* did not start acting as political entities until shortly before Alexander, and even then in a fairly rudimentary fashion. The Trilingual exhibits few of the political institutions that characterize a Greek *polis*. At the same time, some settlements within the *chorai* of *poleis* evolved an identity of their own; note a bilingual inscription from Antiphellus (*TAM* I 56) where the tomb owner can describe himself as part of the community of Phellus in the Lycian text, but an Antiphellite in the Greek.

In Pamphylia the process was rather more advanced, to judge from the Aspendus decree, which does display a number of the typical political institutions. This is probably because of the feeling amongst the settlers of the Pamphylian cities that they were in some sense Greek. In Cilicia it is much less clear what was happening, but given the small degree of Hellenization manifested in the material evidence one suspects that '*polis*-identity' was less advanced in Cilicia than in either Pamphylia or Lycia. All these processes seem to have speeded up after the conquests of Alexander, and by *ca.* 250 BC the Lycian cities certainly had caught up with the Pamphylians; Xanthus is quite happily giving out *proxenia* and hereditary citizenship by 260/59 BC (*SEG* 33 1183. 11-12).

A further interesting aspect is that in Lycia, the inhabitants gradually came more and more to conceive of themselves as citizens of *poleis*, but they also had a strong sense of themselves *as Lycians*. This sense of national identity did not go away, and a tension was created between the national and *polis*-identity. This tension was finally resolved in the creation of the Lycian League, probably around 200 BC, a framework that accommodated both impulses (again, this can be seen as the same solution to the same problems being confronted in e.g. Aetolia where it resulted in the Aetolian League; see on this Funke 1997, esp. 163-8). Such a situation did not arise in Pamphylia, because there was no sense in Pamphylia of Pamphylian nationalism; there was never any unified political state. However, neither did a federal structure arise amongst the cities of Cilicia, where there had been a unified political state. Why the federal process should have happened in Lycia and not in Cilicia is a difficult question to answer, but one might suggest, very tentatively, that the answer lies partially in the different political relations the two areas had with the Hellenistic kingdoms, a matter into which it is not appropriate to go now,[49] and partly in the different speeds of the processes of Hellenization; in Lycia Hellenization was further advanced than in Cilicia at the time of Alexander's conquests, and so the pace of post-Alexandrian Hellenization could be more relaxed and thus allow the traditional nationalism to survive.

Finally, all these areas were within the Persian empire for most of this period. What did the Persians think of these developments? There is no evidence to suggest either that they hindered or assisted; but they probably did not disapprove. Political identity centred upon the nation provoked the great nationalist revolts in Egypt and Babylon, which gave the empire more trouble than anything the Greeks did before Alexander. It can only have been to the Persians' advantage for identity based on the nation to be replaced by identity based on the city.

---

[48] Snyder 1966, 60-1 and Bing 1969, 115 n. 76 raise the possibility that Soli's conscious Rhodian identity is demonstrated by its hostility towards Alexander.

[49] However, it may be that the Lycian League was prompted into existence by Antiochus III in the early 2nd century BC (Keen 1998, 180).

Tracing an 'interface' between the 'barbarian' and 'Hellenic' *polis* in southern Anatolia is, as already stated, no easy task, since not enough is known about the starting point. What can be traced, to a degree, is the use by the inhabitants of these areas of the term *polis* and their development of a political identity as citizens of *poleis*. Yet the ultimate result would not have been necessarily to produce a carbon copy of the Greek *polis* in Anatolia; rather the institutions were adapted to their own needs, the Lycian use of the term *perioikoi* indicating this.

Bibliography

Atlan, S. 1958: Eine in Side geprägte lykische Münze. *Anatolia* 3, 89-95.

Badian, E. 1977: A Document of Artaxerxes IV? In Kinzl, K.H. (ed.), *Greece and the Eastern Mediterranean in Ancient History and Prehistory. Studies Presented to Fritz Schachermeyr on the Occasion of his Eightieth Birthday*, Berlin, 40-50.

Bean, G.E. 1968 (2nd ed 1979): *Turkey's Southern Shore*, London.

Bing, J.D. 1969: *A History of Cilicia during the Assyrian Period*, Ann Arbor: University Microfilms.

Bing, J.D. 1971: Tarsus: a Forgotten Colony of Lindos. *JNES* 30, 99-109.

Boardman, J. 1980: *The Greeks Overseas*[3], London.

Borchhardt, J. 1990: Zêmuri. Die Residenzstadt des Lykischen Königs Perikles. *MDAI(I)* 40, 109-143.

Borchhardt, J. 1993: *Die Steine von Zêmuri. Archäologische Forschungen an den verborgenen Wassern von Limyra*, Vienna.

Borchhardt, J. and Dobesch, G. (eds.) 1993: *Akten des II. Internationalen Lykien-Symposions*, Vienna.

Bousquet, J. and Gauthier, P. 1994: Inscriptions du *Létôon* de Xanthos. *REG* 107, 319-361.

Brandt, H. 1992: *Gesellschaft und Wirtschaft Pamphyliens und Pisidiens im Altertum*, Bonn.

Brixhe, C. 1976: *Le dialecte grec de Pamphylie: documents et grammaire*, Paris.

Brixhe, C. 1991: Étymologie populaire et onomastique en pays bilingue. *RPh* 65, 67-81.

Bryce, T.R. 1986: *The Lycians: A Study of Lycian History and Civilisation to the Conquest of Alexander the Great I: The Lycians in Literary and Epigraphic Sources*, Copenhagen.

Chaniotis, A. 1997: Review of Hansen 1996a. *BMCR* 8, 726-738.

Cook, J.M. 1975: Greek Settlement in the Eastern Aegean and Asia Minor. In *CAH*[3] II.2, 773-804.

Davies, G. 1895: Greek Inscriptions from Lycia. *JHS* 15, 100-115.

De Ste. Croix, G.E.M. 1972: *The Origins of the Peloponnesian War*, London.

Dillery, J. 1995: *Xenophon and the History of His Times*, London.

Duchesne-Guillemin, J. 1975: Syennesis. In *Der Kleine Pauly*, Munich, 440.

Erzem, A. 1940: *Kilikien bis zum Ende der Perserherrschaft*, Leipzig.

Flensted-Jensen, P. 1995: The Bottiaians and their *Poleis*. In Hansen, M.H. and Raaflaub, K. (eds.), *Studies in the Ancient Greek Polis*, Stuttgart, 103-132.

Flensted-Jensen, P. and Hansen, M.H. 1996: Pseudo-Skylax' Use of the Term *Polis*. In Hansen and Raaflaub 1996, 137-67.

Funke, P. 1997: *Polis*genese und Urbanisierung in Aitolien im 5. und 4. Jh. v. Chr. In Hansen 1997a, 145-88.

Gneisz, D. 1990: *Das antike Rathaus*. Vienna.

Goldman, H. 1963: *Excavations at Gözlü Kule, Tarsus* III, Princeton.

Graham, A.J. 1982: The Colonial Expansion of Greece. In *CAH*[2] III.3, 83-162.

Gygax, M.D. 1991: Los periecos licios (siglos IV–III a.C.). *Gerión* 9, 111-130.

Hahn, I. 1981: Periöken und Periökenbesitz in Lykien. *Klio* 63, 51-61.

Hansen, M.H. 1993: The *Polis* as a Citizen-State. In Hansen, M.H. (ed.), *The Ancient Greek City-State*, Copenhagen, 7-29.

Hansen, M.H. 1994: *Poleis* and City-States, 600–323 B.C. A Comprehensive Research Programme. In Whitehead 1994a, 9-17.

Hansen, M.H. (ed.). 1996a: *Introduction to an Inventory of Poleis*, Copenhagen.

Hansen, M.H. 1996b: ΠΟΛΛΑΧΩΣ ΠΟΛΙΣ ΛΕΓΕΤΑΙ (Arist. *Pol.* 1276a23). The Copenhagen Inventory of *Poleis* and the *Lex Hafniensis de Civitate*. In Hansen 1996a, 7-72.

Hansen, M.H. 1996c: City-Ethnics as Evidence for *Polis* Identity. In Hansen and Raaflaub 1996, 169-96.

Hansen, M.H. (ed.). 1997a: *The Polis as an Urban Centre and as a Political Community*, Copenhagen.

Hansen, M.H. 1997b: Hekataios' Use of the Word *Polis* in His *Periegesis*. In Nielsen, T.H. (ed.), *Yet More Studies in the Ancient Greek Polis*, Stuttgart, 17-27.

Hansen, M.H. 1998: Response: Hansen on Chaniotis on Hansen. *BMCR* 98.2.7.

Hansen, M.H. and Fischer-Hansen, T. 1994: Monumental Public Architecture in Archaic and Classical Greek *Poleis*. In Whitehead 1994a, 23-90.

Hansen, M.H. and Hornblower, S. (eds.) forthcoming: *An Inventory of the Ancient Greek Polis*, Oxford.

Hansen, M.H. and Raaflaub, K. (eds.). 1996: *More Studies in the Ancient Greek Polis*, Stuttgart.

Head, B.V. 1911: *Historia numorum: a Manual of Greek Numismatics*[2], Oxford.

Hereward, D. 1958: Inscriptions from Pamphylia and Isauria. *JHS* 78, 57-77.

Hill, G.F. 1897: *Catalogue of the Greek Coins of Lycia, Pamphylia and Pisidia*, London.

Hornblower, S. 1982: *Mausolus*, Oxford.

Keen, A.G. 1996: Alexander's Invasion of Lycia: Its Route and Purpose. *AHB* 10, 110-118.

Keen, A.G. 1998: *Dynastic Lycia: A Political History of the Lycians and Their Relations with Foreign Powers, c. 545–362 B.C.*, Leiden.

Keen, A.G. forthcoming a: An Inventory of Lykian *Poleis* in the Archaic and Classical Periods. In Hansen and Hornblower forthcoming.

Keen, A.G. forthcoming b: An Inventory of *Poleis* on the South Coast of Asia Minor (Pamphylia, Kilikia) in the Archaic and Classical Periods. In Hansen and Hornblower forthcoming.

Keen, A.G. forthcoming c: The 'Kings' of Lycia in the Achaemenid Period. In Brock, R. and Hodkinson, S.J. (eds.), *Alternatives to the Democratic Polis*, Oxford [2000, pp. 269-279].

Kolb, F. (ed.). 1995: *Lykische Studien II: Forschungen auf dem Gebeit der Polis Kyaneai in Zentrallykien. Bericht über die Kampagne 1991*, Bonn.

Kolb, F. and Kupke, B. 1992: *Lykien: Geschichte Lykiens im Altertum*, Mainz.

Larsen, J.A.O. 1945: Representation and Democracy in Hellenistic Federalism. *CPh* 40, 65-97.

Maier, F.G. 1959: *Griechische Mauerbauinschriften* I, Heidelberg.

Melchert, H.C. 1993: *Lycian Lexicon*², Chapel Hill.

Merkelbach, R. and Şahin, S. 1988: Inschriften von Perge. *EA* 11, 97-170.

Metzger, H. 1963: *Fouilles de Xanthos II: L'acropole lycienne*, Paris.

Metzger, H. 1972: *Fouilles de Xanthos IV: les céramiques archaïques et classiques de l'acropole lycienne*, Paris.

Miller, S.G. 1978: *The Prytaneion*, Berkeley.

Neumann, G. 1979: *Neufunde lykischer Inschriften seit 1901*, Vienna.

Neumann, G. 1990: Die lykische Sprache. In *Götter, Heroen, Herrscher in Lykien*, Vienna, 38-40.

Nollé, J. 1988. In Franke, P.R., Leschorn, W., Müller, B. and Nollé J. (eds.), *Side*, Saarbrücken, 45-67.

Olshausen, E. 1972: Pamphylia. In *Der Kleine Pauly*, Munich, 441-4.

Rhodes, P.J., with Lewis, D.M. 1997: *The Decrees of the Greek States*, Oxford.

Robert, L. 1966: *Documents de l'Asie Mineure méridionale: inscriptions, monnaies et géographie*, Geneva.

Ruge, W. 1939: Olympos (21). *RE* XVIII, 315-321.

Schuller, W. 1995: Poleis im Ersten Attischen Seebund. In Hansen, M.H. (ed.), *Sources for the Ancient Greek City-State*, Copenhagen, 165-170.

Schweyer, A.-V. 1993: Essai de définition des χῶραι de Telmessos et de Myra. In Borchhardt and Dobesch 1993, II, 39-45.

Schweyer, A.-V. 1996: Le pays lycien. Une étude de géographie historique aux époques classique et hellénistique. *RA*, 3-68.

Seyer, M. 1991–1992: Die Wohnsiedlung auf den Hangterrassen in Limyra. *ÖJh* 61 Beiblatt, 141-5.

Seyer, M. 1993: Zur Grabung in den Hanghäusern von Limyra. In Borchhardt and Dobesch 1993, II, 171-181.

Shipley, G. 1997: "The Other Lakedaimonians": The Dependent Perioikic *Poleis* of Laconia and Messenia. In Hansen 1997a, 189-281.

Snyder, J.W. 1966: *Alexander the Great*, New York.

Triedler, H. 1969: Mallos. In *Der Kleine Pauly* 3, 935-936.

Whitehead, D. (ed.). 1994a: *From Political Architecture to Stephanus Byzantius: Sources for the Ancient Greek Polis*, Stuttgart.

Whitehead, D. 1994b: Site-Classification and Reliability in Stephanus of Byzantium. In Whitehead 1994a, 99-124.

Wörrle, M. 1978: Epigraphische Forschungen zur Geschichte Lykiens II - Ptolemaios II und Telmessos. *Chiron* 8, 201-246.

Wörrle, M. 1991: Epigraphische Forschungen zur Geschichte Lykiens IV: drei griechische Inschriften aus Limyra. *Chiron* 21, 201-239.

Zimmermann, M. 1992a: *Untersuchungen zur Historischen Landeskunde Zentrallykiens*, Bonn.

Zimmermann, M. 1992b: Die lykischen Häfen und die Handelswege im östlichen Mittelmeer: Bemerkungen zu *P Mich* 1 10. *ZPE* 92, 201-217.

Herodotus on the Black Sea Coastline and Greek Settlements: Some modern misconceptions

John Hind

Herodotus has been charged with exaggeration, errors, lies and even malicious fabrications, at various times since Plutarch's attempted demolition of his reputation in the *De Malignitate Herodoti*. More moderately he is often faulted for retelling tales without checking them, giving versions which he expressly does not believe, reproducing numbers that are impossible. He has also been accused of misrepresenting his own status as eyewitness, traveller and personal collector of information (Fehling 1971; 1989). In particular it has been doubted that he set foot at all on Black Sea shores, though this hyper-scepticism has not found much acceptance (Armayor 1978, 45-62; Pritchett 1993). Like all humankind, Herodotus must be admitted to be fallible, especially about enemy numbers. In his calculation of distances from days-journey, and in descriptions of far-distant peoples. However some of our difficulties appear to lie in modern misunderstanding of what he says. There are, I believe, several passages which, when closely studied, may yield a more intelligible picture of Herodotus' view of the Black Sea region than we have at present, and may add something about the Greek settlements there. This last question has been made more difficult by the fact that Herodotus thought it of greater interest to describe the exotic native and nomadic peoples than the Greek cities of the coast, which are commonly referred to, but without full description. So what is mentioned in connection with the geographical section of his work (continents, long-range land-journeys and voyages) and, conversely, what is not mentioned. In view of his normal practice, may both have some significance.

The General Shape of the Pontus/Black Sea

> No sea can equal the Black Sea; it is 1380 miles long and 410 miles wide at its widest part...... The foregoing measurements were calculated in the following way; in summer in daytime a ship can cover a distance of approximately 70,000 fathoms and at night 60,000. A voyage from the entrance to the Black Sea as far as Phasis, which is its greatest length, takes nine days and eight nights. This makes a distance of 1,110,000 fathoms, or 11,100 stades (or 1380 miles). Across the broadest part, from Sindica to Themiskyra on the Thermodon, it is a voyage of three days and two nights, equivalent to 330,000 fathoms or 3,300 stades (or about 410 miles). I should add that the Pontus is connected with a lake, Maeotis, which is not much less in size than itself.
>
> (Hdt. 4.85-86)

It is accepted that Herodotus' dimensions for the Black Sea (given of course by him in stades, not miles) are greatly exaggerated, and that the size of the Sea of Azov is even more so (Arnaud 1992, 57-59). All editions and commentaries on Herodotus Book 4 have recognized this, though there seems no reason to conclude with Armayor, that such roughness of calculation (from day- and night-voyages) makes it difficult to accept that Herodotus had actually had experience of sailing in the Black Sea. He may well have been to Borysthenes and even to the R. Phasis, but have depended for his fuller concept of the size and shape of the Black Sea on Hecataios, or on *emporoi-traders* within the area. For our present purpose, however, it is not the dimensions of the Pontus, but the shape, which is of interest. In general terms this is thought of, and is presented on maps of the world according to Herodotus, as a long oval with very little, if any, narrowing at the mid-point. However, Herodotus does mention a 'broadest part' (Sindica-Themiskyra; Taman Peninsula to Bay of Bafra), which implies that he knew of narrower parts not mentioned. This narrow waist of the Pontus figures significantly in the works of later geographers (e.g. Strabo 2. 5. 23; 7.4. 3; 12. 2. 10), and is said to allow ships to follow the short crossing from Kriou Metòpon to Cape Karambis (Ai Todor in S. Crimea to Kerempe in N. Turkey). Herodotus makes no mention of this short crossing, but does describe a huge curve (to the south) of the Scythian coastline and a curve back again northwards once Taurica (mountainous Crimea) has been passed, going from West to East.

> Thrace juts out into the sea in front of Scythian territory. A bend is formed by the coast, and Scythia takes over from Thrace, and the Ister flows into the sea with its mouth turned towards the East. I shall now give you some indication of the extent of the Scythian coastline, starting from the Ister. From there stretches what is known as 'Ancient Scythia', lying facing the sea towards the south and south-west as far as the city called Kerkinitis. After that, still bearing out towards the same sea, the land is mountainous and thrusts forward into the Pontus. The tribe of the Tauroi lives here as far as what is called the 'Rugged Chersonesus'. This reaches out into the sea, which is over toward the South-East. For Scythia has two of its sides bounded by seas, one towards its South and one towards the East just as is the case with Attica. The Tauroi live there by that part of Scythia in a similar way, as though some other people and not Athenians lived in the corner

of the land at Sounion, Taurica reaching out into the sea further than the stretch from Thoricos to the deme of Anaphlystos. This is the outline of Taurica, though I describe it as one comparing small with great.' (He then makes a similar comparison of the heel of Italy from Brundisium to Tarentum with Taurica). 'But after Taurica the Scythians live beyond the Tauroi, and range the land along the eastern sea, and that to the West of the Cimmerian Bosporus and the Lake Maeotis as far as the R. Tanais, which flows out into the far corner of this lake.

(Hdt. 4. 99-100)

It is clear from this description that, although Herodotus does not present the explicit picture of a 'Scythian bow-shape' for the Pontus, as do later writers such as Strabo, Mela, Pliny and Ammianus Marcellinus (Hind 2001), he does know of the great curve of the shore between Danube and the northern part of the Crimea, and of the promontory - like nature of the mountainous land of the Tauroi. He also describes the forward-thrusting lie of this part of Scythia, which on one side faces south and south-west (steppeland Ukraine and Crimea as far as Kerkinitis) and on the other faces the eastern sea (steppeland Crimea from Theodosia to the Bosporus). This makes sense, when the huge area of this seaward side of Scythia is compared with the whole of Attica (relatively small though it is), and mountainous Taurica is compared with the Sunium promontory. Thus Scythia is conceived as having one of its sides (the southern) along the Pontus and Taurica, and one (the eastern) partly along the shores of the Pontus. The 'Rugged Chersonesus', which forms the tip of the mountainous Tauric land, and juts out towards the East (from the point of view of someone from Borysthenes) into the sea, must be the southernmost outreach of the Crimean Mountains (and not the Kerch Peninsula, which was never thought of as a peninsula in ancient times). They alone are 'rugged enough' to merit the term (*Trēkheé*) and jut out far into the sea (Hind 2001, 25-32). Once this is realised, one can see that Herodotus did have some notion of the Pontus being narrower at this point by virtue of the huge thrust of the Scythian and Tauric lands southwards into the sea. He also refers to two sections of the Pontus, that to the South and that to the East, separated by the salient of Scythian land and the mountainous seaboard of Taurica. This sounds like a less specific suggestion of the central waist of the Pontus caused by the Crimea, which is described so well by Strabo, likening the effect to be one almost of two seas (2. 5. 23; 7. 4. 3; 12. 2. 10). But Herodotus was here concerned only with delimiting Scythia on its two coastal sides, and not with describing the shape of the Pontus, as a whole, if indeed he knew it. Strabo, who does describe the whole Pontus - configuration, makes it clear that the rugged, mountainous seaboard is Taurica, and the promontory 'stretching far out to the south' is Kriou Metòpon on the southern tip of Crimea (7. 4. 3).

Square Scythia and the Greek Settlements on its Southern Side

On the landward side Scythia is bounded, starting from the Ister, by the following tribes, first the Agathyrsoi, then the Neuroi, the Androphagoi and last the Melankhlainoi. In shape it is a square, of which two sides are along the sea and two reach inland. From the Ister to the Borysthenes it is a journey of ten days, and from the Borysthenes to Lake Maeotis is another ten. From the sea inland to the Melankhlainoi beyond the Scythians is a journey of twenty days. (There follows a calculation of a day's travel as 200 stades, and the sides of Scythia as 4,000 stades each).

(Hdt. 4. 100-101).

Much has been written of this square 'Scythia of Herodotus', particularly concerning the 'Scythian' peoples located within the square, and the 'non-Scythian' peoples around it to the North-West, North, and North-East (Rybakov 1979; Yailenko 1983, 54-65). Here we shall consider only the two sides along the sea (Pontus) and Lake Maeotis (Sea of Azov). In the passage quoted earlier Herodotus distinguishes clearly, as we have seen, between the Pontus (*thalassa*), Bosporus Cimmerius (Straits of Kerch) and Lake Maeotis (*limnè* Sea of Azov). In this continuation he appears at first to make the whole coastal stretch go 'along the sea' (*para tèn thalassan*), then to make the southern side reach as far as Lake Maeotis, and the eastern side reach inland (that is up the western side of Lake Maeotis) from the sea (Pontus). Without actually saying it Herodotus has pinpointed the south-eastern corner of 'Square Scythia' as in the region of the Cimmerian Bosporus, here approaching it from the present-day eastern Crimea (Kerch Peninsula).

The southern side of Square Scythia is elsewhere punctuated by major and lesser rivers, Ister (Danube), Tyras (Dniester), Hypanis and Borysthenes (combined estuary of Bug and Dnieper), Panticapes, Hypaciris, Gerrhos (as yet not located satisfactorily), and the Cimmerian Bosporus (Straits of Kerch). Each river had a Greek/Milesian colony at or near its mouth, Istria (Hdt. 2. 83), Tyras (4. 51), Olbia/Borysthenes (4. 17, 18, 78), Kerkinitis (not far from the mouth of the R. Hypaciris/Gerrhos, 4. 55). Kerkinitis also is said to be on the coast of Scythia, near the beginning of the mountainous region of Taurica (4. 99). Only the easternmost corner of this side (Cimmerian Bosporus region) is left without a stated Greek settlement near or at its mouth. But, if this coincides with the western side of the Cimmerian Bosporus, we may well identify his Kremnoi (4. 20; 110) with the well-known city and *emporion* at Panticapaeum (Strabo 7. 44-5). Although Herodotus puts Kremnoi 'on the Lake Maeotis', one may note that the Cimmerian Bosporus is itself commonly called 'the mouth of Lake

Maeotis' (Strabo 7. 4. 5), and that Herodotus places Kremnoi somewhere in the region of the ditch of the blind slaves (Hdt. 4. 3; 20), which in turn enclosed the western side of the Cimmerian Bosporus (Hdt. 4.28). This ditch is thought to be the Uzunlyarsk Dyke, which cuts off an eastern portion of what is now the Kerch Peninsula. Kremnoi might then be seen as the earlier name of Panticapaeum, serving as the capital of the Archaianactid rulers of Bosporus, and ruling some Scythians within the dyke (Hind 1994, 477-479; 1997, 111-116). It would also serve as the *emporion* for the Royal Scythians, whose 'Square' Territory came down in its south-eastern corner as far to the East as the ditch which the sons of the blind slaves had dug (Hdt. 4. 20).

Herodotus gives some other information about Kremnoi, though in a mythological context (4. 110). He has a party of Amazons cross the Pontus from northern Asia Minor and land directly at Kremnoi, there to become mothers of the Sarmatian people by the Scythians. This crossing is accomplished without mention of passing the Cimmerian Bosporus, which would be odd if Kremnoi were up in the Lake Maeotis proper, but understandable if it were 'at the mouth of Maeotis'. Although Kremnoi is here made the location of a legendary tale, it was also a firmly historical port-of-trade in the 5th century, as was Panticapaeum throughout this time (though perhaps under an earlier name before the 430s BC). Furthermore, Panticapaeum favoured the use of so-called Kerch vases, on which Amazons and horses are frequent decoration, perhaps a visual reference to their local legend.

To summarise, it seems that Herodotus conceived of the southern (Pontus) side of his square Scythia as twenty days in length, with ten from the Ister to the Borysthenes (the half-way point. 4. 17) and ten on to the Lake Maeotis / Pontus corner, which was bounded by 'the ditch of the sons of the blind' and by the Cimmerian Bosporus. Along this side lay Istria (though he does not mention it here), Tyras, Borysthenes/Olbia, Kerkinitis, and at the corner (i.e. on the Kerch Straits) stood Panticapaeum (probably Kremnoi). Out into the Pontus reaches steppeland Crimea, encompassing the Tarkhankut Peninsula to the West, the North Crimea and the Kerch Peninsula to the East, as well as the mountainous southern part of Crimea that was Taurica. Herodotus advisedly spoke of Scythia facing a sea to the South and, beyond Taurica, to the East, which he seems sometimes to have called a sea (*thalassa*), and sometimes to have separated into three elements - sea, straits and the Maeotis lake.

The Sixth River of Scythia and Kerkinitis

> Most of the great rivers of Herodotus' Scythia are easily identifiable. Ister (4. 47-50) is the Danube, Tyras (4. 51) the Dniester. Hypanis (4. 52) is the Bug, which has a joint estuary with the Borysthenes (Dnieper. 4. 53). Hyrgis or Syrgis (4. 57; 123) is probably the Donets, and Tanais (4.20-1; 57; 100; 116) is certainly the Don. Three rather lesser rivers are the subject of dispute, though they are said to be navigable up from the sea (4. 47), which ought to give some clues. The Pantikapes (4. 18; 54) has been thought to be either a tributary of the Dnieper, or the Kalanchak, or the Konka which forms at times a kind of alternative stream of the Dnieper (Rybakov 1979; Yailenko 1983). The Gerrhos (4. 19; 56) is supposed to be the Molochnaya, flowing from near the bend of the Dnieper (Gerrhos region) into the Sea of Azov. The third river, which defies identification, is the Hypaciris, which 'flows into the sea not far from Kerkinitis'.

> The Hypaciris, the sixth river, flows from a lake right through the territory of the Scythian nomads, and reaches the sea near Kerkinitis, leaving Hylaia and the place called Achilles' Racecourse on the right.
>
> (Hdt. 4. 55)

All the rivers of Scythia, except the first, the Ister, are said to take a southerly course into the Pontus (Tyras, Borysthenes, Panticapes), or it is implied that they flow in that direction; the Hypanis at one point flows close to the Tyras; the Gerrhos splits off from the Borysthenes and flows down to the sea; the Tanais flows into the Lake Maeotis from far up country (Fig. 1). The Hyrgis or Syrgis is not given a direction of flow, and the Donets in fact enters the Don from the West. This leaves the Hypaciris, which Herodotus likewise does not say flowed from the North, though he does say that it flowed through the territory of the Scythian Nomads; what is more, although at 4. 18-19, the Panticapes and Gerrhos are crossed in a land-journey through Scythia, the Hypaciris is not mentioned. This observation allows us to look for the outlet of the R. Hypaciris on the coast of Western Crimea near the city of Kerkinitis (Eupatoria) and to seek its full course within the Crimea, a river in fact, which does not flow from the North. Herodotus' Hypaciris may well be a combination of Sasyk liman (an inlet running from the coast into the W. Crimea), plus an overland route to the R. Salgyr, which then flows into the western marshy area of the lake Maeotis (See the Rivers Bukes, Gerrhos (and Pacyris?) flowing from different regions, Pliny *NH* 2. 84), which would allow a further waterway link with Gerrhos, since the Molochnaya flows into the same area of the Lake. At the very least, this observation, that Herodotus does not mention the direction of flow of the Hypaciris, opens up new possibilities in identifying this part of Herodotus' geography, that it was one river or a waterway combining two rivers in steppeland Crimea. Interestingly Pomponius Mela (2. 4) also

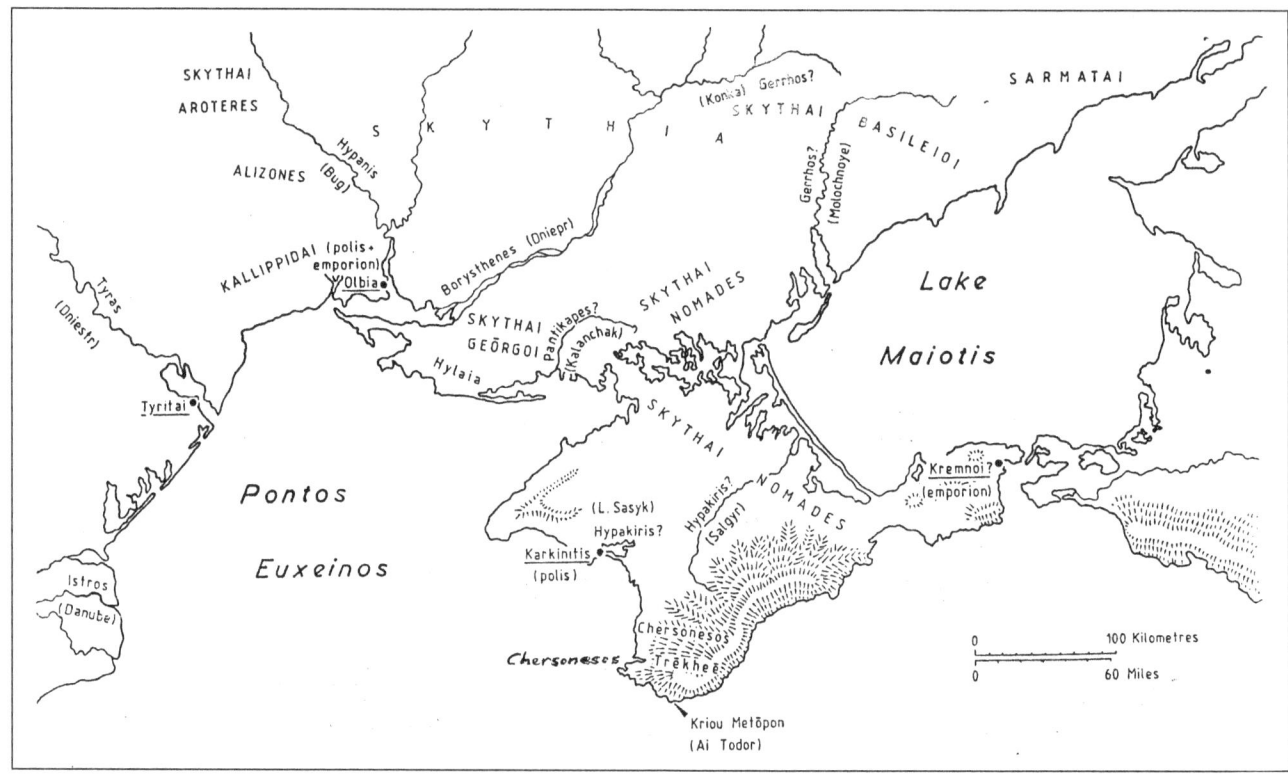

Figure 1.

says that two rivers flowed from 'different headwaters and from different directions'.

Tyras and the Tyritai

> The River Tyras runs southward from its source in a large lake, which forms the boundary between Scythia and the country of the Neuroi. At its mouth live Greeks called Tyritai.
>
> (Hdt. 4. 51).

This brief reference is rarely commented on, and, where it is, it is usually just to say that the site of Tyras was on the south side of the liman, under, and on the river side of, Akkerman/Moncastro castle, at the modern site of Belgorod Dnestrovsk. But it is clear that the plural Tyritai, though vague, is appropriate, since at the time of Herodotus two colonies seem to have existed, Ophiussa (probably Belgorod), and Nikonion on the opposite side of the liman at Roxolanskoe. There were also a large number of small settlements on both sides of the estuary, and these may well have belonged to fishing folk who supplied the *emporoi* mentioned by Ps.-Skymnos (776-800). Some time in the later 4th century BC Tyras was concentrated as one city, when refugees abandoned Nikonion (Karyshkovski and Kleiman 1985, 41. fig. 11; Okhotnikov 1983, 101-2; Sekerskaya and Okhotnikov in Mjelcarek *et al.* 1997, 13-17).

The Colchoi and the R. Phasis

Herodotus mentions the Colchoi and the Phasis (R. Rioni in W. Georgia) surprisingly frequently - Colchoi some twelve times and the R. Phasis seven times. In six separate contexts, but he never even hints at the existence of a Greek city (*polis* or *apoikia*) at the mouth of the river (Fig. 2).

> (a) The Greeks again were responsible for the next outrage. They sailed in an armed merchantman to Aia in Colchis on the R. Phasis, and not content with the regular business that had brought them there, they abducted the king's daughter Medea.
>
> (Hdt. 1.3).

This opening mention of the R. Phasis and Aeetes' legendary city of Aia clearly left no room for mention of a Greek city in connection with the Argonauts, but an aside concerning a subsequent foundation would have been characteristic of Herodotus (see his location of Sinope, where the Cimmerians had once settled (4. 12)). It is also interesting that Herodotus thinks of the Argonauts as going to Colchis for business (*prèxis*), i.e. to get the Golden Fleece, the original intention being to trade for it.

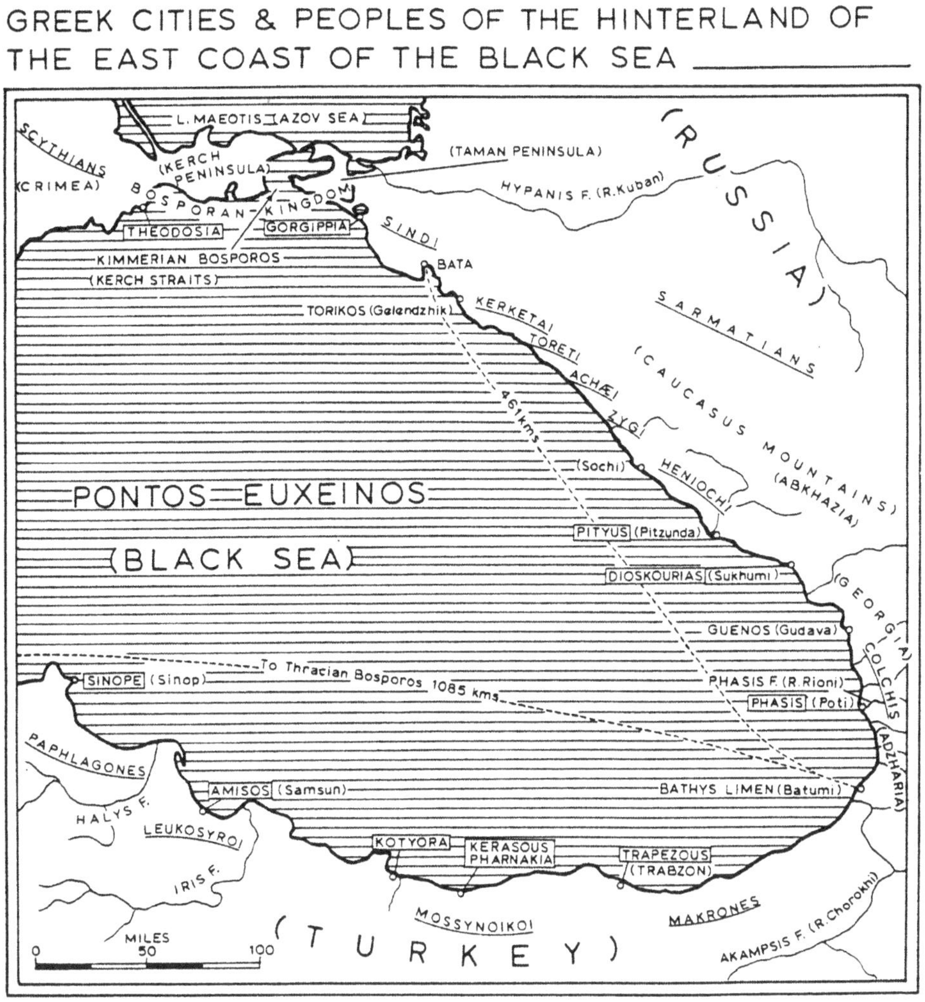

Figure 2.

(b) From the Sea of Azov to the Phasis and the Kolkhians is a thirty day's journey for a quick traveller; but it is not far from Colchis to Media.
(Hdt. 1. 104).

Here the context is the Cimmerian and Scythian invasions of Asia, and the Colchoi are considered a significant region and demarcation line on the way. But no Greek city of the future is mentioned.

(c) Sesostris defeated the Scythians and Thracians; on his way back he came to the R. Phasis, and it is quite possible that he detached a body of his troops and left them behind to settle.... it is undoubtedly a fact that the Colchoi are of Egyptian descent. [There are then several further mentions of Colchoi.]
(Hdt. 2. 103-104)

Again in this third passage Herodotus might have said that he had observed the 'Egyptian' characteristics, while staying in a Greek colony at Phasis (*cf.* Borysthenes 4. 76-78), but he makes no such comment. It has been suggested that he may have made his ethnic observations about the Colchoi at some location outside the Black Sea altogether. It is certain that he displays no knowledge of a Greek colony there in his own time.

(d) and (e) At Book 3. 97 the Colchoi are mentioned, but not the R. Phasis; they are placed outside the satrapal system of the Persian Empire, but are said to give annual gifts (tribute) to the Persians. Again at Bk 7. 79 the Colchoi appear as a contingent of Xerxes' army, bearing their own national arms, but there is no mention of the river, still less of Greeks living there.

(f) Persian territory extends southward to the Red Sea, as it is called; north of them are the Medes, then the Saspires, then the Colchoi, who go as far as the northern sea, where the mouth of Phasis is. Two great continental promontories run out from there; one of which stretches from the Phasis in the north along the Black Sea and the Hellespont to the Mediterranean at Sigeion on the Troad.

(Hdt. 4. 37-38).

This is a very large-scale geographical description of the Near East, but all that need be commented on here is that the 'northern sea' is the Black Sea, and that the R. Phasis is mentioned twice, as being in the land of the Colchoi, but there is no word of any Greek city there, though Sigeion is mentioned at the nearer end of 'this great promontory of land.'

(g) Again at 4.40 the Colchoi are mentioned as one of four tribes between the Red Sea and the Black Sea, but this is done in order to orientate the reader with peoples even further east, and to introduce the Caspian Sea and R. Araxes. There is no mention of Phasis, river or city.

(h) Another thing that puzzles me is why three distinct women's names should have been given to what is really a single land-mass; and why too the Nile and the Phasis - or, according to some, the Maiotic Tanais and the Cimmerian Bosporus - should have been fixed upon for the boundaries.

(Hdt. 4. 45)

Here once more Herodotus is indulging in macro-geography - the continental names he means are Asia, Europe, and Libya. The two rivers, Nile and Phasis are referred to, without in either case a city being mentioned; but the Nile has previously appeared, with Greek Naukratis and Egyptian Memphis brought to our attention. Phasis is here again a river (to Herodotus) with no hint of a Greek colony.

(i) To sail from the entrance to the Black Sea to Phasis is a voyage of nine days and eight nights ... (see p. 41, col. 1).

(Hdt. 4. 85).

This voyage is fixed at the western end by referring to the Thracian Bosporus and to the Greek cities, one on either side, Calchedon and Byzantion, but again there is no hint of a Greek city or colony at Phasis. In six passages (far more references than to other comparable rivers or geographical locations) Herodotus has contrived to mention the R. Phasis, but to say nothing of a Greek city there, and to refer to Colchoi on several other occasions, again without a hint of Greeks in their midst.

Now these omissions might be due to pure chance or to ignorance. However, it would be flatly against his normal practice, where he routinely mentions it, if a Greek city lay at or near the mouth of a major river or waterway. These are Istria on the Ister (2. 33); Sinope (with Pteria some way inland and the R. Halys to the West, 1. 75-6); Borysthenes/Olbia (4. 17, 18, 53, 78); Kerkinitis, near the R. Hypaciris and Gerrhos' joint mouth, 4. 85, 99); Themiskyra on R. Thermodon (a barbarian town at S. end of the longest crossing of the Pontus, 4. 86); Heraioupolis and Apollonia, at either end of an overland route from Propontis to the Pontus (4. 90; 93); Calchedon and Byzantion by the Thracian Bosporus (4. 86); Ainos at the mouth of the R. Hebros (4.90); Naukratis, 'city' and emporion on the W. branch of the Nile delta (2. 97; 178-179); Pyrene, a town, thought by Herodotus to be up in the headwaters of the Danube (2. 38); Babylon, divided in two by the R. Euphrates (1. 178); Nineveh and Opis on the R. Tigris (1. 189, 193); Kaspatyros on the upper reaches of the R. Indus (4. 44); Tartessos, a trading area and kingdom of S. Spain, just beyond the Pillars of Hercules (4. 152). In a remaining notable case, the Tanais (Don) (4. 45, 57, 100), Herodotus mentions no town in this corner of the nomad world, and archaeology seems to show that at the mouth of the Don there was no Greek-style town till the early 3rd century BC (Marchenko 1986, 377-98; Böttger 1996, 41-50).

It is clear that, wherever possible, Herodotus chose to mention it, if a Greek city lay on a major river, when it came up for notice in his geographical sections even on only one or two occasions. In the case of Phasis he mentions only a legendary Colchian town in connection with the Argonauts (1. 3). Yet there were six occasions, when he might have mentioned a Greek city there, had he known of one. The presumption is fairly strong that none existed at the time. And if this seems too vigorous a use of the *argumentum e silentio*, then we may produce the more positive statement of Xenophon about 40 years later (*ca.* 400 BC), that he had had it in mind to lead a colony of his soldiers, about 8,600 men, to the land of the Phasians, where a native Colchian king and descendant Aietes ruled (*Anab.* 5. 6. 36-37). As Xenophon spent some time in the Sinopian colonies of Trapezous, Kerasous and Kotyora, and detained ships both going eastward and coming from the East, he must have been well aware of the potential for settlement in the Phasian *chora* (coastal Colchian territory), and have known that no Greek colony as yet existed there (Hind 1996a; 1996b; *cf.* Braund 1994; Ehrhardt 1984; Tsetskhladze 1992; 1994a; 1994b; 1996; 1997).

Most scholars have been reticent about Herodotus' silence concerning any Greek city at Phasis. My contention is that this is in itself a misconception, and that we can use the silence, along with other evidence, to create a strong case that no Greek city existed at Phasis until the 4th century BC, when Milesians and Sinopians may have collaborated in a belated joint venture.

I am grateful to John Graham for various comments on this paper made while in press (Pers. comm. 22.5.1995).

Bibliography

Armayor, O.K. 1978: Did Herodotus ever go to the Black Sea? *HSCP* 82, 45-62.

Arnaud, P.1992: Les relations maritimes dans le Pont-Euxin d'après les données des geographes anciens. *REA* 94, 1/2, 57-97.

Böttger, B.1994: Joint excavation in Tanais, *New Studies on the Black Sea Littoral.* In Tsetskhladze, G.R. (ed.), Oxford, 41-50.

Braund, D. 1994: *Georgia in Antiquity - A History of Colchis and Transcaucasian Iberia 550 B.C. - A.D. 562,* Oxford.

Ehrhardt, N. 1984: Zur Gründung und zum Charakter der Ostpontischen Griechensiedlungen. *ZPE* 56, 153-158.

Fehling, D. 1971: *Die Quellenangaben bei Herodotus*, Berlin.

Fehling, D. 1989: *Herodotus and his Sources: Citation. Invention and Narrative Art*, Leeds.

Hind, J.G.F. 1988: Herodotus' geography of Scythia: the Rivers and the Rugged Peninsula. In Lordkipanidze, O.D. (ed.), *The Black Sea Littoral in the Seventh-Fifth Centuries B.C. - Literary Sources and Archaeology,* Tbilisi, 137-140.

Hind, J.G.F. 1994: The Bosporan Kingdom. *CAH* VI^2, 476-511.

Hind, J.G.F. 1996a: Traders and Ports-of-Trade (Emporoi and Emporia) in the Black Sea in Antiquity. *Il Mar Nero* 2, 113-26.

Hind, J.G.F. 1996b: The types on the earliest coins of the Phasians – Kolkhidki. In O.D. Lordkipanidzé and P. Leveque (eds.), *Sur Les Traces des Argonautes*, Besançon, 209-211.

Hind, J.G.F. 1997: Colonies and Ports of Trade on the Northern Shores of the Black Sea: Borysthenes, Kremnoi and the other Pontic *Emporia* in Herodotus. In T. Heine Nielsen (ed.), *Yet More Studies in the Ancient Greek Polis,* Stuttgart, 107-116.

Hind, J.G.F. 2001: A Sea 'like a Scythian bow' and Herodotus' 'Rugged Peninsula'. In Tsetskhladze G.R. (ed.), *North Pontic Archaeology. Recent Discoveries and Studies,* Leiden, 25-32.

Karyshkovski, P.O. and Kleiman, I.B. 1985: *Drevni Gorod Tyra,* Kiev.

Marchenko, K.K. 1986: Die Siedlung von Elizavetovka - ein griechisches barbarisches emporion im Don-delta. *Klio* 68, 377-398.

Mjelcarek, K., Okhotnikov, S.B. and Sekunda, N.V. (eds.) 1997: *Nikonion - An Ancient City of the Lower Dniester*, Torun.

Okhotnikov, S.B. 1983: An archaeological map of the Lower Dniester area in the Ancient period (6th/5th cent. B.C. - 3rd cent. A.D. *Materialy po Arkheologii Severnogo Prichernomorya* 9, 101-122 (in Russian).

Pritchett, W.K. 1993: *The Liar School of Herodotus*, Amsterdam.

Rybakov, B.A. 1979: *Gerodotova Skiphia: Istoriko - Geographicheski Analiz*, Moscow.

Tsetskhladze, G.R. 1992: Greek Colonisation of the Eastern Black Sea Littoral (Colchis). *DHA* 182. 224-258.

Tsetskhladze, G.R. 1994a: Colchians, Greeks and Achaemenids in the 7th-5th centuries B.C.: A Critical Look. *Klio* 76, 78-102.

Tsetskhladze, G.R. 1994b: Greek penetration of the Black Sea. In Tsetskhladze, G.R. and De Angelis, F. (eds.) *The Archaeology of Greek Colonisation. Essays dedicated to Sir John Boardman,* Oxford, 111-136.

Tsetskhladze, G.R. 1996: La colonizzazione greca nell' area del Ponto Eusino. Settis S. *et al.* (eds.), *I Greci - Storia, Cultura, Arte, Societa,* Giulio Einaudi, 945-973.

Tsetskhladze, G.R. 1997: Greek Penetration of the Eastern Black Sea littoral, Some Results of Study. *VDI* 2, 100-115 (in Russian).

Yailenko, V.P. 1983: Towards the question of the identification of the rivers and peoples of Herodotus' Scythia. *Sovyetskaya Ethnographya* 1, 54-65 (in Russian).

The Shape of the new Commonwealth
Aspects of the Pontic and Eastern Mediterranean Regions in the Hellenistic Age*

Zofia Halina Archibald

The Black Sea features prominently in any discussion of ancient Greek colonisation. Thereafter it tends to drop from view. General surveys of the Hellenistic period often ignore this area altogether, concentrating on the splendours of the royal courts of Egypt, Pergamon, Sicily or Macedon.

It is true, of course, that the northern shores of the Pontus were not conquered by the Macedonians and never part of any Macedonian kingdom. But its western and southern shores were. The tendency to exclude the Black Sea from Hellenistic surveys is sometimes attributed to a lack of basic information in accessible sources. There has been a change, partly as a result of better co-operation with scholars from Georgia, Bulgaria, Romania, Russia and Ukraine, particularly during the last two decades. The systematic documentation by multinational teams of scholars of particular classes of material, inscriptions and other documents, transport amphorae, pottery and the like, has also engendered a more inclusive approach, which has benefited considerably from enhanced co-operation amongst specialists. Bulletins such as *SEG (Supplementum Epigraphicum Graecum)*, *Bulletin Épigraphique*, published in *Revue des Études Grecques,* reports of numismatic finds in *Coin Hoards* and elsewhere regularly include data from the Black Sea and its environs. A great deal of this material, as well as much of what gets reported in the periodic bulletins on the Black Sea and neighbouring areas in *Archaeological Reports*, *AJA*, and special issues of other journals, dates from the Hellenistic Age. There is therefore a well established working assumption that such regions should command as much attention as those of the Mediterranean proper. But whereas the colonising period of the 7th to 5th centuries BC has been extensively reassessed in a wide range of recent publications, the 4th to 1st centuries BC have not received similar treatment.

Today we are in a better position than was possible, even a decade ago, to see how the Pontic region relates to other kingdoms and neighbouring areas of the pre-Roman Mediterranean. But much of the information we have is complex and difficult to interpret. How does the Pontic region compare with Seleucid Asia or mainland Greece, for example? How comparable was the development of cities? What was distinctive and unique about the Pontic 'Common Market'?[1] How far was this regional economy embedded in the habits and traditions of the Mediterranean? The new data currently at our disposal has not yet been used to answer such questions. Before we can respond, we need to have a clear concept of what the operating factors were in this time and place. Whether or not we view the 'Hellenistic world' as a coherent concept,[2] new perceptions of this period elsewhere in the Mediterranean can provide useful insights for the Black Sea communities and *vice versa*. I want to draw attention here to three interrelated themes:

1. The relationship between urban and rural space;
2. How far non-Greek institutions differed from Greek ones;
3. In the case of colonies, how should we characterize the relationship between indigenous people and newcomers?

Urban and rural space

Although some studies of ancient communities still dispense with them, maps usually form the starting point for any enquiry, particularly of such distant zones as the Black Sea. But the usual representation of historical communities as dots in a white void reinforces the static impression of isolated, nucleated oases. It has become difficult to conceptualize wider social relations because the colonial Greek network is so dominant in historical thinking. The context of colonial activity is rarely examined in an adequate manner and the time scale selected for such analysis is often limited. The gap is gradually being rectified as field studies have embraced wider areas, adopted better sampling strategies and absorbed information drawn from aerial photography. But

---

* This paper was completed in autumn 1997; it has not been feasible, in the time available, to bring the bibliography fully up to date. I have therefore included only a small number of key books and articles of specific relevance to the main arguments. Z.H.A., April 2001.

[1] This concept has been reinforced in a major review by Vinogradov 1987, 9-77 (*non vidi*); some idea of the author's approach can be gleaned from other publications (see esp. the author's own summary in his review of recent epigraphic work on the Black Sea in *REG* 103 (1990/92) 532); a very brief *résumé* is included in Vinogradov and Kryzickij 1995, 90-93.

[2] The most succinct analysis of the problem is provided by Davies 1984, esp. 263-4, 270-85, 298-315: "The Hellenistic World is normally taken to denote areas where the language of government and literature is Greek, where the personnel ...is largely Greek.. where there is interchange of Greek-style goods... This is too one-sided. What we are following is a process of colonial expansion and settlement, wherein Greek culture and institutions spread outwards" (*ibid.*, 263); Davies argues that the increasing intensity of economic activity in the Hellenistic Age "did go some way towards making one world out of what had been hitherto an assemblage of economic zones less intimately and more superficially connected." (*ibid.*, 284). Graham Shipley's struggle to cope with this period in terms of 'World Systems' theory shows the continuing difficulties of trying to explain complex interactions through prescriptive 'top-down' sociological models (Shipley 1993, 271-84). These ideas are discussed further below. (See now Davies 2000 for a more radical reassessment).

remote sensing and intensive survey techniques have yet to be adopted as standard. Traditional archaeological methods give optimum attention to stone and high quality ceramic material. They favour selective rather than quantitative approaches to the evidence. This makes it particularly hard to assess the behaviour of nomadic groups, whose movements and settlements require much more sensitive and advanced techniques of analysis.[3]

Survey archaeology in the eastern Mediterranean area has revealed a great deal about the non-nucleated outliers of known ancient communities, as well as the dynamic, fluctuating character of nucleated settlements.[4] The assumption that we need only concern ourselves with geographical foci, with the core of administrative centres, has been found wanting. But this has yet to translate itself into the way we conceive community behaviour. Historical discussions are concerned with communities as a whole; there is a tendency for these to become monolithic: we speak of the Athenians, the Panticapaeans and others, as though these labels truly represented the entire communities referred to. What we find on the ground are discrete units, farms, villages, towns, rural constructions - the homes of citizens and non-citizens alike. Intensive fieldwork has helped to reinforce our awareness of the close interaction between urban and rural activities. Ancient cities were embedded in a rural landscape. Nucleation was a consequence of rural patterns of land management. This must also have been true in the case of colonies, even though any official foundation had a notional starting point, at which a preliminary land division occurred, perhaps one of several. (Recent work at Chersonesus suggests that notional beginnings may not necessarily have been the most significant events in a site's spatial history: Carter et al. 2000, 709-14). S. Alcock's review of surface surveys conducted in Greece and the islands, Crete, Cyprus, Asia Minor, Syria, Palestine/Israel, Jordan, the Persian Gulf, Iraq, Iran and Afghanistan, has shown that there were wide variations in the pattern and scope of urban and rural development in Hellenistic times (Alcock 1994). It seems clear that a range of factors must be taken into account in assessing the general picture of social and economic evolution in a particular area. The tendency to view the Hellenistic Age according to a unitary chronological scheme based on international political events does not take into account such differences; nor does it correspond with developments in civic institutions.[5]

Future regional Hellenistic histories will have to be more sensitive to local indicators of change and continuity, whether or not political decisions may have altered or enhanced wider trends.

The Black Sea region represents not one, but a series of interconnected areas, whose geography, resources and history differed quite markedly. I will concentrate here on the western and northern shores and their neighbouring hinterlands. In some ways these are quite contrasting zones, not only in terms of resources but also in the character of Greek and native interaction. At the same time, there are important cultural and historical connections between the two regions which illuminate the period under consideration in significant ways. The western margins of the Pontus were populated by Thracian communities whose territorial (and perhaps biological) ancestors had been among the first cereal farmers and stock breeders in Europe. In the 1st millennium BC a pattern of extensive rural settlement developed - large and small villages, not only in lowland plains but also in upland valleys of the Rhodope mountains. Contacts with the Aegean, whether direct or indirect, via rivers - certainly along the Danube and Maritsa (ancient Hebros), perhaps also along other waterways - is reflected in occasional finds of imported ceramic and metal goods, and in the existence of related metallurgical traditions between the Pindus range and the Balkans.[6] During the 5th century BC, a dynasty drawn from the Odrysian 'tribe' acquired power over most of the east Balkan region between the Stara Planina (Balkan Mountain) in the north, the Aegean and Pontic coasts to south and east.[7] Urban centres began to emerge at about the same time in the central or Thracian Plain. The one we know most about is near Vetren, north-west of Pazardjik. Little is yet known about the character of such sites in the late 5th and early 4th centuries. At Vetren substantial and impressive fortifications were built, the beginnings of a paved street plan and the presence of significant quantities of coined money (Fig. 1).[8] Such developments reflect a

---

[3] An international study of nomads and farmers in the Murghab delta of Turkmenistan using intensive survey techniques, selective excavation and computerized mapping has yielded impressive results. I owe my information on this work to an unpublished lecture given by Prof. Maurizio Tosi (Dept. of Archaeology, University of Bologna), to the Theoretical Archaeology Group Conference 1996 in the University of Liverpool. The joint project between the Preserve of Tauric Chersonesus and the Institute of Classical Archaeology, University of Austin, Texas, outlines the potential of sophisticated inter-disciplinary studies (Carter et al. 2000).

[4] Relevant to this discussion are: Bintliff and Snodgrass 1985; Bintliff 1988; Alcock, Cherry and Davis 1994; Bintliff 1994; Cherry 1994.

[5] Alcock 1994, 174-87, esp. 179; Gauthier 1985, 5; note contrasting styles of analysis in Shipley 2000 (esp. 73-83, 120ff., 271-86) and Davies 2000, together with other contributors to Archibald et al. 2000.

[6] Gotsev 1997; bibliography to 1993 in Archibald 1998, chs. 1-3; Bonev and Alexandrov 1996, 33-7, figs. 63-66 (fragments of two (?) Chiot 7th century white slipped amphorae and a tripod; cf. Boardman 1967, 137 "..decoration Protogeometric in spirit but not in date", cf. Pl. 46, nos. 523, 534, 538. Boardman refers to complete examples of similar type from Berezan. Tsetskhladze (1998b, 13-14) has rightly emphasized the fact that Chian parallels date from the end of 7th – first half of 6th century, not 8th century BC, as Bonev and Alexandrov imply.

[7] Archibald 1998, ch.4.

[8] Yourukova and Domaradzki 1990; Domaradzki 1993; 1995; Domaradzki 1996; Bouzek, Domaradzki and Archibald 1996; Archibald (2000-2001); a number of studies in the Études section of BCH volume 123, is devoted to the Pistiros inscription, but not to the site itself at Vetren.

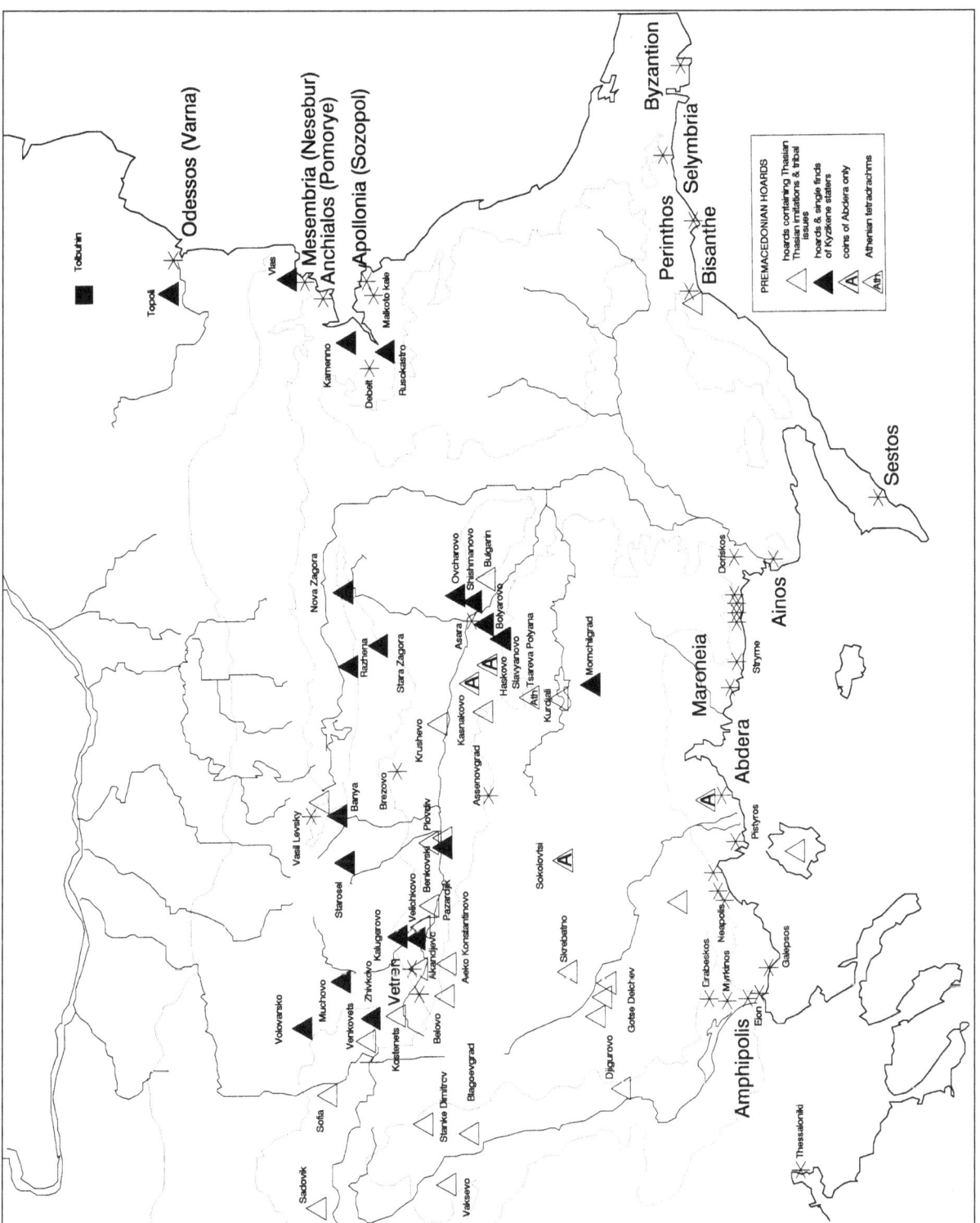

Figure 1a. The Odrysian kingdom of Thrace – the distribution of coin hoards in the 5th and first half of the 4th century BC coincides with the principal centres of power and known mound cemeteries of the princely elite within kingdom.

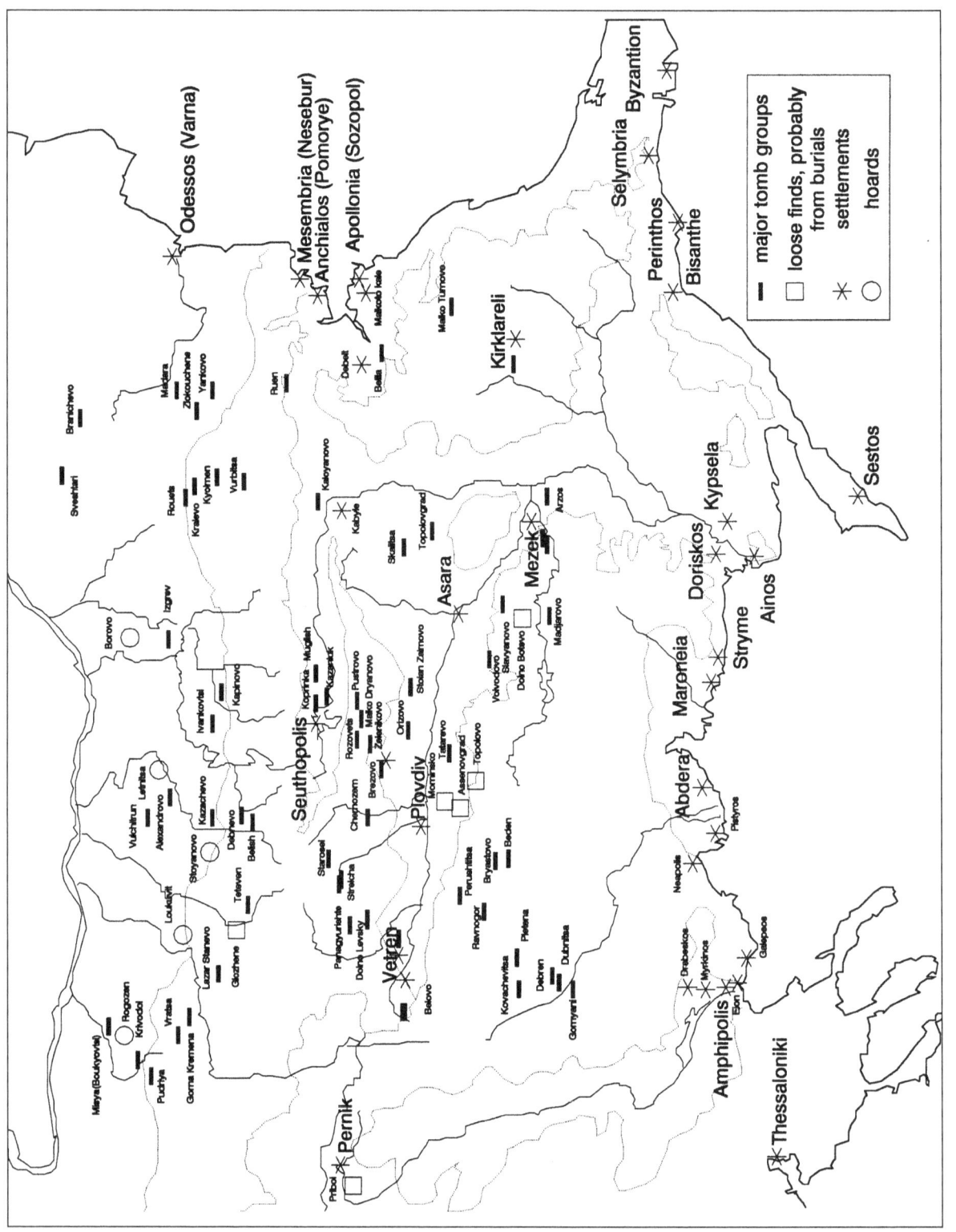

Figure 1b. The Odrysian kingdom of Thrace – from the second half of the 4th century BC onwards, the number and geographical spread of tribal centres, represented by known sites and mound cemeteries, increased.

conscious territorial strategy on the part of Odrysian rulers. The contents of princely burials, including elaborate and highly decorated gilded silver horse trappings, as well as the iconography of individual items, show that the Odrysians prided themselves on their cavalry skills and on their ample resources in livestock.[9] Close similarities between the form of Odrysian élite cavalry gear and those of their contemporary peers among the Royal Scythians have often been noted by archaeologists but rarely considered in the context of political élites in the *urbanized* areas of the Pontic region.[10] People of Thracian or related stock (the identification is archaeological, not ethnic), can be documented along the northern shores of the Pontus in the early centuries of the first millennium BC, together with a variety of identifiably different communities, particularly on the Asiatic side of the Bosporus.[11]

Current archaeological research on ancient Mediterranean economics has focused markedly on the farming of smallholdings; little account has been taken of how more extensive properties, involving larger-scale livestock rearing, might have been managed.[12] Historians and archaeologists have been concerned with the appropriation of landed property by known communities and with the definition of bounded farming plots. The development of more specialized stock breeding is far less easy to follow.

But groups associated with exceptional herds were also those with easy access to water meadows - the Thessalians in the Peneus and Titaresius valleys, the Macedonians along the marshy Loudias and Haliacmon estuaries, the Odrysians along the middle Hebros (Maritsa) banks, in modern times often used for rice and cotton cultivation. The importance of active flood plains in early farming communities has been given prominence in a new series of geomorphological studies.[13] This new emphasis on pastoral strategies at the heart of river valleys rather than on marginal land or hillsides is likely to provide a more fruitful approach to the study of urban development along these major waterways.

Pastoralism in the steppe regions adjoining the northern shores of the Black Sea is often seen as quite distinct from the settled, cereal-growing townships of the coast. What was a literary metaphor in Herodotus, contrasting the mobile (read: uncivilised) Scythians with autocratic Persians on the one hand or Greeks on the other, has too often been taken to represent a fundamental, unbridgeable, difference between Scythians and Greeks.[14] Palaeo-botanical evidence from Scythian steppe settlements such as Belsk on the Vorskla tributary of the Dnieper (occupied from the late 7th century BC onwards), and a host of lesser neighbouring sites, shows that as far as cereal growing is concerned, far from having adopted cereal cultivation late from the Greek colonists, the steppe Scythians planted a wide variety of cereal crops. Bread wheat and rye are already found in the steppe region in pre-Scythian times. The range of crops found on Scythian sites, whether in the steppe regions or in the Crimea (Ust-Alminsk, Verkhne-Sadove, Scythian Neapolis), does not differ substantially from that found in colonial Greek sites, although the proportion of individual crops varies. At Belsk the dominant forms were emmer, hulled and naked barley, spelt and club (durum) wheat, millet and various legumes. R. Sallares has argued that the dominant role of bread wheat varieties in Ukraine and the Crimea from *ca*. 600 BC onwards was the main reason why this region became a magnet for grain importers on behalf of Greek cities, notably Athens.[15] Animals reared by Greek colonists were of local breeds, predominantly sheep and goat, later increasingly more cattle at the expense of ovicaprids, and these were of the native hornless type.[16] Studies of viticulture in the Crimean peninsula have also revealed a

---

[9] Archibald 1998, chs. 8 and 10 with references; Archibald 2000.
[10] Mozolevskii 1973; 1979; Murzin 1979; Melyukova 1979, 196-225 (comparison of harness, weapons and armour); 235-44 (discusses historical and archaeological sources, mainly in the context of Atheas and his kingdom, examining the situation in the Dobrudja in the second half of the 4th century BC); Melyukova 1995 (on the basis of Alekseev's studies and other recent work revises the period of most intensive contact between the Royal Scythians and Getai as the second half of the 4th century BC, thereby dissociating these phenomena from the political history of Atheas' kingdom); Vasilev 1980; Kitov 1980; Fialko 1995; Alekseev 1987a; 1987b.
[11] Melyukova 1979 *passim*; Nikulitse 1987; Kubyshev, Polin and Chernyakov 1985 (with bibliography on 'Thraco-Cimmerian' and related finds in the southern Ukraine and Crimea); Kolotukhin 1985 (the 8th - 6th century BC origins of the Tauri); the second Tskhaltubo Conference was devoted to the subject of indigenous matters (Tskhaltubo 1979); see esp. the articles by K. Marchenko and L.V. Kopeikina on indigenous pottery fabrics; E.A. Rogov on the Crimean lowlands; A.A. Maslennikov on the steppe regions; Y.G. Vinogradov on non-Greek names in Olbian prosopography. Marchenko (1996) refers to new work on the indigenous populations on the Asiatic Bosporus, notably by A.M. Zhdanovskii, which are not currently accessible to me. Solovyov 1999, 93-7, 110, 112, on the relationship between communities of different ethnic complexion at Berezan, and more generally in the Lower Bug estuary. Several papers in volume 6 of *Colloquia Pontica* (*North Pontic Archaeology: Recent Discoveries and Studies*, ed. G.R. Tsetskhladze, Brill 2001) focus on this topic, notably those of V.P. Vanchugov, S.B. Okhotnikov, S.Y. Vnukov, G.M. Nikolaenko, A.A. Maslennikov, A.M. Butyagin and S.L. Solovyov, and V.D. Kuznetzov.
[12] For a conspectus of opinions on pastoral strategies, see Whittaker 1988, esp. J.F. Cherry, Pastoralism and the role of animals in the pre- and protohistoric economies of the Aegean, 6-34.

[13] Lewin, Macklin and Woodward 1995, esp. van Andel *et al.*, 131-43; Barker and Hunt, 145-57.
[14] For an extended exploration of the metaphor, see Hartog 1988; on nomads, see Taylor 1994, esp. 407-10, on ethnic definitions; Sulimirski and Taylor 1991, 547-90, esp. 'Prolegomena', 547-55. The lack of objective evidence behind the metaphor has been demonstrated by Shaw 1982-83.
[15] Kruglikova 1985; Yanushevich and Nikolaenko 1979; Yanushevich 1981; 1989; Shramko and Yanushevich 1985, with distribution map of samples, 58, fig. 8; Sallares 1991, 331-2.
[16] Tsalkin 1960; 1966.

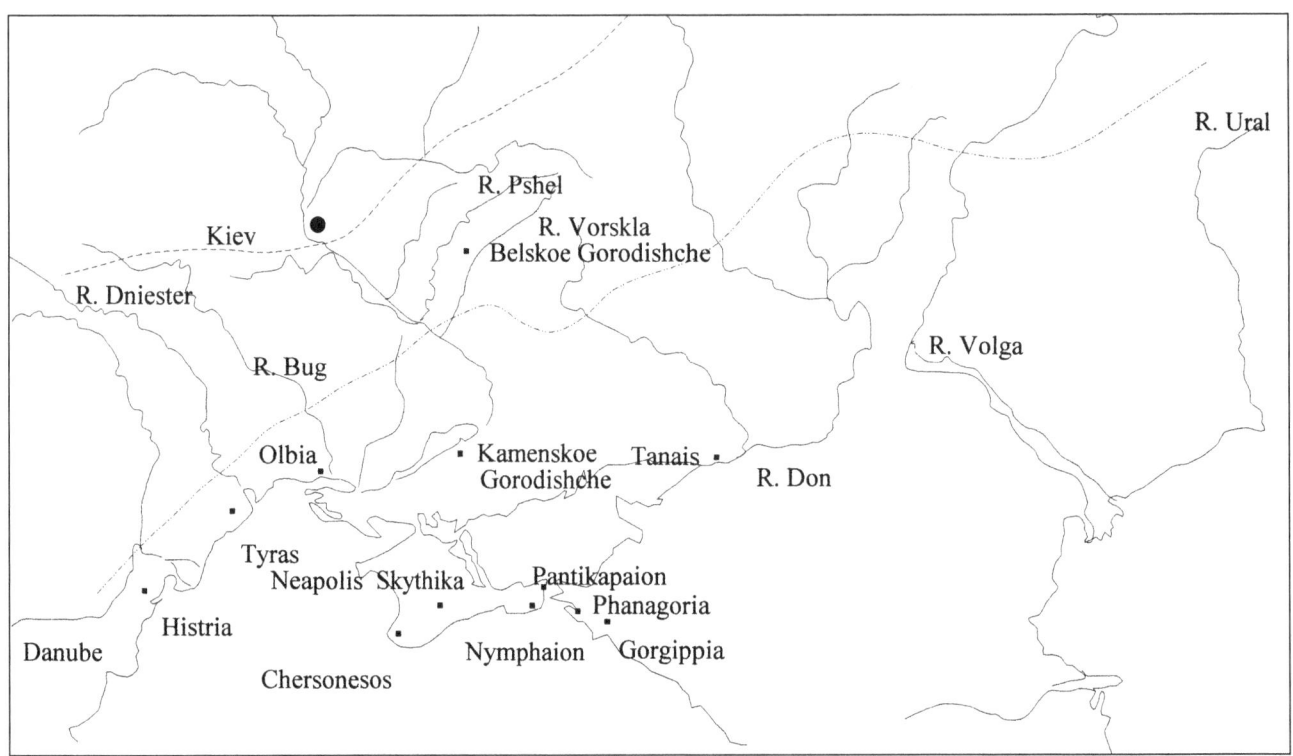

Figure 2. Territory of the Bosporan kingdom and neighbouring regions, with principal sites referred to in text; the dotted line below Kiev shows the transition from forest to forest steppe; the line above Olbia marks the transition from forest steppe to grass steppe.

most interesting symbiotic relationship between natives and Greeks. The cereal varieties grown by the local Tauric population continued and intensified after the colonising period. Vine stocks were selected from the best local varieties to produce cultivated specimens. The Tauri cultivated vines on their own estates. Grapes grown on these estates dating from the 2nd and 3rd centuries AD would have been of similar size to those of modern cultivated vines. The wide variety of cultivated forms documented from these sites has prompted the excavators to speculate that Caucasian or central Asian strains were added to the local stock.[17]

The relationship between city and country has been one of the principal underlying themes in the study of the north Pontic colonies (Fig. 2).[18] Olbia represents a community somewhat apart from the Crimean and Taman peninsula settlements which were gradually subsumed into the Spartocid kingdom of Bosporus or had a very close relationship with it. More research has been devoted to Olbia's rural territory than of any other Pontic city, with the possible exception of Chersonesus. The general outline seems clear; after the early, dramatic expansion into rural terrain during the 6th century BC, there was a marked decline in the 5th, followed by a revival towards the end of the same century. This reinvigoration of rural settlement continued into the 4th and 3rd centuries but diminished once more in the 2nd century BC.[19] Such an analysis, based on gross numbers of settlements, is open to various qualifications. Y. Vinogradov's theory, taken up by K. Marchenko, that the city's rural territory was 'captured' by the nomadic Scythians in the aftermath of Darius' unsuccessful invasion of Scythia, has been criticised and is now apparently rejected by both authors themselves. Changes in the pattern of rural land use are more likely to be the result of a variety of factors, internal as well as external. It is equally possible to argue that a contraction of territory was due to a regrouping or reorganisation of the terrain, with a greater concentration of the rural population in and around the city itself.[20]

---

[17] Z.A. Yanushevich, G. Nikolaenko, and N. Kuzmina, La viticulture à Chersonèse de Taurique aux ive - iie siècles av.n.è. d'après les recherches archéologiques et paléoethnobotaniques. *RA* 1985, 115-22; I.K. Whitbread, *Greek Transport Amphorae. A Petrological and Archaeological Study*, Athens 1995, 13-19 with further references.

[18] V.D. Blavatskii, *Zemlyedelye v Antichnikh Gosudarstvakh Severnogo Prichernomor'ya*, Moscow 1953; Kruglikova 1975.

[19] A.Wąsowicz, La campagne et les villes du littoral Septentrional du Pont-Euxin (Nouveaux témoignages archéologiques). *Dacia* n.s. 13 (1969) 73ff.; Wąsowicz 1975; Ruban 1985; S.D. Kryzhitskii *et al.* 1989, Ch. II, 96ff.; Vinogradov and Kryzickij 1995, 41-54, 72-3; pls. 18; 64.2. Solovyov 1999, 115 and n. 89, dates the critical transition at the end of the first third of 3rd century BC; this may indeed be true of Berezan, and of other sites in the environs of Olbia, but there is a danger of circularity in the assumption that decline occurred at all rural sites at the same time.

[20] Vinogradov 1983, 399-404; K.K. Marchenko in *Tskhaltubo 1977*, 130-8; see review by A. Wąsowicz, *DHA* 6 (1980) 7-20; *cf.* Marchenko, *VDI*

Arguments about land use are affected by assessments of grain production and grain exports to the Aegean, notably Athens, particularly in the 4th century BC. That bread wheat was produced is not in question (though in what quantities and where is hard to demonstrate). How much was exported from the northern shores of the Black Sea and on what time scale are issues of intense debate. Russian and Ukrainian scholars have used rather different arguments from those deployed by western ancient historians.[21] A. Shcheglov has argued that the bulk of cereal production was concentrated in the hinterland of the Greek colonies, to a lesser extent in the forest steppe, separated from the former by the grasslands, which were periodically dominated by nomad Scythian groups. He believes that any grain exported from the forest steppe was mediated by the Royal Scythians and unlikely to have been of any significance, much less regularity, before the 4th century BC.

There are three fundamental objections to the scenario of Greco-Scythian relations as presented by Vinogradov and Marchenko and which underpins Shcheglov's thesis. The first objection is that the thesis does not fit the evidence. In order to deny 'trade' of any significance (and the writers largely ignore the 4th century and later sources in these discussions), it is necessary to explain away the presence of non-native objects. But it does not inspire confidence when the argument against exports depends entirely on the gross numbers of surviving Greek objects imported into the forest steppe (objects which, it is argued, were exchanged for grain). It is precisely in the fortified settlements of the forest steppe that the largest quantities of imported material of the 6th and 5th centuries BC have been found. In this region too a boatload of 5th to 4th century BC metallic vessels, of high quality, was found in peat near Peshchannoe, south-east of Kiev, on a former tributary of the Dnieper, south of the great Dnieper rapids hereabouts, which formed a barrier to direct movement upriver. However we describe what was going on between Greeks and non-Greeks, there was a great deal of exchange involved, for which surviving objects, particularly those from burials, form a rather unreliable numerical indication.[22]

At the same time, Olbian farmers are interpreted as dependent on Royal Scythian patronage for the success of their relations with the forest steppe peoples. The Royal Scythians were numerically insignificant in the Lower Dnieper region before the 5th century BC.[23] The dramatic (and temporary) decline in Olbia's rural settlements around the end of the first quarter of the 5th century BC cannot be accounted for by the arrival of dramatic numbers of nomadic invaders, because the evidence of a Scythian presence on any scale simply is not there. The assumption that grain production and exports fluctuated as relations between the colonies and nomad Scythian groups waxed and waned cannot be sustained. Rich élite burials of the Royal Scythians, reflecting a wealth based, according to the above theory, on the successful exploitation of commercial transactions between Greeks and natives, begin to appear only in the advanced 5th century BC.[24] Herodotus' account of Scythia (4. 16-18; 54-57) refers to a number of agricultural communities, principally on the western and eastern banks of the river Bug and the lower Dnieper. The

---

1981, 1, 142ff.; Marchenko 1982; Vinogradov, Domanskii and Marchenko 1990, esp. 138-9 (repeating theory of Scythian capture of territory); S.D. Kryzhitskii and V.M. Otreshko, On the problem of the formation of Olbia's *polis*, in A.S. Rusyaeva (ed.), *Olbia and its Environs* (Kiev 1986) 14 (in Russian); *cf.* Kryzhitskii *et al.* 1989 for the contrary theory of a regrouping of resources. Vinogradov and Marchenko have since changed their minds about the role of Scythians in exploiting the political situation in the aftermath of Darius' invasion (Marchenko and Vinogradov 1989, 806), though not about the nature of relations between nomadic and settled communities; there are notable differences, not just in nuance but in overall thrust, between this last analysis and another published in German in the same year (Vinogradov and Marchenko 1989, 544-545). Solovyov (1999, 110-115) summarises the arguments with considerable acumen, contrasting the fortunes of Berezan, which never recovered from the multiform difficulties encountered during 5th century BC, with those of Olbia, which continued to flourish.

[21] Shcheglov 1990, 141-59, esp. 149-53, rejecting large scale grain imports before 4th century BC; 156, for finds of *triticum aestivum* (bread wheat) and *triticum compactum* (club wheat) in the rural estates of Olbia (Kozyrka, Boikuch), Chersonesus and elsewhere in the Bosporan kingdom. These are discussed more fully in the specialist article by Shramko and Yanushevich (above n.15). Similar views to Shcheglov's have been expressed by N. Leipunskaya, On the role of trade/exchange relations in the economy of Olbia in the second half of the 6th century BC, in *Tskhaltubo 1977*, 125-30.

[22] Onaiko's classic account (1966) is now sadly out of date; Rolle's survey (Rolle 1985) still uses Onaiko's maps but includes more recent syntheses in her discussion. Area maps of sites and finds have been compiled and published for the Lower Bug (Kryzhitskii, Buiskikh and Otreshko 1990) and Dniester (Okhotnikov 1983). On the hoard from Peshchanoe: O.D.Ganina, *Ancient Bronzes from Petchannoe*, Kiev 1970 (in Ukrainian); the vessels have sometimes been described as gilded or gold-plated (e.g. Rolle 1989, 92); this is incorrect (see Cl. Rolley, *RA* 1987, 2, 352).

[23] Shcheglov 1990, 141-6, 149-51; Shcheglov is prepared even to deny the conventional translation of Herodotus 4. 17. 2, referring to the Σκύθαι ἀροτῆρες as growing corn (σῖτον) not for eating but to sell (ἐπὶ πρήσι). Shcheglov's preference, which would make the root πρήθω (= to heat) renders the whole sentence meaningless, since the contrast is between growing for food and growing for another purpose.

[24] "Out of sixteen princely barrow-graves of the 6th and 5th centuries, as listed by M. Artamonov, found within the territory of the Royal Scythians, none was of the 6th century; five were of the advanced stage of the 5th century, and the latest of this group, the very richly equipped royal barrow-grave of Solokha... was of the turn of the 5th to the 4th century" (Sulimirski and Taylor 1991, 574; M. Artamonov, *Treasures from Scythian Tombs*, London 1969). Rolle's major study of funerary practices (Rolle 1979) is not concerned with the analysis of Royal Scythian tombs and her brief book (Rolle 1985) does not address diachronic matters either. Ilinskaya and Terenozhkin (1983) illustrate 'nomad Scythian' tumuli of the 7th - 5th centuries in the Lower Dnieper and Crimean regions (map p. 88) but their contents are almost exclusively of steppe origin (*cf.* on the other hand map p. 120, with 4th century BC evidence). See also Alekseev 1987a and 1987b.

historian in fact distinguishes the Royal Scythians from their nomadic counterparts (4. 56), as well as indicating that the former dominated the whole region east of the Gerrhus, a tributary of the Dnieper, as far as the Crimea (Taurica) and the River Tanais (Don), regarding the rest of the population as if they were their slaves (4. 19-20). Herodotus' description of the various named communities cannot be made to fit the archaeological pattern of population groups - it is too imprecise. But there are overall correspondences; we cannot account for gaps in the evidence. The historian seems to indicate that nomadic and settled groups were to be found in the same areas. The fact that the Royal Scythians looked down on their fellow inhabitants cannot be assumed to mean that they exercised complete power over them. The historian wants to make it clear that the former regarded themselves as leaders of an otherwise disparate collocation of groups. The palaeo-botanical studies already referred to make it clear that settled communities of Scythian (and non-Scythian or pre-Scythian, indigenous) origin already had a developed system of agricultural production before the advent of any significant demand for grain from Aegean cities, but the range of foodstuffs listed by Herodotus (corn, onions, leeks, lentils and millet: 4. 17) fits the palaeo-botanical samples reasonably well.

The second objection is to the assumption that Scythians were primarily nomads and that they were fundamentally and irrevocably opposed to settled communities. The archaeological evidence indicates that Herodotus' distinction between the settled communities of Scythia and the nomadic Scythians should, if anything, be given more, not less emphasis. The Royal Scythians are presented by him as leaders and military protectors. Shcheglov's view depends too heavily on the metaphor of nomad Scythian behaviour and underestimates not only the rootedness of indigenous agricultural traditions, but equally the scale on which these were adopted by former nomadic groups in the forest steppe zone and from thence into the grasslands.[25]

In the grass steppe settlements were fewer but larger. The best known is Kamenka (Kamenskoe city-site), a fortified site covering 12km^2, on the left bank of the Dnieper opposite Nikopol.[26] Three quarters of the enclosed area, on a peninsula surrounded by the Dnieper and two of its tributaries, the Konka and Bolshaya Belozerka, consisted of sand dunes. In the far south-west was an acropolis, evidently the seat of a local ruler; this was separated physically and geographically from the main area of habitation and industry. Slag and other industrial waste indicates that iron was smelted and processed here on a large scale, the ore being derived from the Krivoi Rog deposits approximately 60km to the west, as well as copper, lead and zinc. Kamenskoe site is surrounded by mound cemeteries which include many spectacular 'chieftain' type burials of similar date (the settlement became active around the turn of the 5th - beginning of the 4th century BC). The proximity of such major sites, both in the forest steppe and grass steppe, to the River Dnieper and its tributaries, underscores the importance attached by their inhabitants to river traffic. The industrial activities at Kamenskoe site required large quantities of wood which would have had to be taken from forests upriver. Grain and other organic materials, as well as manpower, could easily have moved down in the direction of Olbia and beyond. The emergence of sites like Kamenskoe shows that there was no intrinsic contradiction between pastoral nomadism and a sedentary existence. The seasonal needs of large herds could be accommodated from such a base, with the animals being wintered within the fortifications.[27] The industrial and exchange activities of the inhabitants enmeshed them in a network of mutual obligations but need not have affected their traditional preference for rearing livestock. Current evidence does not allow us to make assumptions about how forest and grass steppe communities may have negotiated exchanges with Greek colonists. But there is no reason to believe that the Royal Scythians could or did operate any kind of monopoly. They may well have levied taxes or tribute on transports going upriver; they may even have been encouraged to settle at Kamenskoe and elsewhere along the lower course of the Dnieper in order to do this. But their relationship with communities upriver cannot have been as unequal as Shcheglov would have us suppose. Such power as they did exercise over river traffic is unlikely, on present evidence, to have been significant before 400 BC, when the main settlement's life began. The acknowledged acme of Royal Scythian power in the Lower Dnieper region, the second half of the 4th century BC, coincided with the expansion of many cities within the Bosporan kingdom. This is also the period in which our knowledge of Greek commercial relations with the Bosporan kings is best documented. The fact that Greek colonies and Scythian communities flourished in parallel demonstrates that the benefits were mutual.

Aerial photography of the Taman and Crimean peninsulas has revealed a dense network of rural sites, functioning from 6th century BC, which parallel the creation of new civic centres in both areas during the same period.[28] The

---

[25] For the relationship between these archaeological groups and their possible historical correlates (the Callipidae, Halizones and 'Agricultural Scythians'), see Sulimirski and Taylor 1991, 573-89; B.A. Rybakov, *Herodotus' Scythia*, Moscow 1979 (in Russian); I.V. Kuklina, *The Ethno-geography of Scythia from ancient sources*, Leningrad 1985 (in Russian); Herodotus' geography of Scythia: the rivers and the rugged peninsula, in *Tskhaltubo-Vani V* (1990) 127-36.

[26] B.N. Grakov, *Kamenskoe gorodishche*, Moscow 1954; Rolle 1979, 160ff.; 1985, 480-5;1989, 119-22. For a further refinement of differences between Kamenskoe and sites with mixed evidence, closer to Olbia, see Bylkova 2000 (Belozerskoye city-site).

[27] *Cf.* Rolle 1989, 105.

[28] Shcheglov 1980; *cf.* Wąsowicz 1972; Paromov 1986; *idem*,

attraction of such sites for any nomadic Scythians was not the agricultural land; ploughed fields were of little value except as forfeits - incomers could bribe the farmers with threats to burn their crop. Villages and towns offered rich pickings for a quick raid - the target mobile valuables, including potential slaves. But towns took care to build defences, whether around residential quarters or agricultural land and country estates built walls and towers.

The most detailed archaeological exploration has taken place in the environs of Chersonesus. During the 4th century BC intensive cultivation expanded in the western half of the Crimean peninsula, where, according to Shcheglov, the citizens of Chersonesus measured out plots over the whole of the Mayachnii peninsula (Lighthouse Point: 18ha.), which was sealed off by two parallel walls with towers. Subsequently, during the third quarter of the 4th century BC, the whole Heracleian peninsula, the immediate hinterland of the city itself, was divided up into 402 allotments, which were divided up into plots, numbering as many as 2,400 in the first half of the 3rd century BC, and eventually covering some 1,000km^2.[29] It is assumed that the native Taurians were evicted; their settlements have been documented outside the land division scheme, on the eastern bank of a deep ravine which formed a natural barrier around the *chora* of Chersonesus and further inland, towards the foothills of the Taurian mountains.[30] The relationship between the Chersonesitans and their immediate neighbours in the plain requires clarification. Although the huddling of Tauric settlements just outside the Chersonesitan land division does suggest a relocation, we need to know more about the wider interactions of the two groups.[31] These Tauric communities lay in the path of any incoming nomadic groups from outside the Crimean peninsula.

But the sedentary life held plenty of attractions for the Scythians. At Simferopol, there was a Scythian 'city' from the 3rd century BC onwards, with its own fortifications and an elaborate extra mural mausoleum. The Scythian inhabitants imported amphorae from Heracleia Pontica, Rhodes and Knidos. As in the case of the earlier steppe settlements, this was a community involved in the network of Pontic connections, not outside it.[32]

The gradual encroachment of new groups into already occupied areas, or the expansion of existing communities, no doubt did cause tension. A. Maslennikov has studied the evidence of artillery balls (associated with Greek colonists) and arrow heads (the preferred artillery weapon of the Scythians) at a range of fortified sites on the Crimean peninsula. Many of these seem to date from the 3rd century BC but chance finds of this type are hard to date closely without careful investigation and documentation; the sites studied extend from 6th to 1st century BC. Nevertheless, most probably do belong to the final three centuries.[33] This evidence of manifest aggression needs to be balanced by more systematic examination of rural sites. Maslennikov has also given these his attention, attempting to classify them over time, although his published scheme is rather confusing and difficult to relate both to contemporary communities in different periods and to similar phenomena in the western part of the Crimean peninsula.[34] The existence of forts, fortifications and walled settlements does not mean that communities were constantly under siege; merely that they wanted such reassurance. Far from being a period of decline, as Marchenko and Vinogradov have suggested, the 4th and 3rd centuries BC were one of robust expansion in the Bosporan kingdom.[35] The situation of the Royal Scythians underwent changes *ca.* 300 BC onwards which we cannot as yet explain satisfactorily. Increased sedentarisation in the environs of the Bosporan kingdom

---

Intervention sur la péninsule de Taman, in Lordkipanidzé and Lévêque 1990, 161-4 (citing 217 rural sites); Carter *et al.* 2000.

[29] A. N. Shcheglov, *Polis and chora*, Simferopol 1976 (in Russian); *idem, The north-western Crimea in antiquity*, Leningrad 1978 (in Russian); V.M. Zubar, *The Tauric Chersonesus in ancient times*, Kiev 1993; in Russian; Saprykin 1994, with earlier bibliography; Hind 1992-1993, 96-99, with further refs. to outlying dependencies of Chersonesus, especially Kerkinitis and Kalos Limen; Hind 1998, 146-51; Carter *et al.* 2000, 709-14, confirming a date for the land divisions in the 360s or 350s.

[30] E.I. Solomonik, *Arkheologiya* (Kiev) 20 (1976); A. N. Shcheglov, *Tskhaltubo-Vani* IV (1988), 53-81; see above, n.11.

[31] O.Y. Savelya, On Greek-barbarian relations in the south-western Crimea, 6th - 4th centuries BC, in *Tskhaltubo 1979*, 166-76; A.N. Shcheglov, The Tauri and the Greek colonies in Taurica, in *Tskhaltubo 1979*, 204-18; *idem* in Koshelenko *et al.* 1984, 310-71; Saprykin 1994, 82.

[32] P. Shults, *The Mausoleum of Scythian Neapolis*, Moscow 1953 (in Russian); T. Vysotskaya, *The Scythian fortress*, Simferopol 1975 (in Russian); *eadem, Neapolis, capital of the later Scythian kingdom*, Kiev 1979 (in Russian); *Problems of ancient culture. Résumés of papers presented to the Crimean Conference*, Simferopol 1988, 195-313, esp. those of Khrapunov, 283-4; Zaitsev, 289-90, Puzdrovskii, 303-4 (all in Russian).

[33] A.A.Maslennikov, The new data concerning the history of poliorcetica of the ancient Bosporus, *SA* 1 (1996) 68-78 (in Russian). Solovyov refers to the numbers of burials, from 5th century BC onwards, at Berezan, which were pierced by Scythian style arrowheads (1999, 111 with refs.).

[34] Maslennikov 1989; *cf.* S.Y. Saprykin, The Aspurgians. *SA* 2, 1985, 65-78, who examines coastal and rural sites in a specific time period, 1st century BC - 1st century AD.

[35] Marchenko and Vinogradov 1989, 810-11; *cf.* Vinogradov and Marchenko 1989, 547-9; for the Bosporan kingdom, see Gaidukevich 1971, 65ff., 170-255; Koshelenko *et al.* 1984, 59-84; *GPPAE* 73-5 (Hermonassa); 78-81 (Gorgippia); 208-16 (Panticapaeum); 284-8 (Phanagoria); Kruglikova 1980; 1982; Hind 1994, 493-502, 504 (although Hind dates the 'decline' of the kingdom too early, *ca.* 300 BC); see Hind 1992-93, for more extensive evidence of continuing prosperity: 100-101 (Theodosia and Nymphaeum); 102-3 (Hellenistic Panticapaeum); 103-9 (Taman sites). V.D. Blavatskii, who excavated not only at Panticapaeum but also at Phanagoria, and in the hinterland of Sindice, was convinced that the 3rd century BC was a period of huge expansion (Blavatskii 1964, esp. 94-125). The problem of how to interpret the later stages of the Hellenistic kingdom are discussed further below.

appears to have been accompanied by continuing movement westwards towards the Danube.³⁶ This brings me to the third and most serious objection to Vinogradov and Marchenko's scenario, adopted by Shcheglov. Successive waves of nomadic invaders are invoked to explain all manner of changes. It is taken as axiomatic that Scythian attacks caused extended periods of crisis, particularly from the 3rd century BC onwards. This tendency not only arrogates to vague groups a sweeping power they are unlikely, as mobile groups, to have had. It is inadequate as an explanatory model of change in the final three centuries BC. (If scholars are drawing analogies with the Tartar raids from 13th century onwards, they have not admitted it. There is no reason to believe that the scale and severity of raids were at all comparable, and the practical implications are quite different).

The sedentarisation of the Scythians has taken us some way from the argument about grain exports. Western ancient historians have eschewed any consideration of native production in the Black Sea region, concentrating on the nature of Athenian demand. This is clearly a necessary, but not a sufficient argument for evaluating overall exchange patterns. In 1985 P. Garnsey changed the nature of the debate by re-evaluating the productive potential of Attica in terms of land available for cultivation and the 'carrying capacity' of that land in relation to population estimates. On this basis, Attica could feed much, if not most, of its population, most of the time.³⁷ In the past it was too readily assumed, without any attempts to calculate actual need, that the Athenians could not survive without importing considerable quantities of grain on a regular basis. But the recognition that Athenians could and did find ways of dealing with scarce resources modifies rather than diminishes the significance of imports. M. Whitby now argues that Garnsey has probably underestimated the potential shortfall between grain produced and grain required in Athens. But, more importantly, he has demonstrated that the desire of Athenians to import (and re-export) grain did not depend exclusively on notions of what the community's needs might be at any one time.³⁸ A number of different variables affected the intensity of transactions over grain; these should include the desire for a more varied diet and for what were perceived to be better quality foodstuffs, as well as the capacity of private entrepreneurs to recognize an opportunity when they saw

one. So calculations of productive capacity can only provide us with general theoretical parameters. Athenian strategies with respect to grain imports were based on enabling a plentiful supply, by a combination of regulations and incentives, not on estimates of need.³⁹ Whether or not Demosthenes overestimated, for the private purposes of a particular speech, the role of Pontic grain imports at Athens (20. 29-33: 400,000 *medimnoi*, allegedly equal to the total imported from all other sources), there is enough independent evidence to show that the Athenians did enjoy 'favoured nation' status in the Bosporan kingdom; they and their representatives in Bosporus were exempt from the usual tax of one thirtieth on grain exports, and shipments destined for Athens were given preferential treatment in the harbours. In return, successive Bosporan rulers received the highest formal honours from the Athenians that any individual could hope to receive.⁴⁰ The importance of international exchanges to the economy of the north Pontic cities in general, and of the Bosporan kingdom in particular, is reflected in the writings of ancient geographers from Herodotus (4. 17: the *emporion* of the Borysthenites; 20. 1; 110: Kremni, *emporion* on Lake Maeotis) to Strabo (7. 4. 5, 11. 2. 10-11: Panticapaeum and next in size, Tanais; 7. 3. 17: Olbia, a large *emporion*; 7. 4. 4: Theodosia; 11. 2. 10: Phanagoria).⁴¹ An *emporion* was not simply a port or harbour, although many are on rivers; the prime role of an *emporion* was as a place of regulated exchange for merchants from different origins, often

---

³⁶ Melyukova 1979; 1995; Andrukh and Chernov 1990.

³⁷ P. Garnsey, Grain for Athens, in Cartledge, P. and Harvey, F.D. (eds.), *Crux*, Sidmouth 1985, 62-75; Garnsey 1988, 50-55, 90-9, 139-141. Whitby (1998,118 n.33) has pointed out that Garnsey later reduced his estimates of the resident population of Attica (Garnsey 1988, 90, 104) which would enhance the community's ability to be self-supporting. Whitby believes that Garnsey has underestimated 'by a significant margin' both the numbers of residents in Athens and their food requirements (118). *Cf.* Tsetskhladze 1998a.

³⁸ Whitby 1998, 102-28. I am most grateful to Mike Whitby for allowing me to see a copy of his paper before publication.

³⁹ Whitby 1998, 118-123.

⁴⁰ M.N. Tod, *A Selection of Greek Historical Inscriptions II*, Oxford 1948, no. 167 = P. Harding, *Translated Documents of Greece and Rome 2. From the End of the Peloponnesian War to the Battle of Ipsus*, Cambridge 1985, no. 82 with bibl. *Cf.* Lysias 16. 4; Isocr. 17. 3-5; I.B. Brashinskii, *Athens and the Northern Black Sea littoral in the 6th - 2nd centuries BC*, Moscow 1963, 123-6 (in Russian); G. de Ste. Croix, *Origins of the Peloponnesian War*, Oxford 1972, 47 and App. 8. 314; R. Seager, Lysias against the corndealers. *Historia* 15 (1966) 172-84; C. Tuplin, Satyros and Athens: IG II² 212 and Isokrates 17.57. *ZPE* 49 (1982) 121-8; Hind 1994, 499-500 with bibl.; Heinen 1996.

⁴¹ Panticapaeum is placed among the first class *emporia* of the Mediterranean by R. Etienne (L'*emporion* chez Strabon ' A: Les *emporia* straboniennes: inventaire, hiérarchie et mécanismes commerciaux, in *L'Emporion*, 23-46, esp. 29; P. Rouillard, in the same volume, argues that Strabo uses the term primarily in a descriptive rather than juridical sense, although such sites might acquire a defined juridical status (48-9); the emergence of regulated *emporia*, and the care taken to define such regulations, particularly in 'peripheral' areas, is examined by A. Bresson (Les cités grecques et leur emporia, in *L'Emporion*, 163-226). Hind has argued that Cremni was a predecessor of Panticapaeum or a so far undiscovered site on Lake Maeotis (1994, 477, 479) and that the manner in which Herodotus loosely refers to a self-constituted community like Olbia as an *emporion* underscores the exceptional importance of trading interests (Hind 1985). The association of the terms 'Skythikon' and 'Taurikon' with the *emporion* of Chersonesus surely means that this was the entry point for exchanges with the Scythian and Tauric populations (*contra*: Saprykin 1996, 362, 369, who believes that these are only toponyms, because he assumes that relations between them and the Greeks were poor throughout the 3rd century BC). Horden and Purcell 2000, 395-400, are far more sanguine; *emporia*, were, in their view, cosmopolitan by definition.

located to provide access for outsiders to local resources.[42]

Greek and Non-Greek Institutions

Around the middle of the 4th century BC, an inscription was carved in fine Greek letters at or near Vetren in the Thracian Plain, on behalf of the native ruler, most probably Amadocos II, which provides guarantees for Greek colonists and other Greek citizens, from Thasos, Apollonia and Maronia, at the *emporion* Pistiros and other nearby (?) *emporia*, and cites regulations laid down by Cotys (probably Cotys I: 383/2–359 BC) as a precedent. Provision was also made for the regulation of transports travelling by road between the *emporion* and Maronia on the Aegean coast.[43] The ruler himself acted as guarantor. This duplicates the situation which existed in the Bosporan kingdom, where the Leuconidae, or members of Leucon's family (whose function and titles are variously described) promulgated decrees on behalf of the Bosporan state.[44] In Thrace the Odrysian dynasty held power successfully over many different 'tribes'; its rulers are called kings by Greek writers and orators; inscriptions originating from Greek states often give the ruler's name without any epithet or title, as in the Vetren inscription, although coins and documents do add *basileus* from the 3rd century onwards. This makes it difficult to judge whether use of the title became fashionable, in the style of Hellenistic monarchs, or whether the term copies some local usage.[45] These rulers personally conducted diplomacy with Greek cities of the Aegean, as did the Macedonian kings.[46]

Greek writers never applied the term *tyrannos* to a Thracian ruler, as they did with respect to their Bosporan counterparts. In Odrysian Thrace, as in Macedon, kingship was an institution with established rules of procedure. This does not mean that in Bosporus authority had been seized or arrogated in some irregular manner. The term *tyranos* is misleading, even if some Athenian orators and a few other Greek writers sometimes used it in connection with Bosporan rulers. There is no evidence to show that the Leuconidae held power unconstitutionally. The idea that Spartocus was a mercenary leader who manipulated his way to power during wrangles among the Archaeanactidae is an implausible attempt to explain how Thracians, and with distinguished names at that, should find themselves in control without any apparent opposition.[47] On the contrary, their role as 'chief executives' seems to have been actively sanctioned by the communities over which they had command. Leucon, who came to power in 389/8 BC, is at first styled 'son of Satyrus, the Panticapaean' (*CIRB* 37), later '*archon* of Bosporus'. The title *archon*, which implies that the Leuconidae wished to be seen as legitimate magistrates, not autocrats, reappears on documents of one of his successors, Pairisades I (*CIRB* 10, 11, 1039-40). The choice of term is instructive, because Leucon's ancestors were preceded by the Archaeanactidae, a hereditary dynasty of Milesian, or possibly Mytilenaean origin, which seems to have had no qualms about its lack of accountability. Unfortunately, we know almost nothing about this dynasty and cannot judge how power was exercised in the colonies of Bosporus. Nevertheless, what may have been acceptable or viable in the period after the Persian Wars, was evidently no longer so in 4th century BC. Judging by the epigraphic evidence, Leucon and Pairisades held slightly different roles with respect to the Greek cities on the one hand, and their native subjects on the other. The same documents which call them *archon* of Bosporus refer to them as kings of individually named 'tribes', notably the Sindi, Toreti and Dandarii; other communities are later referred to as well.[48]

The personal names of the Leuconidae, beginning with Spartocus, the man who seems to have taken over from the Archaeanactidae, include many which were popular within the Odrysian dynasty. Spartocus (Sparadocus) is in fact the name of king Sitalces' brother. His inscribed silver coins (there are no coins bearing Sitalces' name), are the earliest types minted on behalf of this dynasty in Thrace (*ca.* 440-30 BC). Although Sparadocus was never king, his son Seuthes was Sitalces' successor.[49] Sitalces and his father Teres had allied themselves in the past with the Royal Scythians through marriage alliance. Sitalces' sister had been married to Ariapeithes, whose other wife was a Histrian woman, the mother of Scyles. The story of Scyles is used by Herodotus as a graphic, aphoristic example of how the Scythians insisted on maintaining their own customs. But that is the gloss the historian chose to put on it. What it tells us about the diplomatic connections of the

---

[42] Ar. *Pol.* 7. 5. 4; cited by Bresson, (above note) 166, 168, 199.
[43] Domaradzki 1993, 41 Fig. 6, Annexe 56, No. 5 (L. Domaradzka); Velkov and Domaradzka 1994; Velkov and Domaradzka, in Domaradzki 1995, 73-85.
[44] Rostovtzeff 1931, 133-4; Hind 1994, 490, 496-7 with discussion.
[45] Archibald 1998, chs. 4, 9, 11 and 13.
[46] M. Hatzopoulos, *Macedonian Institutions under the Kings* vols. I-II, Athens 1996.
[47] This is what Werner believed (1955, 419, 430-5), though he also accepts the premise that the change of power was in some way connected with Pericles' *Periplus* of the Black Sea (*cf.* Rostovtzeff 1930, 565; Hind 1994, 490, 492) and thus imposed from without. The chronological synchronicity may be fortuitous. The foundation of an Athenian 'colony' at Nymphaeum has no particular bearing on the internal affairs of Panticapaeum and its immediate neighbours. Most importantly, the creation of a petty dictator would not only have been a most uncharacteristic move by the Athenians; it was the complete opposite of such political solutions as the Athenians were seeking elsewhere in the Aegean and Black Sea (Plut. *Per.* 20). For the use of the term 'tyrant' with reference to Bosporan rulers, see Werner 1955, 420-21; Hind 1994, 495-8.
[48] Hind 1994, 496 with refs.
[49] Archibald 1998, ch. 4 on Odrysian Sparadocus; the Odrysian origins of Spartocus have been accepted explicitly by Hind 1994, 491, following Gaidukevich 1971, 66-8, implicitly by V.V. Latyshev, W. Tomaschek, E. Minns and R. Werner (Werner 1955, 419 and n. 3 with further refs.).

Odrysians is far more revealing. Scyles was defeated by his step-brother, and Sitalces' half-brother, Octamasades, with Sitalces' active support (Hdt. 4. 80). This means that *ca.* 440 BC, when this incident is usually dated, an Odrysian was already established as the supreme commander of the Royal Scythians. Spartocus the Bosporan ruler, who came to power within these same years (Diod. 12. 31. 1), is unlikely to have been the same man as Sitalces' brother, although the possibility should not perhaps be excluded altogether. In the early years of this century, when Thrace was considered, by such eminent authorities as M. Rostovtzeff, to have been a pale imitation of Scythia, the idea of an Odrysian prince as an eligible, indeed, influential candidate for high office, would have seemed absurd. But Rostovtzeff did not have access to the data we have now, which shows the Odrysians to have been the pioneering leaders of a large territorial state, patrons of the arts and builders of cities; models in these respects for neighbouring regions, whereas 'pan-Scythianism' - the tendency to attribute all innovation to the Scythians - has been discredited by archaeologists.[50] The regular adoption by the Leuconidae of Thracian names, especially names favoured by the Odrysian dynasty, such as Spartocus and Pairisades, cannot be explained except in terms of a special relationship with the Thracian royal house.[51]

Greek writers, particularly those with an Athenian perspective, seem rarely to have considered the problems of social units larger than the kind of *polis* envisaged by Aristotle.[52] Federal structures, which enabled individual communities to participate through elected or appointed representatives, had been attempted in many different forms in Greece. But their effectiveness depended on all kinds of factors, including social cohesiveness, geographical distance, common interests and customs, competition over resources. Such factors were likely to be of even greater significance where the population was of mixed origin, as in the case of the Bosporan kingdom, which included native people organized according to traditional social structures as well as Greek cities. The federal option was not available here, even if it had been desired; federation presupposes constituent members who are in some sense comparable and have some shared characteristics. In this case the constituent members were disparate and had little in common in terms of cultural background. But they had learned to live together over several centuries. The solution adopted by the Bosporan rulers and their advisors is summed up by Rostovtzeff:

I have tried to show that the state of the Bosphorus was originally a military tyranny and remained one: it grew out of a compromise between the native population and the Greek colonists. For the natives, the ruling dynasty was always a dynasty of kings, since it was the kings that for centuries they had been accustomed to obey. The Greeks, in order to preserve their dominant position and the foundation of their economic prosperity, were obliged to abandon their civic liberties to take for their chiefs the hellenized barbarians who ruled the native population. For the Greeks this form of government was a tyranny... This tyranny interests us: it was not a passing incident, like the tyrannies in many Greek cities during the sixth and fourth and third centuries BC, but a form of settled government which existed for centuries and which gradually transformed itself into a Hellenistic monarchy comparable with the monarchies in Asia Minor, Bithynia...[53]

It had the sagacity to invent a semi-Greek constitution, which held the state together for centuries; it contrived to make this form of government popular in Greece, and by means of propaganda issued by its historians, to install Bosporan tyrants, such as Leucon and Pairisades, in the great gallery of famous statesmen whose names were famous in the Greek schools..."[54]

No other author has delineated the Bosporan state with the same degree of passion and eloquence. Rostovtzeff's knowledge both of ancient sources and archaeological material relating to the Bosporan kingdom was unrivalled at the time of writing; but his enthusiasm has rarely been shared by his successors, despite the enormous increase in our knowledge base since that time.[55] His characterisation of the Leuconidae as 'Hellenized barbarians' sounds dated and stereotyped. The idea that the colonial Greeks of Panticapaeum were obliged to give up their liberties is a trifle sentimental. The city was far from being democratic under the Archaeanactidae. If, as I have argued, leading circles in the Bosporan cities did invite a member of the Odrysian family to take over as official 'head of state', they did so for clear political reasons - to improve their bargaining capacity with the Royal Scythians; to enhance their prestige among the local population and to benefit from the network of Odrysian contacts elsewhere in the

---

[50] Rostovtzeff 1931, 487-52 on supposed 'Scythian' features in Thrace; Archibald 1998, chs. 4-12.
[51] For the significance of dynastic names as expressions of mutual friendship, see G. Herman, *Ritualized Friendship and the Greek City*, Cambridge 1987.
[52] On federal organisation, see Rhodes 1993, esp. 169-77, and the introductory chapter by Roger Brock and Stephen Hodkinson to Brock and Hodkinson 2000, 1-31.

[53] Rostovtzeff 1922, 71.
[54] Rostovtzeff 1922, 81.
[55] *Cf.* however, Hind 1994, 510: "The Bosporan Greeks, their barbarian rulers and incorporated peoples, constructed a stable and original society and culture... They had durable and talented individual dynasts in the late 5th and 4th centuries, who ruled for long periods and gave Bosporus a prestige which carried it through the rather more difficult times of the 1st half of the 3rd and early 2nd centuries."

Aegean. The Athenians made their first formal alliance with Sitalces in 431 BC (Thuc. 2. 29), but Attic-style objects, including silverware of the kind that might have been given as a present from one high-ranking (Athenian or other Greek) official to another (at the Odrysian court), as well as the more ubiquitous red figure and black glazed pottery, began to appear in élite burials from the middle of the 5th century onwards.[56]

This was the decision of one particular influential grouping against others. The people of Theodosia were evidently sympathetic to some of those ousted (Anon. *Periplus* 51). Commercial rivalry between the *emporia* of the two principal cities probably explains at least some of the mutual mistrust. Leucon I rebuilt the harbour of Theodosia (Dem. 20. 33) after he had successfully brought the siege of the city, begun by his predecessor, Satyrus, to an end, *ca.* 370 BC.[57] If the leading citizens of Panticapaeum were simply unhappy with the policies of the Archaeanactidae they could have replaced them with someone else from among their number. The choice of an outsider shows that there were good *political* reasons for seeking a different kind of alignment. A leader from among the Royal Scythians was out of the question if the colonists hoped to maintain any serious credibility as independent entities. Aside from them, no native grouping could compete with the prestige of the Odrysians and in any case, any kind of partiality towards one local group could not contribute to a solution for the Crimean region as a whole. The longevity of the dynasty selected is a clear indication of their personal prestige, which was enhanced with successful territorial expansion westwards across the eastern half of the Crimean peninsula and eastwards into the Kuban. What is most surprising is that the solution worked at all.

Rostovtzeff called the constitution of Bosporus 'semi-Greek' and an 'invention' distinct from conventional 'tyranies'. The Athenian family of the Philaidae had created some kind of precedent in the Thracian Chersonesus, ruling over the native Apsinthians and Greek cities alike. Rostovtzeff recognized that the compromise worked out in Bosporus resembled the kinds of solutions attempted by Hellenistic rulers. V. Blavatskii subsequently developed these analogies into a full-blown theory, arguing that the Bosporan kingdom was already a proto-Hellenistic structure early in the 4th century BC.[58] Nor is Bosporus the only region where 'Proto-Hellenism' has been mooted; J.P. Weinberg explored its possible application to the Achaemenid Empire.[59] 'Proto-Hellenistic' presupposes that certain elements anticipated what happened later. Inevitably, it begs all manner of questions about what changes are thought to have taken place and what is understood in this context by 'Hellenistic'. Blavatskii understood the term in its traditional sense, namely the adoption of Greek language and institutions. Weinberg, on the other hand, applied it quite differently, seeing in Achaemenid economic and social institutions features which allegedly anticipated developments after Alexander's conquests. Both authors sought to explain their subjects by reference to something else, rather than analysing them according to some internal scheme. Blavatskii failed to appreciate what Rostovtzeff intuited, namely the unique combination forged by the nascent Crimean state. Neither author was particularly interested in a different set of analogies. The Bosporan kingdom was a constitutional monarchy in all but name. Spartocus and his successors were all drawn from one family and their right to inherit titular authority was not, apparently, disputed by their subjects (even if members of the family sometimes vied for office). Constitutional monarchies had a long tradition both inside and outside the Greek world and were duly included by Aristotle in his political works. The philosopher emphasized the differences between tyrannical government, exercised by unrepresentative individuals or dynasties in support of particular factions, and monarchical government, which supported established power groups, particularly aristocratic ones, although any non-Greek rule was in his eyes tantamount to despotism (*Pol.* 3. 14. 6, 1285a; 5. 9. 10, 1310b - 1315b). Contrary to what Rostovtzeff claimed, the Bosporan rulers were not tyrants, since their position was sanctioned by the very people who had most to lose from a revolutionary take-over. Most importantly, the tenor of government was inclusive rather than exclusive, with individuals of different extraction, Greek and non-Greek, resident in the cities and occasionally named in civic documents, although we know far too little about how wealth and political power may have been distributed.[60]

The historical *caesura* marked by the life and death of Alexander the Great has been an axiom of Greek history ever since J.G. Droysen coined the term 'Hellenismus'. Alexander the Great's eastern conquests have regularly been taken as the model for the Hellenistic kingdoms over the next three centuries. The foundation of colonies, the adoption of Greek urban and community structures and the taste for extravagant courtly fashions, all prominent features of his reign, have been taken as symptomatic of

---

[56] Archibald 1998, chs. 5 and 7.
[57] Shelov-Kovedyaev 1985; *idem*, Die Eroberung Theodosias durch die Spartokiden, *Klio* 68 (1986) 367-76; S.M. Burstein, The war between Heraclea Pontica and Leucon I of Bosporus, *Historia* 23 (1974) 401-16.
[58] V.D. Blavatskii, Il periodo del Protoellinismo sul Bosporo, in *Atti del Settimo Congresso Internazionale di Archeologia Classica*, Rome 1963, vol. III, 49-66.

[59] J.P. Weinberg, Bemerkungen zum Problem "der Vorhellenismus im Vorder Asien", *Klio* 58 (1976) 5-20; see P. Briant's reservations in Briant 1982, 321-5.
[60] V.D. Blavatskii, On the ethnic composition of the population of Panticapaeum in the 4th - 3rd centuries BC, *SA* 28 (1958) 97-106 (in Russian); *cf. SEG* 42 (1992) 189, no. 687.

contemporary developments in many different regions. In particular, the Greek city has been seen as the vehicle through which Greek traditions and institutions were mediated.[61] This traditional scheme is unsatisfactory.[62] A narrative framework based only or mainly on the biography of Alexander the Great and his Successor kings fails to accommodate many of the regions which belonged to the 'Hellenistic World' through diplomacy, economic exchanges or more diffuse cultural interactions. Moreover, the analysis of society by means of a tripartite scheme - kings and kingdoms, Greek cities and rural native populations - fails to take account of existing social and economic patterns, which continued to exert a profound influence on all the areas conventionally encompassed. An exaggerated preoccupation with the 'civilising' influence of the new Graeco-Macedonian regimes has been exposed as the romantic judgement of British, German and French colonialists.[63]

The underlying error, whatever its modern colouring, has been to extend in time and space the categories of a 'Greek history' created for a narrowly delimited horizon (the Greek peninsula plus offshore settlements). This is not to deny that Greek culture and institutions played an important formative role. But they represent elements within a wider, more complex picture and their significance for these wider horizons was for long assumed, on the basis of selective evidence, rather than demonstrated. The most detailed and extensive examination within this broader canvas has been of native institutions in the former Achaemenid empire. These studies have not merely been concerned with continuities and discontinuities, but with the fundamental nature of social and economic relationships. The assumptions made by an older generation of scholars about the feudal nature of land tenure,[64] and about the use of Greek as the language of administration (Sherwin-White and Kuhrt 1993, 48-51), are clearly inaccurate.

Another difficulty is the supposed uniqueness of the Greek *polis*. Not all Greek communities were organized as *poleis* (if we take this to mean self-constituted nucleations) and not all *poleis* were Greek. Early historians such as Hecataeus and Herodotus sometimes applied the term *polis* to non-Greek centres. We also find the same place being given different designations by different authors. In some cases this may reflect the historical fluctuation, whether geographical or social, of a particular settlement. But it surely suggests that rigid distinctions may not be appropriate; indeed, it opens up the possibility that historians may in the past have exaggerated the degree to which Greek cities in general differed from their non-Greek counterparts. Urban centres, however constituted, had existed in Babylonia, Assyria and Egypt, not to say Hittite Phrygia, for many centuries. The emergence of communal institutions and structures in Greece belongs within the context of state (or 'micro'-state) development in contemporary Europe as well as the Near East.[65]

At present it is still difficult to understand how non-Greek institutions differed from Greek ones. The process of urbanisation is indirectly related to that of communal structures. Towns developed with many different forms of administration. In the Hellenistic Age civic institutions are usually seen as part and parcel of the process of town development, although the political and social aspects of city organisation should not be lumped together. The problem is illustrated in a case such as Sardis. The capital city of Lydia has a long urban history, more splendid in many ways than many of its Ionian contemporaries in the 6th century BC. But little is known of its institutions. Early in the final third of the 4th century BC (the precise date is much disputed), the Milesians made a treaty with the Sardians, evidently in response to a deputation from Sardis. The Milesians promised any visiting Sardians the privilege of *asylia*. Milesians visiting Sardis were also

---

[61] J.G. Droysen, *Geschichte des Hellenismus* I-III, Basel (1952, originally published in 1843); B. Bravo, *Philologie, histoire, philosophie de l'histoire: étude sur J.G. Droysen, historien de l'antiquité* (Warsaw, 1968) esp. Ch. 5; *cf.* A. Momigliano and J.G. Droysen between Greeks and Jews, *History and Theory* 9 (1970) 139-53 = *Essays in ancient and modern historiography*, Oxford 1977, 307-23. For the dominance of the city as a structural form, see Jones 1940; W.W. Tarn and G.T. Griffith, *Hellenistic Civilisation*[3], London 1952, ch. III; Cl. Préaux, *Le monde hellénistique* II, Paris 1978, Pt. III, esp. chs. 1-3, although in Pt. IV, chs. 1-2, she qualifies this plan in her detailed discussion of cultural ideology and languages; Walbank 1981, 60-78, 133-42; Davies 1984, 304: (the) 'relentless spread' (of the Greek *polis*) into area after area of erstwhile non-Greek lands'; see now Davies 2000.

[62] For general critiques, see S. Alcock, Surveying the peripheries of the Hellenistic World, in Bilde *et al.* 1993, 162-75; Alcock 1994; see now Davies 2000.

[63] E. Badian, Alexander the Great and the unity of mankind, *Historia* 7 (1958) 425-44; Cl. Préaux, Reflexions sur l'entité hellénistique, *Chronique d'Égypte* 40 (1965) 129-39; *eadem*, Imperialismes antiques et idéologie coloniale dans la France contemporaine: Alexandre le Grand "modèle colonial". *DHA* 5 (1979); Kuhrt and Sherwin-White 1987, ix-xii; *Rois, Tributs et Paysans*, 491-506; Davies 1984, 263-4; Sherwin-White and Kuhrt 1993, 141-87, esp. 186-7.

[64] Briant 1982; Sherwin-White and Kuhrt 1993, 40-113; P. Briant, *Histoire de l'Empire Perse,* Paris 1996; G.D. Aperghis, The Persepolis Fortification Tablets - Another Look, in Brosius, M. and Kuhrt, A. (eds.), *Aspects of Achaemenid History: essays in memory of D.M. Lewis,* Leiden 1998; M. Aperghis, Population – Production – Taxation – Coinage: a Model for the Seleucid Economy, in Archibald *et al.* 2000, 69-102; on land tenure, see Archibald in the same volume, pp. 247-52.

[65] For cities of the Near East and the question of citizen status, see A. Kuhrt, *The Ancient near East, c.3000-330BC*, London 1995, II, 537-40, 610-21; M. Van de Meirop, *The Ancient Mesopotamian City*, Oxford 1997; J.K. Davies, The "Origins of the Greek *Polis*": where should we be looking?, in Mitchell, L.G. and Rhodes, P.J. (eds.), *The Development of the Polis in Archaic Greece*, London 1997, 24-38, forms a useful starting point for discussion of 'micro'-state structure and development; I am grateful to John Davies for our discussions of these and related topics; I have explored some of these problems in Archibald 2000. The publication of Brock and Hodkinson 2000 provides a wide-ranging resource on community structure and organisation in the Aegean region.

granted protection, guaranteed by such persons as the Sardians were to appoint.[66] It is clear that Sardis had its own magistrates; we are not given any technical names in this text but a council of some kind evidently sent its ambassadors to Miletus. The text we have was put up by Milesians for their own records. But during the 3rd century BC Greek terminology came to be applied to the city of Sardis (*polis*) and many of the features which we associate with Hellenistic urban amenities - a theatre, hippodrome and the like, are referred to (*cf*. Plb. 7. 15-17).[67]

The Pistiros inscription from Thrace has shown that the Odrysian kings adopted some Greek practices in the pre-Macedonian period when promulgating decrees. This is reflected not only in language but also in terminology. Since this text was carved primarily on behalf of Greek colonists, we do not know how relations were expressed between princes and towns and whether towns like that at Vetren had decision-making powers of their own. Greek was also the language of decrees made by Bosporan rulers. Both in Thrace as in the Bosporus, the initial motor for the use of Greek may have been commercial exchange. But a profusion of local languages and dialects continued to be used in both regions.

3. Indigenous People and Greeks

Among the most interesting and detailed Hellenistic documents from the northern and western shores of the Black Sea is a series of honorary decrees on behalf of prominent individuals, some Greek citizens, some non-citizens. Both Luigi Moretti and Claire Préaux have given some prominence to these documents in their respective historical and epigraphic surveys of the Hellenistic world.[68] The most celebrated, and the longest, is that in favour of Protogenes of Olbia, now usually dated no earlier than 200 BC.[69] Studies of this growing *corpus* of civic honorary decrees are accumulating. They reflect the strengths and weaknesses of the institutional approach to Hellenistic history. The inscriptions have been published by local scholars, steeped in the history and archaeology of their regions but paradoxically inured to a colonialist perspective. In the absence of a narrative history of the Pontic cities, to say nothing of the regions behind them, there has been a huge temptation to see these decrees as windows onto the wider historical scene. Similarities in phrasing as well as content have been grasped on as indicative of a widespread and growing economic crisis in the Greek colonial cities, increasingly threatened by outside groups or forces, be they Scythian, Sarmatian, Thracian or Galatian. Polybius' brief sketch of Byzantium's strategic position and its interminable quarrels with local Thracians has not only been taken at face value but become a lapidary verdict (4. 45), on malaise in the north. This view, propounded most vigorously in a series of articles by D.M. Pippidi on the Histrian archive and by Y. G. Vinogradov on Olbia, has not been seriously questioned by historians,[70] although archaeologists have adopted different views.

The first error is to project the language of otherness contained in these decrees onto the geographical landscape, identifying with a supposed Greek point of view against the 'others', the outsiders, uniformly styled 'barbarians'. General trends, whether regional or local, must be disentangled from the circumstances described in particular inscriptions. The decrees in question are encomia, not historical *résumés*. P. Gauthier's pioneering study of honorary decrees has revealed the rationale of such grand gestures, which reciprocate and acknowledge remarkable public benefits (Gauthier 1985). Three of his conclusions are of special relevance to the Pontic decrees in question. First, that honours were neither empty nor arbitrary promises but real privileges. Public honours were among the few positive rewards which a community could bestow. Some were of genuine practical advantage to the recipient (*asylia*, *proedria* and the like); others were largely symbolic, even if there were some material benefit therefrom - a gold crown, a statue.[71] The etiquette behind these gestures continued the tendency of Classical civic institutions to rely on the goodwill of its citizens when extraordinary expenditure was required, notwithstanding the fact that service to the state was carried out through elected office. Money drawn from her allies masked this reliance in 5th century BC Athens; the mechanisms became apparent once more in 4th century, when extra-territorial resources were drastically curtailed, at the same time as the needs of expenditure increased. The economic importance,

---

[66] *Syll.*³ 273; Herrmann 1997, 169, no. 135 with bibl.
[67] P. Gauthier, *Symbola*, Paris 1972, 240-2; *idem, Nouvelles Inscriptions de Sardes II: Documents royaux du temps d'Antiochos III; Décret de Sardes en l'honneur de'Heliodoros*, Geneva 1989; Sherwin-White and Kuhrt 1993, 180-83
[68] Moretti, *ISE* II, 134-63, nos. 122-32; Preaux 1978, I, 40-2 with bibl.; II, 520-4.
[69] *IOSPE* I² 32 (= *Syll.*³ 495; Austin 1981, 170-4, no. 97); Vinogradov 1979, 312-3, with *comparanda*).

[70] Pippidi 1962b; 1962c; 1962d; 1965; 1975b, 41 (a constant state of alarm at Olbia) '.. dans des circonstances que différent à peine de celles d'Istros' (seamlessly linking the decree in honour of Agathocles, son of Antiphilos (*I Histria* no. 15; Moretti, *ISE* No. 131) with Polybius' résumé and the Protogenes decree, despite huge gaps in space and time); *cf*. Pippidi and Popescu 1959; Marchenko and Vinogradov 1989, 811; Vinogradov 1981, 28-33; 1983; 1989; Vinogradov and Marchenko 1989, 548-9; Vinogradov and Kryzickij 1995, 93-5, 139-43. The assumptions made by the authors contributing to Welskopf 1974 vol. II, converge with those of Pippidi and Vinogradov (see esp. D.P. Kallistov, Die Poliskrise in den Städten der Nördlichen Schwarzmeerküste, 551-86, 587-607; 608-47 (J. Kruskol); *cf*. A. Stefan (*ibid*, 648-63) and V. Iliescu (664-81) on the west Pontic cities). Boffo (1989) has also tried to use the decree of Chersonesus in favour of Diophantus (*Syll.*³ 709) to make broader claims about contemporary affairs.
[71] Gauthier 1985, 12-30; 67, 92-102, 131-49 (on *proxenia*).

even for such a city as Athens, of wealthy property owners, whether as candidates for various civic liturgies or as sources of extraordinary levies,[72] only emphasises the fact that civic expenditure throughout antiquity depended in varying degrees on private or external resources. Formal recognition of a community's gratitude to an individual with the conferment of *megistai timai* seems to have evolved during the 4th century BC, acquiring particular rules at Athens in the 3rd century.[73] In part this process reflects changes in the relationship between official magistracies and voluntary initiatives, with a growing dependence by the Athenian state on the latter (Gauthier 1985, 115-9). Such grants when inscribed document for us behind - the -scenes activities which imposed real, sometimes huge burdens; for some citizens they were unavoidable duties. Where individual citizens or non-citizens voluntarily chose to take on exceptional responsibilities, the risks were high and incentives were needed. Public recognition served such a need; what survives is frequently the latest, most durable, retrospective gesture, in monumental form.

The second conclusion of Gauthier's book is that, contrary to P. Veyne's thesis, according to which narrow groups of highly privileged individuals effectively ran their city's affairs, civic administrations continued to exercise independent judgement and responsibility.[74] Gauthier is prepared to concede that Veyne is on firmer ground in the 'Late Hellenistic' period, from around the middle of the 2nd century BC onwards.[75] The scale of Roman financial exactions altered the entire framework within which the cities of the eastern Mediterranean operated. Detailed analysis of Hellenistic royal euergetism has shown that the great majority of grants were made in response to requests from cities. In other words, cities successfully lobbied rulers to provide funding for important public works and social welfare schemes. In order to pursue their own policies, and since benevolent despotism was the prevailing style of Hellenistic monarchy, rulers were obliged to negotiate with civic representatives; this provided cities with the leverage to secure their own interests.[76] The success of such strategies would therefore have depended on the ambition and tenacity of individual city administrations to promote suitable representatives at the royal courts.

The third significant outcome of Gauthier's study is that honorary decrees were usually records of a lifetime's achievement. The special rules which applied in Athens concerning when a candidate might hope to receive *megistai timai* may not have applied elsewhere. But the format of many decrees makes it clear that the same general principles were adhered to; ultimate honours were granted to exceptionally distinguished persons, in recognition of a wide range of benefits over many years, in some cases even over several generations.[77] Since the aim was to highlight a man's (and it was usually a man's) good works, the decrees amplify, even dramatise, particular events in order to give due expression to benefits received. The chronology of these events is often hard to reconstruct. The drafters were not recording for documentary purposes, but signalling one individual's role in civic affairs. Little wonder then, that one man takes centre stage, regardless of whoever else may have been involved at the time; such facts were not pertinent to the text.

Gauthier believed that there were no major regional differences in the manner of granting honours, except perhaps in one respect. In some at least of the Pontic cities, notably at Histria, decrees mention conferment of the title *euergetes* on a citizen; such a practice was normally confined to non-citizens.[78] These are subtle niceties. At Histria it appears that the inscription of a man's name as benefactor seems to have represented a kind of premier category of honorand. Likewise, the somewhat less distinguished but no less honourable grants of *proxenia* were not accompanied by formal inscription but by other privileges, *isoteleia* and the like.[79] Does this departure from what we know of honorary inscriptions in the Aegean represent a special nuance, adapted perhaps to suit local society, or were there special conditions which required special recognition? Here we are confronted by problems of signification on the one hand, scale on the other, which no one has seriously attempted to define. Had Histrian society developed its own language of distinction? Was it affected by a symbolic language derived from Getic practice? Or were the pressures exerted on the colonies by non-Greek peoples in some sense more intractable than the problems encountered by Aegean cities?

The former explanation (differences of nuance) seems preferable to the latter (different conditions). Although we may not be able to quantify the scale of civic problems in the Pontic region, we can at least flesh out who the

---

[72] See esp. J.K. Davies, *Wealth and the Power of Wealth in Classical Athens* (New York 1981), chs. V, 73-87; VI, 90-131; T.L. Shear, Jr., *Kallias of Sphettos and the Revolt of Athens in 286 BC*, Princeton, New Jersey 1978; M.M. Austin, Society and Economy, *CAH* VI² (1994) 541-58; see also papers by Bringmann, Oliver in Archibald *et al.* 2000.
[73] Gauthier 1985, 77-91;103-30.
[74] Gauthier 1985, 1-2, 8, 57 n. 162; 68-70; *contra*: P. Veyne, *Le Pain et le Cirque*, Paris 1976, esp. 192, 215; 235-6 on Protogenes of Olbia, holding absolute power like a Cosimo de Medici). See also Gauthier 1984; 1993, esp. 217-25.
[75] Gauthier 1985, 3, 67-8; 1993, 211-2.
[76] J.-L. Ferrary, *Philhellénisme et imperialisme*, Paris 1988, 117-9; Gauthier 1993, 214-5; Bringmann 1993, 7ff., esp. 15; Bringmann and von Steuben 1995 *passim*; Bringmann in Archibald *et al.* 2000.

[77] Gauthier 1985, 82-9; 49, 57-8 for the hereditary element.
[78] Gauthier 1985, 31-6, listing Histrian documents with this anomalous procedure, 33-4.
[79] Gauthier 1985, 10-11; 35, discussing similar examples from other Pontic cities, including Histria, Odessos, Mesambria, Dionysiopolis, Olbia and Chersonesus.

adversaries were. Studies of the epigraphic material almost invariably treat non-Greeks as unjustified aggressors; the nature of their aggression, indeed their power, is left vague. We do know that many cities paid tribute in some form to communities of the interior.[80] But this was by no means a new phenomenon; the Greek cities of Thrace had certainly been subject to such imposts on a regular basis under the Odrysian kings.[81] The same kind of relationship between rulers of the interior and Greek coastal cities seems to have survived into the Hellenistic Age, although the circumstances are obscure. The Histrian decree in honour of Agathocles, son of Antiphilus, which probably dates to the first half of the 2nd century BC,[82] describes a set of nested relationships: between the citizens of Histria and unnamed Thracians under a named leader, Zoltes, whose scratch army was threatening to spoil the city's crops (l. 9-10, 14, 19-21, 30-1, 35, 38-40, 44, 57); an indigenous king (*basileus*) Rhemaxos, evidently in control of some Greek cities as well as inland territories (l. 16-7, 50), and local people who take refuge inside Histria (l. 43-4). The use of the term 'barbarians' further obscures whatever real distinctions existed between the various non-Greek communities involved. Pippidi has argued that the ones who fled into the city were unfree or servile labourers who worked on Greek plots.[83] He was keen to rebut the argument that the Pontic cities used slave labour in the fields. His comparisons with the servile agricultural populations of Heracleia Pontica, Sparta, Crete and elsewhere may or may not be relevant. Much depends on how we envisage mechanisms of social control. The Pistiros inscription expressly forbids Greek settlers from bringing *epaulistae* (soldiers?) into the *emporion* (ll. 12-13).[84] The sentence precedes a prohibition against building forts or defensive structures of any kind (ll. 13-5). Ultimate control over the *emporion* is clearly in the hands of the local ruler granting the stipulated rights. We are still woefully ignorant about the niceties of the socio-economic relations which lie behind these words. But where an indigenous ruler could enforce his power, Greek colonists had no say. Precisely how these various interests were resolved in peripheral territory, particularly in the hinterland of colonies, is still unclear.

In Odrysian Thrace status did depend on birth and wealth, with an agricultural population dominated by aristocratic military élites (Hdt. 5. 6). But the élites maintained their power by networks of personal loyalty, expressed through gift exchange, networks which included the whole social spectrum, as in the case of many other aristocratic followings in Greece and beyond (Thuc. 2. 97. 3-4; Xen. *Anab.* 7. 3. 23ff.). The existence of such networks prevented the emergence of whole servile populations. Servitude or unfree status might result in such a context from the lack of adequate support from such a network, where the leading groups were defeated or killed by rival peer groups, leaving former supporters unprotected. Some such mechanism generated the high quality slaves Polybius speaks of as emanating from these regions (4. 38). The Histrian decree in honour of Agathocles confirms the existence of several interest groups with their own followings. Polybius says that in the region of Byzantium there were great numbers of such aristocratic factions (4. 45), a great nuisance to Byzantines. The pickings were all too apparent there. Without the existence of a supreme authority, competition over resources, between the Greek colonies and indigenous groups or amongst natives themselves, could lead to stalemate. Rhemaxos appears in the former example as the arbiter; he is the most authoritative figure in the situation; Agathocles can only appeal; Rhemaxos is the real 'fixer', providing cavalry on two separate occasions to enforce his will (ll. 50, 56).

Relations between Greek colonists and native people cannot be understood without a clearer picture of power groups within the landmasses behind them. The particular groups in power changed over time and their relationships with the colonies changed likewise. Study of the Thracian interior has shown that the strength of central authority has been seriously underestimated in the period of the Odrysian dynasty's heyday in the second half of the 5th and first half of the 4th century BC. The legacy of Odrysian power under Seuthes III in the Valley of the Roses is still very imperfectly understood. But it was far more significant in local and regional terms than excavation of the one city of Seuthopolis led us to believe.[85] At the same time, the so-called Celtic 'kingdom' based at Tylis, somewhere in the south-east of Bulgaria, has been disclosed as a sham, constructed from disarticulated and ultimately inconsistent historical fragments.[86] If there was Celtic settlement in the Central Plain of Bulgaria, the heartland of the Odrysian kings, it was in the form of isolated strongholds. Field survey suggests that the native settlement pattern continued

---

[80] Pippidi 1975b, 44-5, citing decree in honour of ambassadors to Zalmodegicus (Pippidi 1962b, 78 = *SEG* xviii, 288, ll. 9-10, 11-13; xix, 466; xxv, 788; Moretti, *ISE* II, no. 125); *cf.* Solomonik 1987 and *REG* 103 (1990/92) 549 no. 566: inscribed amphora sherd with note from an Apatourios to a Noumenios, referring to need to find out the level of tribute due to the Scythians.

[81] Archibald 1998, chs. 4 and 9 with full discussion of tribute and of the possibility that some Greek cities were to some degree 'subject' to these rulers.

[82] Pippidi 1975b, 32-33, with revised text, dated *ca.* 200 BC (=Moretti, *ISE* No. 131, pp. 151-60; Austin 1981, no. 98, both dating text *ca.* 200-150 BC); D.M. Pippidi, *Inscripțiile din Scythia Minor: vol. I, Histria*, Bucharest, 1983, no. 15.

[83] Pippidi 1975b, 37-8; 1975c.

[84] Velkov and Domaradzka 1994, 11 with commentary; see now V. Chankowski and L. Domaradzka in *BCH* 123 (1999), 250.

[85] See esp. the collection of articles on Seuthopolis and its region in *Sbornik Kazanluk*; other studies have been confined almost exclusively to mound excavations; the topographic survey of which these form part is not publicly available. Kitov 1992/93; 1994a, 1994b, 1996; Kitov and Krasteva 1992-93; 1994-95.

[86] Domaradzki 1984, 78-88; M. Domaradzki, La diffusion des monnaies de Cavaros au Nord-Est de la Thrace. *Eirene* 31 (1995), 120-28.

along earlier lines, perhaps with some changes of regional focus. At Vetren evolutionary changes in the function and character of the site were due to many factors; such changes as occurred in the mid 3rd century were far less significant in overall terms than those *ca*. 300 BC.[87] The most likely vantage points for an intrusive Celtic community, which could not supplant native princelings, but could adversely affect agricultural and commercial interests of Thracians and Greek colonists alike, was in the Strandja plateau.[88] There, Celtic military bands could maintain themselves in well defended hilltop locations, swooping down on the native agriculturalists or driving a hard bargain with Byzantium. The Greek coastal cities of the west Pontus continued to rely on the superior capacity of local rulers to defend their interests. One of these was Sadalas, a native aristocrat, probably from a princely family, who was declared a benefactor of Mesembria in the mid 3rd century BC.[89]

The situation on the northern shores of the Pontus was rather more complicated. Recent investigations at Olbia have thrown new light on the pre-Roman city. It reached its maximum extent up to and including the mid 3rd century BC at least. The whole area of the upper and lower terraces was intensively utilised.[90] Signs of a radical reorganisation are first visible from the mid 2nd century BC. This is marked by the gradual reduction of activity in the north-west sector of the upper city and the dismantling of architectural elements to reinforce the fortifications. Successive refurbishments of the city walls, and occasionally of rural sites (such as Glubokaya Pristan) confirm the real or anticipated attacks of external forces.[91] But natural factors also intervened; there is evidence of serious landslips on the lower terrace, where building was particularly dense.[92] These seem to have been particularly prevalent from the Middle to Late Hellenistic period, culminating in serious deterioration of the building fabric. By the time the city finally collapsed to Getic or other aggressors in the mid 1st century BC, much of the architecture was already in a dilapidated condition. The possible role of Celtic groups in this situation is ambiguous. Notwithstanding the references to Galatai in the decree honouring Protogenes, there is comparatively little evidence of Celtic activity and what there is can be explained in part as the reflection of a Celtic mercenary presence (Shchukin 1995). Current views of Sarmatian penetration into the Don and Dnieper river valleys are circumspect. Some Sarmatian units are known to have intervened in the struggle for power in Bosporus *ca*. 311 BC, but did not succeed in making any long term impact in the area. Marchenko now calls the 3rd century BC one of 'stabilization', with no new nomadic groups moving west of the Don.[93]

I have tried to show that the evidence from Thrace, and the north Pontic region as well as Scythia, is not consistent with a highly polarized view of Greeks and non-Greeks. There is no evidence to show that non-Greeks were somehow predisposed to attitudes fundamentally at odds with Greek ones, or opposed to civic institutions. A.H.M. Jones only once considered the Pontic region in his survey of the Greek city, and his views can only strike today's reader as bizarre:

> The Thracians were an intractable people, who did not take kindly to Hellenism, and relations between the Greek cities and the neighbouring tribes had usually been hostile. Philip's recent conquest of Thrace and his colonization of the interior seemed to mark the beginning of a new era, but the Gallic invasion was soon to sweep away his work when the foundations were barely laid. Along the northern coast of Asia Minor conditions were similar. The Greek colonies were mere islets of civilization in a sea of barbarism.... The natives differed greatly in their degree of culture, ranging from the utterly savage tribes east of the Halys to the relatively civilised Paphlagonian and Bithynian kingdoms, but none were sufficiently advanced to assimilate Greek culture.[94]

Not only was Jones wrong about the facts; his conception of how these societies developed in the pre-Roman period was founded on a deep misunderstanding. Greeks and non-Greeks did not live in isolated, sealed-off worlds. Interdependence was the normal state of affairs, not the exception.

---

[87] Domaradzki 1987 on the Central Plain as a whole; Domaradzki 1993, 37, 46; Domaradzki 1996, 13-34.
[88] Domaradzki 1984, 87-8.
[89] *IGBR* I² 257-62, no. 307; Moretti, *ISE* II, 136-7, no. 123; *SEG* 30 (1980) 701 (dating too early); Mihailov 1983, 24. For the continuing prosperity of Hellenistic Mesambria see now I. Karayotov, *The Coinage of Messambria*, Burgas 1992.
[90] Vinogradov and Kryzickij 1995, 41-54, pls.18, 64/2; Kryzhitskii in *AKSP*, 36-65 for investigations of the harbour line; Leipunskaya, *ibid*, 65-88 for associated ceramic finds.
[91] Kryzhitskii and Krapivina 1994, 187-97; A.S. Rusyaeva and V.V. Krapivina, Towards a history of Olbia in the 4th - 1st century BC. *Arkheologiya* (Kiev) 1992 (4) 17-34; Leipunskaya 1995, 23-44.
[92] Leipunskaya 1995, 28-9.
[93] Marchenko 1996; 1986; A.Y. Alekseev, *The Scythian Chronicle*, St Petersburg 1992, 140-1 (in Russian).
[94] Jones 1940, 27.

Abbreviations

Actes du IICIThrac.	Actes du IIème Congrès International de Thracologie, 4-10 septembre, 1976 (Bucharest 1980).
AKSP	*Antichnaya Kul'tura Severnogo Prichernomor'ya* (Kiev 1988).
Anali	*Anali - istorya - klasicheska kultura - Izkoustvoznane* (University of Sofia, Kliment Ohridski).
CIRB	*Corpus Inscriptionum Regni Bosporani*, V.V Struve (ed.) (Moscow/ Leningrad 1965).
DHA	Dialogues d'histoire ancienne.
ECM/CV	*Échos du Monde classique / Classical Views*.
GPPAE	D.D. Kacharava and G. Kvirkvelia, *Goroda i Poseleniya Prichernomor'ya Antichnoi Epokhi* (Tbilisi 1991).
IGBR	Sofia G. Mihailov, *Inscriptiones Graecae in Bugaria Repertae*, I² (1970), II (1958), III.1 (1961), III.2 (1964), IV (1966).
IOSPE	V.V. Latyshev, *Inscriptiones Orae Septentrionalis Ponti Euxini* (Petropoli 1885-1916)
Istoricheski Pregled	Historical Review (Sofia).
KSIA	*Kratkie Soobshcheniya Instituta Arkheologii Akademii Nauk SSSR* (Moscow).
L'Emporion	A. Bresson and P. Rouillard, (eds.), *L'Emporion*, Publications du Centre Pierre Paris (URA 991) (Paris 1993).
MEFRA	*Mélanges de l'École française de Rome, Antiquités*.
MIA	*Materiali i Issledovaniya po Arkheologii SSSR* (Moscow).
Moretti, *ISE*	L. Moretti, *Iscrizioni Storiche Ellenistiche*, I-II (Florence 1967, 1976).
Pulpudeva	*Semaines philippopolitaines de l'histoire et de la culture thrace* (Sofia).
RosA	*Rossiyskaya Arkheologiya* - continuation of *SA* (Moscow).
RA	*Revue Archéologique* (Paris).
Rois, Tributs et Paysans	P. Briant, *Rois, Tributs et Paysans. Études sur les formations tributaires du Moyen Orient ancien* (Paris, 1982).
SA	*Sovetskaya Arkheologiya* (Moscow).
Sbornik Kazanluk	M. Chichikova (ed.) *Trakiyskata kultura prez elinisticheskata epoha v Kazanlashkiya kray*, (Kazanluk 1991).
SCIV	*Studii şi cercetari de istorie veche* (Bucharest)
*Syll.*³	W. Dittenberger, *Sylloge Inscriptionum graecarum*, 4 vols. (Leipzig, 1915-1924).
Tskhaltubo 1977	O.D. Lordkipanidze (ed.), *Problems of Greek Colonization of the Northern and Eastern Black Sea Littoral*. Materials of the First All-Union Symposium on the Ancient History of the Black Sea Littoral (Tbilisi 1979) (in Russian).
Tskhaltubo 1979	O.D. Lordkipanidze (ed.), *The Demographic Situation in the Black Sea Littoral in the Period of the Great Greek Colonization*. Materials of the Second All-Union Symposium on the Ancient History of the Black Sea Littoral (Tbilisi 1981) (in Russian).
Tskhaltubo-Vani IV	O.D. Lordkipanidze (ed.), *Local Ethno-political Entities of the Black Sea Area in the 7th - 4th Centuries BC*. Materials of the Fourth All-Union Symposium on the Ancient History of the Black Sea littoral, 1985 (Tbilisi 1988) (in Russian and other languages).
Tskhaltubo-Vani V	O.D. Lordkipanidze (ed.), *The Black Sea Littoral in the 7th to 5th centuries BC: Literary Sources and Archaeology (Problems of Authenticity)* Materials of the Fifth International Symposium on the Ancient History of the Black Sea Littoral, 1987 (Tbilisi 1990) (in Russian and other languages).
VDI	*Vestnik Drevnei Istorii* (Moscow)
ZPE	*Zeitschrift für Papyrologie und Epigraphik*.

Bibliography

Alcock, S.E. 1991: Urban survey and the *polis* of Phlius. *Hesperia* 60, 421-63.

Alcock, S.E. 1994: Breaking up the Hellenistic world, in Morris 1994, 171-190.

Alcock, S.E., Cherry, J.F. and Davis, J.L. 1994: Intensive survey, agricultural practice and the classical landscape of Greece, in Morris 1994, 137-170.

Alekseev, A.Y. 1987a: Scythian chronography of the second half of the 4th century BC. *Arkheologicheskii Sbornik Gosudarstvennogo Ermitazha* 28, 38-51 (in Russian).

Alekseev, A.Y. 1987b: Notes on the chronology of Scythian steppe antiquities of the 4th century BC, *SA* 3. 28-38 (in Russian).

Andrukh, S.I. and Chernov, S.I. 1990: New Scythian sites between the Danube and Dniester. *SA* 2, 149-163 (in Russian).

Archibald, Z.H. 1994: Thracians and Scythians. *CAH* VI[2], 444-475.

Archibald, Z.H. 1998: *The Odrysian Kingdom of Thrace. Orpheus unmasked*, Oxford.

Archibald, Z.H. 2000: Space, Hierarchy and Community in Archaic and Classical Macedonia, Thessaly and Thrace, in Brock and Hodkinson 2000, 212-233.

Archibald, Z.H. (2000-2001): The Odrysian river port near Vetren, Bulgaria, and the Pistiros inscription. *Talanta*, 253-275.

Archibald, Z.H., Davies, J.K., Gabrielsen, V. and Oliver, G. (eds.) 2000: *Hellenistic Economies*, London.

Austin, M.M. 1981: *The Hellenistic World from Alexander to the Roman Conquest. A Selection of Ancient Sources in Translation*, Cambridge.

Barker, G.W. and Hunt, C.O. 1995: Quaternary valley erosion and alluviation in the Biferno Valley, Molise, Italy: The role of tectonics, climate, sea level change and human activity, in Lewin, Macklin and Woodward 1995, 145-157.

Bilde, P., Engberg-Pedersen, T., Hannestad, L. and Randsborg, K. (eds.) 1993: *Centre and Periphery in the Hellenistic World*, Aarhus.

Bintliff, J. and Snodgrass, A. M. 1988: Mediterranean Survey and the city, *Antiquity* 62, 57-71.

Bintliff, J. 1994: in Doukelis, P.N. and Mendoni, L.G. (eds.) *Structures rurales et Sociétés Antiques*, (Paris), 7-15.

Bintliff, J. and Snodgrass, A.M. 1985: The Cambridge/Bradford Boeotia Expedition: the first four years. *Journal of Field Archaeology* 12, 123-161.

Blavatskii, V.D. 1964: *Pantikapei. Ocherki istorii stolitsy Bospora*, Moscow.

Boardman, J. 1967: *Excavations at Chios, 1952-1955. Greek Emporio*, London.

Boffo, L. 1989: Grecità di frontiera: Chersonesos Taurica e i signori del Ponto Eusinio (*SIG*[3] 709). *Athenaeum* 27, 211-259.

Bonev, A. and Alexandrov, G. 1996: *Bagachina. A Late Neolithic-Bronze Age and Thracian cult centre (3rd to 1st millennium BC)*, Montana (in Bulgarian).

Bouzek, J., Domaradzki, M. and Archibald, Z.H. (eds.) 1996: *Pistiros I. Excavations and Studies*, Prague.

Brashinskii, I.B. and Marchenko K. 1980: The Elizavetovka site - an urban type settlement. *SA* 1, 211-18 (in Russian).

Briant, P. 1982: Des Achéménides aux Rois hellénistiques: continuités et ruptures (Bilan et propositions, 1979), in *Rois, Tributs et Paysans*, 291-330.

Bringmann, Kl. 1993: The King as Benefactor: Some Remarks on Ideal Kingship in the Age of Hellenism, in Bulloch, A., Gruen, E.S., Long, A.A. and Stewart, A., (eds.), *Images and Ideologies: Self-Definition in the Hellenistic World*, (Berkley), 7-9.

Bringmann, Kl. and von Steuben, H. (eds.) 1995: *Schenkungen hellenistischer Herrscher an griechische Städte und Heiligtümer*, Teil I, Berlin.

Brock, R. and Hodkinson, S. (eds.) 2000: *Alternatives to Athens. Varieties of political organization and community in ancient Greece*, Oxford.

Bylkova, V.P. 2000: On the cultural traditions in the lower Dnieper region during the Scythian times. *RosA* 2, 26-39 (in Russian).

Carter, J. Coleman, Crawford, M., Lehman, P., Nikolaenko, G. and Trelogan, J. 2000: The *Chora* of Chersonesos in Crimea, Ukraine. *AJA* 104, 707-741.

Cherry, J.F. 1994: Regional Survey in the Aegean: the "New Wave" and after, in Kardulias 1994, 91-112.

Davies, J.K. 1984: Cultural, social and economic features of the Hellenistic world. *CAH* VII Part 1, 257-320.

Davies, J.K. 2000: Hellenistic Economies in the Post-Finley Era, in Archibald *et al.* 2000, 11-62.

Dimitrov, K. 1989: Treasures of autonomous coins, trade relations and infrastructure of Thrace during 4th century BC. *Istoricheski Pregled* 45, 21-35 (in Bulgarian).

Domaradzki, M. 1984: *Keltite na Balkanskiya Poluostrov, IV do I v. pr.n.e.*, Sofia.

Domaradzki, M. 1987: Les données numismatiques et les études de la culture thrace du second Age du Fer. *Numizmatika* (Sofia) 21/4, 4-18 (in Bulgarian).

Domaradzki, M. 1993: Pistiros - centre commercial et politique dans la vallée de Maritza (Thrace). *Archeologia* (Warsaw) 44, 35-57.

Domaradzki, M. 1995: *Emporion Pistiros: Thraco-Greek commercial relations* Pazardjik (in Bulgarian).

Domaradzki, M. 1996: Interim Report on Archaeological Investigations at Vetren - Pistiros, 1988-94. In

Bouzek, Domaradzki and Archibald 1996, 13-34.

Dufkova, M. and Pečirka, J. 1970: Excavation of farms and farmhouses in the *Chora* of Chersonesos in the Crimea. *Eirene* 8, 123-174.

Fialko, E.E. 1995: The Thracian bridle from Oguz Barrow. *RosA* 1, 133-146.

Gaidukevich, V.F. 1971: *Das Bosporanische Reich*, Berlin.

Garnsey, P. 1988: *Famine and Food Supply in the Graeco-Roman World. Responses to Risk and Crisis*, Cambridge.

Gauthier, P. 1985: *Les Cités grecques et leur bienfaiteurs (ive s. av. J.C.) Contribution à l'histoire des institutions*, Paris.

Gauthier, P. 1984: Les cites hellénistiques: épigraphie et histoire des institutions et des régimes politiques, in *Proceedings of the Eighth Epigraphic Congress, Athens, 1982* I, Athens, 82-107.

Gauthier, P. 1993: Les cités hellénistiques, in M.H. Hansen (ed.), *The Ancient Greek City State*, Copenhagen, 211-31.

Gotsev, A. 1997: Characteristics of the settlement system during the Early Iron Age in ancient Thrace. In H. Damgaard Andersen, H.W. Horsnaes and S. Houby-Nielsen (eds.), *Urbanization in the Mediterranean in the Ninth to Sixth centuries BC*, Copenhagen, 407-421.

Hartog, F. 1988: *The Mirror of Herodotus* (Berkeley/Los Angeles, tr. of *Le miroir d'Herodote*, Paris 1980).

Herrmann, P. (ed.) 1997: *Inschriften von Milet* I, Berlin.

Heinen, H. 1996: Statues de Pairisadès I et de ses deux fils érigées sur proposition de Démosthène (Dinarque, *Contre Démosthène* 43), in P. Carlier (ed.), *Le quatrième siècle av. J.C. Approches historiographiques*, Nancy/Paris, 357-368.

Hind, J. 1985: Colonies and ports of trade on the northern shores of the Black Sea - the cases of Olbiopolis and Kremnoi, *Thracia Pontica* II, Yambol, 105-118.

Hind, J. 1992-93: Archaeology of the Greeks and Barbarian Peoples around the Black Sea, 1982-1992. *Archaeological Reports* 39, 82-112.

Hind, J. 1994: The Bosporan Kingdom. *CAH* VI^2, 476-511.

Hind, J. 1998: Megarian Colonisation in the Western Half of the Black Sea (Sister – and Daughter – Cities of Herakleia), in Tsetskhladze 1998b, 131-152.

Horden, P. and Purcell, N. 2000: *The Corrupting Sea. A Study of Mediterranean History*, Oxford.

Ilinskaya, V.A. and Terenozhkin, A.I., 1983: *Scythia in the 7th - 4th centuries BC* Kiev (in Russian).

Jones, A.H.M. 1940: *The Greek City from Alexander to Justinian*, Oxford.

Kardulias, P.N. (ed.) 1994: *Beyond the Site. Regional Studies in the Aegean Area*, University Press of America.

Kitov, G. 1980: Horse harnessing in Thrace, in *Actes du II CIThrac.* I, 295-300 (in Russian).

Kitov, G. 1994a: Thracian tumuli, *Thracia* 10, 39-80 (in Bulgarian).

Kitov, G. 1994b: The Kazanluk Plain: the Valley of the Kings. *Anali* 1, 2-3, 46-76 (in Bulgarian).

Kitov, G. 1996: The Thracian Valley of the Kings in the Region of Kazanluk. *Balkan Studies* 37/1, 5-34.

Kitov, G. and Krasteva, M. 1992-93: A Fourth Century BC Thracian Royal Tomb from the Kazanluk region, Southern Bulgaria. *Talanta* 24/25, 59-75.

Kitov, G. and Krasteva, M. 1994-95: The Thracian Grave and Cult Complex in the Ostrusha Tumulus near Shipka. *Talanta* 26/27, 7-28.

Kolotukhin, V.A. 1985: On the Tauri and the Kizil-Koba culture. *SA* 2, 34-46 (in Russian).

Koshelenko, G.A. et al. (eds.) 1984: *Antichnye goroda Severnogo Prichernomor'ya*, Moscow.

Kruglikova, I.T. 1985: *Agriculture of the Bosporus*, Moscow (in Russian).

Kruglikova, I.T. (ed.) 1980/1982: *Gorgippia. Materials of the Anapa Archaeological Expedition* Krasnodar: I (1980), II (1982) (in Russian).

Kryzhitskii, S.D., Buiskikh, S.B., Burakov, A.V. and Otreshko, V.M. (eds.) 1989: *The Agricultural Environs of Olbia*, Kiev (in Russian).

Kryzhitskii, S.D., Buiskikh, S.B. and Otreshko, V.M. 1990: *Ancient Settlements in the Lower Reaches of the Bug (An Archaeological Map)*, Kiev (in Russian).

Kryzhitskii, S.D. and Krapivina, V.V. 1994: A Quarter Century of Excavations at Olbia Pontica. *ECM/CV* 38 n.s. 13, 181-205.

Kubyshev, A.I., Polin, S.V. and Chernyakov, I.T. 1985: An Early Iron Age Burial on the Ingulets River. *SA* 3, 144-154 (in Russian).

Kuhrt, A. and Sherwin-White, S. (eds.) 1987: *Hellenism in the East. The interaction of Greek and non-Greek civilizations from Syria to Central Asia after Alexander*, London.

Leipunskaya, N.O. 1995: Excavations in the Lower City of Olbia, 1985 1992: Preliminary Results. *ECM/CV* 39 n.s. 14, 23-44.

Lewin, J., Macklin, M.G. and Woodward, J.C. (eds.) 1995: *Mediterranean Quaternary River Environments*, Rotterdam.

Lordkipanidzé, O. and Lévêque, P. (eds.) 1990: *Le Pont Euxin vu par les Grecs. Source ecrites et archeologie*, Besançon.

Marchenko, K. 1980: A model of the Greek colonisation of the Lower Bug region. *VDI* 1, 131-43 (in Russian).

Marchenko, K. 1982: Concerning the so-called 'suburb' of Olbia. *VDI* 3, 126-36 (in Russian).

Marchenko, K. 1986: Die Siedlung von Elizavetovka - ein griechisch-barbarisches Emporion im Dondelta.

Klio 68, 377-398.
Marchenko, K. 1996: The third stabilisation in the northern Pontic area in Antiquity. *RosA* 2, 70-80 (in Russian).
Marchenko, K. and Vinogradov, Y.G. 1989: The Scythian period in the northern Black Sea region (750-250BC). *Antiquity* 63, 803-813.
Maslennikov, A.A. 1989: On the Typology of Rural Settlements in Bosporus. *SA* 2, 66-77.
Melyukova, A.I. 1979: *Scythia and the Thracian World*, Moscow (in Russian).
Melyukova, A.I. 1995: The new data about the Scythians and Thracians' relations in the 4th - 3rd centuries BC. *RosA* 1, 28-35 (in Russian).
Mihailov, G. 1983: Les inscriptions comme source de l'histoire thrace. *Pulpudeva* 4, 21-26.
Morris, I. (ed.) 1994: *Classical Greece. Ancient histories and modern ideologies,* Cambridge.
Mozolevskii, B.N. 1973: Scythian burials at Nagornoe, near Ordjonikidze, Dnepropetrovsk region. *Skifskie Drevnosti*, Kiev, 187-234 (in Russian).
Mozolevskii, B.N. 1975: Thracian harness from Homina Mogila. *Studia Thracica* I, 166-178 (in Russian).
Mozolevskii, B.N. 1979: Scythian barrows near Ordjonikidze, Dnepropetrovsk region (excavations 1972-75), in *Skifiya i Kavkaz*, Kiev, 70-154 (in Russian).
Murzin, V.Y. 1979: On cavalry harnessing methods in the Scythian Age, in *Skifiya i Kavkaz*, Kiev, 155-167 (in Russian).
Nikulitse, I.T. 1987: *The northern Thracians in the 6th - 1st centuries BC*, Kishinyev (in Russian).
Okhotnikov, S.B. 1983: *An Archaeological Map of the Reaches of the Lower Dniester in ancient times (6th - 3rd century BC),* Kiev (in Russian).
Onaiko, N.A. 1966: *Ancient Imports in the Dnieper and Bug estuaries, 7th - 5th centuries BC,* Moscow (in Russian).
Ostroverkhov, A.S. 1980: The periods and character of Greco-Scythian economic relations in the Dnieper and Bug estuaries. In *Investigations on the archaeology of the south-western Ukraine*, Kiev, 23-39 (in Russian).
Ostroverkhov, A.S. 1981: Olbia and the trading routes of the Scythians, in *Ancient Monuments of the North Western Black Sea Littoral*, Kiev, 84-94 (in Russian).
Parkins, H. and Smith, C. (eds.) 1998: *Trade, Traders and the Ancient City*, London.
Paromov, Y.M. 1986: A Survey of the archaeological remains in the Taman peninsula in 1981-3. *KSIA* 188, 69-73 (in Russian).
Pippidi, D.M. 1962a: *Epigraphische Beiträge zur Geschichte Histrias in hellenistischer und römischer Zeit,* Berlin.
Pippidi, D.M. 1962b: Histria und Kallatis im 3. Und 2Jh. V.u.Z. In Pippidi 1962a, 11-34 (originally published in *SCIV* 4 (1953) 487-512, abridged version. *Klio* 37 (1959) 119-134).
Pippidi, D.M., 1962c: Die Agrarverhältnisse in den griechischen Städten der Dobruscha in vorrömischer Zeit. In Pippidi 1962a, 60-74 (also reproduced in Irmscher, J. and Schelow, D.B. (eds.), *Griechische Städte und einheimische Völker der Schwarzmeergebietes*, Berlin 1961).
Pippidi, D.M 1962d: Die Beziehungen Histrias zu den Geten im 3.Jh.v.u.Z. In Pippidi 1962a, 75-88 (=*SCIV* 11 (1960) 39-54).
Pippidi, D.M. 1965: Les colonies grecques de Scythie Mineure à l'époque hellénistique. *Balkan Studies* 6, 95-118.
Pippidi, D.M. 1975a: *Scythica Minora*, Bucharest.
Pippidi, D.M. 1975b: III. Istros et les Gètes au IIe siècle. Observations sur le decret en l'honneur d'Agathoclès, fils d'Antiphilos, in Pippidi 1975a, 31-55.
Pippidi, D.M. 1975c: Le problème de la main d'oeuvre agricole dans les colonies grecques de la mer Noire in: Pippidi 1975a, 65-81 (also reproduced in Finley, M.I. (ed.), *Problèmes de la terre en Grèce ancienne*, Paris 1973, 63-82).
Pippidi, D.M. and Popescu, E.M. 1959: Les relations d'Istros et d'Apollonie du Pont à l'époque hellénistique. *Dacia* n.s. 3, 235-258.
Reeder, E.D. (ed.) 1999: *Scythian Gold. Treasures from Ancient Ukraine*, New York.
Rhodes, P. J. 1993: Demes, Cities and Leagues. In Hansen, M.H. (ed.), *The Ancient Greek City State*, Copenhagen, 161-182.
Rolle, R. 1979: *Totenkult der Skythen I. Das Steppengebiet*, Berlin/ New York.
Rolle, R. 1985: Der griechische Handel der Antike zu den osteuropäischen Reiternomaden aufgrund archäologischer Zeugnisse, in Duwel, K., Jankuhn, H., Siems, H. and Timpe, D. (eds.), *Untersuchungen zu Handel und Verkehr der vor- und frühgeschichtlichen Zeit in mittel und Nordeuropa* I, Göttingen, 460-490.
Rolle, R. 1989: *The World of the Scythians*, London.
Rostovtzeff, M.I. 1922: *Iranians and Greeks in South Russia*, Oxford.
Rostovtzeff, M.I. 1930: The Bosporan kingdom. *CAH* VIII[1], 561-589.
Rostovtzeff, M.I. 1931: *Skythien und der Bosporus*, Berlin.
Ruban, V.V. 1985: Some features of the historical development of the Olbia *chora* in the fourth and third centuries BC. *VDI* 1, 26-46 (in Russian).
Sallares, R. 1991: *The Ecology of the Ancient Greek World*, London.
Saprykin, S.J. 1994: *Ancient Farms and Land-Plots on the Khora of Khersonesos, Taurike. Research in the Herakleian peninsula, 1974 – 1990*, Amsterdam.
Saprykin, S.J. 1996: *Emporion Taurikon* and Scythian Harbour of Kalos Limen on ceramic stamps of

Tauric Chersonesus. *REA* 98 (3-4), 357-370.
Shaw, B. 1982/83: Eaters of flesh, drinkers of milk: the ancient Mediterranean ideology of the pastoral nomad. *Ancient Society* 13/14, 5-31.
Shcheglov, A.N. 1980: Utilisation de la photographie aerienne dans l'étude du cadastre de Chersonesos Taurique. *DHA* 6, 59-72.
Shcheglov, A.N. 1985: On Greco-barbarian relations on the periphery of the Hellenistic world, in Lordkipanidze, O. (ed.), *Prichernomor'ye v epokhu ellinizma*, Tbilisi, 185-198 (in Russian).
Shcheglov, A.N. 1986: The process and nature of the territorial expansion of Chersonesus in the 4th century BC. In *The civic commune in the Antique period*, Leningrad, 152-176 (in Russian).
Shcheglov, A.N. 1990: Le commerce du blé dans le Pont septentrional (2ième moitié du VII ème - Vème s.), in Lordkipanidzé and Lévêque 1990, 141-159.
Shchukin, M.B. 1995: The Celts in Eastern Europe. *Oxford Journal of Archaeology* 14, 201-27.
Shelov-Kovedyaev, F.V. 1985: History of the Bosporus in the 6th - 4th centuries BC. *The Most Ancient States in the territory of the USSR*, 8, 3-187 (in Russian).
Sherwin-White, S. and Kuhrt, A. 1993: *From Samarkhand to Sardis. A new approach to the Seleucid Empire*, London.
Shipley, G. 1993: World-Systems Analysis and the "Hellenistic" World, in Bilde *et al.* 1993, 271-284.
Shipley, G. 2000: *The Greek World after Alexander, 323-30 BC*, London.
Shramko, B.A. and Yanushevich, Z.V. 1985: Scythian agricultural plants. *SA* 2, 47-63 (in Russian).
Solomonik, E.I. 1987: Two ancient letters from Crimea. *VDI* 3, 114-131 (in Russian).
Solovyov, S. L. 1999: *Ancient Berezan. The Architecture, History and Culture of the First Greek Colony in the Northern Black Sea*, Leiden/Boston/Cologne.
Sulimirski, T. and Taylor, T. 1991: The Scythians. *CAH*² III.2, 547-590.
Taylor, T. 1994: Thracians, Scythians and Dacians, 800 BC – AD 300. In Cunliffe, B. (ed.), *The Oxford Illustrated Prehistory of European Society*, Oxford, 373-410.
Tsalkin, V.I. 1960: The domesticated and wild animals of the northern Black Sea region in the Early Iron Age. *MIA* 53, 7-109 (in Russian).
Tsalkin, V.I. 1966: The early animal husbandry of the tribes of eastern Europe and Central Asia. *MIA* 135, 11-12, 93-97 (in Russian).
Tsetskhladze, G.R. 1998a: Trade on the Black Sea in the archaic and classical periods: some observations, in Parkins and Smith 1998, 52-74.

Tsetskhladze, G.R. (ed.) 1998b: *The Greek Colonisation of the Black Sea Area. Historical Interpretations of Archaeology*, Stuttgart.
van Andel, T., Gallis, K. and Toufexis, G. 1995: Early Neolithic farming in a Thessalian river landscape, in Lewin, Macklin and Woodward 1995,131-143.
Vasilev, V. 1978 (1980): Einige charakteristische und traditionelle Methoden in der thrakischen Toreutik. *Pulpudeva* 3, 149-164.
Velkov, V. and Domaradzka, L. 1994: Kotys I (383/2 - 359 av.J.C.) et l'*emporion* Pistiros de Thrace. *BCH* 118, 1-15.
Vinogradov, Y.G. 1979: Griechische Epigraphik und Geschichte des nördlichen Pontusgebietes, in *Actes du VIIe Congrès International de l'épigraphie grecque et latine, Constanza 1977*, Bucharest/Paris, 293-316.
Vinogradov, Y. G. 1980: Die historische Entwicklung der Poleis der nördlichen Schwarzmeergebietes im 5 Jahrht. v. Chr. *Chiron* 10, 63-100.
Vinogradov, Y.G. 1983: The *polis* in the northern Black Sea region, in *Antichnaya Gretsya* I, (Moscow), 366-420 (in Russian).
Vinogradov, Y.G. 1987: Der Pontos Euxeinos als politische, ökonomische und kulturelle Einheit und die Epigraphik. In Fol, Al. (ed.), *IXème Congrès d'épigraphie grecque et latine, Acta Centri Historiae, Terra Antiqua Balcanica* II, Sofia, 9-77.
Vinogradov, Y.G., 1989: *The political history of the polis of Olbia in the 7th - 1st centuries BC. A historico-epigraphic investigation*, Moscow (in Russian).
Vinogradov, Y., Domanskii, I. and Marchenko, K. 1990: Sources écrites et archéologiques du Pont nord-ouest. Analyse comparative. In Lordkipanidze and Lévêque 1990, 121-139.
Vinogradov, Y.G. and Kryzickij, S.D. 1995: *Olbia. Eine Altgriechische Stadt im nördlichen Schwarzmeerraum*, Leiden/Boston/Cologne.
Vinogradov, Y.G. and Marchenko, K. 1989: Das nördliche Schwarzmeergebiet in der skythischen Epoche. *Klio* 71, 539-549.
Walbank, F.W. 1981: *The Hellenistic World*, Glasgow.
Wąsowicz, A. 1972: Traces de lotissements anciens en Crimée. *MEFRA* 84/1, 199-210.
Wąsowicz, A. 1975: *Olbia Pontique et son territoire. L'amènagement de l'espace*, Besançon.
Welskopf, E.C. (ed.) 1974: *Hellenische Poleis II. Krise - Wandlung – Wirkung*, Berlin.
Werner, R. 1955: Die Dynastie der Spartokiden. *Historia* 4, 412-444.
Whittaker, C.R. (ed.) 1988: *Pastoral economies in classical antiquity*, Cambridge.
Whitby, M. 1998: The grain trade of Athens in the fourth century BC, in Parkins and Smith 1998, 102-128.

Yanushevich, Z.V. 1981: Die kulturpflanzen Skythiens. *Zeitschrift für Archäologie* 15, 87-96.

Yanushevich, Z.V. 1989: in Harris, D.R. and Hillman, G.C. (eds.), *Foraging and Farming: the evolution of plant exploitation*, London, 607-619.

Yanushevich, Z.V. and Nikolaenko, G.M. 1979: Fossil remains of cultivated plants in the ancient Tauric Chersonese. In Körber-Grohne, U. (ed.), *Festschrift for Maria Hopf*, Mainz, 115-134.

Yourukova, Y. and Domaradzki, M. 1990: Nouvel centre de la culture thrace - Vetren la rég. de Pazardgik (notes préliminaires). *Numizmatika* (Sofia) 24/3, 3-18 (in Bulgarian).

The myths of Panticapaeum: construction of colonial origins in the Black Sea region

David Braund

The purpose of this paper is to explore the colonial traditions that can be traced among the cities of the Black Sea region. Its primary concern is not with the traditions that are usually deemed historical, such as those of Milesian settlement, though these will arise. Rather, its concern is with the myths which were central to the developing identities of the communities of the region, particularly the city of Panticapaeum. In that sense this paper is both a study of the colonial process in the Black Sea region and an attempted exegesis of what may be termed the 'mythical landscape' there. We will conclude with a consideration of the responses to the Hellenic claims of these Black Sea cities by Greeks of the Mediterranean.

The foundation of Panticapaeum is usually ascribed to Miletus (Ehrhardt 1988). However, our fullest account is quite different: here we find not Milesians but a son of Aeetes:

> It was settled by a son of Aietes, who had taken the place from Agaëtes the king of the Scythians and who named the city from the River Panticapes which flows beside it.
>
> (Steph. Byz. *s.v.* Panticapaeum)

It is usual to dismiss the story as false, being both mythical and late. However, we may benefit by proceeding beyond the basic polarity of truth and falsehood in order to understand the story rather better.

First, some context. It is well-known that the origins of cities were commonly rooted in myths. The city of Athens offers a ready example, for in its case we have more information than usual. N. Loraux, in particular, has shown how the mythical origins and proto-history of Athens were developed and used as the sinews of its social, political and religious life (Loraux 1986). The process is evident also in Athenian overseas ambitions, for example in the case of Delos. In the 4th century BC Hyperides' *Delian Speech* evidently presented the Athenian claim to have been colonists of Delos, while a century earlier Cecrops' son, Erysichthon, could be credited with the construction of the first temple of Apollo there (Parker 1996, 224 for full documentation). This case amply illustrates the dynamic interaction of civic self-image, foundation myth, religion and inter-state relations.

Moreover, the process can also be traced in Greek dealings with non-Greeks. In the 420s BC, when dealing with the Odrysian rulers of Thrace, some at least in the Athenian democracy seem to have exploited the mythical marriage of Thracian Tereus and Athenian Procne to validate the link (Parker 1996, 174-5; Mitchell 1997, 137-9). In this context, it is to be observed that even the hard-headed Thucydides, for all his criticisms of the relevance of that marriage, accepts the principle that such a marriage could be an historical reality and could have a direct bearing on inter-state relations (Thuc. 2. 29).

The Aietes whose son founded Panticapaeum must surely be the Aietes who ruled in Colchis. Throughout antiquity, the name was redolent of Colchis: Xenophon mentions a descendant (literally, grandson) of Aietes ruling there in about 400 BC (Anab. 5. 6. 37), Strabo reports the popularity of the name there down to his day (1. 2. 39, pp. 45-6: his family link with Colchis makes his testimony particularly valuable) and in the 6th century AD Agathias attributes an anti-Byzantine speech to an Aietes of Colchis (alias Lazike: Agathias, 3. 8. 7-9). A speech against Greeks was appopriate enough in the mouth of a man named Aietes. For of course King Aietes appears regularly in Argonautic myth as the keeper of the Golden Fleece and consequently the enemy of Jason and his fellow Greeks. Moreover, his daughter Medea is credited (together with much else that might seem undesirable to a Greek audience) with being the ancestress of the Persians. Indeed, when Herodotus opens his *Histories*, he claims that the Persians regarded Jason's removal of Medea from Colchis as the second wrong which they suffered at the hands of the Greeks (Hdt. 1. 1). In similar vein Homer gives the name of Aietes' mother as Perses (*Od.* 10. 135-139, with Braund 1994, 9 and 35-36).

As such, Aietes' son might seem a strange choice as founder of Panticapaeum. Against the weight of the fairly homogeneous tradition there seems small reason in this context to insist upon the Corinthian tradition that Aietes was once its ruler (Paus. 2. 3. 10) and thereby to claim Greekness for his son, the founder of Panticapaeum. That Aietes was the son of Helius (Homer *Od.* 10. 138) might conceivably have been of some significance, insofar as the cult of Apollo the Healer predominated at Panticapaeum (e.g. *CIRB* 6, 10, 25 etc.). At the same time, political and economic relations with Colchis might help to explain the prominence of Aietes' son at Panticapaeum, but, although there were such connections, they were never anything like important enough to account for his role as founder (Braund 1994). Rather than search in vain for other explanations, we can only acknowledge the Persian aspects of Aietes' son. Significantly, it has often been remarked that the identity of Panticapaeum was not only Greek but also Iranian (the standard work remains Gaidukevich 1971). For the city of Panticapaeum a founder was appropriate who was part of Greek myth but also from the Iranian world and who, as the product of Colchis (as it seems), was at home in the Black Sea world.

At the same time, Aietes' son had taken the site from a Scythian king, though Stephanus' language allows no inference about the manner in which he took it, whether by force or by agreement. Certainly, Aietes could be imagined as the father-in-law of a Scythian king (Diod. 4. 45. 4 and 47. 5). In either case, a role for the Scythian king in the foundation-story of Panticapaeum would suit the changing relations between the city and Scythians. Meanwhile, there was also a tradition that Aietes' brother (tellingly, named Perses) had ruled in the Crimea, as also Perses' daughter Circe (Diod. 4. 45). Further afield, the Sarmatians could be regarded as Aietes' descendants through his grandson, named (tellingly, again) Medus (Pliny *NH* 6. 19).

Stephanus does not give the name of Aietes' son, whether or not he found it in his sources. The name was not needed to explain the name Panticapaeum, which is traced explicitly to a river. Yet the absence of a name suggests that Aietes' only well-known son may be excluded, for if the founder had been Apsyrtus, he would surely have been named as such. In any case, it would be difficult to accommodate the foundation in the story of Apsyrtus, killed young. More broadly, the Colchian chase of the Argonauts across the Black Sea and far beyond seems an unlikely context for the foundation. Where foundations did arise as a result of that chase, they came much later, in the Adriatic, and were explained as the result of Colchian weariness and fear of the consquences of return (Braund 1994, 34; also on Tomi - a name, not a foundation). It is tempting to find some resonance of the Panticapaeum tradition in the story that Phrixus was bequeathed a land by a Scythian king (Diod. 4. 47. 5). Phrixus was not Aietes' son, but he was often imagined as his son-in-law. We may be fairly confident that, as with Apsyrtus, Stephanus (and his sources) would have named Phrixus if he had been reckoned the founder. Yet the Phrixus-story shows a possibility: was it imagined that a Scythian king had bequeathed the site of Panticapaeum to Aietes' son? If so, there would be substantial implications for the self-image of Panticapaeum. For, in any case, the city seems to have projected a measure of Scythianness in its identity in that its coinage of the 4th century BC shows a Scythian bow and arrow (Price 1993, pl. 34), a tendency which Dougherty terms 'native appropriation' (Dougherty 1993, 136-56).

Elsewhere in the Bosporan kingdom lay Kutaia, south along the coast from Panticapaeum. Its name was redolent of Colchis and its homonym there, which may be located with confidence at modern Kutaisi, though excavation there remains inchoate (*schol*. Ap. Rhod. 2. 399, with Braund 1994, 34). Procopius indicates the existence of some debate over the history of Colchian Kutaia (or Kotiaion, as he has it):

> Others say that the place became a city in ancient times and was called Kotiaion; and that Aietes sprang from there...
> (*Wars*, 8. 14. 49)

We are left to wonder whether Bosporan Kutaia claimed any link with its Colchian counterpart, with Aietes, or with Aietes' son.

In most cases the details escape us, but there is no doubt that cities of the Black Sea region, as elsewhere in the Greek world, developed their own myths of origin, replete with the activities of gods and heroes. I. Malkin, in particular, has shed valuable light on the broad phenomenon, not least with regard to Pontic Sinope, on which Strabo observes:

> Lucullus...seized Autolycus (a statue of Sthenis), whom they thought their founder and honoured as a god; there was also his oracle. He seems to have been one of those who sailed with Jason and took possession of this place. Then later Milesians, seeing the quality of the place and the weakness of its inhabitants, appropriated it and sent settlers.
>
> (Strabo 12. 3. 11, with Malkin 1987, 207-208)

Strabo's view of Greek settlement at Sinope presents a two-stage process, which entails an interesting disjunction between the oikist and Milesian settlement. Malkin may well be right to see Autolycus' role as a convenient validation for Milesian settlement (1987, 208). Indeed, Heracles offered further precedent for Greek settlers. According to the *Tabula Albana*, Heracles crossed from Scythia, expelled the Amazons from Sinope and installed Greek settlers there (*FGH* 40 F.1a). Apparently in the same tradition, Valerius Flaccus reports Autolycus' presence at Sinope, with his brothers, as the aftermath of an expedition in the entourage of Heracles (5. 113-115; *cf*. Ap. Rhod. 2. 955). They too could be said to have crossed (Ps.-Scymnus 990; Plut. *Luc*. 23 has them shipwrecked, appropriately for the Black Sea). However, it seems that Sinope made more of Autolycus than of Heracles: the former was more readily appropriated perhaps than the ever-roving Heracles, who was claimed with particular vigour along the coast at Heracleia Pontica (Jonnes and Ameling 1994). Meanwhile, Sinope had to accommodate further founding personnel, notably Koos and Kretines (or Kretines of Kos). There was also a nymph Sinope, whose role is unclear but may have been imagined after the fashion of the nymph Kurene in the foundation of the city of her name (Kacharava and Kvirkvelia 1991, 239-42; Hind 1988). Her head appears often on the city's coinage (Price 1993, nos.1374-1542 *passim*). The existence of multiple and variant traditions of foundation is paralleled at Heracleia Pontica and elsewhere (Burstein 1976, 13-14, and see below on Trapezus). Different contexts and perspectives doubtless generated and encouraged such variety. For example, Burstein observes the absence of any mention of the tradition of the Milesian foundation of Heracleia Pontica in the extant fragments of its own historians (Burstein 1976, 13-15, also rejecting the historicity of Milesian foundation). We are left to wonder whether that absence is a matter of chance or a deliberate choice at Heracleia, preferring to stress its settlement from Megara (and Boeotia).

However, the particular interest of Strabo's passage on Sinope is that it gives some indication of the central role of foundation in the civic ritual of a Black Sea city. The key point is that written accounts of civic foundations may and sometimes do (often, I suspect) reflect the traditions fostered and developed within the founded cities themselves. The myth of Autolycus lay at the very heart of Sinope's communal ritual and religious identity. Accordingly, we should infer a local historical tradition at Sinope which embraced the myth and ritual and doubtless elaborated civic tradition in the communal interest. Although the details remain unclear, it is evident that the elaboration of Sinope's foundation proceeded a long way and it seems reasonable to locate much of the momentum for such elaboration in the city itself.

Further, since the identity of the city is so much at stake in these traditions, we are probably right to expect the maximum exploitation of the city's name. For that reason there is a considerable appeal in the notion that Pan was central to the advertised identity of Panticapaeum and possibly venerated as such there. A Pan-like head on its coinage of the 4th century BC has encouraged the view. On the whole, scholarly opinion now seems inclined to reject that interpretation of the head: D. Shelov authoritatively deems it no more than the head of a satyr, in both bearded or unbearded form (Shelov 1978, 217-23; *cf.* Ehrhardt 1988, 484, no. 977). After all a similar head appears on the coinage of Phanagoria, across the straits from Panticapaeum (Shelov 1978, 230). And it must be acknowledged that there is no trace of a cult of Pan in the numerous inscriptions of the city. However, Price has recently re-asserted the identification of the head as Pan (Price 1993, nos. 855-934, *passim*; *cf.* Roscher, *s.v.* Pan, cols. 1429-30, dismissing objections; an *LIMC* supplement containing Pan is awaited). And his judgment seems to be supported by a *proxenia* decree of the 4th century BC from Cyzicus for a citizen of Panticapaeum: the stone is dominated by a Pan-like bust in a concave medallion over the inscription (Pasinli 1989, 48, no. 43). Certainly, the first three letters of the city's name, Pan, often (though not always) appear isolated on the coinage of Panticapaeum. And while the image of Pan can readily be explained, the prominence of a satyr who is not Pan would remain a conundrum.

At the very least, the image could no doubt be understood as Pan when the occasion arose, as when the Bosporan king was engaged with the Arcadians. They honoured him in an inscription, of which only the opening lines survive:

> Resolved by the Arcadians, [to honour] Leucon, son of Satyrus, of Panticapaeum[....

(*CIRB* 37)

It is worth observing that Leucon I is here referred to (unusually) as a Panticapaean. The particular deity of the Arcadians was Pan: were they oblivious to the echo of his name in the city? If, as seems most likely, the Arcadians derived grain from Panticapaeum, they may well have chosen to interpret the name of their civic benefactor in terms of the Gardens (Cepoi/ Dor. Capoi) of Pan, for all the awkwardness of the Greek. After all, Cyzicus seems to have done as much in the proxenia decree, also in the 4th century.

We happen to know of a scarcely more plausible link between Arcadia and the Black Sea region. Pausanias states that the citizens of Arcadian Trapezus did not wish to participate in the foundation of Megalopolis in 370 BC. He adds that, in order to escape the wrath of their fellow Arcadians, they fled to the city of Pontic Trapezus. They were accepted, says Pausanias, because they came from the latter's mother-city. In this way Pausanias presents a story of foundation which made Arcadian Trapezus the mother-city of Pontic Trapezus (Paus. 8. 27. 6). Other extant sources indicate its foundation from Sinope (Kacharava and Kvirkvelia 1991, 282-3). It is therefore tempting to suppose that the story was a late invention, as it may indeed be (there is no sign of it, for example, in Xenophon's *Anabasis*). However, whatever its novelty, Pausanias' story might serve to account for the notoriously early Eusebian date for the foundation of Trapezus (756 BC), which places it earlier than the foundation of Sinope (Hind 1988 is excellent on the problem). For Pausanias gives no clue as to the imagined date of Trapezus' foundation from Arcadia: in principle it may well have been supposed as earlier than the foundation from Sinope. As with Sinope, Trapezus may well have had a tradition of foundation which encompassed several stages.

Be that as it may, Pausanias' story indicates that there is no great difficulty in the suggestion that Pan may have been accorded a role in the foundation of Panticapaeum. However, Stephanus stresses instead the relevance of the name of the River Panticapes (Pan could be linked with rivers: Wiseman 1998, 60-3). We may compare the river Borysthenes, which gave its name to the city that was also known as Olbia (Hdt. 4. 53, though Olbia lay on the River Bug, usually identified as the River Hypanis). The Borysthenes seems to have had a cult at Olbia, as rivers often did, there apparently as Hypanis-Borysthenes (*SEG* XXX 913, about 400 BC). The river deity on the coinage of the city is presumably Borysthenes (Price 1993, nos.

451-533 and 954, making the identification), rather as the coinage of Istrus presents an image of the Danube, alias the homonymous Istrus (Price 1993, no. 260; *cf.* Alexandrescu 1990, 50-1). Herodotus relates that the Scythians traced their origins to the union of Zeus and a daughter of Borysthenes (4. 5. 1). Rivers were imagined as prolific in their generation of children: their daughters were nymphs. Indeed, an old tradition mentions a nymph Borysthenis, though as a daughter of Apollo (Eumelus fg. 17, Kinkel). At the same time, rivers were readily imagined as the paternalist protectors and nourishers of the peoples who lived by them (Braund 1996, ch.1). Did the River Panticapes provide only a name for the city or was there a myth whereby the River Panticapes took an active or advisory role in the settlement of Panticapaeum, perhaps assisting Aietes' son? We may recall father Tiber's role in the foundation of Rome (Virg. *Aeneid* 8. 31-101).

There is certainly scope for a nymph close to the south at the city of Nymphaeum, whose name is highly suggestive. Indeed, the female head on the coinage of Nymphaeum seems to be a depiction of the nymph, whether or not she is a daughter of the River Panticapes (Shelov 1978, 20; Price 1993, nos. 834-835). We should note the nymphs at Sinope and elsehere, for example at Cyrene (on which, see most recently, Marshall 1998). In the Black Sea region as elsewhere, the colonial landscape was a mythical and ritual landscape (Dougherty 1993). Was the nymph of Nymphaeum a daughter of the River Panticapes? Is the Pan (or satyr) depicted on the coins of Panticapaeum part of a myth (an amorous myth?) involving that nymph or Nymphaeum (on Pan and nymphs, Roscher, *s.v.* Pan, esp. cols.1421-6; *cf.* Plut. *Sulla* 27)?

Place-names must be interrogated, not in etymological quest for positivist realities, but as a guide to the myths of their creation. For example, the city of Cepoi, 'The Gardens', across the straits from Panticapaeum is probably to be understood as the Gardens of a deity. Neighbouring Aphrodite, whose major cult-centre lay close by, would be an obvious candidate, though of course not the only one (Strabo 11. 2. 10, p. 495). Several place-names are redolent of Achilles, whose cult was of the first importance in the north of the Black Sea region, not least on the island of Leuke. The Race-course of Achilles is attested from the 5th century BC (Hdt. 4. 55; 76. 4; *cf.* Eur. *I.T.* 436-438), while a settlement named Achilleum seems to have been occupied from the Hellenistic period, with a shrine of Achilles (Strabo 11. 2. 6; Kacharava and Kvirkvelia 1991, 37-38). Although there seems no direct evidence of Achilles' role in Greek settlement of the region, it is hard to believe that no communities assigned him a role, even beyond his cult on Leuke. It must be stressed that we can see only the merest tip of the iceberg of myth generated in the region. What are we to make, for instance, of Cerberion (Plin. *NH* 6.18; *cf.* Hesychius *s.v.* Cerberioi)? it seems hard to avoid an association with Cerberus, the canine guardian of the underworld. The precise nature of that association is beyond our knowledge, but one possibility must be that Heracles somehow brought him here in the course of his mythical seizure of the dog from Hades: Strabo shows Heracles close by with Aphrodite (11. 2. 10). It is perhaps worth observing the appearance of Heracles on the coinage of the nearby Sindians (Shelov 1978, 28-30. The ant on the coinage of Myrmecium seems to play on the multiple meanings of the place-name: Shelov 1978, 19-20; Price 1993, pl. 32).

We would probably know much more if we had the work of Polemo of Ilion. Around 200 BC he composed a work entitled *Foundations of cities in the Black Sea*, which is unfortunately lost but which has been plausibly taken to have been a significant influence upon later writers on the region (Hind 1988, 210). But of course there were so many others, not least within the Black Sea region, advancing their own local traditions. In Heracleia Pontica there developed a strong tradition of mythography and historical writing, about which we have significant knowledge: for example, there are extant fragments of Herodorus' 17 books on the exploits of Heracles, his city's eponymous divine founder. There can be little doubt that Herodorus took particular care to deal with Heracles' activities in the Black Sea region and that his approach was patriotic (Desideri 1991).

The civic significance of such writing is illustrated by the chance survival of an honorific inscription from the city of Chersonesus, founded in the south-west Crimea from Heracleia Pontica, perhaps around 422 BC (Burstein 1976, 34, but the argument for dating is not strong). The honorand is a historian actively engaged in local history; he seems to be a citizen of Chersonesus, for no other civic affiliation is indicated:

> [Heracl?]idas son of Parmenon spoke: Since Syriscus, son of Heraclidas, carefully composed and read out (his work on) the epiphanies of (the) Maiden and discoursed upon [events concerning?] the kings of Bosporus and inquired into former [acts of philanthropy towards?] the cities suitably for the People, that he should receive concordant honours. It was resolved by the Council and the People to praise him for these things and the summnamones should garland him with a gold crown at the Dionysia upon the 21st day and that the (following) announcement be made: "The People garlands Syriscus, son of Heraclidas, because he wrote about the epiphanies of the Maiden and inquired into former [acts of philanthropy?] towards the cities and the kings, truly and suitably for the People". And that the summnamones should write the decree on a stone stele and place it in the [fore?]temple of the Maiden. And that the treasurer of the sacred funds

should provide for the consequent expense in accordance with what has been decided. Resolved by the Council and People...

(IOSPEI² 344, with minor adjustments. On *summnamones*, see Burstein 1976, 20)

As Chaniotis observes (1988, 300), the precise nature of Syriscus' historical work remains unclear, as does Chersonite historiography in general (see *SA* 1987 (1), 48-57 on the possible derivation of the Byzantine legend of Gykia from a much earlier Chersonite tradition, perhaps of the 1st century BC). Evidently there was a work on manifestations of the Maiden, but the inscription does not show the extent to which she was involved (if at all) in matters concerning the Bosporan kings and the cities, perhaps because it is fragmentary. Syriscus' historical work was both a civic and a ritual matter, as local historical writing very often was (Chaniotis 1988, 164). The cult of the Maiden (Parthenos) was central to the civic life and identity of ancient Chersonesus. In particular, her cult was mentioned in Herodotus' *Histories*, which soon became a canonical text (4. 103). Moreover, it offered a potential link with Athens, through Halai Araphenides and Brauron, as portrayed in Euripides' *Iphigenia among the Taurians*. Although the city seems to have been a 5th century foundation, the cult of the Maiden, once appropriated, gave it a greater antiquity and a place in broader Greek myth and history. The importance of her cult for Chersonesus is illustrated amply by the predominance of her image on the coins of the city - whether only her head or her whole image, kneeling, seated or slaying a stag (Price 1993, nos. 706-832, *passim*).

We may suppose with some confidence that among the epiphanies of the Maiden treated by Syriscus, there was at least one associated with the foundation of the city. The Maiden (alias Artemis Tauropolos, Diod. 4. 44. 7) was renowned for her hatred of Greeks, who were sacrificed to her. The creation of a Greek city at Chersonesus, embracing and promoting her cult as its own, must have entailed her appeasement and conciliation with Greeks. Strabo interprets the Greek settlement of the Black Sea at large as a civilising process, rendering the Inhospitable Sea (*Axenos*) an hospitable one (*Euxeinos*) (7. 3. 6). Accordingly, an Aristotelian tradition preserved by Heraclides Lembus presents the foundation of the city of Phasis as the replacement of man-flaying Heniochi with kindly Milesians (Braund 1994, 75-76, 96). The Heniochi, like the Taurians, were imagined as preying in particular upon victims of shipwreck. The foundation of Chersonesus seems to have been envisaged as a similar process of the replacement of barbarian cruelty with Greek civilization, with the Maiden in a central role.

Herodotus offers further insight into local historical traditions on the north coast of the Black Sea. For he lists competing versions of the origins of the Scythians. The Scythians' own version (as Herodotus claims) traced their origin to the union of Zeus and a daughter of the river Borysthenes. They produced Targitaus, who had three sons, who were each progenitors of a section of the Scythians, whose hierarchy they also established (Hdt. 4. 5-7). The union of Zeus and the nymph seems a rather Greek theme, even allowing that Zeus represents a Scythian deity, so that we may wonder whether Herodotus' Scythian sources had been influenced by Hellenic culture (for he did not travel far from the colonized coast, it seems), whether they presented their myth in a Greek fashion for Herodotus' benefit, or whether Herodotus has himself created so Greek an impression, not necessarily by design.

Herodotus proceeds to present another, substantially different version of Scythian origins, which he attributes to 'the Greeks inhabiting the Pontus' (4. 8. 1). It is worth pausing to observe the implications of the attribution for local myth-making and historiographical activity in the Greek cities of the Black Sea. For the attribution offers broad confirmation of the arguments advanced above: the cities of the region created their own traditions to explain their existence, their environment and their neighbours. For example, we happen to know of a Sosicrates of Phanagoria, who wrote a *Catalogue of Men*, though we know nothing about the work beyond its title (Athenaeus 13. 598b: there seems no reason to imagine an error of author or copyist): it might be a work in a Hesiodic tradition (*cf.* his *Catalogue of Women*) and/or it might have a particular concern with the men of the Black Sea region. In particular, it is worth remembering the concern of Hesiod's work with the periphery of his world (on that concern, see Davison 1991, 50 n. 7). Be that as it may, Herodotus reports a tradition of Scythian descent from Heracles which seems to be an expressly Black Sea Greek tradition: he seems to imply that this tradition of Scythian origins would not be found among Greeks outside the region in his day. After all, the overwhelming weight of Greek accounts of Scythians stresses their fundamental otherness. By contrast, the Black Sea Greek account makes the Scythians quasi-Greek, the descendants of Heracles. We may compare the local tradition at Heracleia Pontica which stressed the friendly relations between Greek heroes important to the city (Heracles, the Argonauts) and its barbarian neighbours, the Mariandyni (Burstein 1976, 6-7). It seems reasonable to suspect that it was the Greek Tyritae who pointed out to Herodotus a giant footprint of Heracles near the River Tyras, final proof for them of his visit there (4. 82; *cf.* 4. 51).

According to this version, Heracles was on his way back from the west with the cattle of Geryon, following the circular river of Ocean around the edge of the world. In an otherwise empty Scythia he encountered an Echidna, who was female in her upper body, but a snake from the buttocks down. Their offspring were the forebears of the

Agathyrsi, the Geloni and the Scythians. The story also embraces aetiological detail, which accounts for the Scythian fondness for the bow and for carrying a vessel on their belts (Hdt. 4. 8-10).

Given Herodotus' influence, it is no surprise that later we find the story elsewhere, as in the *Tabula Albana* (*FGH* 40 F1a). Yet that account is interestingly different: for example, there Echidna is the daughter of a river, which is evidently located in Scythia, but named nevertheless Araxes. The nearest we come to such an account before Herodotus is Stesichorus' *Geryoneis*, an Archaic poem of colonial myth-making from the West. Evidently, Stesichorus mentioned Heracles' return to Tiryns with the cattle of Geryon, but there is no indication of his route. We should probably not expect the *Geryoneis* to take Heracles as far afield as Scythia, for its primary concern was the West (see Page 1973, esp. 145 on Heracles' return).

Further, Herodotus offers a third account of Scythian origins, according to which the Scythians were driven westwards by the Massagetae into the land of the Cimmerians. The Cimmerians could not agree on a strategy: the elite stayed and killed themselves in a staged pitched battle, while the Cimmerians fled and founded a settlement on the peninsula where the Greek city of Sinope was established (Hdt. 4. 11-12). This is a story in which Herodotus expresses particular confidence (4. 11. 1).

Of course, in a sense, this third story is not really an origin-story at all, for it fails to provide a genealogy for the Scythians. Yet, like the version of the Greeks of the Pontus, it deals also in aetiology, for Herodotus informs us that there still remain in Scythia Cimmerian walls, Cimmerian straits, a Cimmerian region and the so-called Cimmerian Bosporus. We should add that there were also cities whose names echoed the name of the Cimmerians, notably Cimmericum (Strabo 11. 2. 5, with Kacharava and Kvirkvelia 1991, 135-8). There can be no real doubt that the inhabitants of these cities made much of the pseudo-history of their names. Indeed, Herodotus himself tells us that the tomb of the Cimmerians who died in Scythia was to be seen beside the River Tyras, presumably pointed out by local inhabitants, perhaps including the people of the city of Tyras (4. 11. 4).

Herodotus presents this third story as common to both Greeks and barbarians (4. 12. 3). It seems likely enough that this too is a Black Sea tradition, fostered particularly by cities with a Cimmerian connection, for it is hard to see where else barbarians (and Greeks for that matter) would be imagined as particularly concerned with it. The suggestion gains some further support from Herodotus' citation of a passing mention of Cimmerians hard-pressed by Scythians in the poem of Aristeas of Proconnesus, for, while Proconnesus (and Cyzicus, where Herodotus had also heard tell of him: 4. 14. 1) is close to the Black Sea,

Aristeas himself claimed to have travelled north from the Euxine to the Issedones, neighbours of the Arimaspians: his was in essence a Black Sea tale, albeit perhaps for a wider audience in the Aegean and beyond.

The exploration of origins seems to have been a primary focus of the earliest Greek prose writing (Pearson 1939 remains valuable). As we have seen, these tales of origins encompassed both men and heroes. And Plato's Hippias peddled such tales, after the fashion perhaps of Sosicrates of Phanagoria:

> SOCRATES: Well, just what is it they [sc. the Spartans] love to hear about from you and applaud ? Tell me yourself; I can't figure it out.
> HIPPIAS: The genealogies of heroes and men, Socrates, and the settlements (how cities were founded in ancient times), and in a word all ancient history - that's what they most love to hear about...

(Plato *Hippias Maior* 285d-e)

The sustained consideration of origins throughout antiquity (Bickerman 1952) provides the broad context for traditions of colonial settlement. It is worth stressing that, as with Hippias, man and myth co-exist in these traditions. We have seen as much in the multiple traditions at Sinope. After all, history and myth resist comfortable distinction, especially in the matter of origins. As we have observed in the case of Tereus, even Thucydides can treat myth as history.

In his famous survey of Sicily, Thucydides begins with the origins of its inhabitants, both Greek and non-Greek. While he expresses some reservation about the presence of Cyclopes and Laestrygonians, he seems to find no difficulty with Trojan settlement in Sicily (6. 2. 3). The three aspects of origin which Thucydides mentions indicate an approach akin to Herodotus on Scythian origins, namely genealogical origin, geographical origin and the place where they went (6. 2. 1). Thucydides (also like Herodotus) indicates the existence of competing accounts of origin (notably, 6. 2. 2 on the Sicanians).

The important thing was that these traditions mattered very substantially. They mattered in cities' internal social, political and religious identities. And they mattered also in inter-state relations, wherein origins and notional kinship played a central role throughout antiquity. It is easy to see why historians - and not only Syriscus of Chersonesus - received honours from cities and why Hippias was in demand (Chaniotis 1988, 163 collects examples to illustrate the case of Hippias). For such traditions established the place of a community in the Greek world. By virtue of their distant locations, the cities of the Black Sea region were readily perceived as marginal to the Greek world. Xenophon's account of his march along its southern shore indicates as much: he shows a sustained concern with the isolation and marginality of such Greek culture as he perceives from Trapezus to Byzantium, where at last he seems to have thought that he had reached Hellas (Braund 1994, 134). The north coast was even more susceptible to such perceptions of its limited Greekness. At the end of the 1st century AD, Dio Chrysostom expatiates on the limited, if traditional, Hellenism of Olbia (*Or.* 36). About a century later, Diogenes Laertius attributes to Bion of Borysthenes (= Olbia) acid rejoinders to barbed queries about his origins. Yet Diogenes describes Borysthenes as 'Scythian land', confirming a perception of its non-Greekness (Diog. Laert. 4. 46-57, esp. 55). Even the Bosporan kingdom (alias Pontus) was readily presented as a cultural backwater, as in one of the anecdotes told of Stratonicus the witty harpist:

> When Stratonicus the harpist sailed to Pontus, to the court of Paerisades who was its king, and when (considerable time having passed) Stratonicus wanted to run off back to Greece and Paerisades apparently would not let him, they say that he gave this answer to the king: "You're not thinking of staying here, are you ?!"

(Athenaeus 8. 349d)

Greek ideas of the north coast of the Black Sea were dominated by images of Scythians. It is characteristic of that broad tendency that Pausanias, in describing the passage of goods from the Hyperboreans through several hands on their way to Delos, has the Scythians take them as far as Sinope, from where, he notes, 'they are carried by Greeks' (Paus. 1. 31. 2). After all, Sinope could claim to have produced such luminaries of Hellenism as Diphilus, Diogenes and the historian Baton, though it is far from clear how far they had developed before they left the city (Strabo 12. 3. 11, p. 546). However, elsewhere Pausanias is even less generous to the Greeks of the region, describing Mithridates Eupator as 'king of the barbarians around the Black Sea' without regard for the many Greek cities in his empire there (Paus. 1. 20. 4).

The local traditions of the Greeks of the Black Sea constituted some response to such perceptions. However, the other principal response served only to confirm the force of their dilemma, for the inhabitants of the region chose to travel to the Aegean world in search of Hellenism. A case in point is the speaker of Isocrates' Trapeziticus, who was a member of the Bosporan élite at the turn of the 5th into the 4th century BC. He claimed to have conceived a desire to visit Athens and the rest of Hellas (Isocrates, *Trapeziticus* 3-4). By the early 3rd century AD the practice was a commonplace (Philostratus *Lives of the Sophists* 553). Even a Bosporan king might journey south in search of Hellenic culture (Philostratus, *Lives of the Sophists* 535), while the cities of the Black Sea patronized the panhellenic sanctuaries at Delphi and Olympia (Burstein 1976, 35). Also familiar was the notion that one or two intelligent Scythians, like Anacharsis or Toxaris, would have had a natural desire for Hellenic culture and would travel to Athens, in particular (e.g. Lucian, *The Scythian* 1; *cf.* Hdt . 4. 76. 1 with Braund 1997).

The creation of the Panhellenion under the emperor Hadrian offered a new focus for Greekness. Much remains unsure about this organisation, but the key concern for the present discussion is its criterion for membership. It seems fairly clear that the primary criterion was proof that a member possessed authentic Greek origins either directly or by colonization' (Jones 1996, 46; *cf.* 41 on colonization). This was a new manifestation of a concern which is traceable through the Hellenistic period back into archaic times. In particular, panhellenic festivals had always required their participants to be Greek: Herodotus mentions a challenge (which failed) to the Greekness of Alexander I of Macedon when he sought to race at the Olympic Games around the end of the 6th century BC (5. 23).

It is striking in this context that there is no evidence that any city of the Black Sea region enjoyed membership of the Panhellenion. Although evidence for the membership of cities is certainly incomplete, we know enough to be fairly confident about its broad pattern. All known members come from the Greek mainland and western Asia Minor, plus Crete and Cyrenaica: there are no cities from the Black Sea region, Perinthus being the nearest member. Another notable omission is Magna Graecia, which also lacks any member. An explanation for this limited membership has been advanced in terms of Roman imperial strategies (Spawforth and Walker 1985, 81; Alcock 1993, 166-7), but the Panhellenion offered no real threat to Roman imperial interests, whether actual or potential. Much more plausible seems to be an explanation in terms of culture and religion (notably, Jones 1996, esp. 42). The absence of the cities of the Black Sea may reasonably be seen as an eloquent expression of the inadequate Greekness of the cities of the region as perceived in Athens and perhaps Rome in the 2nd century AD. The membership of Miletus and of colonial Greek cities outside the Black Sea serves to underline that absence.

We have seen that Black Sea colonial communities, as we may term them, were actively engaged in the construction of their own origins, by which they both established their Greek credentials and incorporated neighbouring barbarians into their traditions. Moreover, we have seen that these local traditions were engaged in dialogues not only with a range of other versions, but more fundamentally with a general sense in the Greek world at large that the Black Sea (except on occasion a few places on its south coast) was not a Greek place, so that proper Hellenism was not sustainable there. At the same time, there have been broad implications for the study of colonial traditions: all the scattered fragments of those traditions that happen to have survived must be examined, however unhistorical they may be considered. No-one would seriously maintain that Panticapaeum was actually founded by a son of Aietes, but that tradition offers insights into its civic identity.

Bibliography

Alcock, S. E. 1993: *Graecia Capta: the landscapes of Roman Greece*, Cambridge.

Alexandrescu, P. 1990: Histria in archaischer Zeit. In P. Alexandrescu and W. Schuller (eds.), *Histria*, Konstanz, 47-102.

Bickerman, E. 1952: Origines Gentium. *CP* 47, 65-81.

Braund, D. 1994: *Georgia in Antiquity*, Oxford.

Braund, D. 1996: *Ruling Roman Britain*, London.

Braund, D. 1997: Greeks and barbarians: the Black Sea region and Hellenism under the early empire. In S. Alcock (ed.), *The early Roman empire in the east*, Oxford, 121-136.

Burstein, S.M. 1976: *Outpost of Hellenism: the emergence of Heraclea on the Black Sea*, Berkeley.

Chaniotis, A. 1988: *Historie und Historiker in den griechischen Inschriften: epigraphische Beiträge zur griechischen Historiographie*, Stuttgart.

Davison, J. 1991: Myth and the periphery. In D.C. Pozzi and J.M. Wickersham (eds.), *Myth and the polis*, Ithaca, 49-63.

Desideri, P. 1991: Cultura Eracleota: da Erodoro a Eraclide Pontico. In B. Rÿeamy (ed.), *Pontica I: recherches sur l'histoire du Pont dans l'antiquité*, Istanbul, 7-24.

Dougherty, C. 1993: *The poetics of colonization*, Oxford.

Ehrhardt, N. 1988: *Milet und seine Kolonien*, Frankfurt am Main.

Gaidukevich, V.F. 1971: *Das bosporanische Reich*, Berlin.

Hind, J. 1988: The colonisation of Sinope and the southeast Black Sea area. In O.D. Lordkipanidze (ed.), *Mestnye etno-politicheskie ob'edineniya Prichernomor'ya v VII-IV vv. do n.e.*, Tbilisi, 207-223.

Jones, C.P. 1996: The Panhellenion, *Chiron* 26, 29-56.

Jonnes, L. and Ameling, W. 1994, *The inscriptions of Heraclea Pontica*, Bonn.

Kacharava, D. and Kvirkvelia, G. 1991: *Goroda i poseleniya Prichernomor'ya antichnoi epokhi*, Tbilisi.

Loraux, N. 1986: *The invention of Athens* (transl.), Cambridge, Mass.

Marshall, E.M. 1998: Constructing the self and the other in Cyrenaica. In R. Laurence and J. Berry (eds.), *Cultural identity in the Roman empire*, London, 49-63.

Mitchell, L.G. 1997: *Greeks bearing gifts*, Cambridge.

Page, D.L. 1973: Stesichorus: the Geryoneis. *JHS* 93, 138-154.

Parker, R. 1996: *Athenian religion: a history*, Oxford.

Pasanli, A. 1989: *Istanbul archaeological museums*, Istanbul.

Pearson, L. 1939: *Early Ionian historians*, Oxford.

Price, M.J. 1993: *Sylloge nummorum graecorum IX: The British Museum 1; The Black Sea*, London.

Shelov, D.B. 1978: *Coinage of the Bosporus, VI-II centuries B.C.*, BAR Int. Ser. 46, Oxford.

Spawforth, A.J.S. and Walker, S. 1985: The world of the Panhellenion I: Athens and Eleusis. *JRS* 75, 78-104.

Spawforth, A.J.S., and Walker, S. 1986: The world of the Panhellenion II: three Dorian cities. *JRS* 76, 88-105.

Wiseman, T.P. 1998, *Roman drama and Roman history*, Exeter.

Ionians Abroad

Gocha R. Tsetskhladze

Ionian colonisation has been studied extensively by scholars, and it will long continue to be in the future thanks to the international nature of the subject and the increasing quantity of archaeological evidence brought to light each year.[1] This paper does not aim to discuss directly the reasons for Ionian colonisation, the foundation of colonies and trade.[2] I would like to attempt to demonstrate the circumstances in which Ionians found themselves as they established their colonies - how they responded to local conditions in the territories they were able to colonise; under what new pressures they laboured, to replace the old pressures they left behind. This is a paper about Ionian behaviour outside their homeland and how they survived in a new environment whilst spreading Hellenic culture[3] among the local population and keeping a firm hold on the way of life they had brought with them. This is the most interesting, the unique phenomenon of Ionian colonisation. To elucidate this I shall concentrate mainly on the area around the Black Sea, where the Milesians established the largest number of their colonies. For comparison - of similarities and differences - I shall discuss other regions in which Ionian colonies existed.[4]

The archaeological material we have to date shows that Greek colonists first appeared in the Pontus in the third quarter of the 7th century BC and by the end of that century the settlements of Berezan, Histria, Apollonia Pontica, Sinope, possibly Trapezus, Amisos and the Taganrog settlement were established (Tsetskhladze 1994a, 115-118; 1998b, 19-22 with literature).[5] Colonisation of the Black Sea occurred in several stages: the vast majority of colonies were founded in the 6th century BC (Tsetskhladze 1994a), with few exceptions by Ionians. Although the written tradition tells us that Miletus was the mother city of the great majority of these settlements, archaeological material allows us to recognise the participation of other East Ionian centres - Samos, Ephesus, Chios, etc. - in the colonisation of the Pontic area (Tsetskhladze 1998b, 36; Treister 1999).

From the outset, Ionians settling in the Black Sea tried to maintain the way of life they had in their homeland. Study of inscriptions and graffiti shows that the population of the Pontic Greek cities worshipped the same cults as in Miletus: *Apollon Ietros*, *Apollon Delphinios*, *Apollon Prostates* and *Apollon Hegemon*; *Glycheia*; *Zeus Soter* and *Theoi*; Athena, Dionysos, etc. In Berezan and Leuke there was a cult of Achilles - which was not very common in Ionia. Many cities had a temple dedicated to these gods, especially to Apollo.[6] In the 5th century BC Hermonassa and Kerkinitis had a temple dedicated to Ephesian Artemis (Treister 1999). Temple architecture had much in common with that in Ionia (Pichikyan 1984, 151-86). The language of the inscriptions and graffiti (for example, in Olbia and Berezan) is typically Ionic and was so until the middle of the 4th century BC when the Ionic dialect was supplanted by *koine* (Vinogradov 1997, 74-99). In many colonies the same political institutions and same calendar existed as in Miletus.[7]

Archaeological excavation shows that the first colonists in the northern Black Sea lived in simple dugouts and semi-dugouts with pitched or flat roofs - the exception to this is on the Taman Peninsula. In Olbia, for example, a whole quarter with dwellings of this sort lining both sides of the main street was found. It is thought that only some 10-20 years later, and in the Bosporus 50-75 years later, did the

---

[1] On Ionian colonisation, see Roebuck 1959; Ehrhardt 1983; Tsetskhladze 1994a, 123-26; Gorman 2001, 47-86; Morel forthcoming. Extensive recent archaeological investigation and publication in Ionia, especially Miletus, helps us to view Ionian colonisation not only from the perspective of the colonies but also from that of the mother cities. See Özyigit (47-60) and Drocourt (61-63) in Phocée 1995; Mitchell 1998-99, 146-64; Friesinger and Krinzinger 1999; Senff 2000a; 2000b; Ersoy 2000a; 2000b; Tuna 2000; Büyükkolanci 2000; Kerschner *et al.* 2000; Greaves 2000; 2000a; Gorman 2001, 87-128; von Graeve forthcoming. In the future, I plan to devote an article to the view from the mother cities.

[2] For the latest discussion, see Tsetskhladze 1998b, 51-67; 1998c; Cook and Dupont 1998, 142-93; Kuznetsov 2000; Domínguez and Sánchez 2001, 84-90; Gorman 2001; 47-83, 243-58.

[3] Usually, the spread of Greek cultural features among the locals is described in the literature as Hellenisation. This term, as many will agree, does not provide a true picture of this complex process. Very often, it misleads us and is misunderstood. Frequently, even the discovery of Greek pottery at a local site is considered as indicating Hellenisation, when finds of isolated Greek objects, including pottery, by no means demonstrate Greek influence on local society. These objects could have arrived in many ways and for a variety of reasons. At present, we are not in a proper position to understand fully how or why Greek features were adopted by local societies to which they were entirely alien. We still have difficulties understanding how local people viewed Hellenic culture, and what it meant to them. Nor should we forget that, when we are talking about the Hellenisation of local society, what we really mean is the Hellenisation of elite culture, not that of the whole society. This process could be very superficial (see below). When using the term 'Hellenisation' throughout this paper, I mean influence: to be more accurate, local elites borrowing some elements from Greek culture.

[4] I shall pay more attention to particular regions, ones that have many similarities with the Black Sea, than to others. The bibliography is vast. I shall cite generally the most recent works that are accessible to Western colleagues. Thus, few Eastern European or other works will be mentioned. There are many citations of my own works, and the reasons for this are that they contain exhaustive bibliographies of Eastern European literature and summarise the achievements of Eastern European scholarship.

[5] For the latest on the Greek colonisation of the Black Sea, see Tsetskhladze 1998a; Alexandrescu 2000; Tsetskhladze and de Boer 2000-01. A few general studies are due to appear soon (Hind, Avram and Tsetskhladze forthcoming; Tsetskhladze forthcoming c).

[6] On religions and cults, see Lordkipanidzé and Lévêque 1999; Hind, Avram and Tsetskhladze forthcoming.

[7] On the political institutions of Milesian colonies, see Nawotka 1997; 1999.

colonists start building stone dwellings. In the literature there is an extensive discussion of whether these pits were dwellings or not.[8] It seems, indeed, that they must have been dwelling houses of a type perhaps copied from the local population. Many such dwellings have been found in the settlements of the locals. Many other pits used for storage and the disposal of rubbish have been found, but these are much smaller and have a different shape. Recently, there were unearthed on Berezan two pit-house constructions (complexes Nos. 6 and 13) with the remains of furnaces for smelting metal, as well as a few hundred copper ingots (whose overall weight was 5.6kg). These complexes have been dated to the last quarter of the 7th-first half of the 6th century BC (Domanskii and Marchenko 2001. No dwellings of any other type have been found on sites dating from the period of the first colonists and investigations of the last ten years have yielded dwelling-pits in every Greek settlement in the region. In the Taman Peninsula, where building stone was absent, Greeks used to inhabit wattle and mud-brick houses - a type (wattle) of dwelling known to them and modern scholarship from the local Maeotian settlements (in the Kuban region not far from the Taman Peninsula) (Kuznetsov 2001). If we turn to Colchis (Tsetskhladze 1997), in the area where the terrain was marshy and wet and the local population lived on artificial hills in wooden dwellings, the Greeks also had to live in wooden houses and probably even built temples of wood. Pit-houses were known in the western Black Sea colonies too. Unfortunately, we have no evidence for the type of dwelling of the first Greeks in the southern Black Sea. According to Xenophon (*Anab.* 5. 4. 26) and Strabo (7. 3. 18), and like Colchis, the local population of the south-eastern Pontus had wooden architecture, living in wooden towers.[9]

It must be pointed out that the question of Archaic domestic architecture in the Black Sea colonies cannot be considered as answered, and discussion will undoubtedly continue. The main problem has been and remains how to interpret dugout constructions. We do not know much about Archaic Greek domestic architecture in general, but especially not from Ionia (Morris 1998, *passim*; Nevett 1999, *passim*). What we have does not look as imposing as that from the Classical and subsequent periods - mainly, small, one-roomed mud-brick houses, either with stone foundations or without. No pit-houses have been discovered so far in Ionia itself,[10] but this type of architecture was not alien to Anatolia, as recent studies have demonstrated (Tsetskhladze 2000a with literature). Similar architecture was very widespread in many periods and many cultures. One cannot expect the first colonists, who were not great in number and whose domestic architecture in their homeland was simple, to build in their new environment grand stone buildings, be they private or public. It would be more logical and practical to have the same architecture as the local peoples, who were established in the area and were familiar with local conditions. We have evidence from Magna Grecia of the existence of buildings sunk into the ground, as was common amongst local people (Mertens 1990, 375). Furthermore, pit-houses are known from Metaponto.[11] Thus, it is quite possible that Pontic dugouts and semi-dugouts are examples of the first colonial domestic architecture there. Maybe we are creating this problem artificially. These dugouts existed until the late 6th century BC, when they were replaced by stone dwellings. For modern shcolars, to connect this simple architecture with our own concept of the *polis* seems unrealistic. At the same time, we should not forget that the classical type of *polis* did not emerge in mainland Greece until the late 6th century,[12] which is indeed the period when Greek colonisation largely ended. The question to be asked is: were all pits dwellings, or did some of them have other purposes? Archaeological material from these pits, and other architectural features, as well as the size of pits, help distinguish dwellings from storage pits and workshops (as was the case in Berezan: see above).[13]

The Ionians faced the local peoples living around the Black Sea: Scythians, Taurians, Maeotians and Sindians on the northern coast; Thracians and Getae in the west; Colchians in the east (Tsetskhladze 1998b, 44-50). Our knowledge of the southern part of the Pontus is insufficient.[14] Some of these tribes were quite hostile: their main activity was piracy (Asheri 1998; Tsetskhladze 2000-01). How were the Greeks to deal with them? What was the reaction of the local population towards the colonists and of the colonists

---

[8] See literature in Kuznetsov 1999; Tsetskhladze 2000a.
[9] Recent archaeological excavation in the land of Diauehi revealed the remains of a stone circle with two or three semi-circular bastions projecting from its outer circumference (Sagona 2002). It is possible that this is indeed the foundation of a wooden dwelling-tower.
[10] I am most grateful to Prof. V. von Graeve for this information (personal letter, 21 July 2000). Material from the excavation of Archaic Miletus will be published soon, see now Senff 2000a. One chapter by R. Senff will appear in the Proceedings of the Taman Conference (BAR), and another by him in the second volume of the Phanagoria Publication Project (*Colloquia Pontica*, Brill). Dr Senff is also completing a monograph.
[11] I am most grateful to Prof. J. Carter for this information.
[12] "... urbanisation was slow and limited in early Greece, and that if we wanted to draw a line between 'city' and 'non-city' stages, it would probably be in the late sixth century. The rise of polis and rise of the city were anything but synonymous" (Morris 1991, 40).
[13] Recently, the opinion has been expressed that there is no need to connect the pit-house architecture of the first Greek colonies in the northern Black Sea with borrowing from the local population. The author thinks that the Ionian colonists were already familiar with it from Asia Minor and had no need to borrow the idea (Butyagin 2001a). I expressed the same opinion a year before (Tsetskhladze 2000a) in an article with which the author is unfamiliar. I intend to devote a large article to the first colonial architecture, including that of the Black Sea.
[14] American colleagues are conducting a survey project around Sinope to study settlement patterns. Surface material found so far dates, in the main, only from the Hellenistic down to the Ottoman period. See Doonan and Smart 2000-01; Doonan *et al.* 2001.

towards the locals? In the answer to these questions the large scale of the adaptation of the Ionian Greeks to local conditions can clearly be seen - and this is so for other regions where Ionian colonies were established. In relations between Greeks and the local populations in Pontus three main periods can be distinguished: from the 7th to the end of the 6th century BC; from the beginning of the 5th to the end of the 4th century BC; and from the 3rd to the 2nd century BC.

The first period is noticeable for one important fact: the levels of the Greek settlements contain hand-made pottery in relatively large quantities: Berezan, about 11%; Myrmekion, 24-37%, etc. Hand-made pottery is known from western Black Sea sites as well (Tsetskhladze 1998b, 44-47). The ethnic attribution of this is a difficult and, frequently, hotly debated question. The vast majority of the pottery has either exact parallels with that from the settlements and graves of the local population or has a very close resemblance to it.[15] As well as this hand-made pottery, there are burials in the necropoleis of Greek colonies with so-called barbarian burial rites, as well as some personal names that do not look Greek at all (Vinogradov 1997, 146-64; Tsetskhladze 1998b, 44-47). All this evidence could indicate the existence of local ethnic groups in Greek cities, but sources of these types need to be approached with caution.[16] Literal interpretation can be misleading.[17]

Another important fact is that there are only about 39 Scythian graves in the northern Black Sea region for the Archaic period. The great majority of Archaic Scythian graves were found in the north Caucasus (Alekseev 1998; Tsetskhladze 1999b, 475-77 with literature; *cf*. Kolotukhin 2000). Although Strabo (11. 2. 5) tells us that the Scythians were expelled by the Greeks, re-examination of the evidence and recent investigations have shown that both before and after their Near Eastern campaign, the Scythians lived not in the northern Pontus but in the Kuban and Stavropol regions (Galanina 1997). Thus, direct contacts between Greeks and Scythians were rather limited, at best. It is crucial to underline that there are (so far) no traces of fire or destruction in the Greek settlements of the entire northern Black Sea region in the 6th century BC. None of the cities had fortification systems - all city walls date from the 5th century BC (Tolstikov 1997; 2001), with the exception of Histria in the west, where the first walls were built in 575 BC (Coja 1990, 160-164). In 1992 excavation of Myrmekion yielded traces of fire and of some kind of monumental masonry and walls. The excavator's interim interpretation is that these are the remains of the Archaic fortification of the city's acropolis but this is conjecture and all of these finds need thorough study and careful interpretation. The same can be said about city walls in Porthmeus. We are keenly awaiting the long-promised detailed publication this very important evidence from these two sites.[18]

The question of the local population in the Archaic period still needs further investigation, particularly in the case of the Scythians. Our present level of knowledge supports the *theory* of peaceful relations between Ionians and the local inhabitants of the western and northern Pontus. From the start, it is possible that Thracians and other locals living in the western as well as the northern Black Sea formed a part of the first Greek settlements - peaceful coexistence was always necessary for emigrants from Ionia settling in a barbarian milieu.

If we turn to the eastern Black Sea, Colchis, we know much less about the Greek cities. The Greek cities of the region have either not been located archaeologically or, if they have, their identification is a matter of doubt.[19] The only thing that can be said is that in northern Colchis, modern Abkhazia, inhabited by the Achaei, Zygi and Heniochi, hostile tribes (like Taurians in the mountains of the south-west Crimea), many Greek weapons were found, including helmets and also a shield of the middle of the 6th century BC, evidence of the less than peaceful relations between the locals and Greeks living in Dioscurias (Asheri 1998; Tsetskhladze 1998e, 15-26; 2000-01). It is most likely that there was a Greek quarter in the local settlement at Pichvnari from the Classical period. This has not yet been found but the discovery of several hundred Greek graves points to its existence.[20] The same can be said of another site, Tsikhisdziri, not far from Pichvnari, where the earliest Greek graves date from the late Archaic period.[21]

In the southern Black Sea some local pottery was also found in the Greek cities (Tsetskhladze 1998b, 47 n. 170). This shows that some kind of relations existed but the material is so sparse that it is very difficult to make any

---

[15] The most widespread opinion is that this hand-made pottery reflects the presence of local ethnic groups in Greek settlements. But could it be that there was no alternative pottery - none made by Greeks locally, and not worth importing any, at least in the initial phase of the colony? Mixed marriages cannot be excluded either.

[16] The question of Greekness, as well as ethnicity, is one to which scholars are paying increased attention (for the latest, see Malkin 2001). Another problem is the degree to which we can rely upon Greek sources giving us information about 'barbarians' (for the latest, see, Coleman and Walz 1997; Tsetskhladze 1999a; Cohen 2000, 313-480; Harrison 2002).

[17] This is very well demonstrated by personal names and their ethnic attribution (see, for example, Hornblower and Matthews 2000, 119-58).

[18] Short information appeared soon after the discoveries – not, as far as I know a full publication. Since then it has been repeated in other publications. For the latest, see Vakhtina and Vinogradov 2001; Tolstikov 2001. On the earliest Greek pottery from Myrmekion, see now Butyagin 2001b.

[19] For the latest discussion, see Tsetskhladze 1998e, 5-70; Lordkipanidze 2000.

[20] There are many publication on this site in Georgian. In Western language, see Tsetskhladze 1999c (contains an exhaustive bibliography). See also Vickers and Kakhidze 2001.

[21] The material from this site has not yet been published. For general information, see Tsetskhladze 1999c, 74-81.

definite interpretation. The only case where we know the details is in Heracleia Pontica. It was founded not by Ionians but Megarians and Boeotians in *ca.* 560 BC. As was characteristic of Megarian colonisation practice, the colonists made the native people, the Maryandinoi, their serfs (Tsetskhladze 1998b, 47 n. 169).

At the end of the 6th/beginning of the 5th century (the second period) the political situation in the Black Sea changed completely. The most commonly and widely accepted opinion in Russian and Ukrainian historiography is that the Scythians migrated from the north Caucasian steppes to the northern Black Sea area, establishing two political centres there, one situated in the Crimea (not far from Panticapaeum) and the other not far from Olbia (see, for example, Vinogradov 1997, 74-132). At the same time they started putting pressure on the Greek cities, which led in due course to the establishment of the Bosporan Kingdom in the Kerch and Taman peninsulas to counter the Scythian threat[22] and to the establishment of a Scythian protectorate over Olbia (Vinogradov 1989, 90-109). Events in the western Black Sea were similar: the Odrysian Kingdom came into being and this newly-established political power also started to put pressure on Greek cities, those of the Thracian Black Sea coast (Archibald 1998, 93-125). In the eastern Black Sea the Colchian Kingdom was created by the end of the 6th century BC (Lordkipanidze 1991a, 109-24). We do not have any evidence of pressure from it on the Greek cities of Phasis, Dioscurias and Gyenos (situated on the Colchian Black Sea coast).

Thus, Ionians found themselves under pressure from local kingdoms, but far less hostile than that which they had experienced in their homeland in Asia Minor as the Lydians, and later the Achaemenids, began their conquest and from which they had fled to establish their colonies in the Black Sea and western Mediterranean (Tsetskhladze 1994a, 123-126; Gorman 2001, 47-86). The Ionians' reaction again was one which showed how practical and adaptable they were.

The relationship between the Odrysian kings and Greek cities is very well described by Thucydides (2. 97)[23] who tells us that it was based on gift giving and tribute - by the Greeks to the Odrysians. The same sort of relationship between the Scythians and Greeks is mentioned in one inscription found in the Crimea.[24] However, these political relationships and obligations, and the protection exerted by local kingdoms, had, from a cultural and artistic point of view, positive consequences: they were the means of spreading Hellenic culture to the local elites and societies and, at the same time, Ionian behaviour in not opposing local kings ensured the survival of the Greeks and their way of life.

It is well known that from the 5th, and especially from the 4th century BC, Greek craftsmen commenced mass production of luxurious objects in gold and silver for the Scythian, Thracian and Colchian elites (Boardman 1994, 182-224; Reeder 1999; Marazov 1998). Thanks to archaeological excavation we know of workshops in Berezan, Olbia and Panticapaeum, centres close to which Scythians were living, producing objects in the Scythian Animal Style (Treister 1998). In Colchis in the 5th century BC, Ionians established special workshops at Vani, in the hinterland where the local elite used to live, for the production of gems, finger rings and golden jewellery (Boardman 1994, 217-224). Many princely graves, whether from the north, east or west of the Pontus, contained large amounts of luxurious Greek objects. I must underline, once again, that these should not be considered as trade objects but as gifts and tribute to the local kings and elite to enable the Greeks to maintain a peaceful and prosperous life (Tsetskhladze 1998c, 63-67).

The question of the origin and development of the Scythian Animal Style is still a matter of scholarly debate. Animal Style was characteristic for many nomadic societies of the Near East, including Anatolia and Asia (Rostovtzeff 1929; Bouzek 1997, 244-46). The Scythians were no exception. Two stages may be distinguished in the development of Scythian Animal Style: Archaic and Classical. Before the Scythians' Anatolian raid, Archaic Animal Style had much in common with the Animal Style of the tribes living in modern day Siberia and Mongolia (Bouzek 1997, 244-245). After the Scythians returned from Anatolia at the end of the 7th to middle of the 6th century there is a noticeable Anatolian influence and the closest parallels can be found amongst objects of the "Treasure" from Ziwiye (Bouzek 2001).[25]

For our discussion, the most remarkable finds are the

---

[22] See Hind 1994, 488-95. On traces of destruction in Bosporan cities at the beginning of the 5th century, see Tolstikov 1997.

[23] "In the reign of Seuthes who was king after Sitalces and raised the tribute to its maximum, the tribute from all the barbarian territory and the Greek cities which they ruled was worth about four hundred talents of silver which came in as gold and silver; and in addition, gifts of gold and silver equal in value were brought, not to mention how many embroidered and plain fabrics and the other furnishings, and all this was not given only to him but also to the other mighty and noble Odrysians. For they had established a custom opposite to that of the kingdom of the Persians, to take rather than to give; this custom was indeed practised by the other Thracians as well (and it was more shameful not to give when asked than not to receive when having asked), but because of their power the Odrysians exploited it even more; as a matter of fact, it was impossible to do anything without giving gifts. Consequently, the kingdom gained great strength." See also Mitchell 1997, 134-47.

[24] '... find out, how great are the taxes due to the Scythians' (*SEG* XXXVII, 665; *Bull. ép.* 1990, 566).

[25] For the latest on the Scythian presence in the Near East, see Ivantchik 1999. On the discovery of objects in Scythian Animal Style in Anatolia, see Bouzek 1997, 244-45; 2001, 40-42. On so-called Scythian-type arrowheads in Anatolia, the most recent work is Derin and Muscarella 2001.

matrices in Scythian Animal Style and punches and formers, all of the Archaic period, from the Greek cities of the north-western Black Sea and the Cimmerian Bosporus. Their detailed study has allowed M. Treister (1998; 2001, 59-78) to suggest the presence of craftsmen of Milesian, Ephesian and Lydian origins. The finds demonstrate that these craftsmen were producing metal objects in Animal Style for the Scythians.[26] The discovery in the Kuban region (Ulyap barrow No. 5) of bronze punches for embossing gold foil plaques with the figure of a panther and melon-shaped beads demonstrates the existence of a local workshop there (Treister 2001, 75). It is appropriate to mention here the find of a late Archaic bronze punch at a Hallstatt settlement in Romania (Oprisor), which enabled Treister (2001, 75-76) to connect metalworking here to the Lydian-Ionian tradition, as can be suggested also for Archaic Thracian metalworking (Treister 2001, 77).

The second stage is from the end of the 6th century BC to the end of the 4th century BC, when Animal Style objects (dress ornaments, weapons and horse harnesses) jewellery, and also vessels and *gorytoi* were produced by Greeks (Boardman 1994, 192-216; Treister 2000). Herodotus (4. 78-80) tells the story about the Scythian king Scyles who had been taught by his Greek mother from Histria to know Greek religion and the Greek way of life. He had a house and a Greek wife in Olbia and regularly stayed there. We have few if any metal objects from the 5th century BC. The vast majority of known Scythian metal objects date from the 4th century BC. Stylistic analysis suggests that the craftsmen were Greek, from the Hellespont, western Asia Minor, as well as from southern Italy and Macedonia (Treister 2001, 159). There is continuing discussion about where these workshops operated: from the Bosporan Kingdom or other centres (Treister 2001, 160). To date, several workshops have been identified, such as the 'Workshop of the Solokha phiale' and the 'Workshop of the Solokha scabbard' (Treister 2001, 159-60).[27] Treister (2001, 159) suggests that the earliest workshops commenced production at the end of the 5th-beginning of the 4th century BC.

Thracian culture and art have elements of the Anatolian and Greco-Persian Animal Style as well, with some features of Scythian Animal Style. But they were more Persianised than Hellenised (Boardman 1994, 183-92). The Odrysian elite preferred silver vessels of Achaemenian type and shape. As elsewhere, the Greeks living there adapted their craftsmanship to the tastes of the local elite. For the Greeks, the shapes of the rhyton, phiale mesomphalos, etc. (most beloved vessels of the Odrysians) were not new.[28]

Indeed, these vessels came to Greece itself from the Achaemenian Empire, so there was no difficulty for Ionians to produce these luxurious silver and gilded vessels for the Thracians. The study of Thracian jewellery has received increasing attention in recent years. From the first half of the 5th century BC there were several local workshops in the Odrysian Kingdom, following the patterns of Greek jewellery but adapting their shapes to fit with local tradition (Tonkova 2000-01). Some ceremonial decorations had Near Eastern models as their inspiration. It is most probable that these workshops employed Ionian jewellers from the western Pontic colonies, but it cannot be excluded that local craftsmen worked there under the instruction of Greek masters (Tonkova 2000-01). The discovery of traces of goldsmith's work allowed M. Tonkova (Tonkova 2000-01) to suggest that such workshops existed in various different centres of the Odrysian state.[29] As to Getic jewellery, although it displays some adaptations of Greek models and decorative techniques by local jewellery workshops, it exhibits a greater eclecticism than Thracian 'resulting from deep cultural contacts with the central Balkan region, the Danube river valley, northern Italy and Scythian territories' (Tonkova 2000-01).

In the 5th-4th centuries BC another practice is noticeable - that of Greeks being employed at the courts of local kings to build their royal residences. As Vasil Levski in the Thracian hinterland demonstrates, Greek architects were employed even from the late Archaic period (Bouzek 2000-01). Here, the large building was constructed of ashlar masonry up to Greek standards. Long known is Seuthopolis, where Greek architects built a system of fortifications, a palace and houses in the Hellenic manner. The decoration of these buildings is Greek (Bouzek 2000-01). More than a decade of study of the settlement at Vetren (Domaradzki 1996; 2000; Velkov and Domaradzka 1996; Archibald 2000-01), most probably wrongly identified as *emporion* Pistiros (Tsetskhladze 2000b; *cf.* Avram 1997/98), has revealed another residence of the Odrysian king (Tsetskhladze 2000b), with typical Greek fortifications. In the 4th century this settlement had a

---

[26] B.V. Farmakovskii was the first to suggest that art in the Animal Style in the Greek cities of the northern Black Sea had Ionian roots (Farmakovskii 1914). See now Tsetskhladze 1999b, 475-78.
[27] See also Williams 1998; Treister 2000.
[28] "One could imagine that at an early stage, demand for precious plate was largely fulfilled by (East) Greek craftsmen. These may have started a

workshop tradition whose regional tendencies increased with time and which later involved Thracian craftsmen as well. If not the work of Thracian craftsmen, demand by Thracian clients led to the creation of at least one characteristic variant of horn-shaped rhyton, and although a homogeneous group of animal head rhyta cannot be recognised for Thrace, the extant examples still demonstrate local interest in this type of vase" (Ebbinghaus 1999, 406; see also Archibald 1998, 318-35: catalogue of metal objects from Thrace, 5th to 4th centuries BC). On Scythian horns and rhyta, see Vlassova 2001.
[29] Increasing numbers of local centres of the Odrysian Kingdom have been discovered and studied by Bulgarian colleagues. The most recent is not far from Khalka Bunar, west of the Omurovska river (Tonkova 2002). Found here were several pottery kilns, the head of a terracotta figurine of Aphrodite, and a fragment of local pottery with an incomplete graffito in Greek ...ATOKOY (name of the Thracian king?). These local centres were not just political but for craft production (including metalworking) too. On the same type of Getic centre at Sboryanovo, see Stoyanov 2000; 2000-01.

regular plan: streets lined with colonnades, and a sewerage system with well-built channels (Bouzek 2000-01). Vetren was a centre for crafts and trades as well as for politics (Tsetskhladze 2000b). The same situation may be seen in Colchis in the 3rd and 2nd centuries BC where Vani was built and decorated in the Greek manner (Lordkipanidze 1991b; Tsetskhladze 1998e, 114-64). In the Crimea the picture is the same in the capital of the later Scythians, Scythian Neapolis (Vysotskaya 1979, 35-72). In both the Crimea (Vysotskaya 1979, 179-205) and Vani (Lordkipanidze 1991b, 177-95; Mattusch 1996, 206-16) there were local workshops of bronzesmiths producing objects and casting bronze sculptures in the Greek style. In Phasis at the end of the 5th century a workshop existed where Greek silver cups were produced (Tsetskhladze 1994b). It is possible that Semibratnee settlement was the residence of the Bosporan kings in Sindice, after it was incorporated into the Bosporan kingdom in the 4th century BC. Here, Greek-type fortification have been discovered (Tolstikov 1997, 212-213, fig. 13), as well as an inscription in Greek (Blavatskaya 1993; Graham 2002)[30] mentioning the name Labrys, most probably the ancient name of this place. Another possibility should not be excluded: that it might have been the residence of local Sindian princeling (the same type of settlement as in Vetren, Seuthopolis, Vani, etc.).[31] The problem with this site (which was established at the end of the 6th century BC) is that it was excavated a long time ago and there is no detailed publication available (see bibliography in Blavatskaya 1993).

Greek architects built not only residences for the living but also for the dead. Spectacular royal chamber tombs under mounds were, in the 5th-3rd centuries BC, built in the Lower Don and Sea of Azov regions of Scythia (Tsetskhladze 1998d, with literature) and in the Thracian Valley of the Kings (Shipka area) and other parts of Thrace (Tsetskhladze 1998d; Archibald 1998, 282-303; Marazov 1998, 72-85; Rousseva 2000) by Ionian Greeks, who painted murals within them (Tsetskhladze 1998d; Archibald 1998, 282-303; Marazov 1998, 72-85; Rousseva 2000; Blanc 1998).[32] They had previously built the same type of tombs for their own kings not far from Panticapaeum, capital of the Bosporan Kingdom (Tsetskhladze 1998d). These architects were familiar with this type of chamber tomb from the Anatolian kingdoms (Tsetskhladze 1998d, with literature). At the same time, such a type of funeral architecture is known from Ionia itself (see, for example, Forbeck and Heres 1997).

The relationship between Greeks and local elites and the process of Hellenisation in the Black Sea resulted from direct contacts. We know of Greek settlements or *emporia* in the hinterlands of Thracia (Pistiros) and Colchis (Sakanchia), in Scythia (Kamenskoe, possibly Belskoe) and the Don area (Elizavetovskoe, Tanais).[33] I think that the architects and artists building and painting royal chamber tombs[34] used also to live in the settlement at Vetren (Tsetskhladze 1998d, 79-80), as is demonstrated by the discovery of the same kind of chamber tombs not far from the site (Bouzek 2000-01). The Semibratnye tumuli are also situated next to Semibratnee/Labrys settlement. In Colchis, in the immediate vicinity of Vani is the Sakanchia settlement, where, in the 3rd-2nd centuries BC, the Greek architects and craftsmen building and decorating the residences of the local elite in Vani lived (Tsetskhladze 1998e, 38-44).

Discussion about Ionian influence through their adaptations to local conditions would not be complete without mention of the spread of the Greek language among the local elites. In Colchis the elite became familiar with Greek script from the 5th century BC, when they began to inscribe vessels they owned in Greek. From the 4th century BC, and especially in the Hellenistic period, inscriptions are found on gems and local coins, and even the state and religious language was Greek (bronze inscriptions from Vani and Eshera) (Tsetskhladze 1998e, 110-64; Vinogradov 1997, 577-601). In Thrace many silver objects from the Rogozen Treasure (Cook 1989, 82-100) and a phiale from Leshnikovata Mogila (Theodossiev 1997b) have inscriptions in Greek.[35] Of crucial importance are the finger-ring from near Ezerovo (Venedikov and Gerasimov 1975, fig. 206) and the Kjolmen inscription (Theodossiev

---

[30] "In accordance with his vow, Leucon, son of Satyrus, *archon* of Bosporus and Theodosia, set up this statue for Phoebus Apollo-in-Labrys, the guardian of the city of the Labrytans, having driven out by battle and force from the land of the Sindians Octamasades, the son of Hecataeus, king of the Sindians, who, after expelling his farther from his ancestral rule, confined(?) him in this city" (translation by A.J. Graham [2002]).

[31] For the continuing discussion on the existence of the native Sindian Kingdom, see Tokhtasev 2001.

[32] On Lydian wall-paintings executed by East Greek artists, see Mellink 1980; Özgen and Öztürk 1996, 36-57, 68-73. On Etruscan mural paintings, see below.

[33] See Tsetskhladze 2000b, with literature. On Tanais, see Koshelenko and Marinovitch 2000. On the Greco-native settlement of Albesti near Tomis, see Radulescu *et al.* 2000-01.

[34] On newly-discovered murals in Bulgaria, see *Trud* 19 December 2000, 11. I am most grateful to Dr M. Vassileva for the information. See now *Minerva* 13.3 (2002), 42-5.

[35] There are not many inscriptions known from Getic land. The only example comes from Sveshtari, where Greek letters were incised on a stone lintel in the interior of a Getic royal tomb of *ca.* 300 BC. "The inscriptions consist of separated words which can be reconstructed as AP↑ (...; the inscription appears at the bottom angle) and ИНΔA (...; on the left, from top to bottom, appear the widely-spaced letters ИНΔ; on the right, the overlapping print shows the letters ИНΔ). I interpret the two enigmatic signs as Doric/Carian forms, И=b, ↑=s/t. The site is near Doric Mesambria, and we know of Carian settlements in the area, according to historical evidence. ИНΔA would thus appear as related to Βέδυ, 'water'/'air', in Thraco-Phrygian ritual practice; AP↑ would be read as αρς/αρτ, a common prefix in Thracian names" (Theodossiev 1995). Another interpretation of these letters is that they are the numbers of the Greek acrophonic system and were used to mark rows of stones (Fol *et al.* 1986, 54-55).

1997a), inscribed in the Thracian language but using Greek letters.[36] Some Scythian finger-rings produced by Greeks had inscriptions in Greek - for example, the finger-ring of Scyles (Vinogradov 1997, 613-33). From the Scythian Nemirovskoe city-site originated a fragment of local pottery with Greek letters. Belskoe city-site has yielded Greek letters on an arrowhead and a spindle.[37] All of these could have been inscribed by Scythians just as well as by Greeks.

The material presented and discussed above shows clearly that the Ionians were either quite prepared and willing or obliged to pay attention to local political conditions and developments. Being surrounded by a local population and, from the 5th century BC, under pressure from local kings, they showed an exceptional ability to adapt in order not just to maintain peaceful relations but, at the same time, through their adaptability, spread Hellenic culture among local societies. Of course, Hellenisation was only superficial: the production of luxurious objects such as gifts and tributes, and building and decorating elite residences and tombs using Greek technique and style, but not penetrating too far below the surface of everyday life and ideology. Ionians were employed by local kings to create, under their control, royal and elite culture. In these circumstances, they had to take account of their employers' tastes and wishes. A deeper influence can be noticed on Sindian society, especially on Sindian sculpture, particularly from the 4th century BC when Sindice was peacefully incorporated into the Bosporan Kingdom (Sokolskii 1967). There is Greek influence on Scythian anthropomorphic tomb-stones, especially from the Hellenistic period (Popova 1976).[38]

Was the situation discussed above characteristic for the Ionians only in the Black Sea? What situation do we find in other regions of Ionian colonisation?

Abdera, a wealthy colony situated in Aegean Thrace, was founded twice: the first time in the second half of the 7th century BC by Clazomenians; the second in ca. 545 BC by Teans.[39] Excavation of the city cemetery indeed shows an Ionian presence here.[40] There is information about the exclusion of the *oikistes* by the Thracians in the Clazomenian period. The relationship between Tean Abdera and the Thracian Kingdom is not very clear but, as the literature supposes (Graham 1992), Abdera probably either paid tribute to the Odrysian Kingdom or gave it gifts. Written sources enable us to conclude that there was a permanent threat of Thracian attack (Graham 1992). Another Tean colony, Phanagoria on the Taman Peninsula, was established at the same time as Abdera (Tsetskhladze 2002, with literature). This maintained a quite peaceful relationship with local Maeotians and Sindians, who were Hellenised.

Phocaeans were famous in the ancient world for their trading activities (Hdt. 1. 163). After the disaster of Lydian invasion, they too had to leave their homeland and plan the establishment of colonies.[41] Their principal colonies were established in southern France and Spain, territories quite heavily populated by local peoples. The main Phocaean colony, Massalia, was founded in ca. 600 BC, east of the mouth of the River Rhône. This colony had to deal with local people. For their continued prosperity and survival the Massaliot Greeks had to enjoy peaceful and friendly relations with the Hallstatt chiefs. The well-known bronze crater from Vix (Boardman 1999, 220) is a clear example of a diplomatic gift - illustrating the same sort of relationship as existed in the Black Sea. The discovery of a mud-brick structure at the Heuneburg (Boardman 1999, 224) demonstrates that Greek architects visited the site. The question is whether other travelling craftsmen visited Heuneburg or not. I am not, however, excluding the possibility, because we have much evidence of something similar from Thracian, Scythian and Colchian society, where, as I demonstrated, the Greeks even established their own settlements in the hinterland. Now, with the publication of quite a considerable quantity of the Greek pottery from Heuneburg, it should again be considered (Kimmig 2000).

Let us return to examine Massalia itself.[42] Ancient tradition tells of the welcome the colonists received from a local chief and of their obligation to intermarry with native women (Justin 43. 3. 8-11; Athenaeus 13. 576a-b). About 30% of the pottery excavated in the earliest levels of Massalia is local. It is even supposed that local people established a new settlement next to the Greek. It is interesting to note that the earliest dwellings of Massalia are of mud-brick on a stone foundation. The territories around Massalia and Hyele, another Phocaean foundation,

---

[36] "...the local tribes borrowed the archaic script from some Greek colonies along the Aegean coast of Thrace, or even from Ionia through possible direct contact" (Theodossiev 1997b). See also Theodossiev 1994. The best evidence that the Thracian elite used the Greek language is contained in a new article publishing a chamber-tomb of the first half of the 4th century in the valley of the Kamchiya. The inscription above the entrance records the name of the deceased, the wife of probably a local prince or ruler: ΓΟΝΙΜΑΣΗΖΗ/ΣΕΥΘΟΥΓΥΝΗ (G. Atanasov and N. Nedelchev in *ΠΙΤΥΗ, Studia in honorem Prof. Ivani Marazov*, Sofia 2002, 550-557, in Bulgarian).

[37] See literature in Tsetskhladze 1998b, 50.

[38] On Bosporan anthropomorphic tomb-stones, mainly from Nymphaeum and surroundings, see Moleva 1991; 1999. The same types of monuments are now known from the Taman Peninsula (Tsetskhladze and Kondrashev 2001).

[39] on Abdera, see Graham 1991; 1992.

[40] See the bibliography in Kuznetsov 2000-01.

[41] On Phocaean colonisation, see Morel forthcoming.

[42] On Massalia and territories around it, as well as the relationship between Greeks and Gauls, see Arcelin et al. 1995; Bats et al. 1992; Hermary et al. 1999; Hermary and Tréziny 2000; Hesnard et al. 1999; Phocée 1995; Shefton 1994; Ugolini 1997; Voyage en Marseille 1990; Morel forthcoming.

were stony, unsuited to cultivating grain but good for grapes and olives. For a long time Massalia had no *chora*, both because of the landscape and the proximity of local settlements to the city walls. Massaliots needed grain as well as metals and had to maintain friendly relations with the locals, at least in the early stages of the colony's existence, in order to acquire these commodities.

Massalia started to establish trading posts (*emporia*) on the territory of the local population. The number of Massaliot settlements or sub-colonies increased from the Hellenistic period. Archaeological excavation at Arles, about 30km from the sea, has demonstrated that a local settlement existed here, where Greeks settled from the middle of the 6th century BC. Greek influence on local society around Massalia was quite noticeable. At Glanon, for example, public buildings imitated Greek models.

Another region of Phocaean colonisation, the Iberian Peninsula, has much in common with the situation in the Black Sea.[43] Probably only two Greek colonies existed: Rhode and Emporion (modern Ampurias). There is not much evidence about Rhode in the written sources or archaeologically. Now we know that Emporion was founded at the same time as Massalia directly by Phocaeans. Initially a small settlement was established on an island and in *ca.* 575 BC it moved to the shore of the mainland, an area populated by locals. New excavations on this small island, now attached to the mainland, have revealed very interesting material, including the remains of local pottery production (Bonet and Retolaza 2000, 285-346). From the beginning, locals formed part of the Emporion. The two parts of the colony, Greek and local, were divided by a wall, which is the same situation we find in Tanais on the River Don, established by Bosporan Greeks in the Hellenistic period (Koshelenko and Marinovitch 2000). Emporion had practically no *chora* (Marzoli 2000), at least until the 5th-4th centuries, thanks to the marshy nature of the surrounding territory and the existence of local settlements.

Since Emporion was surrounded by a local population, the relationship between colonists and natives was very important for ensuring the survival of the Greeks here: Iberian society was highly organised, although not centralised.[44] The Ullastret settlement, about 20km from Emporion, was the residence of the Iberian elite in the hinterland and, situated on a hill, it controlled the whole of the territory surrounding Emporion. Hence the relationship between Emporion and Ullastret settlement was not only one of trade but also political. It is noticeable that the city walls of Ullastret were not constructed until about 500 BC, long after the final establishment of Emporion. Greek pottery was found in large quantities at Ullastret, in almost every house. The planning of the settlement clearly shows Greek influence: an acropolis with its own inner walls and small temples, and a porticoed market place.

Another settlement is Tivisa, overlooking the Ebro river and controlling the entrance to the interior. It has very strong fortifications and a gateway closely modelled on Greek plans of the 4th century. Greek pottery was found here as well. Thus these two show that the Greeks established close and peaceful relationships with the Iberian elite living in very well fortified settlements controlling the interior territories so important to the Greeks for trade. The Emporitans could derive little benefit from their own surrounding, marshy territory. In the southeast of the Iberian Peninsula the most important illustrations of Iberian-Greek relations are the local settlements of Porcuna and Castulo, as well as Huelva.[45]

Tartessian/Iberian culture, although strongly indigenous, was more Phoenicianised than Hellenised.[46] More Greek influence can be traced from the 4th century BC, when the Punic world fell to Rome and Iberian-Phoenician links became exiguous. Ionian influence on Iberian stone sculpture is very well known.[47] Local, very Hellenised sculpture workshops existed in Castulo and Obulco. In these workshops very probably Greeks and locals worked side by side, the former adapting their artistic skills to the tastes of the local elite and the latter working under Greek instruction. (The same can be said of Sindian sculpture in the Kuban region - see above.) Tomb monuments show Anatolian influence which came here through the Ionians.[48] Important from this point of view are funeral stelai which carry depictions of Ionic columns, etc., as well as chamber tombs of exactly the same plan as royal tombs in Thracia and the Bosporan Kingdom, and with exactly the same design of pillars as chamber roof-supports in both places. Iberian small bronze figures as well as gilt silver phialai from Tivisa and Santiesteban show Greek influence. It is very difficult to identify the ethnic origin of the craftsmen producing them but it is possible that they were made by Greeks.

---

[43] On Emporion, and Greeks in Spain, see Aguilar 1999; Bonet and Sánches 1998; Jaeggi 1999; Olmos and Rouillard 1996; Rouillard 1991; Rouillard and Villanueva-Puig 1989; Domínguez 1996; 1999; forthcoming.

[44] On Iberia, see Boardman 1994, 49-74; Cunlife and Keay 1995; Ruiz and Molinos 1998.

[45] On Greek pottery from the territory of Portugal, see Arruda 1997, 76-109.

[46] "Iberia was not Hellenised. She assumed Greek cultural features and reinterpreted them, frequently on her own account. Or she used Greeks, in the best of cases, to express in a Greek manner, truly Iberian ideas-but little more" (Domínguez 1999, 324).

[47] Now see Aguilar 1999; Peraile 2000.

[48] It is interesting to note that in one of the Galera tombs of the 4th century BC a sculpture of a goddess on her throne, made in north Syria in about 700 BC, was found. Chamber tombs are known in the Phoenician colonial cemetery at Trayamar, and they are considered as remote prototypes of Iberian chamber tombs. (I am most grateful to A. Domínguez for this information.)

Greco-Iberian script is another example of the Hellenisation of the elite and the whole Iberian society. Nowadays in general about 2000 inscriptions are known in Iberian script. Iberian script is a very complicated matter. From perhaps the 7th century BC to the 5th, a 'Southern' script, influenced by the Phoenicians, was used to write the 'Tartessian' language. Slightly later (from the 6th century?), a derivative of it, the Iberian script, was used to write the eponymous language. There are two varieties of the script: one used in Andalusia and south-eastern Spain; the other in eastern and north-eastern Spain and in the Iberian regions of southern France. Independently and contemporaneously, a script heavily dependent on the Ionian arose in a part of south-eastern Iberia called Contestania, beginning in the 5th century although most of the known material written in it dates from the 4th century; perhaps, indeed, it did not survive beyond the end of that century.[49] Inscriptions in Iberian script were found not just at local sites but in Emporion as well, and on both Greek and local pottery. One type of inscription, letters on lead, is known from both Emporion and the northern Black Sea area: the examples from the latter vastly outnumber those from the former (Vinogradov 1998).

In Magna Grecia we do not have many Ionian colonies.[50] Let us mention Etruria first of all. Ionians established their quarter at Gravisca (the harbour of Tarquinia) about 600 BC. This was not just a centre of trade between Greeks and Etruscans but a production centre too. Ionian influence on early Etruscan tomb-painting and some tomb architecture is very well known (Naso 1996; Steingräber 1986, 18-52, 283-288; *cf.* Prayon 2001).[51] It has been suggested that

Ionian Greeks also established a gem workshop in the late 6th century BC in Etruria (Spier 2000). Thus the Ionians were controlled by the Etruscan elite and were used to create their culture. Greek craftsmen adapted their skills to meet the tastes and demands of their employers. From the outset, Hyele was entirely Greek. There is no evidence so far to suggest that locals formed any part of it. The city, at least initially, enjoyed friendly relations with local chiefs, but later, about 520 BC, it had to erect walls. Alalia too was surrounded by a local population, but we know little about its relationship with them.

In Egypt, from the beginning of the 7th century BC, kings employed Ionians and Carians as mercenaries. Mercenary settlements are known to us (Möller 2000, 32-38). Naucratis was a trading port *emporion* without a single mother-city and organised under strict Egyptian control.[52] It was the only port in Egypt to which Greek merchants were allowed to sail. Its government was in the hands of the Greek states whose citizens lived there, listed by Herodotus (2. 178-179): Chios, Teos, Phocaea, Clazomenae, Rhodes, Cnidus, Halicarnassus, Phaselis and Mytilene, sharing the Hellenion; and three further states with separate sanctuaries: Aegina, Samos and Miletus. Local workshops in Naucratis produced Greek-style pottery for local use, votives and scarabs. There is practically no Greek influence on Egyptian art (Guralnick 1997).

To summarise, every Ionian colony was established in a place which already possessed a strong local population, with its own institutions, culture and ideology. The colonies were either independent or under the strict control of local rulers. For a colony to survive and thrive it had to maintain a peaceful relationship with its neighbours, allowing them settle there, paying tribute and making gifts to local kings and, at the same time, producing luxurious objects for the local elite and establishing special workshops for the production of goods to satisfy the local upper classes. Ionian architects and artists used to build for the kings and elites residences for life and tombs for death, as well as decorating these with sculptures and paintings in the Greek style. The only example of serious hostility on the part of the Ionians comes from Corsica, where the Phocaeans established a colony at Alalia in *ca.* 565 BC. In *ca.* 545 BC a large number of refugees arrived there from Phocaea, under the leadership of Creontiades. This extra population needed immediately a new means of support and succumbed to temptation by plundering their

---

[49] I am most grateful to A. Domínguez for discussing these complexities with me. On Etrusean and Lycian script written using the Greek alphabet, see Bonfante 1986, 215-31; Keen 1998, 67-68.

[50] On Magna Grecia, and Etruscans, see Carratelli 1996; Krinziger 2000, 203-328; Andersen *et al.* 1997; Di Vita 2002; Fischer-Hansen 1995; Greco 2002; La Colonisation Grecque 1999; Herring and Lomas 2000; Smith and Serrati 2000; Ridgway D. *et al.* 2000; d'Agostino forthcoming.

[51] I think it appropriate to give a long citation. I hope that the author of it and readers will forgive me. "A number of recent discoveries and publications have shown that monumental art began in Etruria in the early, and not in the late, 7th century BC, with strong suggestions that for all three arts involved, namely architecture, sculpture and painting, the first impulse and quite probably the artists themselves reached Italy from the Near East, rather than from (or through) Greece... But it is also generally accepted that within a couple of generations, still within the 7th century, there was a sharp turn - represented by the story of Demaratus of Corinth in the ancient written sources - towards all things Greek; after which Near Eastern and traditional local traits remained as no more than faintly disreputable 'contaminations' in the essentially Hellenized Etruscan culture... The second part of this assessment appears to me rather questionable, and I shall discuss it here on the basis of two examples of monumental sculpture from the territory of Caere: the stone statues of Ceri and the terracotta cut-out akroteria from Acquarossa. Taken together with their probable antecedents and successors, these monuments, in my view, offer evidence for a strong strain of Oriental inspiration that remained active in Etruscan art (and beyond) across all the Archaic Greek influences. Such an inspiration was however (and this

is my main contention) entirely absorbed, transformed and adapted according to local needs, ideas and tastes, without thereby losing any of its power of representation and communication. In this respect it is perhaps necessary to make it clear at once that I shall refer throughout to subjects and iconographies rather than to style" (Ridgway, F. 2001, 351). On same situation on the Black Sea and similar conclusions, see Tsetskhladze 1999b.

[52] On Naucratis now see Möller 2000; Höckmann and Kreikenbom 2001.

neighbours. In response, Etruscans and Carthaginians came together and, after the Battle of Alalia in *ca.* 540 BC, the Phocaeans had to abandon Corsica, establishing a new colony at Elea on the west coast of Italy (Graham 1982, 142).

Finally, we need to turn to Asia Minor and Anatolia itself, where all the Ionians' problems began and events drove them on their voyages of colonisation. In the 7th century BC there was a very close artistic relationship between Ionians, Phrygians, Lydians and other Anatolian kingdoms.[53] Quite often it is impossible to distinguish Ionian and Lydian styles in sculpture, architecture and painting from each other, hence the term 'semi-Greek' Lydian culture. The Lydians had become the dominant local power, conquering Ionia and other neighbouring states. Ionian craftsmen and artists began producing objects and buildings for the Lydian kings in a mixture of Ionian, Lydian and Phrygian styles - a situation later paralleled in the Ionian colonial world (see above). In the middle of the 6th century BC the establishment of the Persian Achaemenian Empire brought fresh disaster to the Ionians (Tsetskhladze 1994a, 123-126). Ionia was not just incorporated in the Empire; its cities were destroyed. Anatolia under Persian rule was heavily Hellenised thanks to Ionian culture (Boardman 1994, 28-48).

The question of the Ionian role in the creation of Achaemenid royal art has long been studied and disputed. Until relatively recently, Archaemenid art had been considered to be provincial Greek. All the evidence and information to which classical scholars paid most attention came from the Greeks themselves. Nowadays the situation is changing, with more attention being paid to the evidence from the East, which reflects the reality more fully.[54]

It is very difficult to discern different specific styles in Achaemenian art because so many people living in this huge empire participated in its creation (Boardman 2000, 128-39). This is best reflected in the Susa Foundation Charter of Darius :

> The silver and the ebony were brought from Egypt. The ornamentation with which the wall was adorned taht from Ionia was brought. The ivory which was wrought here, was brought from Ethiopia and from Sind and from Arachosia. The stone columns which were here wrought, a village by the name of Abiradu, in Elam - from there they were brought. The stone cutters who wrought the stone those were Ionians and Sardians. The goldsmiths who wrought the gold, those were Babylonians. The men who adorned the walls, those were Medes and Egyptians."[55]

The role of the Ionians, according to the latest investigations, was quite limited (Boardman 1994, 28-42; 2000, 33-37, 117-134, 203). They were mostly stonecutters and architects - indicated not only by style but by masons' marks, which could be Lydian as well. The Ionian style can be distinguished in some decoration and sculpture - only the drapery in the sculpture looks Ionian. Ionians introduced the toothed chisel to Persia. Inscriptions from Persepolis dating from the late 6th/early 5th century BC are in Ionian lettering. The ration accounts for workmen at Persepolis mention very few Ionians: there are only four references. There is proof of the existence of someone able to understand Greek within the Persian administration but of the many tablets from Persepolis, most are in Elamite, one in Phrygian and only one is in Greek (with Ionian script). It seems that the Carians were more privileged than the Ionians (Cool Root 1997).

Everything discussed above shows that the way of life of the Ionians abroad and their responses to particular circumstances were heavily influenced by their experiences in Ionia itself. Their colonisation was driven by necessity after the Lydian and Archaemenian conquests of their homeland. Ionian colonisation started late, when the territories still available for colonisation were limited. In effect, they had no choice of what to colonise nor of whether to colonise. All available territories had considerable local populations. In their new homes they found themselves in circumstances reminiscent of those they had left in their homeland. If in Asia Minor the pressure was from the Lydians and Persians, in the colonial territories it was from Scythians, Thracians, probably Colchians, Gauls, Hallstatt chiefs and Iberians. There was no way back,[56] and to survive they had to adapt, but they had experience of this back home in responding to the Anatolian kingdoms and Persians; moreover, the type of states and structures they had to deal with in the colonies were practically the same - monarchies whose elites shared similar tastes. And I believe that the peaceful character of Ionian colonisation and their exceptional ability to adapt physically and artistically was not just a means of survival and prosperity but, from the 5th century BC, a way of influencing local society and particularly its leaders. In this Ionian colonisation differs from Dorian, which was extremely hostile towards the native peoples.[57]

---

[53] See Ramage 1987; De Vries 1980; Keen 1998, 66-70; Robinson 1999; Voigt and Young 1999, 197-220; Boardman 1999, 84-102
[54] See Boardman 2000; Stronach 2001; Bouchartat 2001.
[55] For the latest, see Boardman 2000, 130.
[56] There is known only one case when Abdera refounded Teos (Graham 1991).
[57] On the differences between Ionian and Dorian colonisation, see Nawotka 1997, 196-215.

Acknowledgments

This paper has been long in preparation. It is a pleasure to thank many colleagues and friends for their assistance. A. Domínguez and R. Olmos helped with my understanding of Iberian culture and for showing me relevant sites, museums and material during my visits to Spain. J. Véla Tejada kindly took me to Emporion and Ullastret. Thanks to J.-P. Morel and A. Fraysse I was able to visit Massalia and many neighbouring local sites. I am most grateful to P. Dupont for his invitation to Lyons and the opportunity this provided to work in the fine library of the Maison de l'Orient Méditerranéen. Thanks to V. von Graeve and his team I was able to see material and visit sites in Ionia. My time as a Visiting Professor at the Institute of Archaeology and Ethnology, University of Copenhagen in 1998 helped me better to understand ancient Italy in general and the Etruscans in particular. I am most grateful to A. Rathje and L. Sørensen. J. Boardman, A. J. Graham, A. Domínguez and A. Snodgrass commented upon the first version of this paper.

Bibliography

Abbreviations

BAR	British Archaeological Reports
CAH	Cambridge Ancient History
JHS	Journal of Hellenic Studies
OJA	Oxford Journal of Archaeology
OpRom	Opuscula Romana
RosArkh	Rossiiskaya Arkheologiya
SA	Sovetskaya Arkheologiya
TÜBA-AR	Türkiye Bilimler Akademisi Arkeoloji Dergesi - Turkish Academy of Sciences Journal of Archaeology
VDI	Vestnik Drevnei Istorii

d'Agostino, B. forthcoming: The First Greeks in Italy. In Tsetskhladze forthcoming a.

Aguilar, S. 1999: Dama de Elche: Embodying Greek-Iberian Interaction. In Tsetskhladze 1999a, 331-351.

Alekseev, A.Y. 1998: Periodizatsiya istorii Evropeiskoi Skifii: traditsii i sovremennoe sostoyanie. *Problemy arkheologii* 4, 118-126.

Alexandrescu, P. 2000: Colonisation occidentale et colonisation pontique. In Krinzinger 2000, 515-520.

Andersen, H.D., Horsnaes, H.W., Housby-Nielsen, S. and Rathje, A. (eds.) 1997: *Urbanization in the Mediterranean in the 9th to 6th Centuries BC*, Copenhagen.

Arcelin, P., Bats, M., Garcia, D., Marchand, G. and Schwaller, M. (eds.) 1995: *Sur les pas des Grecs en Occident...*, Paris.

Archibald, Z.H. 1998: *The Odrysian Kingdom of Thrace*, Oxford.

Archibald, Z.H. 2000-01: The Odrysian River Port near Vetren, Bulgaria and the Pistiros Inscription. In Tsetskhladze and de Boer 2000-01, 253-276.

Arruda, A.M. 1997: *As cerâmicas áticas do Castelo de Castro Marim no quadro das exportaçoes gregas para a Península Ibérica*, Lisbon.

Asheri, D. 1998: The Achaeans and the Heniochi. Reflections on the Origins and History of a Greek Rhetorical *Topos*. In Tsetskhladze 1998a, 265-286.

Avram, A. 1997/98: Notes sur l'inscription de l'*emporion* de Pistiros en Thrace. *Il Mar Nero* III, 37-46.

Bats, M., Bertucchi, G., Conges, G. and Tréziny, H. (eds.) 1992: *Marseille grecque et la Gaule*, Paris.

Blanc, N. 1998: *Au royaume des ombres. La peinture funéraire antique*, Paris.

Blavatskaya, T.B. 1993: Posvyashchenie Levkona I. *RosArkh* 2, 34-47.

Boardman, J. 1994: *The Diffusion of Classical Art in Antiquity*, London.

Boardman, J. 1999: *The Greeks Overseas*[4], London.

Boardman, J. 2000: *Persia and the West. An Archaeological Investigation of the Genesis of Achaemenid Art*, London.

Bonet, P.C. and Retolaza, M.S. (eds.) 2000: *Ceràmiquez jònies d'època arcaica: centres de producció i comercialitzacio al Mediterrani Occidental*, Barcelona.

Bonet, P.C. and Sánchez, C. (eds.) 1998: *Los griegos en España*, Madrid.

Bonfante, L. (ed.) 1986: *Etruscan Life and Afterlife. A Handbook of Etruscan Studies*, Warminster.

Boucharlat, R. 2001: The Palace and the Royal Achaemenid City: two Case Studies - Pasargadae and Susa. In I. Nielsen (ed.), *The royal Palace Institution in the First Millennium BC. Regional Development and Cultural Interchange between East and West*, Aarhus, 113-124.

Bouzek, J. 1997: *Greece, Anatolia and Europe: Cultural Interrelations During the Early Iron Age*, Jonsered.

Bouzek, J. 2000-01: The First Thracian Urban and Rural Dwellings, and Stonecutting Techniques. In Tsetskhladze and de Boer 2000-01, 243-252.

Bouzek, J. 2001: Cimmerians and Early Scythians: the Transition from Geometric to Orientalising Style in the Pontic Area. In G.R. Tsetskhladze (ed.), *North Pontic Archaeology. Recent Discoveries and Studies*, Leiden, 33-44.

Bouzek, J., Domaradzki, M. and Archibald Z.H. (eds.) 1996: *Pistiros I. Excavations and Studies*, Prague.

Butyagin, A.M. 2001a: Zemlyachnoe stroitel'stvo na arkhaicheskom Bospore (genezis i razvitie). In Zuev 2001, 36-341.

Butyagin, A.M. 2001b: Painted Pottery from the Early

Levels of Myrmekion (1992 Field Season). In J. Boardman, S.L. Solovyov and G.R. Tsetskhladze (eds.), *Northern Pontic Antiquities in the State Hermitage Museum*, Leiden, 179-198.

Büyükkolanci, M. 2000: Excavations on Ayasuluk Hill in Selçuk/Turkey. A Contribution to the Early History of Ephesus. In Krinzinger 2000, 39-44.

Carratelli, G.P. (ed.) 1996: *The Western Greeks. Classical Civilization in the Western Mediterranean*, London.

Cohen, B. (ed.) 2000: *Not the Classical Ideal. Athens and the Construction of the Other in Greek Art*, Leiden.

Coja, M. 1990: Greek Colonists and Native Populations in Dobruja (*Moesia Inferior*). In J.-P. Descoeudres (ed.), *Greek Colonists and Native Populations*, Oxford, 157-168.

Cook, B.F. (ed.) 1989: *The Rogozen Treasure*, London.

Cook, R.M. and Dupont, P. 1998: *East Greek Pottery*, London/New York.

Cleman, J.E. and Walz, C.A. 1997: *Greeks and Barbarians*, Bethesda.

Cool Root, M. 1997: Cultural Pluralisms on the Persopolis Fortification Tablets. *Topoi* Suppl. 1, 229-262.

Cunliffe, B. and Keay, S. (eds.) 1995: *Social Complexity and the Development of towns in Iberia*, Oxford.

De Vries, K. 1980: Greeks and Phrygians in the Early Iron Age. In K. De Vries (ed.), *From Athens to Gordion*, Philadelphia, 33-50.

Derin, Z. and Muscarella, O.W. 2001: Iron and Bronze Arrows. In A. Çilingiroglu and M. Silvini (eds.), *Ayanis I. Ten Years' Excavations at Rusahinili Eiduru-kai 1989-1998*, Rome, 189-218.

Di Vita, A. 2002: Urbanistica della Sicilia greca. In *Greek Archaeology without Frontiers*, Athens, 209-222.

Domaradzki, M. 1996: Interim report on archaeological investigations at Vetren-Pistiros, 1988-94. In Bouzek, Domaradzki and Archibald 1996, 13-34.

Domaradzki, M. 2000: Poblèmes des emporia en Thrace. In L. Domaradzka, J. Bouzek and J. Rostropowicz (eds.), *Pistiros et Thasos. Structures économiques dans la Péninsule balkanique aux VIIe-IIe siècles avant J.-C.*, Opole, 29-38.

Domínguez, A. 1996: *Los griegos en la Península Ibérica*, Madrid.

Domínguez, A.J. 1999: Hellenisation in Iberia?: The Reception of Greek Products and Influences by the Iberians. In Tsetskhladze 1999a, 301-330.

Domínguez, A.J. forthcoming: Greeks in the Iberian Peninsula. In Tsetskhladze forthcoming a.

Domínguez, A.J. and Sánchez, C. 2001: *Greek Pottery from the Iberian Peninsula. Archaic and Classical Periods*, Leiden.

Domanskii, Y.V. and Marchenko, K.K. 2001: Borisfen: k voprosu o bazovoi funktsii kolonii. Nachalo. In A.Y. Alekseev (ed.), *Otdelu arkheologii Vostochnoi Evropy i Sibiri 70 let*, St Petersburg, 16-18.

Doonan, O. and Smart, D. 2000-01: Gerna Dere, Roman and Byzantine Settlement in Sinop Province, Turkey. In Tsetskhladze and de Boer 2000-01, 17-24.

Doonan, O., Gantos, A., Hiebert, F., Besonen, M. and Yaycioglu, A. 2001: Sinop Regional Archaeological Survey 1998-99: The Karasu Valley Survey. *TÜBA-AR* 4, 113-135.

Ebbinghaus, S. 1999: Between Greece and Persia: Rhyta in Thrace from the Late 5th to Early 3rd Centuries B.C. In Tsetskhladze 1999a, 385-426.

Ehrhardt, N. 1983: *Milet und seine Kolonien*, Frankfurt.

Ersoy, Y. 2000a: East Greek Pottery Groups of the 7th and 6th Centuries B.C. from Clazomenae. In Krinzinger 2000, 399-406.

Ersoy, Y. 2000b: Archaic Clazomenae. In Solovyov and Tsetskhladze 2000, 124.

Farmakovskii, B.V. 1914: Arkhaicheskii period v Rosii. *Materialy po arkheologii Rossii* 34, 15-78.

Fischer-Hansen, T. (ed.) 1995: *Ancient Sicily*, Copenhagen.

Fol, A., Chichikova, M., Ivanov, T. and Teofilov, T. 1986: *The Thracian Tomb near the Village of Sveshtari*, Sofia.

Forbeck, E. and Heres, H. 1997: *Las löwengrab vom Milet*, Berlin.

Friesinger, H. and Krinzinger, F. (eds.) 1999: *100 Jahre Österreichische Forschungen in Ephesos*, Vienna.

Galanina, L.K. 1997: K voprosu o kubanskom ochage panneskifskoi kul'tyry. *VDI* 3, 125-138.

Gorman, V.B. 2001: *Miletos, the Ornament of Ionia. A History of the City to 400 B.C.E.*, Ann Arbor.

von Graeve, V. (ed.), forthcoming: *Frühes Ionien: Eine Bestandaufnahme*, Mainz.

Graham, A.J. 1982: The Colonial Expansion of Greece. *CAH* III.3^2, Cambridge, 83-162.

Graham, A.J. 1991: Adopted Teians: a passage from the new inscription of public imprecations from Teos. *JHS* 111, 176-178.

Graham, A.J. 1992: Abdera and Teos. *JHS* 112, 44-73.

Graham, A.J. 2002: Thasos and the Bosporan Kingdom. *Ancient West & East* 1.1, 90-103.

Greaves, A. M. 2000a: The Shifting Focus of Settlement at Miletos. In P. Flensted-Jensen (ed.), *Further Studies in the Ancient Greek Polis*, Stuttgart, 57-72.

Greaves, A.M. 2000b: Miletos and the Sea: a Stormy Relationship. In G.J. Oliver, R. Brock, T.J. Cornell and S. Hodkinson (eds.), *The Sea in Antiquity*, Oxford, BAR, 39-62.

Greco, E. 2002: In Magna Grecia: la cultura greca ed il milieu italico. In *Greek Archaeology without Frontiers*, Athens, 197-208.

Guralnick, E. 1997: The Egyptian-Greek Connection in the 8th to 6th Centuries B.C.: An Overview. In Cleman and Walz 1997, 127-154.

Harrison, T. (ed.) 2002: *Greeks and Barbarians*,

Edinburgh.

Hermary, A., Hesnard, A. and Tréziny, H. (eds.) 1999: *Marseille grecque. 600-49 av. J.-C. La cité phocéenne*, Paris.

Hermary, A. and Tréziny, H. (eds.) 2000: *Les Cultes des cités phocéennes*, Aix-en-Provence.

Herring, E. and Lomas, K. (eds.) 2000: *The Emergence of State Identities in Italy in the First Millennium BC*, London.

Hesnard, A., Moliner, M., Conche, F. and Bouiron, M. 1999: *Parcours de villes. Marseille: 10 ans d'archéologie, 2600 ans d'histoire*, Aix-en-Provence.

Hind, J. 1994: The Bosporan Kingdom. *CAH* VI^2, Cambridge, 476-511.

Hind, J., Avram, A. and Tsetskhladze, G. forthcoming: The Black Sea Region. In M. Hansen et al. (eds.), *The Ancient Greek Polis* (Copenhagen Polis Centre), Oxford.

Höckmann, U. and Kreikenbom, D. (eds.) 2001: *Naukratis. Die Beziehungen zu Ostgriehenland, Ägypten und Zypern in archaischer Zeit*, Möhnesee-Wamel.

Hornblower, S. and Matthews, E. (eds.) 2000: *Greek Personal Names. Their Value as Evidence*, Oxford.

Ivantchik, A. 1999: The Scythian 'Rule Over Asia': the Classical Tradition and the Historical Reality. In Tsetskhladze 1999a, 497-521.

Jaeggi, O. 1999: *Der Hellenismus auf der Iberischen Halbinsel. Studien zur iberischen Kunst und Kultur: Das Beispiel eines Rezeptionsvorgangs*, Mainz.

Keen, A.G. 1998: *Dynastic Lycia*, Leiden.

Kerschner, M., Lawall, M., Scherrer, P. and Trinkl, E. 2000: Ephesos in archaischer und klassischer Zeit. Die Ausgrabungen in der Siedlung Smyrna. In Krinzinger 2000, 45-54.

Kimmig, W. (ed.) 2000: *Importe und mediterrane Einflüsse auf der Heuneburg*, Mainz.

Kolotukhin, V.A. 2000: *Kimmeriitsy i skify Stepnogo Kryma*, Simferopol.

Koshelenko, G.A. and Marinovitch, L.P. 2000: Three Emporia of the Kimmerian Bosporus. In G.R. Tsetskhladze, A.J.N.W. Prag and A.M. Snodgrass (eds.), *Periplous. Papers on Classical Art and Archaeology Presented to Sir John Boardman*, London, 171-178.

Krinzinger, F. (ed.) 2000: *Die Ägäis und das westliche Mittelmeer. Beziehungen und Wechselwirkungen 8. bis 5. Jh.V.Chr.*, Vienna 2000.

Kuznetsov, V.D. 1999: Early Types of Greek Dwelling Houses in the North Black Sea. In Tsetskhladze 1999a, 531-564.

Kuznetsov, V.D. 2000: Nekotorye problemy torgovli v Severnom Prichernomor'e v arkhaicheskii period. *VDI* 1, 16-40.

Kuznetsov, V.D. 2000-01: Phanagoria and its Metropolis. In Tsetskhladze and de Boer 2000-01, 65-76.

Kuznetsov, V.D. 2001: Archaeological Investigations in the Taman Peninsula. In G.R. Tsetskhladze (ed.), *North Pontic Archaeology. Recent Discoveries and Studies*, Leiden, 319-344.

La Colonisation Grecque 1999: *La colonisation greque en Méditerranée occidentale*, Rome.

Lordkipanidze, O.D. 1991a: *Archäologie in Georgien*, Weinheim.

Lordkipanidze, O.D. 1991b: Vani: An Ancient City of Colchis. *Greek, Roman and Byzantine Studies* 32.2, 151-195.

Lordkipanidze, O.D. 2000: *Phasis. The River and City in Colchis*, Stuttgart.

Lordkipanidzé, O. and Lévêque, P. (eds.) 1999: *Religions du Pont-Euxin*, Paris.

Malkin, I. (ed.) 2001: *Ancient Perceptions of Greek Ethnicity*, Cambridge, Mass./London.

Marazov, I. (ed.) 1998: *Ancient Gold: the Wealth of the Thracians. Treasures from the Republic of Bulgaria*, New York.

Marzoli, D. 2000: Emporion und sein Hinterland. Ergebnisse einer interdisziplinären Untersuchung. In Krinzinger 2000, 117-128.

Mattusch, C.C. 1996: *Classical Bronzes. The Art and Craft of Greek and Roman Statuary*, Ithaca/London.

Mellink, M.J. 1980: Archaic Wall Painting from Gordion. In K. De Vries (ed.), *From Athens to Gordion*, Philadelphia, 91-98.

Mertes, D. 1990: Some Principal Features of West Greek Colonial Architecture. In J.-P. Descoeudres (ed.), *Greek Colonists and Native Populations*, Oxford, 373-384.

Mitchell, L.G. 1997: *Greeks Bearing Gifts. The Public Use of Private Relationships in the Greek World, 435-323 BC*, Cambridge.

Mitchell, S. 1998-99: Archaeology in Asia Minor 1990-98. *Archaeological Reports for 1998-1999*, 125-191.

Moleva, N.B. 1991: O nekotorykh osobennostyakh pogrebal'nogo obryada na Bospore (po materialam antropomorfnykh izviyanii). In B.A. Khrshanovskii (ed.), *Rekonstruktsiya drevnykh verovanii: istochniki, metod, tsel'*, St Petersburg, 130-136.

Moleva, N.B. 1999: Antropomorfnye pamyatniki iz nekropolya Nimfeya. In N.L. Grach, *Nekropol' Nimfeya*, St Petersburg, 315-328.

Möller, A. 2000: *Naukratis. Trade in Archaic Greece*, Oxford.

Morel, J.-P. forthcoming: Phocaean Colonisation. In Tsetskhladze forthcoming a.

Morris, I. 1991: The early polis as city and state. In J. Rich and A. Wallace-Hadrill (eds.), *City and Country in the Ancient World*, London/New York, 25-58.

Morris, I. 1998: Archaeology and Archaic Greek History. In N. Fisher and H. van Wees (eds.), *Archaic*

Greece: *New Approaches and New Evidence*, London, 1-92.

Naso, A. 1996: Osservazioni sull' origine dei tumuli monumentali nell'Italia centrale. *OpRom* 20, 69-85.

Nawotka, K. 1997: *The Western Pontic Cities. History and Political Organization*, Amsterdam.

Nawotka, K. 1999: *Boule and Demos in Miletus and its Pontic Colonies from Classical Age until Third Century A.D.*, Wroclaw.

Nevett, L.C. 1999: *House and Society in the Ancient Greek World*, Cambridge.

Olmos, R. and Rouillard, P. (eds.) 1996: *Formes archaïques et arts ibériques. Formas arcaicas y arte ibérico*, Madrid.

Özgen, I. and Öztürk, J. 1996: *Heritage Recovered. The Lydian Treasure*, Istanbul.

Peraile, I.I. 2000: *Monumentos Funerarios Ibéricos: Los Pilares-Estela*, Valencia.

Phocée 1995: *Phocée et la fondation de Marseille*, Marseilles.

Pichikyan, I.R. 1984: *Malaya Aziya - Severnoe Prichernomor'e*, Moscow.

Popova, E.A. 1976: Ob istokakh traditsii i evolyutsii form skifskoi skul'ptury. *SA* 1, 108-121.

Prayon, F. 2001: Near Eastern Influences on Early Etruscan Architecture? In L. Bonfante and V. Karageorghis (eds.), *Italy and Cyprus in Antiquity: 1500-450 BC*, Nicosia, 335-350.

Radulescu, A., Bozoianu, L., Barbulescu, M. and Georgescu, N. 2000-01: Albesti (Depart. de Constanza), Site Fortifié Greco-Indigène. In Tsetskhladze and de Boer 2000-01, 189-206.

Ramage, N.H. 1987: The Arts at Sardis. In E. Guralnick (ed.), *Sardis: Twenty-Seven Years of Discovery*, Chicago, 26-35.

Reeder, E.D. (ed.) 1999: *Scythian Gold. Treasures from Ancient Ukraine*, New York.

Ridgway, D., Ridgway, F.R.S., Pearce, M., Herring, E., Whitehouse, R.D. and J.B. Wilkins (eds.) 2000: *Ancient Italy in its Mediterranean Setting. Studies in Honour of Ellen Macnamara*, London.

Ridgway, F.R.S. 2001: Near Eastern Influences in Etruscan Art. In L. Bonfante and V. Karageorghis (eds.), *Italy and Cyprus in Antiquity: 1500-450 BC*, Nicosia, 351-360.

Robinson, T. 1999: Erbina, the 'Nereid Monument' and Xanthus. In Tsetskhaladze 1999a, 361-378.

Roebuck, C. 1959: *Ionian Trade and Colonization*, New York.

Rostovtzeff, M. 1929: *The Animal Style in South Russia and China*, Princeton.

Rouillard, P. 1991: *Les Grecs et la Péninsule Ibériqiue du VIIIe au IVe siècle avant Jésus-Christ*, Paris.

Rouillard, P. and Villanueva-Puig, M.-C. 1989: *Grecs et Ibères au IVe siècle avant Jésus-Christ. Commerce et iconographie*, Paris.

Rousseva, M. 2000: *Thracian Cult Architecture in Bulgaria*, Jambol.

Ruiz, A. and Molinos, M. 1998: *The Archaeology of Iberians*, Cambridge.

Sagona, A. 2002: Archaeology at the Headwaters of the Aras. *Ancient West & East* 1.1, 46-50.

Senff, R. 2000a: Die archasche Wohnbebauung am Kalabaktepe in Milet. In Krinzinger 2000, 29-38.

Senff, R. 2000b: Archaic Miletus. In Solovyov and Tsetskhladze 2000, 120-121.

Shefton, B.B. 1994: Massalia and Colonization in the North-Western Mediterranean. In G.R. Tsetskhladze and F. De Angelis (eds.), *The Archaeology of Greek Colonisation. Essays Dedicated to Sir John Boardman*, Oxford, 61-86.

Smith, C. and Serrati, J. (eds.), *Sicily from Aeneas to Augustus. New Approaches in Archaeology and History*, Edinburgh.

Sokolskii, N.I. 1967: Sindskaya skul'ptura. In T.V. Blavatskaya *et al.* (eds.), *Antichnoe obshchestvo*, Moscow, 193-203.

Solovyov, S.L. and Tsetskhladze, G.R. (eds.) 2000: *Greeks and Natives in the Cimmerian Bosporus (7th-1st Centuries BC)*, St Petersburg.

Spier, J. 2000: From East Greece to Etruria: A Late Sixth-Century BC Gem Workshop. In G.R. Tsetskhladze, A.J.N.W. Prag and A.M. Snodgrass (eds.), *Periplous. Papers on Classical Art and Archaeology Presented to Sir John Boardman*, London, 330-335.

Steingräber, S. (ed.) 1986: *Etruscan Painting*, New York.

Stoyanov, T. 2000: Notes on the Toreutic Workshops: Production in Northeastern Thrace 4th-3rd Centuries BC. In A. Avram and M. Babes (eds.), *Civilisation grecque et cultures antiques périphériques*, Bucharest, 88-93.

Stoyanov, T. 2000-01: The Getic Capital at Sboryanovo (North-Eastern Bulgaria). In Tsetskhladze and de Boer 2000-01, 207-222.

Stronach, D. 2001: From Cyrus to Darius: Notes on Art and Architecture in Early Achaemenid Palaces. In I. Nielsen (ed.), *The Royal Palace Institution in the First Millennium BC. Regional Development and Cultural Interchange between East and West*, Aarhus, 95-112.

Theodossiev, N. 1994: The Thracian Ithyphallic Altar from Polianthos and the Sacred Marriage of the Gods. *OJA* 13, 313-323.

Theodossiev, N. 1995: Two Early Alphabetic Inscriptions from Bulgaria. *Kadmos* 34, 163.

Theodossiev, N. 1997a: On the Reading and Date of the Kjolmen Inscription. *Indogermanische Forschungen* 102, 216-229.

Theodossiev, N. 1997b: A New Early Thracian Inscription from Bulgaria. *Kadmos* 36, 174.

Tolstikov, V.P. 1997: Descriptions of Fortifications of the Classical Cities in the Region to the North of the

Black Sea. *Ancient Civilizations from Scythia to Siberia* 4.3, 187-232.

Tolstikov, V.P. 2001: Arkheologicheskie otkrytiya na akropole Pantikapeya i problema bosporo-skifskikh otnoshenii v VI-V vv. do n.e. In Zuev 2001, 45-57.

Tokhtasev, S.P. 2001: Eshche raz o sindskikh monetakh i sindskom tsarstve. In Zuev 2001, 63-79.

Tonkova, M. 2000-01: Classical Jewellery in Thrace-Origin and Development: Archaeological Context. In Tsetskhladze and de Boer 2000-01, 277-288.

Tonkova, M. 2002: Novootkrit trakiiski tsent'r. *Nashe Minalo* 23, 5-10.

Treister, M.Y. 1998: Ionia and the North Pontic Area. Archaic Metalworking: Tradition and Innovation. In Tsetskhladze 1998a, 179-200.

Treister, M.Y. 1999: Ephesos and the Northern Pontic Area in the Archaic and Classical Periods. In Friesinger and Krinzinger 1999, 81-86.

Treister, M.Y. 2000: Early Classical Motifs in the 4th Century BC Toreutics from the North Pontic Area (The Ways of Style Transfer in the Toreutics). In A. Avram and M. Babes (eds.), *Civilisation grecque et cultures antiques périphériques*, Bucharest, 94-101.

Treister, M.Y. 2001: *Hammering Techniques in Greek and Roman Jewellery and Toreutics*, Leiden.

Tsetskhladze, G.R. 1994a: Greek Penetration of the Black Sea. In G.R. Tsetskhladze and F. De Angelis (eds.), *The Archaeology of Greek Colonisation. Essays Dedicated to Sir John Boardman*, Oxford, 111-136.

Tsetskhladze, G.R. 1994b: The Silver Phiale Mesomphalos from the Kuban (Northern Caucasus). *OJA* 13, 199-216.

Tsetskhladze, G.R. 1997: How Greek Colonists Adapted Their Way of Life to the Conditions in Kolkhis. In J.M. Fossey (ed.), *Proceedings of the First International Conference on the Archaeology and History of the Black Sea*, Amsterdam, 121-136.

Tsetskhladze, G.R. (ed.) 1998a: *Greek Colonisation of the Black Sea Area. Historical Interpretation of Archaeology*, Stuttgart.

Tsetskhladze, G.R. 1998b: Greek Colonisation of the Black Sea Area: Stages, Models, and Native Population. In Tsetskhladze 1998a, 9-68.

Tsetskhladze, G.R. 1998c: Trade on the Black Sea in the Archaic and Classical Periods: some observations. In H. Parkins and C. Smith (eds.), *Trade, Traders and the Ancient City*, London/New York, 52-74.

Tsetskhladze, G.R. 1998d: Who Built the Scythian and Thracian Royal and Elite Tombs?. *OJA* 17, 55-92.

Tsetskhladze, G.R. 1998e: *Die Griechen in der Kolchis (historisch-archäologischer Abriß)*, Amsterdam.

Tsetskhladze, G.R. (ed.) 1999a: *Ancient Greeks West and East*, Leiden.

Tsetskhladze, G.R. 1999b: Between West and East: Anatolian Roots of Local Cultures of the Pontus. In Tsetskhladze 1999a, 469-497.

Tsetskhladze, G.R. 1999c: *Pichvnari and Its Environs, 6th c BC-4th c AD*, Paris.

Tsetskhladze, G.R. 2000a: Note on Semi-Pithouses and Hand-made Pottery from Gordion. In A. Avram and M. Babes (eds.), *Civilisation grecque et cultures antiques périphériques*, Bucharest, 165-171.

Tsetskhladze, G.R. 2000b: Pistiros in the System of Pontic Emporia (Greek Trading and Craft Settlements in the Hinterland of the Northern and Eastern Black Sea and Elsewhere). In L. Domaradzka, J. Bouzek and J. Rostropowicz (eds.), *Pistiros et Thasos. Structures économiques dans la Péninsule balkanique aux VIIe-IIe siècles avant J.-C.*, Opole, 233-246.

Tsetskhladze, G.R. 2000-01: Black Sea Piracy. In Tsetskhladze and de Boer 2000-01, 11-16.

Tsetskhladze, G.R. 2002: Phanagoria: Metropolis of the Asiatic Bosporus. In *Greek Archaeology without Frontiers*, Athens, 129-150.

Tsetskhladze, G.R. (ed.) forthcoming a: *Greek Colonisation. An Account of Greek Colonies and Other Settlements Overseas*, Vol. 1, Leiden.

Tsetskhladze, G.R. (ed.) forthcoming b: *Greek Colonisation. An Account of Greek Colonies and Other Settlements Overseas*, Vol. 2, Leiden.

Tsetskhladze, G.R. forthcoming c: Greeks in the Black Sea. In Tsetskhladze forthcoming b.

Tsetskhladze, G.R. and de Boer, J.G. (eds.) 2000-01: *The Black Sea Region in Greek, Roman and Byzantine Periods (Talanta XXXII-XXXIII)*, Amsterdam (2002).

Tsetskhladze, G.R. and Kondrashev, A.V. 2001: Notes on the Rescue Excavation of the Tuzla Necropolis (1995-1997). In G.R. Tsetskhladze (ed.), *North Pontic Archaeology. Recent Discoveries and Studies*, Leiden, 345-364.

Tuna, N. 2000: Archaic Teos: Preliminary Survey Results. In Solovyov and Tsetskhladze 2000, 121-124.

Ugolini, D. (ed.) 1997: *Languedoc occidental protohistorique. Fouilles et recherches récentes (VIe-IVe s. av. J.-C.)*, Aix-en-Provence.

Vakhtina, M.Y. and Vinogradov, Y.A. 2001: Eshche raz o rannei fortifikatsii Bospora Kimmeriiskogo. In Zuev 2001, 41-45.

Velkov, V. and Domaradzka, L. 1996: Kotys I (383/359 B.C.) and emporion Pistiros. In Bouzek, Domaradzki and Archibald 1996, 205-216.

Venedikov, I. and Gerassimov, T. 1975: *Thracian Art Treasures*, Sofia/London.

Vickers, M. and Kakhidze, A. 2001: The British-Georgian Excavation at Pichvnari 1998: The 'Greek' and 'Colchian' Cemeteries. *Anatolian Studies* 51, 65-90.

Vinogradov, Y.G. 1989: *Politicheskaya istorya ol'viiskogo*

polisa, VII-I vv. do n.e., Moscow.

Vinogradov, Y.G. 1997: *Pontische Studien. Kleine Schriften zur Geschichte und Epigraphik des Schwarzmeerraumes*, Mainz.

Vinogradov, Y.G. 1998: The Greek Colonisation of the Black Sea Region in the Light of Private Lead Letters. In Tsetskhladze 1998a, 153-178.

Vlassova, E.V. 2001: The Scythian Drinking-Horn. In J. Boardman, S.L. Solovyov and G.R. Tsetskhladze (eds.), *Northern Pontic Antiquities in the State Hermitage Museum*, Leiden, 71-112.

Voigt, M.M. and Young, T.G. 1999: From Phrygian Capital to Achaemenid Entrepot: Middle and Late Phrygian Gordion. *Iranica Antiqua* XXXIV, 191-242.

Voyage en Marseille 1990: *Voyage en Marseille. 100 ans d'archéologie en Gaule du sud*, Marseilles.

Vysotskaya, T.N. 1979: *Neapol' - stolitsa gosudarstva pozdnikh skifov*, Kiev.

Williams, D. 1998: Identifying Greek Jewellers and Goldsmiths. In D. Williams (ed.), *The Art of the Greek Goldsmith*, London, 99-104.

Zuev, V.Y. *et al.* (ed.) 2001: *Bosporskii fenomem: kolonizatsiya regiona, formirovanie polisov, obrazovanie gosudarstva* I, St Petersburg.

Archaische attische Keramik in Ionien

Yasemin Tuna-Nörling

Schrieb Ingeborg Scheibler zur Verbreitung attischer Keramik in Ionien noch 1983 "Sieht man von den rhodischen Funden ab, ist diese Keramik allerdings im ionischen Osten spärlicher vertreten als etwa in den griechischen Kolonien Unteritaliens und Siziliens",[1] läßt der Foschungsstand nach fast zwei Jahrzehnten eine differenziertere Aussage zu. Neue Publikationen zu Grabungsfunden in Ionien und den benachbarten Regionen des westlichen Kleinasiens zeigen, daß die bemalte Keramik aus Athen auch hier geschätzt und in größeren Mengen importiert wurde.[2]

Von den Städten des ionischen Zwölfstädtebundes, nämlich Milet, Myus, Priene, Ephesos, Kolophon, Lebedos, Teos, Klazomenai, Phokaia, Samos, Chios und Erythrai, sind nicht alle in gleichem Maße archäologisch untersucht worden. Kenntnisse über den Import attischer Keramik sind nur für sechs dieser Städte verfügbar, zu denen die als zwar nicht zum Städtebund gehörige, aber noch vor der 23. Olympiade (688 v. Chr.) ionisch gewordene Stadt Alt-Smyrna (Bayraklı) hinzuzufügen ist.[3]

Alt-Smyrna (Bayraklı)

Die frühesten Importe attisch schwarzfiguriger Keramik in Ionien wurden in Alt-Smyrna und im Heraion von Samos gefunden. Es sind Amphorenfragmente nahe dem Nettos Maler um 610/600.[4]

Ohnehin weisen diese beiden Fundorte die größten Mengen attischer Keramik während des gesamten 6. Jhs. auf, wobei die Funde aus dem Heraion in Qualität und Vielfalt unübertroffen bleiben.

Die aus der Siedlung und dem Bereich des Athena-Tempels stammenden Funde nehmen in Alt-Smyrna[5] im Laufe des 6. Jhs. zu und erreichen hinsichtlich der Menge im letzten Viertel des Jhs. ihren Höhepunkt. Während im frühen 6. Jh. große Mischgefäße wie Dinoi und Kratere vor allem des Sophilos (Abb.1) sowie Lekanai/Lekaniden des KX-Malers und der Maler der Dresdner-Lekanis mehrfach vertreten sind, wird mit den ab *ca.* 570 einsetzenden Komasten- und Sianaschalen, welche ab der Jahrhundertmitte von den Band- und Randschalen abgelöst werden, die Schale zur beliebtesten Gefäßform (Abb. 2). Im letzten Drittel bzw. Viertel des Jhs., in dem die attische Keramik das breiteste Spektrum an Formen aufweist, kommen Schalen, vor allem Droop- u. Kasselschalen, aber auch des Typ A u. C nach wie vor am häufigsten vor. Daneben wurden Amphoren, Kratere und Lekythen bevorzugt. Um die Jahrhundertwende sind Lekythen und Skyphoi z. B. der CHC-Gruppe und zu Beginn des 5. Jhs. Schalen der Leafless-Gruppe in großen Mengen vertreten (Abb. 3); diese werden um *ca.* 490/70 von zahlreichen Schalen, Schalenskyphoi und Lekythen, überwiegend der Haimon- Gruppe und deren Umkreis, abgelöst.

Rotfigurige Keramik der archaischen Zeit wurde bisher in Alt-Smyrna vereinzelt gefunden: es ist ein Schalenfrgt. des späten 6. Jhs.[6] und ein Stamnosfrgt. der Syriskos-Gruppe aus den Jahren 480/70.[7]

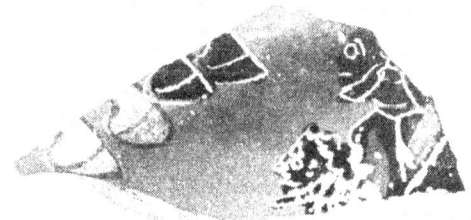

Abb. 1. Dinos (?) aus Alt-Smyrna, Nr.254, Sophilos, 580/75 v. Chr., Leichenspiele zu Ehren des Patroklos?

Danksagung

Bettina Kreuzer danke ich ganz herzlich für Auskünfte über die unpublizierte attisch-rotfigurige Keramik und die Panathenäischen Amphoren aus dem Heraion von Samos sowie ihre Bereitschaft, das Manuskript der vorliegenden Untersuchung durchzulesen und zu kommentieren. Für alle Fehler und Mißverständnisse bin natürlich ich allein verantwortlich. Danken möchte ich ferner Norbert Kunisch, der mir bei einem Besuch in Oxford bereitwillig alle Unterlagen zur attischen Keramik von Milet zeigte und Photos zur Verfügung stellte.

Abbildungsnachweis: Abb.1-5 von der Verfasserin. Abb.5 Milet AT 57.0.149.1 Neg. der Milet- Grabung. Abb.7 Samos, Vathy K 898, DAI Athen Neg.2293.

[1] Scheibler 1983, 173.
[2] In Kap. III der Arbeit "Alt-Smyrna & Pitane" wurde eine Bestandsaufnahme der attisch-schwarzfigurigen Keramik im westlichen Kleinasien vorgelegt. Im folgenden Beitrag wird weitgehend an die dort unter "Ionien, Chios und Samos" besprochenen und in Tabellen verzeichneten Funde verwiesen. Desweiteren werden diese durch Neufunde ergänzt und stellenweise korrigiert.
Nach der Drucklegung von "Alt-Smyrna & Pitane" sind zu diesem Thema in chronologischer Reihe erschienen: Ephesos XII,1.- Mytilene.- Assos I.- Assos II.- Assos III.- Phokaia I.- Klazomenai.- Sardeis.- Samos XXII.- Rf. Alt-Smyrna.- Daskyleion I.- Daskyleion II.- Phokaia II.- Add. Alt-Smyrna (die letzten beiden in Druck). Zur älteren Literatur s. Alt-Smyrna & Pitane 101-123.
[3] Zur Landschaftsbegrenzung s. Roebuck 1959, 5-6. Zu Alt-Smyrna s. Roebuck 1959, 28-29.- Akurgal 1983, 21.

[4] Bayraklı Nr. 192, Alt-Smyrna & Pitane 40-41. Kat. 169.- Vathy K 9797, Samos XXII 107 Kat. 1.
[5] Old Smyrna.- Alt-Smyrna & Pitane 3-51. 108-112. 136-149 mit Tab. 3 und 9 mit Nachw. Zu Neufunden s. Add. Alt-Smyrna.
[6] Old-Smyrna 174 Nr. 136.
[7] Rf. Alt-Smyrna 180 Kat. 16.

Abb. 2. Knopfhenkelschale aus Alt-Smyra, İzmir Museum 9920, Maler der Smyrna-Knopfhenkelschale, 560/50 v. Chr.

Abb. 3. Schale aus Alt-Smyra, Inv.Nr. 51, Tondo, Leafless- Gruppe, Anf. 5. Jh. v. Chr.

Phokaia

Im Bereich der archaischen Siedlung und des Athena-Tempels der Stadt Phokaia[8] setzen die frühesten attischen Importe um 600/590 mit einem Kolonettenkrater des Gorgo-Malers ein. Auffällig ist, daß es sich bei den frühen und qualitätvollen Vasen nicht wie anderenorts um vereinzelte Funde, sondern um bis zur Jahrhundertmitte relativ gleichbleibende größere Mengen handelt. Es sind überwiegend Kratere und Dinoi, u. a. des Malers von Berlin F 1659, des Sophilos, in der Art des Gorgo-Malers, später des Dammhirsch-Malers (Abb. 6), einige in der Art

---

[8] Alt-Smyrna & Pitane 105-108. 136-149 mit Tab. 2 u. 9 mit Nachw.; Phokaia I; Phokaia II (Die Anzahl der Vasen in der Auflistung von Alt-Smyrna 106-107 Tab. 2 stimmt mit dem neuen Katalog von Phokaia II nicht ganz überein, da sich bei der Aufnahme des stark fragmentierten Materials die Zusammengehörigkeit mancher Fragmente zum selben bzw. zu einem anderen Gefäß ergeben hat; ferner konnte in einzelnen Fällen erst durch Profilzeichnungen die genaue Gefäßform bestimmt werden, so daß hier geringfügige Korrekturen nötig waren.). Zu den Ausgrabungen s. ferner: Akurgal 1993.- Akurgal 1995.

Abb. 4. Randschale aus Phokaia, Nr. 52, Sakonides, 550/40 v. Chr.

Abb. 5. Lekanis aus Phokaia, Inv.Nr. 53, Art des Lydos, 560/50 v. Chr.

Abb. 6. Volutenkrater aus Phokaia, Izmir Mus. Inv.Nr. 9634, Dammhirsch-Maler, 550/40 v. Chr.

des Lydos, Lekanen/Lekaniden des KX-Malers und in der Art des Lydos (Abb. 5), Amphoren sowie einige Schalen. Geht man davon aus, daß die zahlreichen Gefäße, nämlich die um 550/30 anzusetzenden Band- u. Randschalen (Abb. 4), Phokaia im ersten der beiden Jahrzehnte erreichten, fällt die höchste Fundkonzentration in die Zeit um 550/40. Neben Schalen behaupten sich auch Kratere, Amphoren, Lekanen/Lekaniden und Pyxiden. In dem darauffolgenden Jahrzehnten sinkt die Zahl wieder auf das Niveau der ersten Jahrhunderthälfte; ab 510 ist attische Keramik nur noch in geringen Mengen oder vereinzelt anzutreffen. Die Schale bleibt im weiteren Verlauf des 6. Jhs. und im frühen 5. Jh. die meist importierte Gefäßform; daneben kommen einige Skyphoi, Amphoren, Olpen, Pyxiden u. a. vor.

Rotfigurige Vasen haben die Ausgrabungen in Phokaia bislang nur wenige hervorgebracht: unter den in der archaischen Zeit entstandenen Gefäßen sind einige Schalen, darunter eine nahe dem Scheuerleer-Maler (um 520/10), eine Amphora oder Hydria und wenige Kratere zu nennen.

Klazomenai

Attische Keramik wurde in Klazomenai[9] sowohl auf der Akropolis und Siedlung als auch in den Nekropolen gefunden. Die frühesten Funde sind Olpen des Gorgo-Malers und seines Umkreises um 590/80, denen eine Lekanis des Sophilos (Abb. 7) und ein Krater/Dinos des Polos-Malers folgen. Trotz einiger weiterer Schalen und Kratere bleibt der Import bis zur Jahrhundertmitte relativ gering. Danach nehmen die Funde schlagartig zu: es sind vor allem Band- u. Randschalen sowie wenige Skyphoi und Amphoren. Die meisten attischen Vasen erreichen Klazomenai im letzten Viertel des 6. Jhs. Die Schale bleibt auch jetzt die meist vertretene Gefäßform (Droop-, Kassel, Typen A. u. C, auch einige rotfigurige Schalen); daneben behaupten sich Lekanai/Lekaniden z. B. der Leagros-Gruppe und aus dem Umkreis des Antimenes-Malers, Lekythen u. a. der Phanyllis-Gruppe und Amphoren, darunter einige aus dem Umkreis des Antimenes-Malers, sowie in geringen Mengen andere Gefäßformen. Für das

---

[9] Alt-Smyrna & Pitane 108-112. 136-149 Tab. 3 u. 9 mit Nachw. ; Klazomenai mit weiterer Lit. zur Grabung.

frühe 5. Jh. sind vor allem zahlreiche Schalen der Leafless-Gruppe und Schalenskyphoi der Haimon-Gruppe belegt.

Unter den wenigen rotfigurigen Vasen der archaischen Zeit überwiegen Schalen: es sind qualitätvolle Stücke, u. a.

Augenschalen um 520/500, Schalen des Typs C, die stilistisch an Epiktetos/Oltos erinnern (Abb. 8) sowie solche aus dem weiten Umkreis des Nikosthenes-Malers. Ferner ist eine Bauchamphora des frühen 5. Jhs. zu nennen.

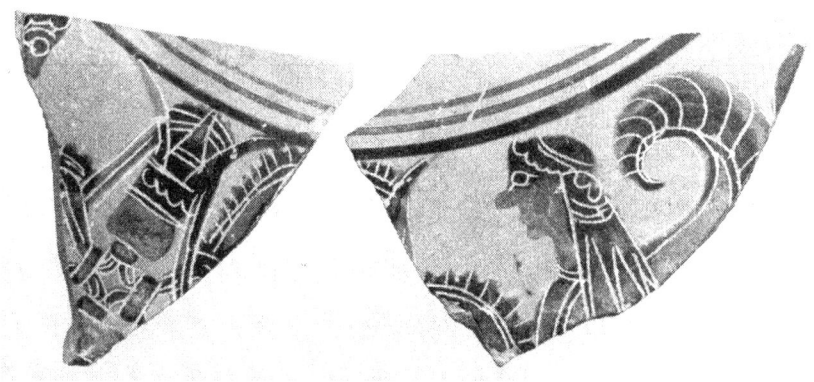

Abb. 7. Lekanisdeckel aus Klazomenai, KLAZ 82 Akropolis Südabhang TN 049, Sophilos, 580/70 v. Chr.

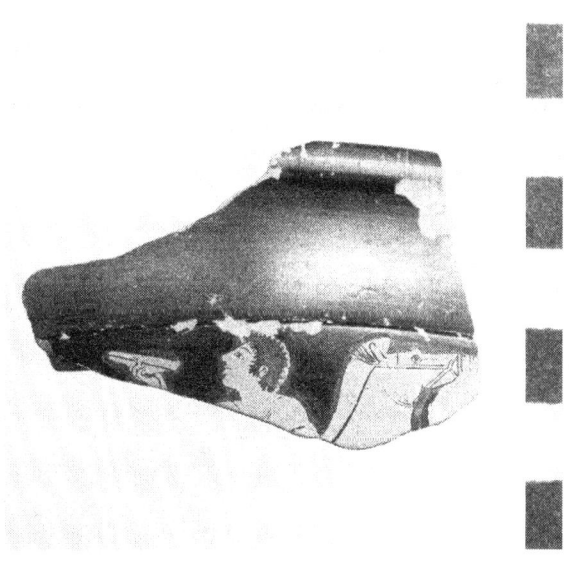

Abb. 8. Schale aus Klazomenai, KLAZ 86 FGT TN 013, 510/490 v. Chr.

Chios

Auf der ionischen Insel Chios[10] ist attische Keramik bislang recht wenig nachgewiesen. Der früheste Fund ist ein Deckel der Komasten-Gruppe um 570 in Chios-Stadt, dem ein weiterer Deckel, eine Schale und eine Oinochoe folgen. In der 2. Hälfte des Jhs. sind es weiterhin drei Schalen, darunter eine rotfigurige, zwei Amphoren, ein Krater, zwei Deckel, ein Epinetron und im frühen 5. Jh. eine Lekythos.[11]

In dem im Süden der Insel gelegenen Emporio wurden Fragmente attischer Vasen im Hafen- und Athena-Heiligtum sowie in der Nekropole gefunden. Die ältesten Stücke sind eine Siana- und eine Knopfhenkelschale, denen in der 2. Hälfte des Jhs. drei Droop-u. Kasselschalen und ein Krater folgen. In das frühe 5. Jh. zu datieren sind einige Schalen, u. a der Leafless-Gruppe, eine rotfigurige sowie eine Lekythos.[12]

Auch Phanai weist im 3. Viertel des 6. Jhs. Funde auf: es sind zwei Bandschalen und wenige geschlossene Gefäße.

Ephesos

In Ephesos sind der Altar und Altarhof des Artemisions und die spätarchaische Nekropole im Osten der oberen Agora, dem sog. Staatsmarkt, als Fundorte attischer Keramik bekannt;[13] ferner wird von Funden aus der archaisch-klassischen Nekropole im Bereich der römischen Tetragonos-Agora und der Siedlung Smyrna berichtet.[14] Der älteste Fund ist eine Sianaschale aus dem Artemision, dem um 540 eine Amphora in der Art des Exekias folgt. Die Funde nehmen hier aber erst im letzten Drittel des 6. Jhs. zu und dauern im frühen 5. Jh. an. Es sind Droopschalen, eine Pelike, eine Oinochoe der Werkstatt des Athena-Malers, eine Lekythos der Phanyllis-Gruppe und später Schalenskyphoi und mehrere Lekythen der Haimon-Gruppe. Von den Funden aus der Nekropole ist als frühester Fund eine Kasselschale zu nennen, der einige Amphoren und Olpen, ein Krater sowie Lekythen der Phanyllis- und Hahn-Gruppe und später eine weitere nahe der Kleine-Löwen-Gruppe folgen; hinzu kommt ein Schalenskyphos der Haimon-Gruppe.[15]

Die rotfigurige Keramik der archaischen Zeit ist im Artemision bislang nur durch eine Schale des Pithos-Malers vertreten.

Milet

Von der attischen Keramik Milets ist bislang wenig publiziert worden.[16] Nach den Vorberichten zu den Ausgrabungen zu urteilen, ist der früheste Beleg für attischen Import eine Pferdekopfamphora um 580/70 aus dem Norden des Athena-Tempels. Jüngste Funde, vor allem aus dem Aphrodite-Heiligtum des Zeytintepe zeigen, daß dies kein Einzelfund ist:[17] Kratere mit Tierfriesen sowie zahlreiche Komasten- und Sianaschalen zeugen von regem frühen Import. Bekannt sind aus dieser Zeit desweiteren zwei Amphoren aus dem Umkreis des Kleitias und des Lydos und einige Lekanen/Lekaniden (Abb. 9).[18] Im 3. Viertel des 6. Jhs. nehmen die Fundmengen auch in Milet zu: zu den bisher publizierten sechs Band- und der einen Randschalen[19] kommen nun zahlreiche Exemplare vom Zeytintepe und Kalabaktepe hinzu, denen einige Kassel- und zahlreiche Droopschalen folgen. Ferner sind Kratere des Lydos-Umkreises, einige Hydrien und Kelchpyxiden belegt. Zu den vereinzelten bekannten Stücken[20] des letzten Viertels des 6. Jhs. können nun auch Lekaniden, Amphoren, Olpen, Augenschalen, Schalen des Typs C, u. a. der Gruppe der Kamiros-Palmetten, Skyphoi u. a. der F. P.-Klasse und der CHC-Gruppe um 500 und wenige Lekythen gezählt werden (Abb. 10). Lekythen, jetzt mit ornamentaler Verzierung, bleiben auch im frühen 5. Jh.[21] selten. Daneben sind Schalen des Typ A der Leafless-Gruppe und Schalenskyphoi der Haimon-Gruppe vertreten.

Rotfigurige Keramik der archaischen Zeit ist bislang in geringen Mengen nachgewiesen: es sind an Oltos/Epiktetos erinnernde Augenschalen vom Zeytintepe, ein Schalenfrgt. vom Kalabaktepe und ein Askos aus dem Umkreis des Douris.[22]

---

[10] Alt-Smyrna & Pitane 108-112. 136-149 Tab. 3 u. 9 mit Nachw.
[11] Rf. Schale des Pithos-M. s. ARV² 141,70.
[12] Boardman 1967, 156, 697 Taf. 57.
[13] Alt-Smyrna & Pitane 108-112. 136-149 mit Tab. 3 und 9 mit Nachw. (die in den Nachw. angegebenen Seiten- und Tafelnummern haben sich beim endgültigen Druck geändert, Kat. Nrn. stimmen jedoch überein); Ephesos XII,1.
[14] Trinkl 1999, mit Anm. 1. Zu weiteren archaischen Gräbern in Ephesos s. Knibbe und Langmann 1993, 52-53.
[15] Trinkl 1999.

[16] Alt-Smyrna & Pitane 108-112. 136-149 mit Anm. 600, Tab. 3 und 9; hinzuzufügen zu Nachw. 312 ist: Kraterfrgt., Schiering 1979, 106, Taf. 24,8. Ferner Müller-Wiener 1983, 249 Abb. 8 auf S. 493; Kerschner 1995, 216-217 Nr. 1-2 , Abb. 18,1; Kerschner 1999, 48 , Nr. 82 Abb. 17. 28b.
[17] Die freundliche Auskunft verdanke ich Norbert Kunisch, der die gesamte attische Keramik zur Publikation vorbereitet. Demnach handelt es sich um ca. 200 Frgte. vom Zeytintepe, ca. 100 Frgte. vom Kalabaktepe und weitere 300-350 Frgte. aus den alten Grabungen. Zu den Ausgrabungen auf dem Zeytintepe s. Gans 1991.- Senff 1992.- Heinz und Senff 1992. Zu den Ausgrabungen auf dem Kalabaktepe mit dem Heiligtum der Artemis Kithone und dem archaischen und frühklassischen Wohnviertel s. V. Graeve 1986.- V. Graeve 1987.- V. Graeve 1990- V. Graeve und Senff 1991.- Heinrich und Senff 1992.- Senff 1995.- Kerschner 1995- Kerschner 1999.
[18] Alt-Smyrna & Pitane 108-112 Tab. 3 mit Nachw. 307. 308 (nur 1 x).
[19] Zusätzlich: Schiering 1979, 106 Taf. 24,8.
[20] Alt-Smyrna & Pitane 108-112 Tab. 3 mit Nachw. 313-315.
[21] Hinzu kommt: Kerschner 1995, 216,1 (Lekythos, Umkr. d. Haimon-M.).
[22] Auskünfte von N. Kunisch.- Kerschner 1995, 216, 2.- Voigtländer 1982, 87 Taf. 29,5.

Abb. 9. Lekanisdeckel aus Milet, BN 87.17.1, 2. Viertel 6. Jh. v. Chr.

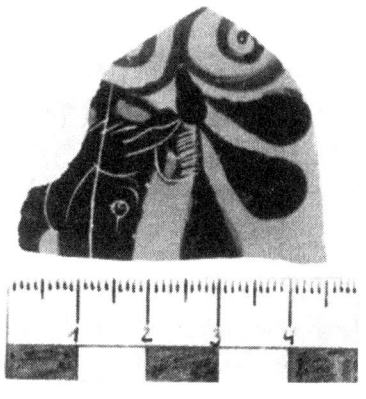

Abb. 10. Halsamphora aus Milet, AT 57.0.149.1, Anf. 5. Jh. v. Chr.

Didyma

Im Apollontempel von Didyma ist attische Keramik in sehr geringen Mengen belegt.[23] Es sind vereinzelte Schalen und Skyphoi, darunter eine Kasselschale, eine der Leafless-Gruppe und ein hermogenischer Skyphos sowie je ein Amphoren- und Kraterfrgt., die sich vom 3. Viertel des 6. Jhs. bis in das frühe 5. Jh. datieren lassen.

Samos

Das Heraion von Samos liefert die reichsten Funde attischer Keramik im ionischen Küstenbereich;[24] weitere Funde wurden in Pythagoreion in der Westnekropole,[25] im Artemis-Heiligtum[26] und Stadtgebiet[27] sowie auf dem Kastrohügel[28] gemacht.

Der Import beginnt im Heraion um 600 mit einer Bauchamphora nahe dem Nettos-Maler. Bereits im frühen 6. Jh. sind die Fundmengen beachtlich. Dabei handelt es sich in erster Linie um Amphoren, Lekanen/Lekaniden, Hydrien und Skyphoi, u. a. des Kerameikos-Malers, in der Art des Gorgo-Malers und des KX-Malers. Von besonderer Bedeutung sind die zahlreichen Schalen des KX-Malers um 575/70, denen einige Komasten- u. Sianaschalen folgen. Im 2. Viertel des 6. Jhs. bleiben Amphoren, Hydrien und Lekanen/Lekaniden, u. a. des Kleitias, Lydos, Polos-Malers und deren Umkreise, am häufigsten vertreten (Abb.11). Ab der Jahrhundertmitte, in der die Importmengen ihren Höhepunkt erreichen, sind Kleinmeisterschalen mit über 100 Stück eindeutig die beliebteste Gefäßform. Daneben behaupten sich weiterhin Amphoren, u. a. des Exekias, Amasis-Malers (Abb. 12), Elbows-Out-Malers und Affekters, aber auch Schalen des Typs A und Kelchpyxiden, u. a. der Princeton-Gruppe und des Malers der Nikosia Olpe. Im späteren 6. Jh. nehmen die Fundmengen allmählich ab. Schalen (Band-, Droop-, Kassel-, Blütenbandschalen sowie Typ A) kommen weiterhin häufig vor, daneben sind Kratere, einige Amphoren und weiterhin Kelchpyxiden, eine davon in der Art des Lysippides-Malers, mehrfach vertreten. Aus dem 1. Viertel des 5. Jhs. sind lediglich Schalen des Typs A, vor allem der Leafless-Gruppe, und einige Lekythen hervorzuheben.

---

[23] Alt-Smyrna & Pitane 108-112. 136-149 Tab. 3 u. 9 mit Nachw.
[24] Alt-Smyrna & Pitane 108-112. 136-149 Tab. 3 mit Nachw.; Samos XXII. In der Endfassung von Samos XXII bekamen alle Einträge Inv. Nrn.; ferner haben sich durch Einschübe und Korrekturen die Kat. Nrn. verschoben, die Reihenfolge der in den Nachw. von Alt-Smyrna & Pitane laut Manuskript zitierten Stücke stimmt aber im großen und ganzen noch überein.
[25] Boehlau 1898, 48-51.- CVA Kassel 2, Taf. 52.- Yfanditis 1990, 101-102 Nr. 102.- Löwe 1996, 50-55. Grab. 40; 81 Brandschicht 22.
[26] Tsakos 1980a, 305-318.- Tsakos 1980b, 460-372 Taf. 274.
[27] Tsakos 1970, 416 Taf. 350
[28] Tölle-Kastenbein 1974, 147.

Abb. 11. Hydria aus dem Heraion von Samos, Vathy K 1427, Kleitias-Umkreis, 570/60 v. Chr.

Abb. 12. Amphora aus dem Heraion von Samos, Vathy K 898, Amasis-Maler, um 540 v. Chr.

Rotfigurige Vasen des späten 6. Jhs. sind im Heraion zwar von bester Qualität, jedoch in geringen Mengen vertreten: es sind sieben Schalen und sechs Kratere, darunter zwei Kratere, ein Stamnos und ein Teller. Von den Krateren erinnert einer stilistisch stark an Euphronios, während eine Schale die Signatur des Töpfers Kachrylion trägt. Die Mehrzahl der rotfigurigen Vasen läßt sich in die 1. Hälfte des 5. Jhs. datieren, darunter zahlreiche Schalen, zwei Pyxiden und Lekythen.[29]

Gefäßformen

Symposionsgeschirr

Mischgefäße

Kratere[30] und Dinoi (Lebetes)[31] (Diagramm 1)

Der Krater und der Dinos als wichtige Bestandteile des Symposiongeschirrs, die zum Mischen von Wasser und Wein dienten, gehören bereits seit dem frühen 6. Jh. zum Repertoire der aus Athen importierten Gefäße.[32] Unter den

---

[29] Nach schriftlicher Mitteilung Bettina Kreuzers vom 9. September 2000.

[30] Zu Krateren s. Schiering 1983, 146-147.- Scheibler 1983, 18.- Agora XXIII 23-29.- Schleiffenbaum 1991.- Frank 1990. Zum Stellenwert des Kraters beim Symposion s. Lissarrague 1990a, 196-209.- Zur gesellschaftlichen Stellung des Besitzers eines Kraters s. Luke 1994, 23-32.

[31] Zu Dinoi (Lebetes) s. Schiering 1983, 149.- Agora XXIII 33-35.

[32] Bei kleinen Wandungsfragmenten läßt sich oftmals nicht entscheiden, ob sie von einem Kolonettkrater oder Dinos stammen, jedoch kommen Dinoi nach 550 kaum mehr vor. Dinosständer sind auf Samos mehrfach gefunden worden: Alt-Smyrna & Pitane 108- 112 Tab. 3 mit Nachw. 368. 386. 405; Samos XXII 125-126 Kat. 51-54.

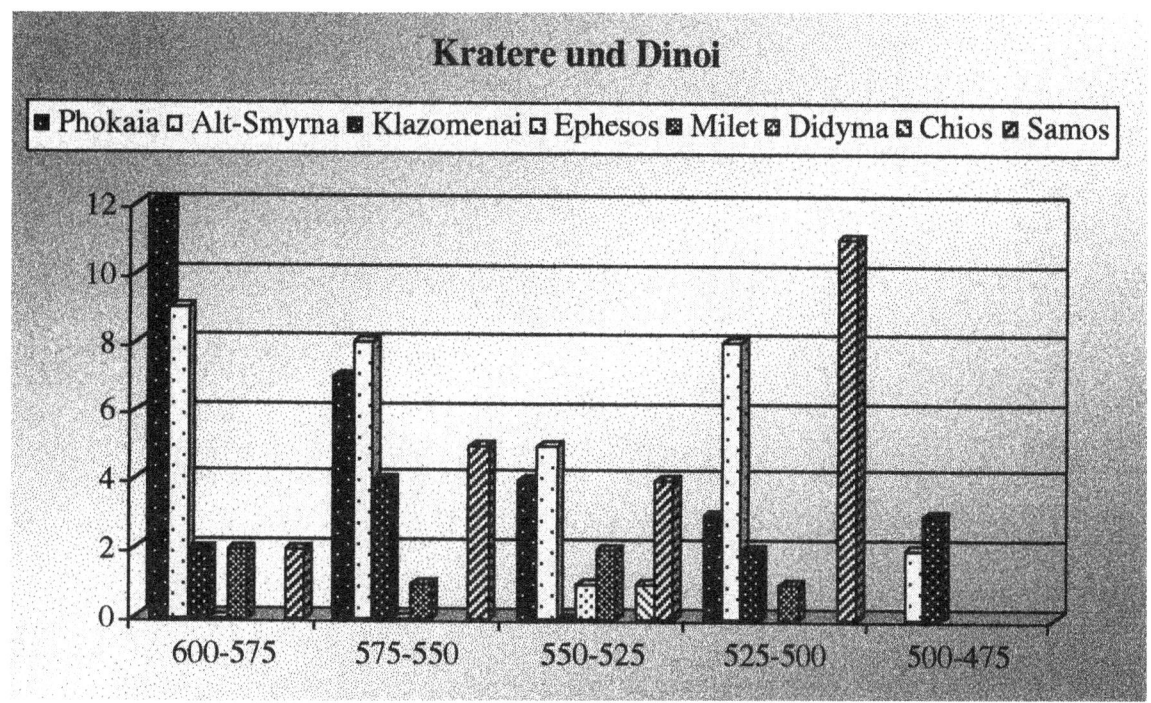

Diagramm 1. Kratere und Dinoi.

ionischen Fundorten weisen Phokaia und Alt-Smyrna im frühen 6. Jh. u. a. mit Exemplaren des Gorgo-Malers u. Umkreises, des Malers v. Berlin 1659, des Sophilos (Abb. 1) und später in der Art des Lydos die höchste Dichte auf, die bis zum Ende des Jhs. mit leicht abnehmender Tendenz anhält.[33] Aus Milet wird von einigen Krateren um 580/70 berichtet.[34] Auf Samos und in Klazomenai sind im 2.-3. Viertel des 6. Jhs. je 4-5 Exemplare belegt, die im letzten Viertel des Jhs. sogar etwas zunehmen.[35] Auch Ephesos, Didyma und Emporion weisen vereinzelte Kraterfunde auf. Dabei sind Kolonettenkratere naturgemäß in der Überzahl, aber auch Volutenkratere kommen in Phokaia bereits im zweiten Jahrhundertviertel (Abb. 6)[36] und später auch in Alt-Smyrna vor;[37] Kelchkratere lassen sich im späten 6. Jh. sowohl in Klazomenai und als auch in Samos nachweisen.[38]

In den benachbarten Landschaften Kleinasiens sind Kratere und Dinoi in den Satrapensitzen Daskyleion[39] und Sardeis[40] recht früh ab 590 belegt, wobei sie im ersteren zahlreicher sind; aus Gordion ist bislang ein Krater um 560 bekannt.[41] Im lykischen Xanthos kommen Kratere ab 570 ebenfalls häufig vor.[42] Vereinzelte Funde wurde in der Äolis ab 590 in der Nekropole von Pitane[43] und in Larisa, später auf Lesbos gemacht.[44] Wenige Kratere sind im karischen Iasos,[45] auf Rhodos in Lindos[46] ab dem frühen 6. Jh. und erst später in anderen Orten nachgewiesen.[47]

Als Mischgefäß dienten ferner Stamnoi und Amphoren.[48] Bislang sind nur ein schwarzfiguriger Stamnos[49] des letzten Viertels des 6. Jhs. sowie ein rotfiguriger aus den Jahren um 480/70 in Alt-Smyrna belegt.[50]

---

[33] Alt-Smyrna & Pitane 105-108 Tab. 2 mit Nachw. 133-34. 140-41. 151. 157; 108-112 Tab. 3 mit Nachw. 197-98. 207-08. 218-19. 231-32; Phokaia II Kat. 97-121; Add. Alt-Smyrna Kat. 40-56.

[34] Da mir keine genauen Fundzahlen aus Milet vorliegen, konnten in den Graphiken nur die publizierten und die mir von N. Kunisch erwähnten Stücke berücksichtigt werden.

[35] Alt-Smyrna & Pitane 108-112 Tab. 3 mit Nachw. 278. 282. 362-63. 379. 399. 418; Klazomenai Kat. 115-128; Samos XXII.

[36] Phokaia I 19-20 Abb. 8-9; Y. Tuna- Nörling in: APP 435- 438.- Phokaia II Kat. 114-115.

[37] Add. Alt-Smyrna Kat. 55.

[38] Alt-Smyrna & Pitane 112-115 Tab. 3 mit Nachw. 262. 265. 278. 282. 362-3. 379. 399. 418; Klazomenai Kat. 121. 125; Samos XXII 128 Kat. 63-64. 129 Kat. 70.

[39] Daskyleion I Kat. 155-176, neben Kolonettenkrateren auch ein Volutenkrater Kat. 167 und ein Kelchkrater Kat. 168, beide spätes 6. Jh; Daskyleion II 70-73 Kat. 196-215.

[40] Alt-Smyrna & Pitane 115-117 Tab. 5 mit Nachw. 651. 658, ferner Sardeis 79-81 Att 35-43.

[41] Alt-Smyrna & Pitane 118-199 Tab. 6 mit Nachw. 692; DeVries 1997,447 Abb. 1.

[42] Alt-Smyrna & Pitane 115-117 Tab. 5 mit Nachw. 613. 621. 631. 637.

[43] Alt-Smyrna & Pitane 77-78 Kat. 97-98;105-108 Tab. 2 mit Nachw. 65.

[44] Alt-Smyrna & Pitane 105-108 Tab. 2 mit Nachw. 117-118. 168-169. 171.

[45] Alt-Smyrna & Pitane 112-115 Tab. 4 mit Nachw. 460.

[46] Alt-Smyrna & Pitane 112-115 Tab. 4 mit Nachw. 558. 560. 563.

[47] Alt-Smyrna & Pitane 112-115 Tab. 4 mit Nachw. 502 (Kamiros). 582 (Fikellura).

[48] Zur Verwendung von Amphoren auch als Mischgefäße s. Scheibler 1987, 70-73.- Kaeser 1990, 192-193. Zu Amphoren in Ionien s. unten.

[49] Zu Stamnoi s. Schiering 1983, 158-159 mit Lit.- Philippaki 1967

[50] Alt-Smyrna & Pitane 112-115 Tab. 3 mit Nachw. 233. Rf. Alt-Smyrna 180 Kat. 16.

Psyktere[51]

Zu den selten erhaltenen Gefäßen zählen Psyktere, die man zum Kühlen des Wein in Kratere stellte. Der Fuß eines Psykters mit Efeufries auf der Standplatte sowie ein weiteres wohl zur Schulter eines solchen Gefäßes gehöriges Fragment des späten 6./frühen 5. Jhs. wurden in Alt-Smyrna gefunden.[52]

Serviergefäße

Olpen und Oinochoen[53] *(Diagramm 2)*

Schankkannen, mit denen man Wein aus Mischgefäßen schöpfte und den Teilnehmern des Gelages einschenkte, sind in Ionien seit dem frühen 6. Jh. belegt. Sie sind während der gesamten archaischen Zeit in relativ geringen Mengen vertreten,[54] dennoch fällt auf, daß sie im frühen 6. Jh. - vor allem Olpen des Gorgo-Malers und seines Umkreises[55]- und am Ende des Jhs., u. a. der 'Dot-Ivy'-Gruppe,[56] häufiger vorkommen.

In den benachbarten Regionen sind Olpen und Oinochoen in der äolischen Nekropole von Pitane,[57] ähnlich wie in Ionien, ab dem frühen 6. Jh., auf Lesbos[58] ab 550 bezeugt. In Daskyleion sind sie im späten 6. Jh.[59] mehrfach, in Sardeis[60] vereinzelt gefunden worden. Besonders zahlreich sind Kannen im lykischen Xanthos[61] und ab der 2. Jahrhunderthälfte in den Nekropolen von Rhodos, wo sie vor allem im Kamiros des frühen 5. Jhs. zur beliebtesten Grabbeigabe avancieren.[62]

Lekanen/Lekaniden[63] *(Diagramm 3)*

Schüsseln mit und ohne Deckel, die man zur Aufnahme und zum Servieren von Speisen benutzte, gehören zu den Gefäßtypen, die ab dem frühen 6. Jh. in Ionien importiert wurden. In Phokaia, Alt-Smyrna und im Heraion von Samos sind vor allem Lekaniden des KX-Maler, des Malers der Dresdner-Lekanis und des Kerameikos-Malers mehrfach gefunden worden.[64] Diesen folgen im 2. Jahrhundertviertel Lekaniden des Sophilos, des Polos-Malers und des Lydos-Umkreises (Abb. 5,9).[65] Nach einem einzelnen Deckel des Sophilos (Abb. 7) nehmen in Klazomenai Lekaniden erst im späten 6. Jh. zu: es sind Vasen der Leagros-Gruppe und aus dem Umkreis des Antimenes-Malers.[66]

In den benachbarten Landschaften sind einige wenige frühe Lekaniden in Troja, in Daskyleion und auf Rhodos in Ialysos zu erwähnen;[67] ab dem 2. Viertel des 6. Jh. erscheinen sie in Thymbra, Mytilene, Kamiros, Daskyleion und ab der 2. Jahrhunderthälfte zahlreich im lykischen Xanthos.[68]

Teller[69]

Teller sind in Ionien selten. Neben dem Teller aus Alt-Smyrna in der Art des Lydos sind zwei Exemplare des 2. Viertels des 6. Jhs. aus dem Heraion von Samos und ein weiteres, an den Lysippides-Maler erinnerndes Stück aus Phokaia zu nennen.[70]

Außerhalb Ioniens sind vier Teller um 520/10 hervorzuheben, die in einem Grab der Nekropole von Pitane gefunden wurden und alle von einer Hand nahe dem Maler von Toronto 283 stammen;[71] desweiteren sind drei Tellerfragmente der ersten Jahrhunderthälfte, darunter

---

[51] Zu Psyktern s. Schiering 1983, 156.- Scheibler 1983, 18-20.- Agora XXIII 20-22.

[52] Rf. Alt-Smyrna 186 Kat. 52.- Alt-Smyrna & Pitane 108-112 Tab. 3 mit Nachw. 234.

[53] Zu Olpen u. Oinochoen s. Schiering 1983, 152-153.- Scheibler 1983, 20.- Agora XXIII 39-43.

[54] Zum Fehlen von Kannen in den östlichen Gebieten des Persischen Reiches im Gegensatz zu den westlichen Satrapien, s. DeVries 1977.- Daskyleion I 16.

[55] Phokaia I 16 Abb. 1; Phokaia II Kat. 85-86.- Add Alt-Smyrna Kat. 35.- Klazomenai Kat. 129-130.

[56] Alt-Smyrna & Pitane Kap. I. Kat. 181.- Add. Alt-Smyrna Kat. 38-39.

[57] Alt-Smyrna & Pitane 105-108. Tab. 2 mit Nachw. 64. 71. 88-89. 96-97.

[58] Alt-Smyrna & Pitane 105-108. Tab. 2 mit Nachw. 175. 183. 188 (Mytilene).

[59] Daskyleion I Kat. 202-209A; Daskyleion II 73f. Kat. 217-222.

[60] Alt-Smyrna & Pitane 115-117 Tab. 5 mit Nachw. 678. 684, ferner Sardeis 77 Att 19-20.

[61] Alt-Smyrna & Pitane 115-117 Tab. 5 mit Nachw. 632. 638.

[62] Alt-Smyrna & Pitane 112-115 Tab. 4 mit Nachw. 483. 494. 501. 509-10. 522. 533. 540. 546-47. 562. 566. 581. 595-96. 605.

[63] Zu Lekanen und Lekaniden s. Schiering 1983, 150.- Scheibler 1983, 21-22.- Agora XXIII 51-53.- Lioutas 1987. Zum Gebrauch bei Mahlzeiten zum Auftragen von Speisen: Rotroff und Oakley 1992, 35 mit Anm. 1.

[64] Alt-Smyrna & Pitane 105-108 Tab. 2 mit Nachw. 136; Phokaia II Kat. 123-124. 131-132.- Alt-Smyrna & Pitane 108-112 Tab. 3 mit Nachw. 199. 365; Add. Alt-Smyrna Kat. 57. 59.

[65] Alt-Smyrna & Pitane 105-108 Tab. 2 mit Nachw. 143; Phokaia II Kat. 125-129. 133-136.- Alt-Smyrna & Pitane 108-112 Tab. 3 mit Nachw. 209. 380; Add. Alt-Smyrna 58. 60-61; Samos XXII Kat. 131-140.

[66] Klazomenai Kat. 176-187.

[67] Alt-Smyrna & Pitane 103-105 Tab. 1 mit Nachw. 29; 112-115 Tab. 4 mit Nachw. 516.- Daskyleion II 61-63 Kat. 157-160.

[68] Alt-Smyrna & Pitane 103-105 Tab. 1 mit Nachw. 30. 43; 105-108 Tab. 2 mit Nachw. 176; 112-115 Tab. 4 mit Nachw. 476; 115-117 Tab. 5 mit Nachw. 614. 634.- Mytilene Kat. 62.- Daskyleion I Kat. 235-36 (2. V. 6.-frühes 5. Jh.).

[69] Zu Tellern s. Schiering 1983, 159.- Callipolitis- Feytmans 1974.- Agora XXIII 53-56.

[70] Alt-Smyrna & Pitane 105-108 Tab. 2 mit Nachw. 158; Phokaia I Abb. 20-21; Phokaia II Kat. 144.- Alt-Smyrna & Pitane 108-112 Tab. 3 mit Nachw. 210. 383.

[71] Alt-Smyrna & Pitane 105-108 Tab. 2 mit Nachw. 91.

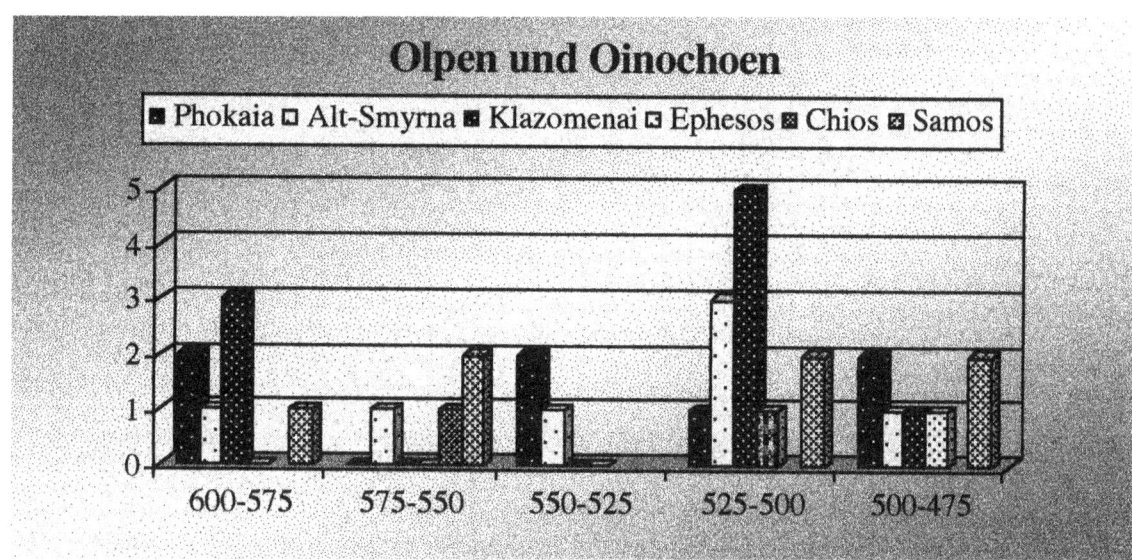

Diagramm 2. Olpen und Oinochoen.

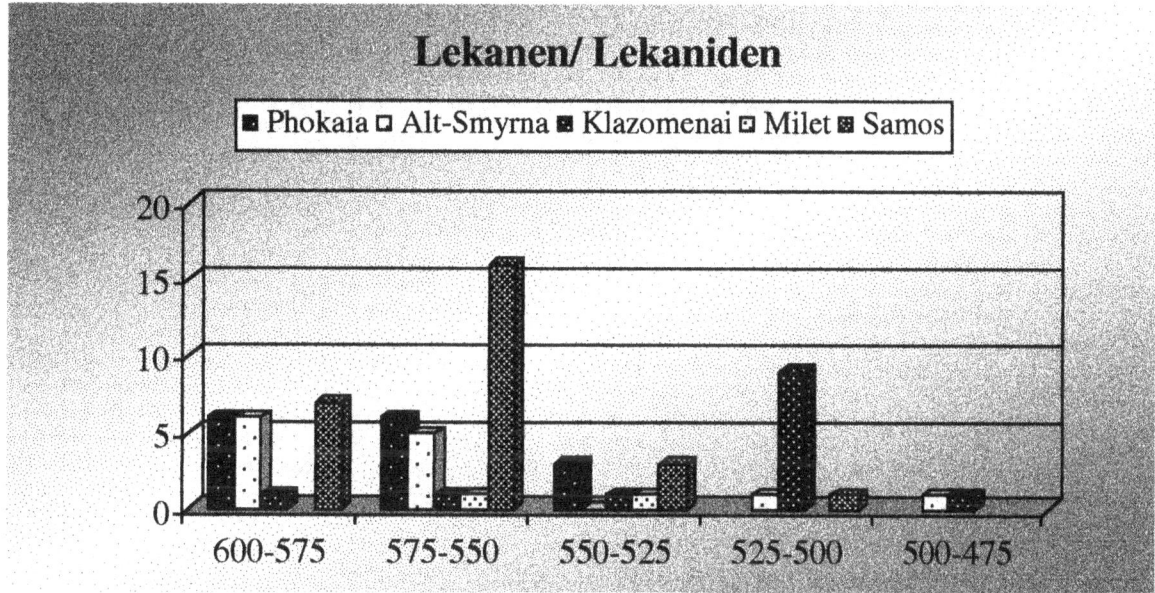

Diagramm 3. Lekanen und Lekaniden.

eines des Polos-Malers, auf der Akropolis von Mytilene belegt.[72]

Trinkgefäße

Schalen[73] *(Diagramm 4)*

Ioniens bevorzugter Importartikel aus dem athenischen Kerameikos war ab dem 2. Viertel des 6. Jhs. eindeutig die Trinkschale. Die frühesten Funde setzen um 580/70 in Phokaia, Alt-Smyrna, Klazomenai, Milet und Samos mit Komastenschalen, u. a. des KY-Malers, und Schalen des KX-Malers ein;[74] diesen folgen Sianaschalen, u. a. des Taras-Malers und C-Malers, die vor allem in Alt-Smyrna, Milet und Samos in größeren Mengen vertreten sind.[75] Auch Knopfhenkelschalen kommen vor (Abb. 2).[76] Als die

---

[72] Mytilene Kat. 63-65.
[73] Zu Schalen s. Schiering 1983, 148.- Scheibler 1983, 20-21.- Agora XXIII 62-68.- "Schale".

[74] Alt-Smyrna & Pitane 105-108 Tab. 2 mit Nachw. 137; Phokaia II Kat. 1-2.- Alt-Smyrna & Pitane 108-112 Tab. 3 mit Nachw. 200. 258. 369. 335. 372; Add. Alt-Smyrna Kat. 1.- Klazomenai Kat. 1-2.- Nach Auskünften N. Kunischs mehrfach vom Zeytintepe.
[75] Alt-Smyrna & Pitane 105-108 Tab. 2 mit Nachw. 138; Phokaia II Kat. 3-5.- Alt-Smyrna & Pitane 108-112 Tab. 3 mit Nachw. 201. 264. 347. 370; Add. Alt-Smyrna Kat. 2; Klazomenai Kat. 3-4; nach Auskünften N. Kunischs zahlreich gefunden auf dem Zeytintepe.
[76] Phokaia II Kat. 6; Alt-Smyrna & Pitane 108-112 Tab. 3 mit Nachw. 202 (Alt-Smyrna). 348 (Emporio). 388 (Samos).

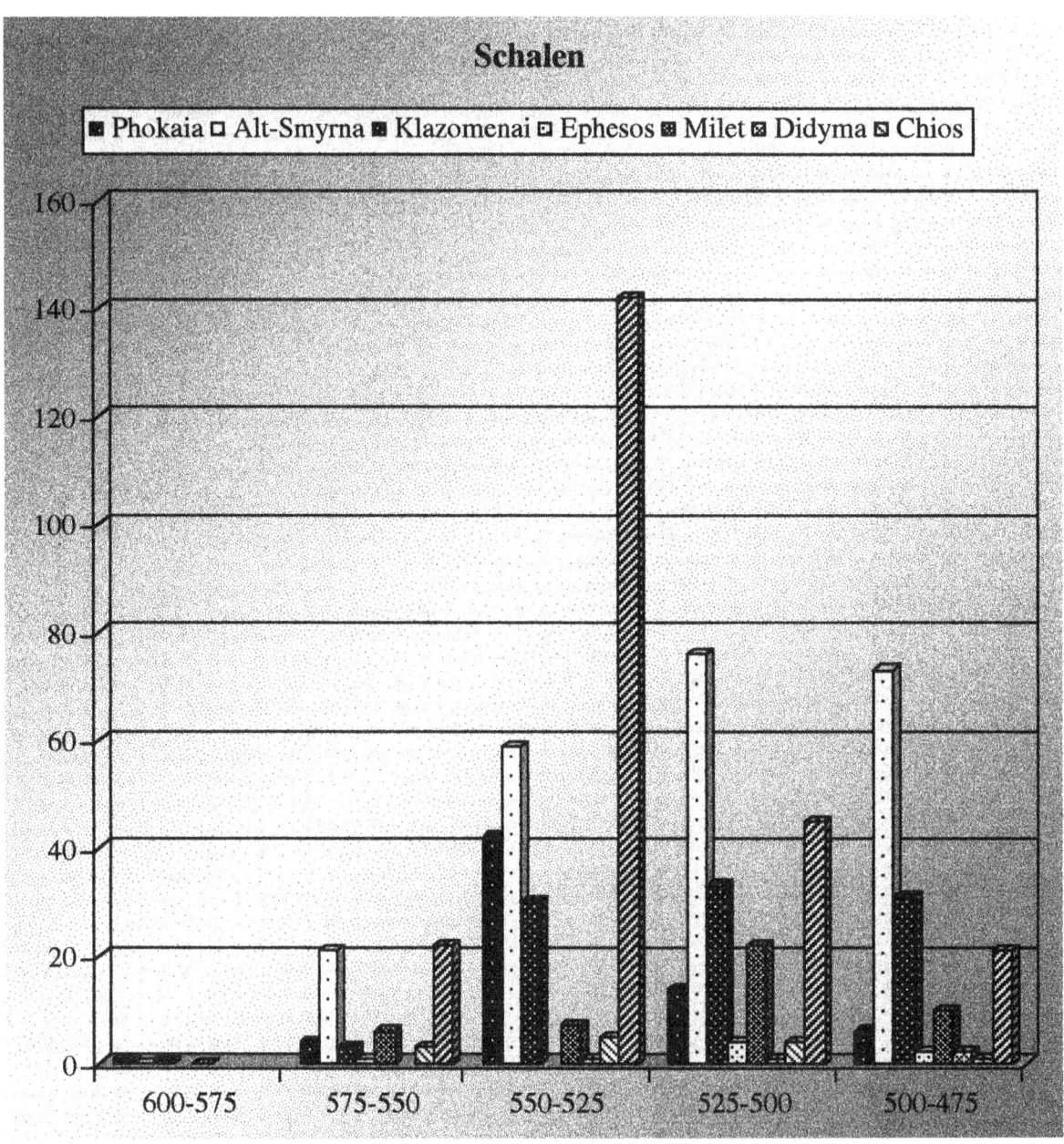

Diagramm 4. Schalen.

beliebtesten Schalentypen erweisen sich Rand- und Bandschalen, die den ionischen Kleinmeisterschalen Konkurrenz machten und diese wohl allmählich vom Markt verdrängten.[77] Zahlreich wurden sie im Heraion von Samos gefunden, aber auch in Phokaia, Alt-Smyrna, Klazomenai und Milet, darunter Stücke des Tleson und Tleson-Malers, des Läufer-Malers, des Amasis und seines Umkreises u. a. (Abb. 4).[78] Im letzten Drittel des 6. Jhs. erfreuen sich Droop- und Kasselschalen, vor allem in Alt-Smyrna an Beliebtheit, sind aber ebenso auf Samos, und in geringeren Mengen, in Klazomenai, Milet, Ephesos und Phokaia zu finden.[79] Weiterhin häufen sich in dieser Zeit auf Samos, in Alt-Smyrna, Klazomenai und Milet Schalen des Typs A, zu denen sich bald die des Typs C gesellen, u. a. der Gruppe der Kamiros-Palmetten.[80] Diesen folgen im frühen 5. Jh. zahlreiche Schalen der Leafless-Gruppe und ihres Umkreises (Abb. 3).[81] Unter den wenigen rotfigurigen

---

[77] Roebuck 1959, 82-82.- Sardeis 72

[78] Alt-Smyrna & Pitane 105-108 Tab. 2 mit Nachw. 144-45. 160; Phokaia II Kat. 7-44.- Alt-Smyrna & Pitane 108-112 Tab. 3 mit Nachw. 212-14. 221. 267-68. 280. 309-10. 332. 338. 389-91. 407; Add. Alt-Smyrna Kat. 3-13; Klazomenai Kat. 5-36.

[79] Alt-Smyrna & Pitane 105-108 Tab. 2 mit Nachw. 154; Phokaia II Kat. 45-46.- Alt-Smyrna & Pitane 108-112 Tab. 3 mit Nachw. 222-223. 288-89. 351-52. 408-409; Add. Alt-Smyrna Kat. 14; Klazomenai 37-45.

[80] Alt-Smyrna & Pitane 108-112 Tab. 3 mit Nachw. 225. 274. 411; Add. Alt-Smyrna Kat. 15-19; Klazomenai Kat. 46-63; nach Auskünften N. Kunischs.

[81] Alt-Smyrna & Pitane 108-112 Tab. 3 mit Nachw. 240. 426; Add. Alt-

Vasen der archaischen Zeit in Phokaia, Klazomenai und Samos dominieren ebenfalls Schalen des Typs A und C (Abb. 8).[82]

Die Schale war nicht nur in Ionien sondern im gesamten westlichen Kleinasien in der zweiten Hälfte des 6. Jhs. und mancherorts auch im frühen 5. Jh. die bevorzugte attische Gefäßform.[83] Von den frühen Schalen sind Komastenschalen im äolischen Pitane, auf Rhodos in Lindos, in Daskyleion, Sardeis und Gordion nachgewiesen,[84] während Sianaschalen in Elaious, Pitane und Mytilene, im karischen Labraunda, auf Rhodos in Kamiros und Ialysos, in Sardeis sowie in Xanthos z. T. mehrfach vorkommen und somit einen größeren Verbreitungsgrad zeigen.[85] Weitaus verbreiteter und in größerer Anzahl zu finden sind alle Varianten der Kleinmeisterschalen und deren Nachfolger, die Schalen des Typs A.[86]

Skyphoi[87] (Diagramm 5)

Skyphoi (Kotylai) des frühen 6. Jhs. sind bislang nur im Heraion von Samos gefunden worden, davon zwei von der Hand des KX-Malers.[88] Diesen folgen dort um 570 weitere Stücke und in Alt-Smyrna sind es drei Skyphoi des KY-Malers und der Gruppe des Oxforder Deckels.[89] Im 3. Viertel des 6. Jhs. kommen in Klazomenai, Didyma, Milet und auf Samos wenige Bandskyphoi vor.[90] Erst im späten 6. Jh. und um die Jahrhundertwende häufen sich Skyphoi, u. a. der Heron-Gruppe, CHC-Gruppe, F. P.-Gruppe in Milet, Alt-Smyrna und Klazomenai.[91] Im frühen 5. Jh. erfreuen sich Schalenskyphoi der Haimon-Gruppe und ihres Umkreises, wie zahlreiche Exemplare aus den letzten beiden Fundorten zeigen, einer großer Popularität.[92]

In den benachbarten Landschaften haben sich Skyphoi (Kotylai) des frühen 6. Jhs. vereinzelt in Troja, in Elaious und in Sardeis sowie mehrfach in Pitane erhalten.[93] Einige Bandskyphoi sind ab der Jahrhundertmitte in Elaious, Kamiros, Ialysos, Sardeis belegt, jedoch nimmt die Anzahl der Skyphoi und Schalenskyphoi erst gegen Ende des Jhs. zu. Nun sind sie in Troja, Thymbra, Pitane, Mytilene, Labraunda, Kamiros, Ialysos, Daskyleion, Sardeis u. Xanthos ebenfalls zu finden.[94]

Kantharoi und Mastoi[95]

Zu zwei Kantharoi gehören möglicherweise Fragmente aus Alt-Smyrna, von denen einer dem C-Maler um 565/60 zugewiesen werden kann.[96] Im Heraion von Samos haben sich ebenfalls zwei Kantharoi gefunden, davon einer des KX-Malers um 580/75.[97] Ein einziger Mastos um 530/20 ist im Heraion von Samos belegt.[98]

Vorratsgefäße

Amphoren und Peliken[99] (Diagramm 6)

Die frühesten attischen Vasen in Ionien, bzw. im gesamten westlichen Kleinasien sind Amphoren nahe dem Nettos-Maler um 610/600, die sich in Alt-Smyrna und im Heraion von Samos gefunden haben.[100]

Amphoren, die sowohl zur Aufnahme und Aufbewahrung von Flüssigkeiten (Wein, Öl, Milch u. a.) als auch fester Nahrung (Getreide, Hülsenfrüchte, Nüsse u. a.) dienten,

---

Smyrna Kat. 20-24; Klazomenai Kat. 64-89.
[82] s. oben unter den Fundorten.
[83] Zusammenfassend Alt-Smyrna & Pitane 119-123.
[84] Alt-Smyrna & Pitane 105-108 Tab. 2 mit Nachw. 67; 112-115 Tab. 4 mit Nachw. 559, 575; 115-117 Tab. 5 mit Nachw. 653; 117-119 Tab. 6 mit Nachw. 689.- Daskyleion I Kat. 1-2, darunter Schalen des KY-Maler mehrfach vertreten.
[85] Alt-Smyrna & Pitane 103-105 Tab. 1 mit Nachw. 3; 105-108 Tab. 2 mit Nachw. 68. 172; 112-115 Tab. 4 mit Nachw. 435 (16 Stück). 468. 517. 576; 115-117 Tab. 5 mit Nachw. 610. 654.- Sardeis Kat. Att 47-53.
[86] Alt-Smyrna & Pitane 103-105 Tab. 1 (Elaious, Troja, Thymbra) Nachw. 4-5. 7-11. 14. 16-17. 31-32. 36. 39. 45. 47. 51. 57-58; 105-108 Tab. 2 (Pitane, Gryneion, Myrina, Larisa, Mytilene) mit Nachw. 69. 76-78. 82-85. 92. 105. 109. 119-22. 125. 128. 173. 177-78. 185; 112-115 Tab. 4 (Labraunda, Mylasa, Iasos, Kamiros, Ialysos, Lindos u. weitere FO auf Rhodos) mit Nachw. 436-43. 445-46. 449-51. 454-58. 477-79. 485-89. 497. 504-05. 525-529. 534-38. 543. 549. 561. 565. 577-79. 584-86. 591. 600-01; 115-117 Tab. 5 mit Nachw. 617-18. 623-26. 635-36. 640-41. 646-48. 661-62. 667-70. 680-81; 117-119 Tab. 6 mit Nachw. 690. 693-95, ferner Daskyleion I Kat. 5-85. 241-274; Daskyleion II Kat. 5-121.- Sardeis Kat. Att 55-78. 91-106.- Tenedos 1-9.- Gryneion Abb. 5. 11.- Mytilene Kat. 69-71. 77.
[87] Zu Skyphoi s. Schiering 1983, 158 (Skyphos). 146 (Kotyle).- Agora XXIII 58-61.
[88] Alt-Smyrna & Pitane 108-112 Tab. 3 mit Nachw. 357.
[89] Alt-Smyrna & Pitane 108-112 Tab. 3 mit Nachw. 204. 373; Add. Alt-Smyrna Kat. 25.
[90] Alt-Smyrna & Pitane 108-112 Tab. 3 mit Nachw. 270. 323. 394; Klazomenai Kat. 90-91.
[91] Alt-Smyrna & Pitane 108-112 Tab. 3 mit Nachw. 226. 241; Klazomenai Kat. 92-102; nach Auskünften N. Kunischs.

[92] Alt-Smyrna & Pitane 108-112 Tab. 3 mit Nachw. 249-50. 284; Add. Alt-Smyrna Kat. 28; Klazomenai Kat. 103-113.
[93] Alt-Smyrna & Pitane 103-105 Tab. 1 Nachw. 1. 26. Tab. 2 Nachw. 70 (Nahe d. Gr. d. Oxforder Deckels). Tab. 5 Nachw. 649.
[94] Alt-Smyrna & Pitane 103-105 Tab. 1 Nachw. 33-34. 37. 48; 105-108 Tab. 2 Nachw. 86. 93-94. 100-01. 179. 186; 112-115 Tab. 4 mit Nachw. 444. 447. 498. 506. 550. 592. 603; 115-117 Tab. 5 mit Nachw. 627. 642. 676. 682-83, ferner Mytilene Kat. 66-68; Daskyleion I Kat. 86-154; Daskyleion II 124-155; Sardeis Kat. Att. 80-83.
[95] Zu Kantharoi und Mastoi s. Schiering 1983, 145. 151.- Scheibler 1983, 20-21. 38-40.
[96] Alt-Smyrna & Pitane Kap. I Kat. 166-167.
[97] Samos XXII Kat. 184-185.
[98] Alt-Smyrna & Pitane 108-112 Tab. 3 mit Nachw. 396.
[99] Zu Amphoren u. Peliken s. Schiering 1983, 140-141. 153.- Scheibler 1983, 1-2. 32-35.- Agora XXIII 4-18. 20.- Scheibler 1987, 58-118. Bei fragmentierter Grabungskeramik erweist sich die genaue Bestimmung von Wandungsfragmenten geschlossener Gefäße als schwierig, so daß die Zugehörigkeit zu einer Amphora, Hydria, Olpe oder Oinochoe nicht immer sicher ist.
[100] Alt-Smyrna & Pitane Kap. I Kat. 169; Samos XXII Kat. 1.

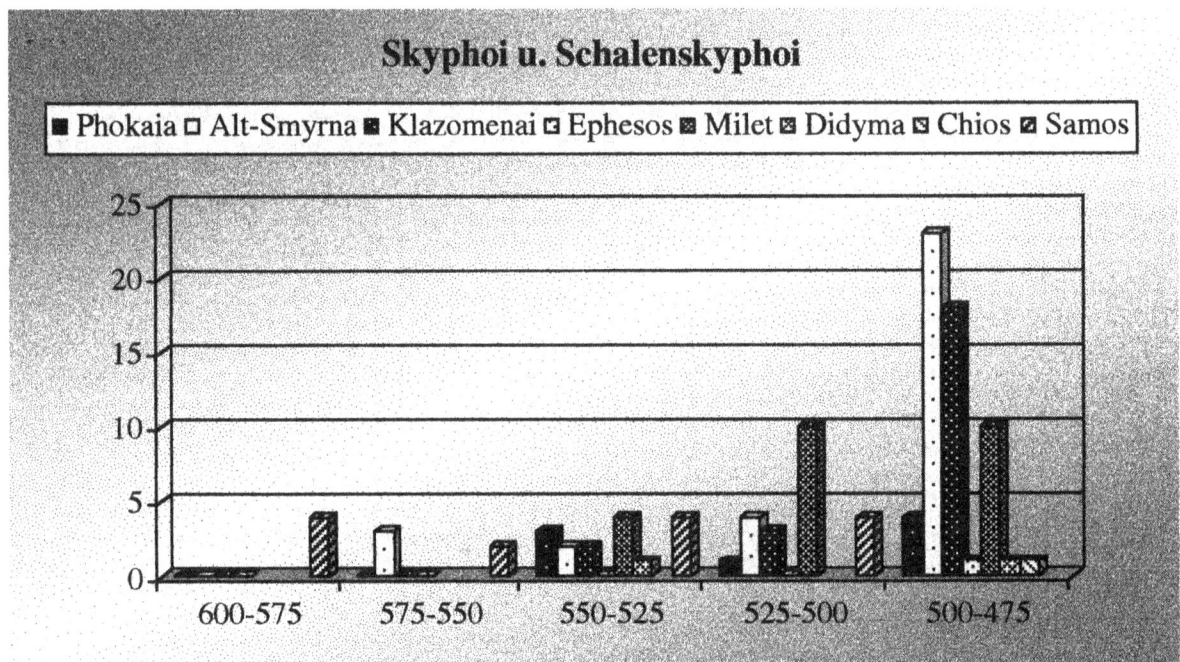

Diagramm 5. Skyphoi und Schalenskyphoi.

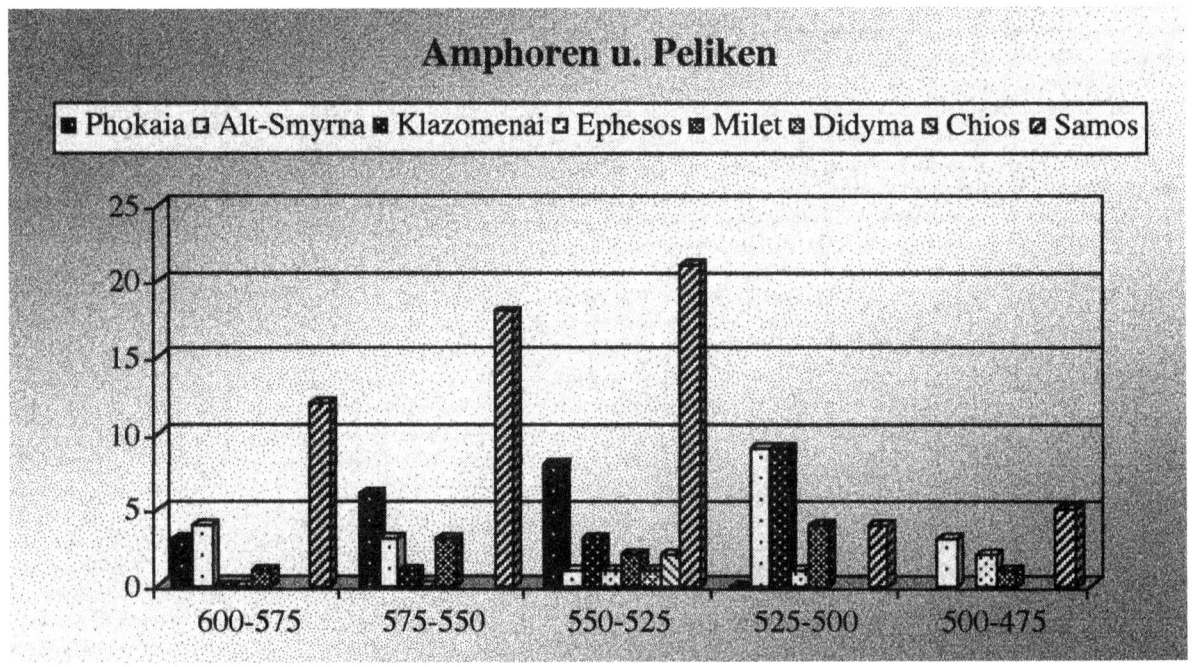

Diagramm 6. Amphoren und Peliken.

aber auch manchmal als Mischgefäße Verwendung fanden,[101] kommen in Samos in den ersten drei Jahrhundertvierteln sehr häufig und mit zunehmender Tendenz vor: hervorzuheben sind hier Amphoren in der Art des Gorgo-Malers, des KX-Malers, des Kleitias und seines Umkreises, denen die des Lydos und seines Umkreises, des Amasis-Malers (Abb. 12) und später des Affekters und Exekias folgen.[102] In Phokaia sind sie mit ähnlicher Tendenz in geringeren Mengen vertreten. Hier ist das früheste Exemplar eine Bauchamphora wohl des KX-Malers, dem weitere, u. a. des Camtar-Malers um 560/50,

---

[101] Scheibler 1983, 1-2.- s. Anm. 48.

[102] Alt-Smyrna & Pitane 108-112 Tab. 3 mit Nachw. 358-59. 375-76. 397. 414. 423. 427-28; Samos XXII Kat. 1-50.

folgen.[103] Nach ein paar frühen Stücken, u. a. des Sophilos und in der Art des Gorgo-Malers, kommen Amphoren in Alt-Smyrna und Klazomenai erst im letzten Viertel des 6. Jhs. u. a. aus dem Umkreis des Antimenes-Malers häufiger vor[104]. Aus Milet wird von einer Pferdekopfamphora, einer Amphora des Kleitias- und des Lydos-Umkreises berichtet. Vereinzelt wurden Amphoren in Ephesos, Didyma und in Chios-Stadt gefunden.[105]

Als spezielle Amphorenform ist ferner eine, bislang einzige 'Tyrrhenische'-Amphora des Castellani-Malers in Alt-Smyrna zu erwähnen.[106] Eine rotfigurige Amphora des frühen 5. Jhs. ist in Klazomenai belegt.[107]

Auch einige Panathenäische Amphoren fanden den Weg nach Ionien: in Phokaia kamen Fragmente von zwei Exemplaren des 3. Viertels des 6. bzw. frühen 5. Jhs. zutage. Zahlreich wurden sie im Heraion von Samos gefunden: es sind vor allem Gefäße aus dem späten 6. und frühen 5. Jh. des Malers der samischen Preisamphoren und des Eucharides-Malers.[108]

Amphoren sind außerhalb Ioniens im äolischen Pitane vom frühen 6. bis in das frühe 5. Jh. in geringen Mengen vertreten; in den rhodischen Nekropolen Kamiros und Ialysos kommen sie ab dem 2. Viertel bis zum Ende des Jhs., ähnlich wie in Xanthos, recht häufig vor. Auch die Satrapensitze Sardeis und Daskyleion weisen ab dem 2. Viertel bzw. 2. Hälfte des 6. Jhs. reiche Funde auf.[109]

Salb- und Ölgefäße

Lekythen[110] (Diagramm 7)

Die frühesten Lekythen in Ionien sind in Alt-Smyrna und Samos im 3. Viertel des 6. Jhs. vereinzelt nachweisbar. Sie sind dem Maler von Rhitsona 49. 261, der Delphin-Gruppe und der Schwarzhals-Klasse zuzuweisen.[111] Häufiger werden sie erst im späten 6., vor allem aber im frühen 5. Jh. Mehrfach belegt sind in Alt-Smyrna und Klazomenai Lekythen der Phanyllis-Gruppe, während hier ebenso wie in der archaischen Nekropole von Ephesos um 500 auch die Hahn-Gruppe, die Hund- und- Hase-Gruppe sowie der Gela-Maler vertreten sind; in Milet wird aus dem letzten Viertel von nur wenigen Stücken berichtet. Unter den zahlreichen Lekythen des 1. Viertels des 5. Jh., die in Alt-Smyrna besonders häufig vorkommen, dominieren die der Haimon-Gruppe; ferner fallen einige ornamentverzierte Lekythen mit Palmetten auf.[112]

In der Troas und an den Dardanellen sind Lekythen ab dem letzten Viertel des 6. Jhs. in den Nekropolen von Elaious und Thymbra, im frühen 5. Jh. auch in den Nekropolen von Assos und Antandros sowie in Troja belegt. In der äolischen Nekropole von Pitane sind sie bereits im frühen 6. Jh. nachgewiesen, zahlreich werden sie aber erst im letzten Viertel des 6. und frühen 5. Jh.; ab dem 3. Viertel des 6. Jhs. kommen sie auf Lesbos und im frühen 5. Jh. auch in Gryneion, Myrina, Kyme und Larisa vor. Ähnlich verhält es sich auf Rhodos: in Kamiros ist eine Lekythos des frühen 6. Jhs. gefunden worden, doch größere Mengen lassen sich, wie auch in Ialysos, Lindos und dem festländischen Iasos und Mylasa, erst im letzten Viertel des 6. und ersten Viertel des 5. Jhs. nachweisen. Die gleiche Tendenz läßt sich im lykischen Xanthos und den Satrapensitzen Daskyleion und Sardeis beobachten.[113]

Die Fundmengen zeigen, daß die Lekythos im späten 6. und frühen 5. Jh. im gesamten westlichen Kleinasien neben der Schale die am häufigsten aus Athen importierte Gefäßform war.[114] Diese Zunahme attischer Lekythen

---

[103] Alt-Smyrna & Pitane 105-108 Tab. 2 mit Nachw. 131. 139. 148; Phokaia II Kat. 66-82.
[104] Alt-Smyrna & Pitane 108-112 Tab. 3 mit Nachw. 195-96. 206. 228-29. 239. 243. 251. 271. 277; Add. Alt-Smyrna Kat. 29-34; Klazomenai Kat. 131-138. 141. 146-149. 152.
[105] Alt-Smyrna & Pitane 105-108 Tab. 2 mit Nachw. 290-91. 295-96 (Pelike). 304-5. 311. 319. 333. 340-41. und nach Auskünften N. Kunischs.
[106] Add. Alt-Smyrna Kat. 31.
[107] Klazomenai Kat. 255.
[108] Phokaia I 24 Abb. 22; Phokaia II Kat. 74-75; Alt-Smyrna & Pitane 108-112 Tab. 3 mit Nachw. 414. 428.- Kreuzer, Preisamphoren.
[109] Alt-Smyrna & Pitane 105-108 Tab. 2 mit Nachw. 63. 80. 87. 95; 112-115 Tab. 4 mit Nachw. 470-72. 482. 491-92. 499. 519-20. 531. 539. 544-45. 507. 580. 587-88. 593-94. 603 (inkl. weitere FO auf Rhodos); 115-117 Tab. 5 mit Nachw. 611-12 (3 Pferdekopfamph.) 620. 628-29. 643. 657. 665. 671. 677.- Sardeis Kat. Att 1-16.- Daskyleion I Kat. 177-201 (auch ein Frgt. einer Panathenäischen Amph.?); Daskyleion II Kat. 161-195.

[110] Zu Lekythen s. Schiering 1983, 150.- Scheibler 1983, 22. 35-37.- Agora XXIII 43-47. Zur Benutzung der Lekythos im Persischen Reich s. DeVries 1977.
[111] Alt-Smyrna & Pitane 108-112 Tab. 3 mit Nachw. 220. 400.
[112] Alt-Smyrna & Pitane 108-112 Tab 3 mit Nachw. 235. 245. 252. 283. 285. 292. 298. 301. 315-316 (keine Amp./Hyd.). 331. 346. 355. 433.- Add. Alt-Smyrna Kat. 62- 68.- Klazomenai Kat. 153-167.- Samos XXII Kat. 97-100. App. 2-5 (1 x weißgrundig).- Kerschner 1995, 216,1 und Auskünfte N. Kunischs.
[113] Alt-Smyrna & Pitane 103-105 Tab. 1 Nachw. 12. 15. 20. 46. 50. 52. 54. 59-60.; Tab. 2 mit Nachw. 66. 81. 90. 98. 102. 107. 111. 115. 127. 129. 184. 192; 112-115 Tab. 4 mit Nachw. 453. 463. 467. 474. 484. 496. 503. 512. 541. 548. 554. 564. 567. 569. 583. 590. 598. 606; 115-117 Tab. 5 mit Nachw. 633. 639. 666. 679. 685. 688.- Assos II 119ff Kat. 26-28. 36.- Assos III 112-115 Kat. 35-36. 38.- Antandros I Abb. 26.- Antandros II Abb. 5.- Gryneion Abb. 12.- Daskyleion I Kat. 210-229.- Daskyleion II Kat. 223-251.
[114] Alt-Smyrna & Pitane 119-123 mit Tab. 7.

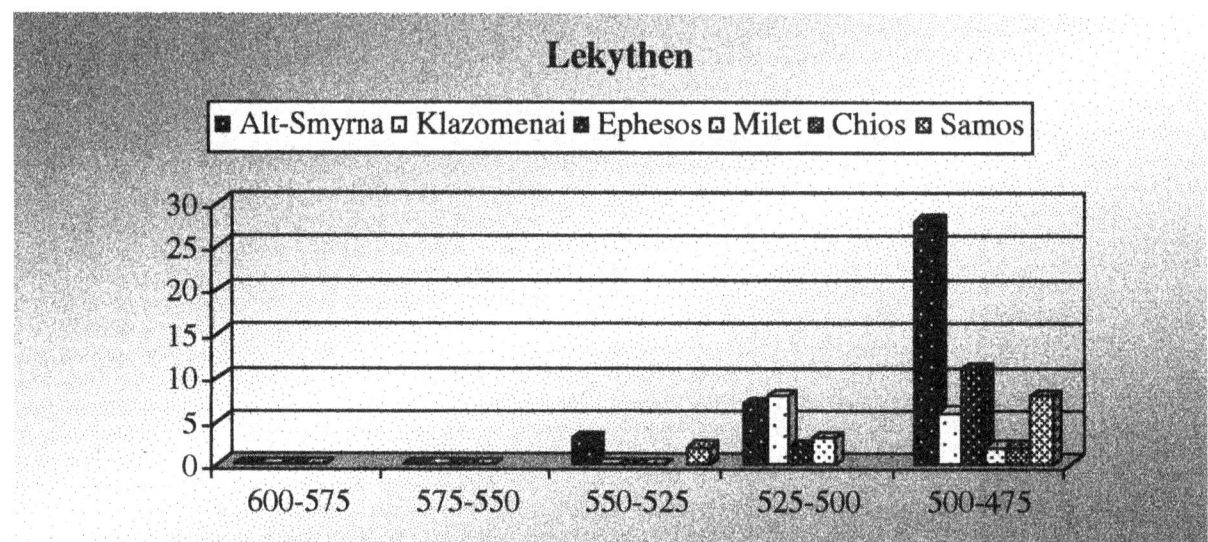

Diagramm 7. Lekythen.

könnte nach Carl Roebuck ein Indiz dafür sein, daß sich die Duftöle aus Athen allmählich gegen die bis dahin marktführenden lydischen Parfüme durchsetzten.[115]

Alabastra und Aryballoi[116]

Alabastra kommen in der archaischen Zeit in Ionien gar nicht vor,[117] in den benachbarten Landschaften vereinzelt im frühen 5. Jh., wie z. B. in Elaious und in Kamiros.[118] Geläufiger werden sie, sowohl figürlich als auch ornamentverziert, im 2. Viertel des 5. Jhs., wie ein Beispiel in Milet[119] sowie andere in Myrina, Kamiros, Ialysos, Lindos und Daskyleion zeigen.[120]

Von den ohnehin seltenen attischen Aryballoi ist einer möglicherweise im 3. Viertel des 6. Jhs. nach Phokaia gelangt.[121] Ein weiterer ist im 2. Viertel des 6. Jhs. in Kamiros belegt.[122]

Pyxiden[123]

Pyxiden, die zur Aufbewahrung von Salben, Kosmetika und Schmuck dienten, sind ab der Mitte des 6. Jhs. in Phokaia und im späten 6. Jh. in Klazomenai in geringen Mengen belegt,[124] während Samos, vor allem das Heraion ab 560/50, eine auffallend große Menge Kelchpyxiden aufweist, u. a. des Amasis-Malers, des Lydos-Umkreises, der Princeton Gruppe III und des Malers der Nikosia-Olpe.[125] Ferner wurden einige Kelchpyxiden in Milet gefunden. Zu einer Kelchpyxis um 540/30 gehören wohl Fragmente aus Phokaia, die stark an die Archippe-Gruppe erinnern.[126]

Pyxiden zählen in den benachbarten Landschaften zu den seltenen Gefäßen: eine Pyxis ist im lykischen Xanthos und eine weitere des C-Malers oder Umkreises im mysisch/phrygischem Daskyleion nachgewiesen.[127]

Exaleiptra[128]

Zwei Fundorte haben in Ionien diese eher seltenen Toilettengefäße für Salben oder Öl hervorgebracht: das Heraion von Samos und Alt-Smyrna. Das früheste

---

[115] Roebuck 1959, 81-81.- Sardeis 72.
[116] Zu Alabastra und Aryballoi s. Schiering 1983, 140-141- Scheibler 1983, 22-24.- Agora XXIII 47-48.
[117] Das möglicherweise als Alabastron angesprochene Fragment aus Milet könnte m. E. auch von einer Olpe/Oinochoe stammen, Alt-Smyrna & Pitane 108-112 Tab. 3 mit Nachw. 320.
[118] Alt-Smyrna & Pitane 103-105 Tab. 1 Nachw. 21; 112-115 Tab. 4 mit Nachw. 513.
[119] Alt-Smyrna & Pitane 108-112 Tab. 3 mit Nachw. 321; 105-108 Tab. 2 mit Nachw. 113; 112-115 Tab. 4 mit Nachw. 515. 556. 571-72. 607.- Daskyleion I Kat. 373-74.
[120] Alt-Smyrna & Pitane 105-108 Tab. 2 Nachw. 113; 112-115 Tab. 4 Nachw. 515. 256. 571. 607.- Daskyleion I Kat. 373-74.
[121] Phokaia II Kat. 122.
[122] Alt-Smyrna & Pitane 112-115 Tab. 4 mit Nachw. 475.

[123] Zu Pyxiden s. Schiering 1983, 156-157.- Scheibler 1983, 24. 44-46.- Roberts 1978.- Agora XXIII 49-50.
[124] Phokaia II Kat. 140-143.- Klazomenai Kat. 173-175 (u. a Dreifußpyxis?; Pyxis?, CHC-Gr.).
[125] Alt-Smyrna & Pitane 108-112 Tab. 3 mit Nachw. 381-82. 402-03. 419. 425. Zu Kelchpyxiden s. Samos XXII 13-17 mit Lit in Anm. 115.- CVA Malibu 2, 21. Weitere Kelchpyxiden wurden auf Samos im Artemision und in der Nekropole gefunden, s. Samos XXII 13-17.
[126] Nach Auskünften N. Kunischs; Phokaia I 19-21. Abb. 10-11.- Tuna-Nörling 1997, 438-440. Abb. 8-11; Phokaia II Kat. 140.
[127] Alt-Smyrna & Pitane 115-117 Tab. 5 mit Nachw. 615.- Daskyleion I Kat. 234.
[128] Zu Exaleiptra s. Schiering 1983, 142-143.- Scheibler 1983, 24.- Agora XXIII 49.

Exemplar aus Samos ist ein Werk des Kerameikos-Malers um 600/590, dem zwei des Kleitias und ein weiteres aus dem Umkreis des Lydos folgen. Das Fragment aus Alt-Smyrna, das möglicherweise zu solch einem Gefäß gehört, stammt aus dem Umkreis des Sophilos.[129]

In den benachbarten Landschaften brachten die rhodischen Nekropole von Ialysos und das lykische Xanthos Exaleiptra hervor.[130]

Wassergefäße

Hydrien[131]

Eine große Anzahl von Hydrien, jenen Krügen, mit denen Frauen das Wasser vom Brunnen holten,[132] sind im Heraion von Samos gefunden worden. Sie setzen mit Stücken um 590/80 u. a. des KX-Malers ein und dauern bis ins frühe 5. Jh. an, die meisten gelangten jedoch im 2. Viertel des 6. Jhs. hierher. Sie stammen mehrfach von der Hand des Kleitias und aus seinem Umkreis (Abb. 11), aus dem Umkreis des Polos-Malers sowie des Lydos und von der Hand des Nearchos. In Phokaia ist ein wohl zu einer Hydria gehöriges Fragment des Sophilos und ein weiteres um die Jahrhundertmitte belegt, während in Alt-Smyrna und Klazomenai im 3. bzw. letzten Viertel des 6. des Jhs. vereinzelte Exemplare nachgewiesen sind.[133]

In den benachbarten Landschaften kommen Hydrien in den Nekropolen von Kamiros und Ialysos ab dem 2. des 6. Jhs., vor allem um die Jahrhundertwende und im frühen 5. Jh., häufig vor; auch Xanthos weist einige Stücke im 3. Viertel des 6. Jhs. auf; desweiteren sind sie vereinzelt auf Lesbos und in Sardeis belegt.[134]

Louteria,[135] *Lebetes Gamikoi*[136] *und Phormiskoi*[137]

Die Existenz von Louteria (Wasserbecken) und Lebetes Gamikoi (Hochzeitskessel) ist schwierig nachzuweisen, da sie in fragmentierter Form meist für Kratere oder Dinoi (Lebetes) gehalten werden. Wegen des guten Erhaltungszustandes eindeutig als Louterion erkannt wurde das Becken des Sophilos aus Phokaia um 590/80; ein Becken anderer Form auf hohem Ständer des KX-Malers um 580/75 kam im Heraion von Samos zutage.[138] Der einzige gesicherte Lebes Gamikos Ioniens ist der des Sophilos oder seines Umkreises um 580/75 aus Alt-Smyrna.[139] Sowohl Lebetes Gamikoi als auch Loutrophoren (zum Holen des Brautbadwassers), die im attischen Hochzeitsritual und Todeskult eine wichtige Rolle spielten, zählen zu den am seltensten exportierten Gefäßen des attischen Kerameikos.[140] So ist im gesamten westlichen Kleinasien bislang keine Loutrophoros belegt. Ähnlich verhält es sich mit den kalebasseförmigen Phormiskoi, die als Sprenggefäße im Totenkult zum Einsatz kamen. Ob es sich bei dem kleinen bauchigen Gefäß mit schlankem Hals des frühen 5. Jhs. aus Phokaia um einen Phormiskos oder eine kleine Olpe handelt, läßt sich wegen des Erhaltungszustandes schwerlich entscheiden.[141]

Miniaturgefäße

Wohl attischer Herkunft, wenn auch z. T. angezweifelt, sind eine Miniaturoinochoe, zwei Miniaturdinoi und ein Miniaturskyphos aus der Westnekropole von Samos, die alle aus einem von Johannes Boehlau als Kindergrab angesehenen reichen Grab des mittleren 6. Jhs. stammen.[142]

Miniaturgefäße kommen auch in Nekropolen der benachbarten Landschaften vor: ein Amphoriskos des frühen 6. Jhs. ist in Antandros belegt, ein weiterer des 2. Viertel in Assos, während Elaious im späten 6./frühen 5. Jh. einen Amphoriskos, zwei Miniaturskypoi und eine Miniaturhydria aufweist. Besonders zahlreich sind Miniaturgefäße in der äolischen Nekropole von Pitane: es sind einige Miniaturskyphoi und lekanai der Gruppe des Oxforder Deckels und deren Umkreis um 570 sowie zahlreiche Amphoriskoi und eine Miniaturolpe um 580/50. Die rhodischen Nekropolen von Kamiros und Ialysos weisen in der ersten Hälfte des 6. Jhs. vereinzelte Amphoriskoi auf; zahlreicher belegt sind hier Miniaturskyphoi im frühen 5. Jh.[143]

Außer in Nekropolen sind Miniaturgefäße, nämlich weißgrundige Miniaturskyphoi des frühen 5. Jhs. der Lindos-Gruppe, im Satrapensitz Daskyleion und in außergewöhnlich großen Mengen im Athena-Heiligtum auf der Akropolis von Lindos gefunden worden.[144]

---

[129] Alt-Smyrna & Pitane 108-112 Tab. 3 mit Nachw. 211. 366. 385.
[130] Rhodos 13099 (10501), ClRh 3, 32-34 Nr. 2 Abb. 16-17.- Alt-Smyrna & Pitane 112-115 Tab. 4 mit Nachw. 542, Tab. 5 mit Nachw. 622.
[131] Zu Hydrien s. Schiering 1983, 144.- Agora XXIII 35-38.
[132] Scheibler 1983, 17-18.
[133] Alt-Smyrna & Pitane 105-108 Tab. 2 mit Nachw. 132; Tab. 3 mit Nachw. 217 (216). 276. 360. 377. 415. 432.- Phokaia II Kat. 83-84.- Klazomenai Kat. 144.
[134] Alt-Smyrna & Pitane 105-108 Tab. 2 mit Nachw. 170. 181; 112-115 Tab. 4 mit Nachw. 473. 521.- Mytilene Kat. 57.
[135] Zu Louteria s. Schiering 1983, 150-151 mit Lit.- Callipolitis-Feytmans 1965.- Agora XXIII 32-33.
[136] Zu Lebetes Gamikoi s. Schiering 1983, 149.- Agora XXIII 27-29.
[137] Zu Phormiskoi s. Schiering 1983, 154f.- Agora XXIII 48. Zur Benutzung: Touchefeu-Meynier 1972, 93-102.
[138] Alt-Smyrna & Pitane 105-108 Tab. 2 mit Nachw. 135; Phokaia II Kat. 96 (jetzt İzmir Mus. 9537); Tab. 3 mit Nachw. 364.
[139] Alt-Smyrna & Pitane 108-112 Tab. 3 mit Nachw. 197.
[140] Old Smyrna 161 mit Anm. 51.- Scheibler 1983, 35-39. 51-56.- Agora XXIII 18-20.
[141] Alt-Smyrna & Pitane 105-108 Tab. 2 mit Nachw. 159; Phokaia II Kat. 92.
[142] Löwe 1996, 50-55 Kat. 40,4. 8. 10-11; 98 mit Anm. 31; Samos XXII App. 7.
[143] Alt-Smyrna & Pitane 103-105 Tab. 1 Nachw. 13. 22-23. 53; Tab. 2 mit Nachw. 72-75; 112-115 Tab. 4 mit Nachw. 465. 514. 524. 555.- Antandros II Abb. 18.
[144] Daskyleion I Kat. 237-240.- Alt-Smyrna & Pitane 112-115 Tab. 4 mit

Gefäße im Gebrauch

Siedlungen

Bis auf wenige Fragmente aus dem Bereich des Athena-Tempels in Phokaia stammen alle Funde aus den Siedlungsschichten der archaischen Stadt.[145] Ähnlich muß die Keramik aus Alt-Smyrna gewertet werden, da genaue Anhaltspunkte über die Fundplätze z. Zt. noch nicht vorliegen, aber davon ausgegangen werden kann, daß es sich überwiegend um Siedlungskeramik handelt.[146] Genau informiert sind wir über die Fundumstände in Klazomenai, in der bislang der größte Anteil attischer Keramik in der archaischen Siedlung gefunden wurde.[147] Die drei Siedlungen vermitteln für Ionien einen repräsentativen Überblick über die importierten Gefäßtypen im häuslichen Gebrauch: am häufigsten ist Symposionsgeschirr gefunden worden, wobei unter den Trinkgefäßen die Schale mit Abstand die wichtigste Rolle spielt, zu der sich im frühen 5. Jh. der Skyphos bzw. Schalenskyphos gesellt. In der ersten Hälfte des 6. Jhs. fallen in Phokaia und Alt-Smyrna Mischgefäße auf, während in Klazomenai im späten 6. Jh. Vorratsgefäße wie Amphoren stärker vertreten sind.

Die große Anzahl von Lekythen im frühen 5. Jh. in Alt-Smyrna zeigt, daß dieses Salbgefäß, sei es wegen seines Inhaltes oder als Behälter, im Haushalt zur Körperpflege oder bei Tisch häufig Verwendung fand,[148] ein Phänomen, das im Satrapensitz Daskyleion, im heimischen Athen und in Siedlungen Nordgriechenlands ebenfalls beobachtet wurde.[149]

Heiligtümer

Das Heraion von Samos ist zweifellos das Heiligtum mit der größten Ansammlung attischer Keramik in Ionien. Reich an Funden erweisen sich weiterhin die jüngsten Grabungen im Aphrodite-Heiligtum auf dem Zeytintepe und im Heiligtum der Artemis Kithone auf dem Kalabaktepe in Milet. Spärlicher sind bislang Funde in den Athena-Tempeln von Phokaia, Emporio auf Chios und Milet, im Artemision von Ephesos und im Apollon-Tempel von Didyma.

Mehr als die Hälfte der im Heraion von Samos gefundenen attischen Vasen sind Trinkgefäße, vor allem Kleinmeisterschalen des 3. Viertels des 6. Jhs. Eine große Gruppe bilden Amphoren, danach kommen Mischgefäße (überwiegend Kratere), Salbgefäße (insbes. Kelchpyxiden) und Hydrien in größeren Mengen vor.[150] Sie wurden im Rahmen des Kultes zum Essen und Trinken, zur Spende, zur rituellen Reinigung und, z. T. gefüllt mit Wein, Öl, Getreide u. a., als Weihgaben an die Göttin benutzt. Das Trinkgeschirr, das in einigen Fällen wohl sogar als komplettes Set in Auftrag gegeben wurde, wie im Fall der Gefäße des KX-Malers, dürfte bei den rituellen Symposien anläßlich der Feste für Hera zum Einsatz gekommen sein.[151] Frauen weihten der Göttin bei Anlässen wie der Hochzeit oder der Geburt eines Kindes Gefäße aus ihrem Lebensbereich: große Hydrien, die das Wasser für die rituelle Reinigung im Kult enthielten,[152] und mit Kosmetika gefüllte Salbgefäße wie die Kelchpyxiden.[153]

Unter den wenigen attischen Fragmenten, die im Bereich des Athena-Tempels von Phokaia freigelegt wurden, sind eine Lekanis, ein Krater und mehrere Schalen zu nennen,[154] während im Altarbereich des Artemisions neben Schalen und Lekythen auch einige Kratere und Vorratsgefäße belegt sind.

Das Vorkommen von Trinkgeschirr, zahlreiche Schalen und einige Kratere, im Aphrodite-Heiligtum auf dem Zeytintepe in Milet und im Athena-Heiligtum von Emporio auf Chios könnte ebenfalls für ihre Verwendung bei rituellen Symposia sprechen.[155] Eindeutig in diese Richtung weist auch der Befund im karischen Heiligtum des Zeus Labraundos, wo sich ausschließlich Schalen und Skyphoi gefunden haben.[156]

Einige Gefäße wurden aber nicht wegen ihres Inhaltes, sondern ihrer selbst wegen der Gottheit dargebracht, wie

---

Nachw. 570. 191 Stück wurden in einem großen Votivdepot außerhalb des Heiligtums geborgen, weitere Skyphoi dieser Art kamen an verschiedenen Fundplätzen im Heiligtum zutage, s. Blinkenberg 1931, 7. 629-630.
[145] Phokaia II.
[146] s. Old Smyrna 152 mit Anm. 2 und Kat., die meisten Funde aus Graben C und H der Siedlung; Nr. 39 vom Tempeltor.- Alt-Smyrna & Pitane 3.
[147] Klazomenai 15-25.
[148] Phanagoria Kap. III Kommentar zu Lekythen. Da Funde in Phokaia zu dieser Zeit abnehmen und die festländische Siedlung von Klazomenai nach der Eroberung Klazomenais durch die Perser in Folge des Ionischen Aufstandes 494/93 verlassen wird, läßt sich in den beiden Siedlungen wenig zur Verwendung von Lekythen sagen.
[149] Daskyleion I 9-15 Diagramm 4 und Kat. 210-233. 296-372. Allerdings stammen viele dieser Lekythen aus dem sog. Areal der Temenosmauer, wo sich möglicherweise ein Temenos für Kybele und andere Gottheiten befunden hat - Daskyleion II Kat. 223-251. Agora: Hannestad 1988, 226.- Shear 1993, 383-482 Tab. 1-2.- Rotroff und Oakley 1992, 12. 25. Nordgriechenland: Tiverios, Manakidou und Tsiafaki 1994, 197-202 Abb. 3.- Koukouli- Chrysanthaki 1983, 123-146 Abb. 17.

[150] Samos XXII 31-32. Zur kultischen Verwendung von Hydrien s. Diehl 1964, 171-209.
[151] Samos XXII 33-40. Zur Verwendung des Geschirrs bei rituellen Symposia in Heiligtümern s. auch: Schaus 1985, 94-95.- Simon 1986, 314. 316. Nach ihrer Benutzung blieb das Geschirr im Heiligtum und wurde der Göttin geweiht, s. Schaus 1985, 95. Zu Importen in Form von Sets bzw. "lots" aus einer Werkstatt s. auch Miller 1997, 68 (Al Mina).
[152] Samos XXII 33 mit Anm. 285. 40.- Schaus 1985, 95.
[153] Samos XXII 40-41.- Roberts 1978, 4.
[154] Phokaia II Abschnitt "Schnitt H".
[155] Simon 1986, 316 (allerdings in Emporio nur wenige attische figürliche Stücke der archaischen Zeit).
[156] Alt-Smyrna & Pitane 112-115 Tab. 4 mit Nachw. 435 (16 Stück!)- 447.

die im Athena-Heiligtum von Alt-Smyrna gefundene Schale des 7. Jhs. mit der Inschrift "Ich bin die Kyliche des Dolion" sowie die Lekythos mit der Inschrift "Ich bin die Lekythos des Derippos" verdeutlichen.[157] Dies dürfte auch für die zahlreichen an die Athena Lindia geweihten Miniaturskyphoi der Lindos-Gruppe gelten.[158]

Nekropolen[159]

In den drei Nekropolen (Yıldıztepe, Kalabak und DSİ) von Klazomenai wurden attische Beigaben des 6. Jhs. überwiegend als Streufunde geborgen. Auch hier spielt Trinkgeschirr eine wichtige Rolle, wobei neben einigen Skyphoi, Krateren, Lekythen und einer Olpe Schalen am häufigsten vertreten sind. Als interessantes Beispiel für Fundvergesellschaftung ist eine Gruppe zu erwähnen, die eine Olpe des Gorgo-Malers (um 590/80) und eine Komastenschale des KY-Malers (um 575/65) barg.[160]

Unter den Beigaben in der spätarchaischen Nekropole von Ephesos sind Lekythen am häufigsten, ferner einige Olpen/Amphoren, eine Schale und ein Krater belegt,[161] während bei der Notgrabung in der archaischen Nekropole von Milet in Yeni Balat einige Lekaniden und Lekanen, zwei Lekythen, ein Skyphos und eine Schale zutage kamen.[162] Von der Nekropole an der Straße nach Pyrgi bei Emporio auf Chios wird lediglich vom Fund einer Schale und einer Lekythos berichtet.[163] Die Westnekropole von Samos brachte, soweit bekannt, wenig attische Keramik hervor: neben einer Kleinmeisterschale sind vor allem die vier Miniaturgefäße aus einem reich ausgestatteten Kindergrab hervorzuheben.[164]

Reicher an attischen keramischen Funden und daher aussagekräftiger sind Nekropolen der benachbarten Landschaften: Während die Nekropolen von Elaious und Thymbra ab den 2. Viertel des 6. Jhs. sowohl Trinkgeschirr, vor allem Schalen und Skyphoi, als auch im frühen 5. Jh. verstärkt Lekythen, aber auch einige Miniaturgefäße aufweisen, sind in den Gräbern von Assos nach vereinzelten Vorläufern zu Beginn des 5. Jhs. an attischen Beigaben fast nur Lekythen nachgewiesen.[165] In der Nekropole von Pitane gehören attische Vasen seit dem frühen 6. Jh. zu den Beigaben.[166] Dabei dominiert eindeutig Trinkgeschirr, vor allem Schalen, aber auch einige Kannen, wobei Lekythen die Schalen im frühen 5. Jh. allmählich ablösen. Als Set gekauft und einer Bestattung beigegeben sind vier Teller von der Hand desselben Malers um 520/10.[167] Auffällig sind zahlreiche Miniaturgefäße aus dem 2. Viertels des 6. Jhs., die häufig mehrfach in einem Grab oder mit anderen Beigaben kleinen Formats, wie Spielknöchel oder eine Schnabeltasse, sowie mit zahlreichen großen Gefäßen vorkommen. Daß es sich hierbei um Kinderbestattungen handeln muß, beweist nicht zuletzt der Fund eines Miniaturskyphos in einem Kindersarkophag.[168] In den rhodischen Nekropolen Kamiros und Ialysos dominiert beim Trinkgeschirr im 6. Jh. die Schale, während die Kanne im frühen 5. Jh. in der Überzahl ist. Beide rhodische Nekropolen weisen eine enorme Formenvielfalt an Gefäßen auf: es kommen während der gesamten archaischen Zeit auch Vorratsgefäße, Hydrien, Miniaturgefäße und Salbgefäße, insbes. Lekythen vor, letztere verstärkt im frühen 5. Jh.[169]

Symposiongeschirr, das sowohl in den Gräbern als auch außerhalb gefunden wurde, könnte vor Ort beim Totenmahl benutzt und danach dort abgelegt oder anschließend, wie auch die Vorratsgefäße, z. T. mit Inhalt, als Grabbeigabe zur Versorgung im Jenseits dem Toten mitgegeben worden sein.[170] Die große Anzahl von Lekythen im frühen 5. Jh., die möglicherweise Salbgefäße anderer Herkunft ablösten,[171] hängt vermutlich mit dem Bestattungsritual

---

[157] Simon 1986, 315.- Şahin 1983, 113-114 Taf. 124c.- Jeffery 1964, 12, 20, Taf. 6a, Abb. 1 (beide Gefäße nicht -attischer Herkunft).

[158] Alt-Smyrna & Pitane 112-115 Tab. 4 mit Nachw. 570.- Simon 1986, 314-315.

[159] Zu ostgriechischen Nekropolen allg. s. Philipp 1981, 149-166.

[160] Klazomenai 23-25 In den klazomenischen Nekropolen wurden neben Sarkophagen Pithos- und Amphoragräber sowie einfache Erd- und Brandbestattungen freigelegt. Zu Vasen mit einem Zeitabstand von 10-20 Jahren s. Klazomenai 29.

[161] Langmann 1967, 103.

[162] V. Graeve 1988, 267-272. Der Deckel Nr. 2 gehört wohl zu einer Lekanis; die Randfragmente Nr. 20 und 23 dürften nach Profilvergleichen zu urteilen Lekanen sein, während die Fragmente geschlossener Gefäße Nr. 11-12 wohl von Lekythen stammen.

[163] Boardman 1967, 155, 693. 695.

[164] a. O. Anm. 25, ferner Löwe 1996, 54, Nr. 40,17. Die keramischen Funde verschiedener Herkunft in der Nekropole lassen sich in vier Gruppen aufteilen: Salbgefäße, Trinkgeschirr, Essgeschirr und Vorratsgefäße, s. Löwe 1996, 98.

[165] Alt-Smyrna & Pitane 103-105 Tab. 1 mit Nachw. 1-25. 41-55.- Von den 709 Gräbern der Nekropole von Elaious, 390 Pithoi und 319 Sarkophage, s. Waiblinger 1978, 845-846.- Assos I.- Assos II.- Assos III (Funde überwiegend aus Sarkophagen).- s. ferner: Utili 1999 mit ostgriechischer, korinthischer und Buccherokeramik sowie anderen Beigaben, dabei auch einige attische Schalen des 2.- 3. V. des 6. Jhs., Kat. 111-114.

[166] Alt-Smyrna & Pitane 53-99. Auch hier wurden sowohl Sarkophage und Pithosgräber als auch Erd- und Brandbestattungen freigelegt. Zu den Grabkontexten s. Alt-Smyrna & Pitane 99.

[167] Zu Sets s. Anm. 151.

[168] Alt-Smyrna & Pitane 99. Vgl. Miniaturgefäße in Kindergräbern: a. O. Anm. 142 (Samos).- Blegen et al. 1964, 78. 80 mit Anm. 84.- Kerameikos IX 14.- Dunbabin 1962, 290.

[169] Alt-Smyrna & Pitane 112-115 Tab. 4 mit Nachw. 465-556.

[170] z. B. Sianaschale oder Skyphos im Sarkophag oder Olpe bei Brandbestattung in Pitane: Alt-Smyrna & Pitane Kap. II Kat. 7; 65; 75.- Zwei Skyphoi auf Brandbestattung 1. Hälfte 7. Jh. in der Yıldıztepe Nekropole, Klazomenai: Bakır 1982, 64-65.- Löwe 1996, 98-100.- Kurtz und Boardman 1985, 174. 242-243. Zu Bestattungsritualen am Verbrennungsplatz für Brand- u. Urnenbestattungen in Assos, Utili 1999, 143-144; auf Samos, Philipp 1981, 160-161. Zum Totenmahl und Trankopfer bei Besuchen am Grab s. Garland 1985, 110-115.

[171] Auf Samos sind in den Gräbern des mittleren 6. Jhs. lokale Fläschchen, figürliche Salbgefäße, Lekythen und Lydia, korinthische Aryballoi und ägyptische Alabastra aus Alabaster belegt: Löwe 1996, 24-71. Auch in Assos kommen im 6. Jh. korinthische Aryballoi und Alabastra, Fayence- Aryballoi und ostgriechische Salbgefäße vor: Assos I

zusammen. Zum einen wurde die Leiche gewaschen und eingeölt, zum anderen wurde das Öl am Grab als Opferspende dargebracht, weswegen man die Ölbehälter wohl auch mit ins Grab gab.[172]

Maler, Gruppen und Werkstätten

Es ist bekannt, daß Amphoren der 'Tyrrhenischen'- Gruppe sich in Etrurien sehr gut verkauften und der Töpfer Nikosthenes sogar speziell für diesen Markt produzierte.[173] Zählungen der zugewiesenen attischen Vasen in Ionien und den benachbarten Landschaften haben gezeigt, daß sich zwar keine bestimmte Werkstatt auf den Export in dieses Gebiet spezialisiert hatte, dieser Markt dennoch für einige Maler und Werkstätten des Kerameikos nicht unbedeutend war.[174]

Im folgenden werden einige Maler und Gruppen, die mit mehr als 13 Vasen im griechischen Osten vertreten sind, besprochen und die Verbreitung ihrer Produktion in andere Gebiete zum Vergleich herangezogen. Charlotte Scheffer beobachtete, daß die Gefäßform für den Verkauf und die Verbreitung von Vasen ausschlaggebend war.[175] Zu recht kommentierte Robin Osborne diese Beobachtung dahingehend, daß nicht allein die Gefäßform, sondern die Spezialisierung der Maler bzw. Gruppen auf Gefäßformen wie Schalen und Lekythen eine große Rolle spielte.[176] Die Nachfrage gab auch im westlichen Kleinasien immer mehr Spezialisten den Vorrang: im späten 6. und frühen 5. Jh. sind die Lekythen der Phanyllis-Gruppe, Hahn-Gruppe und Haimon-Gruppe sowie die Schalen der Leafless-Gruppe marktführend.

Der *Gorgo-Maler und sein Umkreis* (600/580), deren Vasen erstmalig auch zum Export gelangten, sind in Ionien mit 14, im gesamten westlichen Kleinasien mit 28 Vasen vertreten. In Phokaia fand sich der erste bislang bekannte Kolonettenkrater des Malers, eine Olpe und ein Dinos/Krater aus seinem Umkreis. Zwei Amphoren und eine Lekane in der Art des Malers kamen in Alt-Smyrna zutage, während Klazomenai zwei Olpen und eine aus seinem Umkreis hervorbrachte, eine davon als Grabbeigabe. Unter den fünf im Heraion von Samos geweihten Vasen befinden sich zwei Bauchamphoren, eine Olpe und zwei Deckel. Von den 129 bislang gezählten Gefäßen sind 38% (49 Stück=49) für den heimischen Markt in Athen bestimmt gewesen, während 22% (28) den griechischen Osten, 18% (23) Griechenland und 13% (17) das östlichen Mittelmeer, vor allem Naukratis erreichten.[177]

Bedingt durch die reichen Funde im Heraion von Samos (28) sind Vasen des *KX-Malers und seines Umkreises* (585/70) mit 44 Stück in Ionien besonders zahlreich. Bei den Weihgaben im Heraion handelt es sich um 12 Schalen (davon eine Komastenschale in der Art des Malers), zwei Kotylen, einen Kantharos, sechs Amphoren, eine Hydria, ein Becken, drei Lekanen/Lekaniden und einen Ständer. In Phokaia wurde eine Lekanis im Bereich des Athena-Tempels, drei weitere Lekaniden, eine Schale, eine Bauchamphora und ein Fragment eines großen kelchartigen Gefäßes in der Art des KX-Malers in der Siedlung gefunden. Die Siedlungsschichten von Alt-Smyrna brachten ebenfalls zwei Lekaniden hervor. In Alt-Smyrna und Klazomenai wurden Komastenschalen in der Art des Malers, eine weitere in Sardeis gefunden. Bei den 133 Vasen des KX-Malers, deren Fundort bekannt ist, zeichnet sich ab, daß 44% (59) im heimischen Athen blieben, während 33% (44) in den griechischen Osten (einschließlich der zwei Lekaniden in der rhodischen Nekropole von Ialysos u. einem Krater in Daskyleion) gelangten; weitere 10% (13) erreichten verschiedene Landschaften Griechenlands und 9% (12) die Gebiete des östlichen Mittelmeeres, davon einige auch Naukratis.[178]

Durch neue Funde in Alt-Smyrna, Samos und Sardeis gewinnen auch die Vasen des *Sophilos und seines Umkreises* (590/70) mit 17 Stücken in Ionien, bzw. 23 Stücken im griechischen Osten an Gewicht. Phokaia brachte neben einem Louterion eine Lekanis und möglicherweise eine Hydria hervor. Dem bekannten Lebes

---

63-64 Kat. 1-3.- Assos II Kat. 1-13. 132.- Assos III Kat. 1-20.- Utili 1999, 43-56. 63. 66-70. 215-223. 226. 228-230. Zu korinthischen und lokalen Aryballoi in Pitane zwischen 575- 510 s. z. B. Alt-Smyrna & Pitane Kap. II Kat. 1-2. 19. 58-59. 141-144 (Beifunde).

[172] Kurtz und Boardman 1985, 248.- Löwe 1996, 98. In Athen werden Lekythen und Alabastra auch bei späteren Besuchen am Grab aufgestellt, s. Garland 1985, 107-108.

[173] Boardman 1974, 40-41. 71-72.- Boardman 1979, 34.- Scheibler 1983, 172-173- Scheffer 1988, 536-537.- Kluiver 1997, Kap. 5.

[174] Alt-Smyrna & Pitane 136-149 mit Tab. 9 und Abb. 31. Zur Landschaftsaufteilung s. ebenda 145 Anm. 689. Die Zahlen zur Verbreitung der Maler und Gruppen beruhen grundsätzlich auf ABV und Para, die durch die Neufunde im untersuchten Gebiet sowie Brijder, Siana Cups I-III, Grabungspublikationen und Museums- und Ausstellungskataloge der letzten Jahre ergänzt wurden, jedoch ohne Anspruch auf Vollständigkeit.

[175] Scheffer 1988, 544.

[176] Osborne 1996, 33.

[177] Alt-Smyrna & Pitane 136-149 Tab. 9 mit Nachw.; zu den Zahlen s. 146-147 mit Anm. 690. Hinzu kommen: Phokaia II Kat. 85. 97. 101 (Kolonettenkrater).- Add. Alt-Smyrna Kat. 57.- Klazomenai Kat. 129-130.- Daskyleion I Kat. 155.- Daskyleion II Kat. 157.- Antandros 177 Abb. 18 (M. v. Istanbul 7314). Neuzugänge ferner: Athen: Agora XXIII Kat. 12. 123. 140. 142-143. 532. 709. 777. 1370. 1857.- Griechenland: Ägina I Kat. 117-131.- Etruskische Gebiete: Tronchetti 1983, Taf. 1,a-b.- Cristofani 1981, 205 Abb. 180.- Boitani 1971, 243 Nr. 2025.- Cortona: Paribeni 1972, 392-393,3 Taf. 65.- Martelli 1985,196 Nr. 1.- Westl. Mittelmeer: Villard 1992, 164.- Östl. Mittelmeer: Naukratis Kat. 267-268.- Schwarzmeer: Histria IV Kat. 300, s. auch Samos XXII 86.

[178] Alt-Smyrna & Pitane 136-149 Tab. 9 mit Nachw.; Kap. I. Kat. 2-3 (M. v. NY 22. 139. 22); zu den Zahlen s. 146-147 mit Anm. 691. Hinzu kommen: Phokaia II Kat. 2. 66. 118. 123- 124. 131-132.- Klazomenai Kat. 1 (M. v. NY 22. 139. 22).- Daskyleion II 159.- Siana Cups III 713-14, K 6-10. Neuzugänge außerdem: Athen: Agora XXIII Kat. 1310.- Nymphenheiligtum Kat. 105-145.- Griechenland: Ägina I Kat. 138. 146.- Korinth I Kat. 2.- Griechischer Westen: Pagliardi 1972, 112 Nr. 203.- Sabbione 1987, Abb. S. 114.- Östliches Mittelmeer: Kyrene Kat. 152, s. auch Samos XXII 87-88.

Gamikos aus der Siedlung von Alt-Smyrna, folgen fünf Fragmente, die zu drei bis fünf Dinoi gehören, sowie eine Bauchamphora und ein Exaleiptron aus des Malers Umkreis. Dabei ist das kleine Dinosfragment, das eine Wiederholung der Leichenspiele von Patroklos auf dem Pharsalos-Dinos wiedergeben könnte, von besonderer Bedeutung (Abb.1).

In Klazomenai ist eine Lekanis (Abb. 7) und in Milet möglicherweise ein Krater gefunden worden, während das Heraion von Samos eine Amphora des Malers und zwei Lekaniden aus dem Umkreis hervorbrachte. In den benachbarten Landschaften kamen eine Lekanis aus dem Umkreis in Troja, ein Dinos oder Krater in Lindos, zwei Dinoi des Malers und eine Amphora in seiner Art in Sardeis zutage. Die Auswertung der 99 gezählten Vasen zeigt, daß nach Athen mit 33 % (32) und Griechenland mit 30 % (29), der griechische Osten mit ca. 20 % (20-22) beim Export der Vasen der Sophilos-Werkstatt eine bedeutende Rolle spielte.[179]

Von den Komastenschalen-Malern erfreute sich im westlichen Kleinasien vor allem der *KY-Maler* (575/65) an Beliebtheit. In Ionien wurden fünf, im gesamten griechischen Osten 15 seiner Vasen sowie zwei seines nahen Kollegen, des *Falmouth-Malers*, gefunden. Schalen des KY-Malers kamen in Phokaia, Alt-Smyrna, Klazomenai, möglicherweise in Milet, mehrfach in Pitane, in Lindos und in Daskyleion zutage, während ein Krater in Alt-Smyrna, ein weiterer Krater und eine Lekanis Sardeis erreichten. Alt-Smyrna und Rhodos brachten je eine Schale des Falmouth-Malers hervor. Von den gezählten 87 Vasen stammen 28 % (24) aus Griechenland, 15 % (13) aus Athen und 19,5 % (17) aus dem griechischen Osten.[180]

Der *C-Maler und sein Umkreis* (575/55), der sich in erster Linie auf Sianaschalen spezialisiert hat, ist in Ionien mit 16, im gesamten griechischen Osten mit 33 Vasen vertreten. Während Phokaia eine Lekanis des Malers und zwei Sianaschalen des *Taras-Malers* hervorgebracht hat, wurden in Alt-Smyrna möglicherweise ein Kantharos und drei Sianaschalen des Malers bzw. seiner Werkstatt gefunden. In Klazomenai fand sich eine Sianaschale des Malers und wohl eine des Taras-Malers, in Milet eine weitere Sianaschale von seiner Hand, eine seiner Werkstatt und eine des Taras-Malers, desweiteren im Heraion von Samos erneut eine Sianaschale des Malers, zwei Skyphoi seiner Werkstatt und ein Ständer des *Malibu-Malers*. In den benachbarten Landschaften kamen in Elaious ein Skyphos und in den Nekropolen von Rhodos, in Sardeis und Daskyleion Sianaschalen zutage, im letzteren auch eine Pyxis des Malers selbst. Wertet man die vergleichsweise große Anzahl von 439 Vasen mit bekanntem Fundort aus, zeigt sich, daß der griechische Osten mit 7,5% (33) für diese Werkstatt im Vergleich zu Griechenland mit 48% (210) und dem griechischen Westen mit 24% (107) relativ unbedeutend war.[181]

Von *Lydos* (560/40) selbst sind eine Schale in Phokaia und eine Amphora im Heraion von Samos belegt. Sehr viel häufiger gibt es Vasen *seines Umkreises*, nämlich 20 Stück in Ionien und sieben weitere in den benachbarten Landschaften sowie Vasen des *Malers von Louvre F 6*, der in der Region mit weiteren 11 Gefäßen vertreten ist, davon eines aus Ionien. In der Art des Lydos wurden zwei Kratere und drei Lekaniden in Phokaia (Abb. 5), eine Sianaschale, ein Krater, eine Lekanis und ein Teller in Alt-Smyrna, eine Amphora und ein Krater in Milet sowie vier Amphoren, ein Ständer, ein Krater, eine Hydria und zwei Kelchpyxiden im Heraion von Samos gefunden. Vasen dieser Werkstatt sind ferner in den benachbarten Landschaften in Thymbra, Byzantion, Xanthos, Daskyleion und Sardeis belegt. Bislang hat in Ionien nur Phokaia einen Krater des Malers von Louvre F 6 hervorgebracht, weitere seiner Vasen wurden jedoch in Antissa auf Lesbos, in Ialysos auf Rhodos, in Xanthos, Daskyleion und Sardeis gefunden. Nach den 356 gezählten Vasen zu urteilen, blieb mit 42% (149) der größte Produktionsanteil der Lydos-Werkstatt im heimischen Athen, während 15% (53) nach Griechenland, 14% (49) in etruskische Gebiete und weitere 11% (38) in den griechische Osten gelangten.[182] Nach Michalis

---

[179] Alt-Smyrna & Pitane 136-149 Tab. 9 mit Nachw. (s. auch Korfu-M.); Kap I. Kat. 183.- Phokaia II Kat. 83. 96. 125.- Add. Alt-Smyrna Kat. 29. 42 (Leichenspiele?)- 45.- Klazomenai Kat. 176.- Nach Auskunft N. Kunischs.- Sardeis Att 1. 36-37. Zahlen zur Verbreitung ermittelt nach ABV 38- 43; Para 19.- Ferner Athen: Nymphenheiligtum Kat. 171. 176-180.- Griechenland: Ägina I Kat. 156-159. 161-164.- Korinth I Kat. 3. 5.- Östliches Mittelmeer: Naukratis Kat. 265.- Kyrene Kat. 256, s. auch Samos XXII 88-89.

[180] Alt-Smyrna & Pitane 136-149 Tab. 9 mit Nachw. 760. 825. 1083. 1098.- Phokaia II Kat. 1.- Add. Alt-Smyrna Kat. 1.- Klazomenai Kat. 2.- Nach Auskunft N. Kunischs.- Sardeis Att 40. 45. Zahlen zur Verbreitung ermittelt nach ABV 31-36; Para 16-17; Siana Cups I 224-228, K23. K30. K34. K45. K53. K 66-67. K 71. K 77-78.- Siana Cups II 473, 1. 3-4. 9.; 1.- Brijder, Siana Cups III 714-15, K 11-25. K 2-4.- Korinth I Kat. 11.

[181] Alt-Smyrna & Pitane 136-149 Tab. 9 mit Nachw.; zu den Zahlen s. 146-147 mit Anm. 692.- Phokaia II Kat. 3-4. 133.- Klazomenai Kat. 3-4.- Nach Auskunft N. Kunischs.- Daskyleion I Kat. 3. 234.- Daskyleion II Kat. 1.- Sardeis Att 49; Siana Cups II 478-479, 4-21;480-481, 8-10. 15-17. 23; 482, 3. 7-10; 482,1-3; 483-485, 1. 3-37.- Siana Cups III 717-719, 23-24. 26-28. 30-33. 35-39; 719, 1-2; 719, 1-2; 719- 723, 24-28. 32-41. 46. 53-54. 55-68; 723-724, 12-19; 724-725, 6-8; 725, 1-12; 726-727, 38-64. 66-67.- Nymphenheiligtum Kat. 245.- Griechenland: Ägina II Kat. 16.

[182] Alt-Smyrna & Pitane 136-149 Tab. 9 mit Nachw.; zu den Zahlen s. 146-148 mit Anm. 695. Hinzu kommen: Phokaia II Kat. 48. 107-08. 111. 128. 134-35.- Add. Alt-Smyrna Kat. 2. 58.- Nach Auskunft N. Kunischs.- Daskyleion I Kat. 163. 178.- Daskyleion II Kat. 163.- Sardeis Att 2-3. 5.- Fıratlı 1978, 570 Taf. 164,5 (Zuweisung Tiverios 1981, 164). Neuzugänge ferner: Athen: Agora XXIII Kat. 50-51. 172. 430. 437. 440-441. 449. 628. 790. 1475.- Südl. d. Akropolis Kat. 15-17. 20. 107.- Nymphenheiligtum Kat. 318-357.- Griechenland: Ägina I Kat. 189. 192-195. 200-204.- Ägina II Kat. 4-7. 91-92.- Korinth II Kat. 47.- Sindos Kat. 372.- Tiverios 1981, 163-164 (Vrasta/Chalkidiki, Nausas, Tragilo, Oisyme). Griechischer Westen: Morgantina Kat. 17-1.- Östliches Mittelmeer: Naukratis Kat. 235-236. 258. 260-261.- Kyrene Kat. 7-8. 43. 93-96. 261.- Cyprus Kat. 499. 506.- Schwarzmeer: Histria IV Kat. 301.

Tiverios, der mit Neufunden in der nördlichen Ägäis ihre Verbreitung in diesem Gebiet und entlang der Schwarzmeerküsten aufzeichnet, beginnt der großflächige Export attischer Vasen mit dieser Werkstatt.[183]

Vasen der 'Tyrrhenischen'-Gruppe (560/30) sind in Ionien zwar nicht häufig belegt, allein die Tatsache jedoch, daß sie außerhalb Etruriens gefunden worden sind, ist bemerkenswert. Demnach hat die Werkstatt nicht nur für den etruskischen Markt produziert, sondern auch Kunden im griechischen Osten gefunden, die wohl eher Abnehmer anderer Gefäßtypen als die typischen ovoiden Amphoren waren. In Phokaia wurden in einer Abfallgrube der in mehreren Fragmenten erhaltene Volutenkrater des Dammhirsch-Malers sowie Fragmente einer Kelchpyxis, die wohl der mit der ,Tyrrhenischen'-Gruppe verwandten Archippe-Gruppe zuzuordnen sind, gefunden. Der Krater des Dammhirsch-Malers ist der einzige bisher bekannte Volutenkrater der 'Tyrrhenischen'-Gruppe und als früher Vertreter dieser Vasenform für die attische Vasenkunst von großer Bedeutung (Abb. 6). Desweiteren brachte die Siedlung von Alt-Smyrna Fragmente einer Amphora des Castellani-Malers und die Yıldıztepe Nekropole von Klazomenai den in zahlreichen Fragmenten erhaltenen Kolonettenkrater des Prometheus-Malers hervor.[184] In den benachbarten Landschaften sind zwei Amphoren aus Ialysos und Kamiros und möglicherweise eine weitere aus Daskyleion zu nennen.[185]

Der Antimenes-Maler und sein Umkreis (525/10) ist in Ionien mit sechs, im gesamten griechischen Osten mit 13 Vasen vertreten. Ein Volutenkrater in Alt-Smyrna, zwei Amphoren in Klazomenai sowie ein Kelchkrater, eine Hydria und eine Kelchpyxis aus dem Heraion von Samos können dem Umkreis des Malers, u. a. einmal der Gruppe von Würzburg 199 zugewiesen werden. In den benachbarten Landschaften sind drei Vasen von der Hand des Malers belegt: es sind zwei Amphoren auf Rhodos, davon eine aus Kamiros sowie eine Lekanis in Xanthos. Weitere Amphoren aus dem Umkreis sind in Ialysos, Xanthos und Daskyleion nachgewiesen. Die meisten Vasen dieser Werkstatt mit bekanntem Fundort (105) wurden in etruskischen Gebieten (74=70%), vor allem in Vulci gefunden, wobei der griechische Osten mit 12 % (13) der Funde offenbar eine bedeutendere Rolle als Athen (3=3%) und Griechenland (4= 4%) spielte.[186]

26 Lekythen der Phanyllis-Gruppe und Umkreis (Ende 6. Jh.) sind im gesamten griechischen Osten nachgewiesen, davon sieben in Ionien. Ein Exemplar wurde in Alt-Smyrna gefunden, vier weitere in Klazomenai, davon eine mit einer Kriegerabschiedszene. In Ephesos wurde eine Lekythos im Artemision und eine weitere in der Nekropole freigelegt. In den benachbarten Landschaften kommen sie vor allem in den Nekropolen von Elaious, Pitane, Gryneion und Rhodos, aber auch in Daskyleion vor. Betrachtet man die Verbreitungsstatistik, fällt auf, daß der ostgriechische Markt auch für diese Werkstatt eine untergeordnete Rolle gespielt hat. Von 367 Lekythen sind lediglich 7 % (26) hierher gelangt, während der griechische Westen mit 45 % (164), Griechenland mit 17 % (61), etruskische Gebiete mit 12 % (45) wichtigere Märkte waren.[187]

Die Hahn-Gruppe (Ende 6./Anf. 5. Jh.) ist in Ionien mit drei, im gesamten griechischen Osten mit 19 Lekythen vertreten. Die ionischen Stücke wurden in Alt-Smyrna und in der Nekropole von Ephesos gefunden. Weitere vier Lekythen kamen in Pitane, zwei in der Troas, je eine in Daskyleion und Mysien sowie acht in den Nekropolen von Ialysos und Kamiros zutage. Von 124 Lekythen mit bekanntem Fundort sind 31% (39) in Athen geblieben, 32% (40) gelangten in die verschiedenen Regionen Griechenlands, während 15% (19) den griechischen Osten, 15% (19) die Gebiete des östlichen Mittelmeers und 8% (10) den griechischen Westen erreichten.[188]

Mindestens 25 Vasen (hauptsächlich Skyphoi) der CHC-Gruppe und Umkreis (um 500) wurden im griechischen Osten, davon neun in Ionien verkauft. Sechs Skyphoi wurden in Alt-Smyrna, eine Pyxis in Klazomenai und mindestens zwei bis drei Skyphoi in Milet gefunden. In den benachbarten Landschaften kamen CHC-Skyphoi vereinzelt in Elaious, Pitane, Kamiros, Patara, Sardeis und zahlreich in Daskyleion zutage, im letzteren auch eine Bandschale. Von den gezählten 208 Vasen sind 30% (63) in Griechenland, 26% (55) in Athen, 12% (25) im griechischen Osten und 10% (20) im griechischen Westen

---

305-311. 339.- CVA Pushkin State Museum, Taf. 20,1-5. 46, 1-6 (Pantikapaion).
[183] Tiverios 1981, 151-171.
[184] Phokaia I 18-21 Abb. 8-11.- Y. Tuna- Nörling in: APP 435-446.- Phokaia II Kat. 115. 140.- Add. Alt-Smyrna Kat. 31.- Klazomenai Kat. 118.
[185] Rhodos 6589, ABV 99,55 (O. L. L.- Gruppe).- London B 25, ABV 106,1 (Nahe O. L. L.- Gruppe). Einige Forscher sehen allerdings die O. L. L.- Gruppe nicht als 'Tyrrhenisch' an, s. dazu: ABV 94ff; Kluiver 1992, 74.- Daskyleion II Kat. 166.
[186] Alt-Smyrna & Pitane 136-149 Tab. 9 mit Nachw. Zahlen ermittelt nach ABV 266- 291; Para 117-122; Burow 1989, 106.- Add. Alt-Smyrna Kat. 55.- Klazomenai Kat. 135- 137.- Samos XXII Kat. 63. 85. 122.- Daskyleion I Kat. 189. Neuzugänge ferner: Athen: Agora XXIII Kat. 391.- Griechenland: Ägina I Kat. 255.- Etruskische Gebiete: L Tomay in: Fratte 193- 202 Nr. 9.- Östliches Mittelmeer: Cyprus Kat. 501-502.- Westliches Mittelmeer u. a.: Heuneburg Kat. 1.- Schwarzmeer: CVA Pushkin State Museum, Taf. 22,2. 25,4 (Pantikapaion).
[187] Alt-Smyrna & Pitane 136-149 Tab. 9 mit Nachw.; zu den Zahlen s. 146-148 mit Anm. 698. Hinzu kommen: Klazomenai Kat. 154-157.- Gryneion Abb. 12.- Daskyleion I Kat. 212.- Daskyleion II Kat. 226. Neuzugänge ferner: Athen: Kerameikos VII,2 Gräber 242,5-6. 267,1. 408,1. 462,1-2. S 97.- Etruskische Gebiete: L. Tomay in: Fratte 193-202 Nr. 10.- F. Gilotta in: Caere 3. 1 C 109.- Schwarzmeer: Histria IV Kat. 331.- Tracia Bulgara Kat. 86-87 (Apollonia).- CVA Pushkin State Museum, Taf. 31,1 (Pantikapaion).- Phanagoria Kat. 48.
[188] Alt-Smyrna & Pitane 136-149 Tab. 9 mit Nachw.; zu den Zahlen s. 146-148 mit Anm. 700. Hinzu kommen: Daskyleion II Kat. 234. Neuzugänge ferner: Athen: Agora XXIII Kat. 858.- Südl. d. Akropolis Kat. 199. 200.- Griechenland: Ägina II 18. 68-69.- Corinth II Kat. 83-87.- Griechischer Westen: Morgantina Kat. 4-6. 4-8. 4-9. 17-3.

gefunden worden, was zeigt, daß die Hälfte der Produktion in näherer Umgebung abgesetzt wurde und der Osten eine untergeordnete Rolle spielte.[189]

Von Bedeutung war dieser Markt jedoch für die 'Dot- ivy'- Gruppe und Umkreis (um 500), die sich auf Olpen spezialisiert hatte: 19 Olpen der Gruppe wurde im griechischen Osten gefunden, davon vier in Ionien. Drei der Olpen stammen aus Alt-Smyrna, eine weitere befindet sich im Museum von Selçuk und kam wohl in Torbalı zutage. In den benachbarten Landschaften ist eine in Pitane, mehrere auf Rhodos, vor allem in den Nekropolen von Kamiros und Ialysos, drei in Daskyleion und eine in Sardeis belegt. Von 43 Vasen sind 44% (19) in den griechischen Osten gelangt und weitere 33% (14) in etruskische Gebiete. Geringere Mengen wurden in Athen, im griechischen Westen, auf Zypern und im Schwarzmeergebiet gefunden.[190]

Im frühen 5. Jh. wurde der griechische Osten für zwei Werkstätten des Kerameikos, nämlich für die *Leafless-Gruppe* (500/490) und die *Haimon-Gruppe* (480/60) ein wichtiger Absatzmarkt:

153 Schalen der Leafless-Gruppe und Umkreis erreichten den griechischen Osten, davon mindestens 74 Stücke Ionien. 40 Schalen wurden in Alt-Smyrna (Abb. 3), 18 in Klazomenai und 14 auf Samos gefunden, während Phokaia zwei, Milet mindestens drei bis vier und Didyma sowie Emporion auf Chios jeweils eine aufweisen. In den benachbarten Landschaften sind sie mehrfach in der Nekropolen von Elaious, Ialysos und Kamiros sowie in den Siedlungen Xanthos, Daskyleion und Sardeis gefunden worden; vereinzelt kommen sie auch in Thymbra, Pitane, Gryneion, Myrina, Larisa, Mytilene und Labraunda vor. 46% der 332 Vasen sind demnach in den griechischen Osten verkauft worden; 15% (50) blieben im heimischen Athen, während 13% (42) in verschiedene Landschaften Griechenlands, 9% (31) in etruskische Gebiete und 8% (27) an die Küsten des Schwarzmeers gelangten.[191]

Die Haimon-Gruppe und ihr Umkreis, die in erster Linie Schalenskyphoi und Lekythen herstellten, sind in Ionien mit 40 und im gesamten griechischen Osten mit 454 Vasen vertreten, wobei die Miniturskyphoi der Lindos-Gruppe einen hohen Anteil ausmachen (267 Stück). 19 Vasen wurden in Alt-Smyrna, neun in Klazomenai, sieben im Artemision und eine weitere als Grabbeigabe in Ephesos sowie zwei andere im Heraion von Samos gefunden. In den benachbarten Landschaften sind sie besonders zahlreich in den Nekropolen von Kamiros und Ialysos sowie im Athena-Lindia-Heiligtum in Lindos (allein hier 242 Miniturskyphoi) und im Satrapensitz Daskyleion vertreten. Mehrfach kommen sie in den Nekropolen von Elaious und Assos, vereinzelt in Thymbra, Pitane, Myrina, Larisa, Labraunda und Sardeis vor. Weitere Vasen der Gruppe ohne Fundortangabe befinden sich in den Museen der Region, darunter auch eine auf Kos. Von 1495 gezählten Vasen blieb ca. ein Drittel, nämlich 35,5% (531) im heimischen Athen, 16% (246) gelangten in die verschiedenen Landschaften Griechenlands, während 30% (454) in den griechischen Osten exportiert wurden.[192]

---

[189] Alt-Smyrna & Pitane 136-149 Tab. 9 mit Nachw. Zahlen ermittelt nach ABV 617- 626; Para 306-308, zum Umkreis der CHC- Gruppe gehören die Hund- Gruppe und die Gruppe von Theben R. 102; Klazomenai Kat. 174.- Nach Auskunft N. Kunischs.- Daskyleion I Kat. 86.- Daskyleion II Kat. 43. 126- 131. 133. 152-154.- Sardeis Att 80. Neuzugänge ferner: Athen: Agora XXIII Kat. 1578. 1589. 1600-1603.- Südl. d. Akropolis Kat. 67-81.- Griechenland: Sindos Kat. 105.- Ägina II Kat. 29. 80-81.- Korinth III Kat. 239-242.- Griechischer Westen: Morgantina Kat. 9-158. 39-4. 50-2.- Etruskische Gebiete: F. Gilotta in: Caere 3. 1 Grab C 160.- L. Tomay in: Fratte 193-202 Nr. 7. 11.- Östliches Mittelmeer: Kyrene Kat. 194-197.- Schwarzmeer: Histria IV Kat. 347- 355.- Tracia Bulgara Kat. 70 (Apollonia).- CVA Pushkin State Museum, Taf. 49,2-5. 50,1-3 (Pantikapaion, Harmonassa).- Phanagora Kat. 110-114.

[190] Alt-Smyrna & Pitane 136-149 Tab. 9 mit Nachw. 778. 850. 887. 992. 1069-70. 1085. 1153, zu den Zahlen s. 146-148 mit Anm. 699. Hinzu kommen: Add. Alt-Smyrna Kat. 38-39.- Daskyleion II Kat. 217-218. 220.- Sardeis Att. 20. Neuzugänge ferner: Athen: Agora XXIII Kat. 749. 755.- Etruskische Gebiete: F. Gilotta in: Caere 3. 1 C104.- Östliches Mittelmeer: Kition Kat. 5.- Schwarzmeer: CVA Pushkin State Museum, Taf. 30,3. 5 (Pantikapaion).- Phanagora Kat. 26.

[191] Alt-Smyrna & Pitane 136-149 Tab. 9 mit Nachw.; zu den Zahlen s. 146-148 mit Anm. 701. Hinzu kommen: Phokaia II Kat. 57-58.- Add. Alt-Smyrna Kat. 20-22.- Klazomenai Kat. 64-76. 78-80. 82-83.- Nach Auskunft N. Kunischs.- Gryneion 13 Abb. 11.- Daskyleion I Kat. 69. 74-75. 80.- Daskyleion II Kat. 103.- Sardeis Att 70. 73-74. Neuzugänge ferner: Athen: Agora XXIII Kat. 1833-1835.- Südl. d. Akropolis Kat. 15-17. 20. 107.- Griechenland: Sindos Kat. 373.- Ägina I Kat. 265.- Korinth III Kat. 273-275.- Etruskische Gebiete: D. Dannaruma- L. Tomay in: Fratte 207-275 Grab LXII,4; VI-XV,7.- F. Gilotta in: Caere 3. 1 C152-154.- Östliches Mittelmeer: Kition Kat. 16.- Kyrene Kat. 235-240. 282.- Westliches Mittelmeer u. a.: Heuneburg Kat. 9.- Schwarzmeer: Histria IV Kat. 437-438.- Tracia Bulgara Kat. 77-79 (Apollonia).- CVA Pushkin State Museum, Taf. 61,1-2 (Kormilitsyn). 61,3. 62,1-4. 63,1-4 (Pantikapaion).- Phanagora Kat. 233-239. 241-245.

[192] Alt-Smyrna & Pitane 136-149 Tab. 9 mit Nachw.; zu den Zahlen s. 146-148 mit Anm. 703. Hinzu kommen: Klazomenai Kat. 104-107. 110-113. 164.- Trinkl 1999.- Daskyleion I Kat. 93. 95. 97-106. 108-109. 116-117. 119. 121. 125. 127-128. 133. 153. 219. 222. 225. 237-240- Daskyleion II Kat. 135-136. 138-143. 145-148. 228. 230. 232-233.- Sardeis Att 81. Neuzugänge ferner: Athen: Agora XXIII Kat. 970. 975. 1184-1185. 1222-1236. 1286. 1514-1530. 1534-1535. 1572. 1577.- Südl. d. Akropolis Kat. 24-26. 28. 94-101. 128-129. 180. 225-231.- Kerameikos VII,2 Grab 3,2. 9,3-4. 10,1-2. 15,1-2. 20,1-4. 24,1-2. 29, 1-3 39,2. 40,1-4. 44,1. 45,1. 48,1-2. 49,1. 51,2-3. 55,1. 63,1-3. 64,1. 71,4. 73,1-3. 74,1. 78,1-15. 82,1-2. 84,1. 85,2. 9-10. 86,1. 87,1. 88,1-2. 91,1-2. 92,1-2. 97,1-4. 111,4. 117,1. 126,1. 129,1. 131,1-2. 210,3. 216,1. 220. 221,1. 223,1. 246,2. 265,1. 273,4-11. 276,4-5. 278,3-4. 285,1-6. 308,1-2. 413,1. 482,5-20.- 483,4-13. 485, 2. 538,1-3. 35 HTR Bezik 44 II,1-2. 599,1-2.- Kerameikos IX Grab 21,1. 29,2. 34,2. 45,2. 51. 54,1-3. 57,4. 61,1-2. 64,1. 3. 68,7-8. 69,1. 76,1. 81,1. 84,1. 85,4. 89,1. 91,1. 96,1. 97,1. 98,1-2. 99,1. 105,1. 109,1-7. 111,2. 116,1. 117,1. 4-13. 120,1-2. 122,1. 126,1. 127,1. 128,3-4. 129,1. 130,1. 132,1-5. 134,2. 136,2. 138,1. 139,1-2. 143,1. 145,1. 153,1-2. 8. 155,1. 156,1. 170,2. 181,1-6. 196,2-3. 202. 206,1-2. 210,1-2. 212,1. 214,3-6. 217,1. 220,1-3. 238,3. 144,1. 250,2. 289,1.- Griechenland: Ägina II Kat. 36. 75-76. 100-101.- Korinth III Kat. 193-201. 234. 260-265. 267-269. 272.- Thorikos VII.- Griechischer Westen: Morgantina Kat. 4-3. 4-4. 4-7. 4-10. 6-4. 6-5.- San Pietro 1991, Kat. 1-15.- Etruskische Gebiete: L. Tomay in: Fratte 193-

Themen

Da die Trinkschale die beliebteste Gefäßform war, verwundert es nicht, daß Darstellungen von Dionysos und seinem Gefolge, den Satyrn und Mänaden, am häufigsten zu finden ist. Maßgeblich daran beteiligt war die Leafless-Gruppe mit ihrer Spezialisierung auf Schalen und ihren sich immer wiederholenden Themen. Bei mythologischen Themen überwiegen die Taten des Herakles, der als beliebtester Held im peisistratidischen Athen besonders häufig auf Vasen erscheint.[193] Nach den zahlreichen Tierfriesen, die im frühen 6. Jh. verschiedene Gefäßformen und im dritten Viertel zahlreiche Bandschalen verzieren, kommen desweiteren Kampfszenen, Kriegerauszug, Reiter und Wagenrennen sowie Sportszenen (Lauf, Ringen etc.) vor.[194] Verbunden mit der Qualität weisen die attischen Vasen im Heraion von Samos ein reichhaltiges Repertoire an mythologischen Themen auf.[195]

Eine speziell für den westkleinasiatischen Markt zugeschnittene Themenauswahl konnte bislang nicht festgestellt werden. Für Kunden im Persischen Reich sollen die Schalen des Pithos-Malers mit der Darstellung gelagerter Jünglinge mit 'Baschlik' und Trinkhorn hergestellt worden sein.[196] Grund für diese Annahme sind zahlreiche Funde in Al Mina und weitere in Palästina. Zwei Schalen des Pithos-Malers haben sich in Ionien gefunden, davon eine im Artemision von Ephesos und eine weitere auf Chios. Der Satrapensitz Daskyleion brachte ein weiteres Exemplar hervor.[197] Allerdings waren diese Schalen nicht ausschließlich für den östlichen Markt hergestellt, wie die Fundverbreitung in Griechenland, Sizilien und italischen Gebieten zeigt. Ferner ist kaum erklärbar, warum persische Kunden besonderen Gefallen an diesen nachlässig gemalten Schalen finden sollten, nur weil darauf ein kaum erkennbarer 'Perser' dargestellt war.[198]

Handel und Politik

Ionien weist unter den Landschaften des westlichen Kleinasiens die größten Mengen attischer Keramik auf und zwar, wie überall dort, mit einer starken Zunahme nach der Eroberung durch die Perser im Jahre 546.[199] Allem Anschein nach waren die wirtschaftlichen Verhältnisse nach der Machtübernahme so gut, daß der Keramikhandel reibungslos funktionieren konnte.[200]

Nach Jack Martin Balcer erlebten die ionischen Poleis nun eine wirtschaftliche Blüte, die sich in den neuen Münzprägungen der Städte (z. B. Teos, Kolophon, Phokaia) und später in der Höhe ihrer Beitragszahlungen an den Delisch-Attischen Seebund bemerkbar macht. Angst vor Repressionen der neuen Machthaber und die damit verbundenene politische 'Unfreiheit' ließen zwar die Kunstentwicklung, Lyrik und Philosophie der Ostgriechen stagnieren, Wirtschaft und Handel konnten sich aber uneingeschränkt weiterentwickeln.[201]

Inwiefern dies für Phokaia zutrifft, läßt sich an Hand der dort gefundenen attischen Keramik nicht eindeutig nachvollziehen. Herodot (1. 163) berichtet, daß die Phokaier während der Belagerung duch die Perser ihr gesamtes Hab und Gut auf Schiffe luden und fortsegelten. Als es ihnen nicht gelang, den Chioten eine Inselgruppe abzukaufen, fuhren sie weiter gen Westen und ließen sich in Alalia (Aleria) auf Kyrnos (Korsika) nieder. Einige von Heimweh geplagte Phokaier kehrten aber bald zurück (Hdt. 1. 165- 166; Strabo 3. 252). Analysiert man die attische Keramik vor diesem Hintergrund, zeigt sich, daß die höchste Konzentration in das Jahrzehnt 550/40 fällt, in dessen Mitte die Eroberung und Zerstörung der Stadt durch die Perser stattfand. In dem darauffolgenden Jahrzehnt sinkt die Zahl der Funde plötzlich wie vor 550 wieder unter die Hälfte. Dieses Phänomen, das sicherlich mit der Eroberung Phokaias zusammenfällt, wird man zwar nicht als Hiatus, aber als deutliche Zäsur interpretieren dürfen. Fraglich ist, ob die von anderen *Poleis* der Region abweichende Abnahme der Vasenfunde attischer Herkunft erst nach 510 als ein Indiz der brachliegenden Wirtschaft und der damit verbundenen fehlenden Kaufkraft der Phokaier zu bewerten ist. Möglicherweise werden künftige Untersuchungen im klassischen Phokaia ein anderes Bild vermitteln.[202]

Schwerwiegender als die erste Eroberungswelle waren für einige *Poleis* die Folgen des Ionischen Aufstandes, mögen

---

202 Nr. 2.- D. Donnaruma- L. Tomay in: Fratte 207-275 Kat. Grab XV,4. CI (1929),2.- F. Gilotta in: Caere 3. 1 C 159.- Östliches Mittelmeer: Naukratis Kat. 273. 293.- Kition Kat. 8-9. 11-12. 17.- Kyrene Kat. 146. 190-193.- Cyprus Kat. 393. 485.- Schwarzmeer: Histria IV Kat. 359-362. 364-65. Tracia Bulgara Kat. 4 (Varna). 83. 88. 99-112 (Apollonia).- CVA Pushkin State Museum, Taf. 35,5-6. 41,3-4. 52,1-2 (Olbia). 39,2-4. 52,3-. 5. (Pantikapaion). 40,1-2. 52,4 (Kormilitsyn). 53,3 (Harmonassa).- Morgan 1999, Kat. 117 (Harmonassa). 153-154 (Phanagoria).- Phanagoria Kat. 119-125. 128. 131-137. 140. 142. 215.

[193] Boardman 1974, 236. Bsp. Alt-Smyrna & Pitane Kap. I Kat. 23. 119. 132. 145.- Klazomenai 118. 184.- Phaokaia II Kat. 41. 48. 91. 115.

[194] Bsp. Kampf: Alt-Smyrna & Pitane Kap. I Kat. 134.- Klazomenai 209.- Phokaia II Kat. 84. 115.- Samos XXII App. 2.- Kriegerauszug: Klazomenai Kat. 135.- Wagenrennen: Alt-Smyrna & Pitane Kap. I Kat. 34. 159. 181. 186.- Klazomenai 175. 178.- Samos XXII Kat. 159.- Reiter: Alt-Smyrna & Pitane Kap. I Kat. 5.- Klazomenai Kat. 3.- Phokaia II 73. 115. 142.- Sport: Alt-Smyrna & Pitane Kap. I Kat. 12. 19.- Phokaia II Kat. 137.

[195] s. Samos XXII 43- 83.

[196] ARV² 139ff, 23-37.- De Vries 1977, 546.

[197] ARV² 141,70.- Ephesos XII,1 Kat. A 37.- Daskyleion I Kat. 380.

[198] Ähnlich argumentieren auch: Lissarrague 1990b, 145-146.- Miller 1997, 69.

[199] Zur persischen Eroberung Kleinasiens s. Balcer 1995, 43-73.

[200] Zum Handel mit attischer Keramik im Persischen Reich s. Miller 1997, 65-72 (hier sind die Funde von Alt-Smyrna, Klazomenai, Phokaia und Daskyleion nicht berücksichtigt).- Daskyleion I 18-22.- Daskyleion II 15-26.

[201] Balcer 1991, 57-65.- Balcer 1995, 75-99. Ähnliche Beobachtungen bereits von Hornblower 1983, 67.- Roebuck 1988, 452-453.

[202] s. Diskussion Phokaia II.

die Gründe dafür politischer oder wirtschaftlicher Art gewesen sein, und dessen Niederschlagung (499/493). [203] Zu den betroffenen Städten zählt Klazomenai. Ein kurzer Hiatus von der Mitte des 6. Jhs. bis *ca.* 530, der mit der persischen Eroberung 546 in Verbindung gebracht wird,[204] und ein zweiter Hiatus vom frühen 5. Jh. bis *ca.* 400, der von der Umsiedlung der Bevölkerung nach der zweiten persischen Invasion um *ca.* 494/3 zeugt, spiegelt sich auch im attischen Keramikbefund wieder. In den untersuchten Siedlungsschichten und auf der Akropolis sind kaum Funde belegt, die sich genau in die 40er und 30er Jahre des 6. Jhs. datieren lassen. Im letzten Jahrhundertviertel nimmt die attische Keramik hier wieder deutlich zu, hört aber im frühen 5. Jh. abrupt auf. Die spätesten Funde sind Werke der Leafless-Gruppe, Haimon-Gruppe und CHC-Gruppe.[205]

In welchem Ausmaß sich die Zerstörung Milets im Jahre 494 anhand der attischen Keramik nachvollzeihen läßt, wird die geplante Publikation Norbert Kunischs zur gesamten attischen Keramik zeigen.[206]

Im Heraion von Samos erreichen die Keramikimporte aus Athen im dritten Viertel des 6. Jhs. ihren Höhepunkt, nehmen dann ab und sind im frühen 5. Jh. nur noch spärlich vertreten. Vermutlich muß diese Abnahme attischer Vasen im Zusammenhang mit der Ermordung des Polykrates im Jahre 522 und den darauffolgenden Unruhen gesehen werden.[207]

Weniger betroffen von den politischen Ereignissen scheint Alt-Smyrna gewesen zu sein. Zwar nimmt Ekrem Akurgal für die Stadt eine Blütezeit zwischen 600-545 an,[208] der Import attischer Keramik reicht aber weit über dieses Datum hinaus. Vielmehr erreichen die größten Mengen attischer Keramik die Stadt erst im letzten Viertel des 6. Jhs. Die Zahl der Vasen nimmt im frühen 5. Jh. zwar etwas ab, übertrifft aber mengenmäßig die aller anderen ionischen *Poleis*.

Laut Überlieferung blieb Ephesos von den Zerstörungen infolge des Ionischen Aufstandes weitgehend verschont, was sich, trotz geringer Mengen, in der attischen Keramik, die ohne Unterbrechung bis in das frühe 5. Jh. hineinreicht, wiederzuspiegeln scheint.[209]

Genaue Zahlen zur Verbreitung attisch-rotfiguriger Keramik in Ionien liegen bislang nicht vor. Nach Henri Metzgers Beobachtungen sind in Kleinasien kaum rotfigurige Vasen des späten 6. Jhs. nachgewiesen. Erst im Laufe des 5. Jhs., überwiegend in der zweiten Hälfte und im 4. Jh. nehmen Funde etwas zu.[210] Neue Funde in Alt-Smyrna und Klazomenai bestätigen einstweilen dieses Bild.[211] Auch im Artemision von Ephesos lassen sich die wenigen rotfigurigen Vasen bis auf eine archaische Schale alle in das späte 5. und 4. Jh. datieren.[212] Die ebenfalls nicht zahlreichen Funde aus dem Heraion von Samos stammen wiederum überwiegend aus der ersten Hälfte des 5. und aus dem 4. Jh.[213] Im Satrapensitz Daskyleion nimmt der Import erst im zweiten Viertel des 5. Jhs. ab, um im frühen 4. Jh. wieder zuzunehmen, wobei die Mengen weit über der den ionischen Fundorte liegen.[214] Geringer sind sie im Satrapensitz Sardeis: nach vereinzelten Funden des späten 6. und frühen 5. Jhs (u. a. Oltos?) konzentrieren sich die rotfigurigen Vasen auf das späte 5. und 4. Jh.[215]

Sicher wurde ein Teil der Importkeramik durch die in dieser Zeit ebenfalls geschätzte Schwarzfirniskeramik aus Athen abgedeckt. Über diese ist bislang wenig bekannt.[216] Das Fehlen archaischer rotfiguriger Keramik mag noch mit dem konservativen Geschmack der Ostgriechen und der Lokalbevölkerung erklärt werden,[217] aber für den geringen Import klassischer Keramik im Verlauf des 5. Jhs. müssen andere Gründe vorliegen. Vermutlich lag es an der Armut, an der einige ionische Städte im 5. Jh. unter dem Joch Athens zunehmend litten, während die Zunahme im frühen 4. Jh. mit dem erneut einkehrenden Wohlstand nach der Wiedereinverleibung in das Persische Reich in Verbindung zu bringen ist.[218]

Auf welchem Wege gelangten die Produkte des Kerameikos nach Ionien?[219] Eingeritze Händlerzeichen

---

[203] Zum Ionischen Aufstand s. Walser 1984, 27-35.- Murray 1988, 461-490.- Dandamaev 1989, 153-167.- Balcer 1995, 169-191 mit Lit. Wirtschaftliche Gründe hinter dem Austand vermuten: Lenschau 1913, 175-183.- Högemann 1992, 290-293.
[204] Ähnliche Situation auch in Xanthos, s. Xanthos IV, 194-196.
[205] s. Klazomenai.
[206] Zum Zerstörungshorizont in Milet s. v. V. Graeve 1986.- v. V. Graeve 1990.- Kerschner 1995. s. auch Tuchelt 1988.
[207] Samos XXII, 101.- Walter 1990, 154-189.- Balcer 1995, 119-121.- Ob Samos von den Persern 545 erobert wurde, ist nicht gesichert, s. Shipley 78-80.- Balcer 1995, 64-65. 92. Gesichert scheint hingegen, daß der sog. Rhoikostempel dabei nicht abgebrannt ist, sondern wegen mangelnder Fundamentierung abgetragen wurde, s. Kienast 1998.
[208] Akurgal 1950, 18. 66.- Akurgal 1983, 49.- Akurgal 1993, 48.

[209] Knibbe 1998, 83-84 mit Anm. 141.- Karwiese 1995, 46-47.- Balcer 1995, 86-89.
[210] Metzger 1989, 187-193.
[211] Rf. Alt-Smyrna mit Diagramm 2 zu dem gesamten attischen Keramikimport Alt-Smyrnas.- Klazomenai mit Diagrammen 1-3. Attische Keramik dürfte auf der dem Festland vorgelagerten Insel Karantina, auf die sich die Klazomenier im 5. Jh. zurückzogen, noch zu erwarten sein, wie Sondagen gezeigt haben, s. Klazomenai 22. 26-27.
[212] Ephesos XII,1 93-99.
[213] Briefliche Mitteilung B. Kreuzers vom 11. 9. 2000.
[214] Daskyleion mit Diagramm 4. Hierbei darf nicht vergessen werden, daß im Diagramm nur Stücke berücksichtigt wurden, die mindestens auf eine Jahrhunderthälfte datierbar sind. 135 nicht genauer datierbare Vasen könnten Daskyleion ebenfalls innerhalb dieses Zeitraums erreicht haben.
[215] Sardeis Att 108-136.
[216] Old Smyrna 176-181.- Sardeis Att 137- 586. Att. App. 29-38.- Polat 1988 (Klazomenai).- Güngör 1994, 5-29 (Klazomenai).- Çoşkun (Daskyleion).
[217] Boardman 1979, 37.
[218] Cook 1961, 9-18.- Meiggs 1972, 270-271.- Starr 1975, 83-87.
[219] Dazu zuletzt ausführlich unter besonderer Berücksichtigung von

verraten, daß vor allem Ionier, aber auch Ägineten und Etrusker mit attischen Vasen handelten.[220] Bei attischer Keramik im westlichen Kleinasien kommen sie hingegen selten vor und bieten bislang wenig Anhaltspunkte.[221] Doch die meisten ionischen *Poleis* waren am Seehandel beteiligt und unterhielten Kolonien und Handelsplätze in Übersee. Es ist deshalb anzunehmen, daß die Handelsflotte der Ionier, allen voran der Samier, Mileser, Phokaier und Chioten, für den Großteil der Keramiktransports aus Athen selbst zuständig war.[222] Welche Routen ihre Schiffe in der Ägäis verstärkt einschlugen und welche Häfen sie anliefen, dürfte durch die geographische Lage ihrer Kolonien und Handelsniederlassungen, durch ihre Handelspartner und freundschaftlichen bzw. feindlichen Beziehungen zu den einzelnen Staaten bestimmt gewesen sein. Die Schiffe, die wegen ihrer Bauweise keine langen Strecken ohne Zwischenstop durchsegeln konnten, fuhren in der Regel entlang der Küsten und zwischen den Inseln in Tagesetappen, wie Herodot berichtet (7. 193; 8. 22). Daß sie tatsächlich von Hafen zu Hafen fuhren, um Teile der mitgeführten Ware zu veräußern und dafür neue Ware einzuladen, haben die Mischladungen unterschiedlicher Herkunft auf versunkenen Schiffen wie z. B. dem Porticello oder Giglio-Schiffswrack gezeigt.[223]

In Richtung Norden fuhren Schiffe der *Poleis*, die am Seehandel in der Propontis und dem Pontus Euxeinus beteiligt waren, wobei Milet mit seinen zahlreichen Kolonien an erster Stelle zu nennen ist.[224] Phokaia, Samos, Erythrai, Teos und Rhodos traten hier ebenfalls in Erscheinung.[225] Chios' einzige Kolonie Maroneia lag in Thrakien, doch nahm die Insel wohl mit Hilfe ihres Verbündeten Milet schon früh am Handel im Schwarzmeergebiet teil. Verbindungen zu Abdera in Thrakien hatten die Klazomenier vorübergehend, später die Teer.[226] Die Chioten waren ferner am Handel in Naukratis beteiligt, so daß ihre Schiffe auch entlang der kleinasiatischen Küste die südliche Route einschlugen, während sich ihre Handelsbeziehungen zum griechischem Mutterland erst im 5. Jh. etablierten.[227] Am Hellenion von Naukratis waren von den ionischen Staaten ferner Teos, Phokaia und Klazomenai beteiligt; Samos und Milet unterhielten ihre eigenen Heiligtümer (Hdt. 2. 178).[228] Es ist also im 6. Jh. auf der Route in Richtung Ägypten mit einem regen Schiffsverkehr der Ionier zu rechnen. Bedingt durch ihre Koloniengründungen in Südfrankreich und Nordspanien konzentrierten sich die Phokaier (möglicherweise auch die Samier) schon früh auf Verbindungen mit dem westlichen Mittelmeer. Sie werden für die Verbreitung griechischer Handelsgüter, u. a. attischer Keramik, in der Region verantwortlich gemacht.[229] Umgekehrt dürften ihre Schiffe auf der Heimreise Athen angesteuert und einige Produkte des Kerameikos eingeladen haben. Dies erklärt auch die Menge und Qualität der in Phokaia gefundenen attischen Keramik in der ersten Hälfte des 6. Jhs. Denkbar ist, daß sie von hier aus an andere äolische und ionische Poleis wie Alt-Smyrna oder Pitane, die selbst keinen nennenswerten Anteil am Seehandel hatten und auch keine Kolonien unterhielten, aber reiche attische Keramikfunde aufweisen, weiterverhandelt wurden.[230] Für Samos ist Bettina Kreuzer durch Nachrichten über politische und kommerzielle Beziehungen zu anderen Staaten sowie der Exporte dieser im Heraion zu dem Schluß gekommen, daß zum größten Teil die Samioten selbst als Transporteure der attischen Keramik in Frage kommen.[231]

Nicht nur die Handelsschiffe der Ionier, sondern auch die der anderen Staaten fuhren durch die Gewässer der östlichen Ägäis. Rhodos hatte zwar seine Interessensgebiete schwerpunktmäßig im Westen und Osten, aber möglicherweise waren sie zusammen mit Milet an der Gründung Apollonias beteiligt; neue Funde in Sindos auf der Chalkidike deuten auf Beziehungen zu Ägypten, in der die Rhodier als Vermittler agierten, so daß wir mit ihrer Präsenz in der Region rechnen müssen.[232] Auch megarische Schiffe müssen auf dem Weg zu den Kolonien in der Propontis und später im Schwarzmeer die Gewässer durchsegelt haben.[233] Athen hatte wenig

---

Samos: Kreuzer 1994.
[220] Johnston 1979, 22-31. 48-53.- Austin und Vidal-Naquet 1984, 93.- s. ferner: Figuera 1986, 270-271.
[221] Johnston 1979, 19.- Neu ist ein Krater des Syleus-Malers aus Tekirdağ mit einer bislang unbekannten Händlermarke, s. Tuna- Nörling 1999; Tuna- Nörling 2001.- Zu verschiedenartigenen Graffiti auf Vasen s. ferner Sardeis 71.- Bakır und Gusmani 1993.
[222] Shipley 1982, 69.
[223] Kreuzer 1994,104-105 mit Anm. 7-9. Zur Bauweise der Schiffe s. Höckmann 1985, 52-74.
[224] Ehrhardt 1983, 31-86. Über die Rolle der Milesier als Transporteure attischer Keramik in das Schwarze Meer und nach Naukratis, s. Figuera 1986, 273.
[225] s. dazu: Roebuck 1959, 110-115. 119-124.- Boardman 1980, 238-245.- Tsetskhladze 1994, 111-135.- Langlotz 1966, 10. 14.- Shipley 1987, 51-52.- Bayburtluoğlu 1975, 71.
[226] Roebuck 1959, 106-107.- Boardman 1980, 230-231.- Koukouli-Chrysanthaki 1994, 33-77. Zu neuen Funden, die von frühen Verbindungen der Ionier und Äolier zur nördlichen Ägäis zeugen, s. Vokotopoulou 1994, 79-98.- Vokotopoulou 1996, 319-328.

[227] Roebuck 1950, 240.- Roebuck 1951, 217-218.- Roebuck 1959, 126.- Boardman 1967, 253.- Boardman 1980, 243.- Roebuck 1986, 83-84.- Sarikakis 1986, 123.- Kreuzer 1994,115. Zur chiotischen Keramik im Schwarzmeergebiet s. auch: Bouzek 1990, 34-35.
[228] Roebuck 1951, 212-220.- Roebuck 1959, 134- 135.- Boardman 1980, 118-133.- Braun 1982 36-43.- Ehrhardt 1983, 87-95 (mit Angabe weiterer Handelsplätze Milets im östl. und westl. Mittelmeer) und jetzt Möller 2000 (das Buch war mir leider noch nicht zugänglich).
[229] Roebuck 1959, 94-96. 134.- Langlotz 1966,14-19.- Figuera 1986, 248. 264-265.- Boardman 1980, 216-224.- Kreuzer 1994, 115.- Shefton 1994, 61-86,
[230] Cook 1958, 16-17.- Langlotz 1966, 13-14.
[231] Kreuzer 1994, 113-118.
[232] Gelder 1900, 65-71.- Roebuck 1959, 122.- Boardman 1980, 46-51. 119-142. 176-177.- Tiverios 1985, 82-83.
[233] Roebuck 1959,110-115. 119-124.- Boardman 1980, 241-243.- Legon 1981, 78-85 mit Karte Nr. 4.

Ambitionen in Koloniegründungen, versuchte jedoch seit dem frühen 6. Jh. am Hellespont in Sigeion, an der gegenüberliegenden Nordküste und auf der Thrakischen Chersonesos Fuß zu fassen.[234] Allerdings ist mit Getreideimporten für die Stadt aus dem Schwarzmeergebiet im 6. Jh. noch nicht zu rechnen.[235] Ägina konnte sich im Seehandel erst im späteren 6. Jh. behaupten, als die Tätigkeit der ionischen *Poleis* auf diesem Gebiet allmählich stagnierte; sie übernahm den Handel mit attischer Keramik in Etrurien, trat im Schwarzen Meer und Naukratis jedoch kaum in Erscheinung.[236] Auch Korinth scheint überwiegend im westlichen Mittelmeerbereich Handel getrieben zu haben; das Vorkommen korinthischer Keramik im Osten und im Schwarzmeergebiet zusammen mit ionischer Keramik gilt als Hinweis auf ionische Zwischenhändler.[237] Somit scheiden Athen, Ägina und Korinth im wesentlichen als Transporteure attischer Keramik im 6. Jh. für das westliche Kleinasien aus.[238]

Der Handel in Ionien und in den benachbarten Landschaften sowie der Transport in das Landesinnere lag wohl in griechischer Hand, denn "der Handel an sich war eine griechische Angelegenheit".[239] Dies wird sich auch nach der Machtübernahme der Perser kaum geändert haben, da bei den Persern das Geldwesen und der Handel weniger entwickelt und Marktplätze unbekannt waren (Hdt. 1. 153; Strabo 15. 3. 19).[240] Vorteilhaft für den Handel waren vor allem die gut ausgebauten und gesicherten Karawanenstraßen, die alle Provinzen des Persischen Reiches miteinander verbanden.[241] Die sog. Königsstraße (Hdt. 5. 52- 53) begann im lydischen Satrapensitz Sardeis und führte über Phrygien und den Halys durch Kappadokien und Kilikien, ferner über den Euphrat durch Mesopotamien entlang des Tigris, östlich des Zagros-Gebirges bis Susa.[242] Auf diesen Straßen wird auch die attische Keramik in die Satrapensitze Sardeis und Daskyleion bis nach Gordion in Zentralanatolien transportiert worden sein.[243]

Der Wert bemalter attischer Keramik als Handelsgut ist Gegenstand langjähriger Diskussionen.[244] Nach den eingeritzten Angaben auf Vasen des 5. und 4. Jhs., ergaben sich die Preise durch die Größe der Gefäße und aus der Anzahl der dargestellten Figuren in ihrer Bemalung. So konnte eine bemalte Hydria zwischen 1,5 bis 3 Drachmen, eine Amphora zwischen 5-7 Obole (6 Obole=1 Drachme), ein Kolonettenkrater 10 Obole, eine Lekythos zwischen 2/3 bis 6 Obole und ein Skyphos 1/2 Obol kosten. Es dürfte sich bei diesen Angaben um Werkstattpreise im Kerameikos handeln und nicht um Endabnehmer-Preise. Waren die Gefäße gefüllt (mit Oliven, Öl, Duftöl u. a.), werden sie entsprechend teurer gewesen sein. Ob die Preise nun als teuer oder billig anzusehen sind, kann nur anhand der Lebenshaltungskosten erschlossen werden. Der Tageslohn eines Schreiners oder Matrosen betrag im 5. Jh. eine Drachme, sicherlich doppelt soviel mußte ein Käufer für eine Amphora aus Athen in Ionien bezahlen. Die Zahlen sprechen dafür, daß bemalte attische Keramik über einen beträchtlichen Wert als Handelsware verfügte.[245] Wie kostbar attische Vasen dem Endabnehmer im fernen Kleinasien waren, zeigen auch die zahlreichen Reparaturlöcher, mit denen zerbrochene Gefäße zusammengeflickt und zur Zierde weiterbenutzt wurden.[246]

Abkürzungsverzeichnis

Außer den Abkürzungen der Archäologischen Bibliographie und des *Archäologischen Anzeigers* 1997, 699ff. gelten hier:

Add. Alt-Smyrna	Y. Tuna-Nörling, 'Addenda zur attisch-schwarzfigurigen Keramik aus Alt-Smyrna (Bayraklı)' (in Druck)
Ägina I	W. Felten, 'Attische schwarzfigurige und rotfigurige Keramik' in: *Alt-Ägina*, II,1 (Mainz 1982)
Ägina II	M.B. Moore, 'Aegina, Aphaia-Temple VIII, The Attic Black-Figure Pottery', *AA* 1986, 51-73
Agora XXIII	M.B. Moore and M.Z. Pease Philippides, *The Athenian Agora XXIII, Attic Black-Figured Pottery* (Princeton 1986)
Alt-Smyrna & Pitane	Y. Tuna-Nörling, 'Die Ausgrabungen von Alt-Smyrna und Pitane. Die Attisch-Schwarzfigurige Keramik und der Attische Keramikexport

---

[234] Roebuck 1959, 109-110.- Boardman 1980, 264-266.
[235] Garnsey 1988, 107-113.- Tsetskhladze 1998, 54-57.
[236] Figueira 1986, 246-247. 272-277.- Kreuzer 1994, 113-115.
[237] Salmon 1984, 139-144. Zur korinthischen Keramik im Schwarzmeergebiet s. Bouzek 1979, 38-39 mit Lit.
[238] Entgegen der Meinung von Roebuck 1950, 238.- Roebuck 1959, 81.- Tiverios 1985, 84.
[239] Braund 1995, 168.
[240] Dandamaev und Lukonin 1989, 195-206. 212-213.- Högemann 1992, 220.
[241] s. dazu: Dandamaev-Lukonin 1989, 210.- Wiesehöfer 1982, 5-14.- Graf 1994, 167-180.
[242] Zu den verschiedenen Theorien zum Verlauf der sog. Königsstraße s. Graf 1994, 175-180.
[243] Birmingham 1961.- Langlotz 1966, 11-13.- Miller 1997, 71.- Zu den Funden: Sardeis.- Daskyleion I und II.- Sams 1979.- De Vries 1997.

[244] Johnston 1979, 33.- Vickers 1985.- Boardman 1987.- Boardman 1988a und 1988b.- Gill und Vickers 1989.- Gill und Vickers 1990.- Vickers und Gill 1994, 4. 13. 85-88. 106. 149.- Arafat und Morgan 1994, 108-110.- Kreuzer 1994, 106-107.
[245] Boardman 1988a, 29-30.- Sparkes 1991, 129-131.- Kreuzer 106.
[246] Phokaia II Kat. 5.- Klazomenai Kat. 21.- Daskyleion I 16.

Antandros I	nach Kleinasien', *IstForsch* 41 (Tübingen 1995) B. Yalman, 'Antandros Nekropol Kazısı', *III. Müze Kurtarma Kazıları Semineri 1992* (Ankara 1993) 449-487	Gryneion	1990) T. Özkan, '1992 yılı Gryneion Kazısı Çalıµmaları', *IV.* In: *Müze Kurtarma Kazıları Semineri 1993* (Ankara 1994) 1-15.
Antandros II	Ö. Özeren, F. Ünal and A. Üner, 'Antandros Nekropolü 1995 yılı Kurtarma Kazısı', *VII. Müze Kurtarma Kazıları Semineri 1996* (Ankara 1997) 161-177	Heuneburg	E. Böhr, 'Die griechische Keramik der Heuneburg' in: W. Kimmig (eds.), Importe und mediterrane Einflüsse auf der Heuneburg, *Heuneburg Studien XI, Römisch-Germanische Forschungen* 59 (Mainz 2000) 1-26
APP	J. H. Oakley, W. D. E. Coulsen and O. Palagia (eds.), *Athenian Potters and Painters. The Conference Proceedings* (Oxford 1997)	Histria IV	P. Alexandrescu, *Histria IV. La céramique d'époque archaique et classique (VIIe-Ive s.)* (Bukarest 1978)
Assos I	Chr. Ellinghaus, 'Korinthische und attische Keramik' *Asia Minor Studien* 2 (Bonn 1990) 63-67	Kerameikos VII,2	E. Kunze, Götte, K. Tancke und K. Vierneisel, *Kerameikos VI,2. Die Nekropole von der Mitte des 6. bis zum Ende des 5. Jhs.* (München 1999)
Assos II	A. Filges, 'Korinthische und attische Keramik der archaischen und klassischen Zeit' in: *Asia Minor Studien* 5, Ausgrabungen in Assos 1990 (Bonn 1992) 109-140	Kerameikos IX	U. Knigge, *Kerameikos* IX. Der Südhügel (Berlin 1976)
		Kition	M. Robertson, 'Attic Black-Figure and Red-Figure Pottery'. In: *Excavations at Kition* IV. The Non- Cypriote Pottery (1981) 51-73
Assos III	A. Filges, 'Korinthische und attische Keramik der archaischen und klassischen Zeit II' in: *Asia Minor Studien* 10, Ausgrabungen in Assos 1991 (Bonn 1993) 101-130	Klazomenai	Y. Tuna-Nörling, *Attische Keramik aus Klazomenai* (Saarbrücken 1996)
Caere 3.1	M. Cristofani (eds.), *CAERE 3.1 Lo scavico arcaico della vigna parrocchiale*, I (Rom 1992)	Korinth I	A.B. Brownlee, 'Attic Black-Figure from Corinth: I', *Hesperia* 56, 1987, 73-95
Cl Rh 3	G. Jacopi, *Clara Rhodos III. Scavi nella Necropoli Jalisso 1924-1928* (Rhodos 1936)	Korinth II	A.B. Brownlee, 'Attic Black-Figure from Corinth: II', *Hesperia* 58, 1989, 361-395
Cyprus	E. Gjerstad, *Greek Geometric and Archaic Pottery found in Cyprus* (Stockholm 1977)	Korinth III	A.B. Brownlee, 'Attic Black-Figure from Corinth: III', *Hesperia* 64, 1995, 337-375
Daskyleion I	Y. Tuna-Nörling, *Daskyleion I. Die attische Keramik*, Arkeoloji Dergisi VI, 1998 (İzmir 1999).	Kyrene	M.B. Moore, 'Attic Black Figure and Attic Black Pattern'. In: *The Extramural Sanctuary of Demeter and Persephone at Cyrene, Libya. Final Reports* III,II (Philadelphia 1987) 1-41
Daskyleion II	K. Görkay, 'Attic black-figure pottery from Daskyleion', *Asia Minor Studien* 34, Studien zum antiken Kleinasien IV, 1999, 1-100	Morgantina	C.L. Lyons, *Morgantina Studies* V. The Arcaic Cemeteries (Princeton 1996)
Ephesos XII, 1	A. Gasser, *Die korinthische und attische Importkeramik vom Artemision in Ephesos, Forschungen in Ephesos* XII/1 (1989)	Mytilene	G.F. Schaus, 'Archaic imported fine ware from the Acropolis, Mytilene', *Hesperia* 61, 1992, 355-374
Fratte	G. Greco e A. Pondraldolfo (eds.), *Fratte. Un insedia-mento etrusco-campano* (Modena	Naukratis	M.S. Venit, *Greek Painted Pottery fron Naukratis in*

Nymphenheiligtum	Ch. Papadopoulou-Kanellopoulou, *IEPO THΣ NYΦEΣ* (Athen 1997)
Old Smyrna	J. Boardman, 'Old Smyrna: The Attic Pottery', *BSA* 53-54, 1958/59, 152-181
Phanagoria	C. Morgan, *Attic Pottery from Phanagoria* (im Druck)
Phokaia I	Y. Tuna-Nörling, 'Phokaia Attika Seramiğinden Seçmeler', *Arkeoloji ve Sanat* 59, 1993, 16-27
Phokaia II	Y. Tuna-Nörling, *Attische Keramik aus Phokaia* (im Druck)
Rf. Alt-Smyrna	Y. Tuna-Nörling, 'Die attisch rotfigurige Keramik von Alt-Smyrna', *IstMitt* 48, 1998, 173-191
Samos XXII	B. Kreuzer, *Die attisch schwarzfigurige Keramik aus dem Heraion von Samos*, Samos XXII (Mainz 1998)
Samothrake	M.B. Moore, 'Attic Black Figure from Samothrace', *Hesperia* 44, 1975, 234-250
Sardeis	N.H. Ramage, 'The Attic Pottery'. In: The Corinthian, Attic and Laconian Pottery from Sardis, *Archaeological Exploration of Sardis* 10 (Cambridge, Massachusetts, London 1997) 63-121
"Schale"	K. Vierneisel und B. Kaeser (eds.), *Kunst der Schale. Kultur des Trinkens* (München 1990).
Siana Cups I	H.A.G. Brijder, *Siana Cups I and Komast Cups* (Amsterdam 1983)
Siana Cups II	H.A.G. Brijder, *Siana Cups II The Heidelberg Painter* (Amsterdam 1991)
Siana Cups III	H.A.G. Brijder, *Siana Cups III. The Red-Black Painter, Griffin-Bird Painter and Siana Cups resembling Lip-Cups* (Amsterdam 2000)
Sindos	*ΣΙΝΔΟΣ. ΚΑΤΑΛΟΓΟΣ ΤΗΣ ΕΚΘΕΣΗΣ* (Athen 1985)
Südl. d. Akropolis	Ch. Papadopoulou-Kanellopoulou, Ἀνασκαφὴ "Νοτίως Ἀκροπόλεος". Μελανόμορφη κεραμεικὴ, *ADelt* 27, 1972, Meletai, 185-302
Tenedos T.	Özkan, '1990 yılı Tenedos Nekropol çalışmaları'. In: *II. Müze Kurtarma Kazıları Semineri 1991* (Ankara 1992) 1-9
Thorikos VII	Th. K. Cheliotis, 'A Haimonian Kylix'. In: *Thorikos* VII, 1970/71 (Gent 1978) 131-154
Tracia Bulgara	M. Reho, *La ceramica attica a figure nere e rosse nella Tracia Bulgara* (Rom 1990)
Xanthos IV	H. Metzger, *Fouilles de Xanthos* IV. *Les céramique archaiques et classiques de l'acropole lycienne* (Paris 1972)

Bibliographie

Akurgal, E. 1950: 'Bayraklı Kazısı/Bayraklı', *Ankara Üniversitesi, Dil ve Tarih-Coğrafya Fakültesi Dergisi* 8/1, 1950, 1-97 (Ankara).

Akurgal, E. 1983: *Eski İzmir I. Yerleşme Katları ve Athena Tapınağı* (Ankara).

Akurgal, E. 1993: *Eski Çağda Ege ve İzmir* (İzmir) 55-59

Akurgal, E. 1995: 'La Grèce de l'est berceau de la civilisation occidentale'. In *Phocée et la fondation de Marseilles, Musées de Marseille*, Ausstellungskatalog (Marseille) 31-46.

Arafat, K. und Morgan, C. 1994: 'Athens, Etruria and the Heuneburg: mutual misconceptions in the study of Greek- barbarian relations'. In: Morris, I. (eds.), *Classical Greece: Ancient Histories and Modern Archaeologies* (Cambridge) 108-134

Austin, M. und Vidal-Naquet, P. 1984: *Gesellschaft und Wirtschaft im alten Griechenland*, München.

Bakır, G. 1982: 'Urla/Klazomenai kazısı 1981 yılı çalışmaları raporu', *IV. Kazı Sonuçları Toplantısı*, (Ankara) 63-68.

Bakır, T. und Gusmani, R. 1993: 'Graffiti aus Daskyleion', *Kadmos* 32, 135-144.

Balcer, J.M. 1991: 'The East Greeks under Persian Rule: a Reassessment'. In: Sancisi-Weerdenburg, H. and Kuhrt, A. (eds.), *Achaemenid History VI, Asia Minor and Egypt: Old Cultures in a New Empire. Proceedings of the Groningen 1988 Achaemenid History Workshop* (Leiden) 57-65.

Balcer, J.M. 1995: *The Persian Conquest of the Greeks 545-450 BC*, Xenia Heft 38 (Konstanz).

Bayburtluoğlu, C. 1975: *Erythrai. Coğrafya-Tarih-Kaynaklar-Kalıntılar*, Ankara.

Birmingham, J.M. 1961: 'The overland route across Anatolia in the eighth and seventh centuries B.C.', *Anatolian Studies* 11, 185-195.

Blegen, C.W., Palmer, H. und Young, R.S. 1964: *Corinth XIII, The North Cemetery*, Princeton.

Blinkenberg, C. 1931: *Lindos. Fouilles de l'Acropole 1902- 1914, I*, Berlin.

Boardman, J 1967: *Excavations at Chios 1952-1955, The Greek Emporio*, London.
Boardman, J. 1974: *Schwarzfigurige Vasen aus Athen*, Mainz.
Boardman, J. 1979: 'The Athenian Pottery Trade', *Expedition* 21, Summer 1979, 33-39.
Boardman, J. 1980: *The Greeks Overseas*, 3rd Ed., London.
Boardman, J. 1987: 'Silver is white'. *RA*, 279-295.
Boardman, J. 1988a: 'Trade in Greek decorated pottery'. *OJA* 7, 27-33.
Boardman, J. 1988b: 'The trade figures'. *OJA* 7, 371-373.
Boehlau, J. 1898: *Aus Ionischen und Italischen Nekropolen*, Leipzig.
Boitani, F. 1971: 'Ceramiche e lucerne di importazione greca e ceramiche locali dal riempimento del Vanoc'. *NSc* 25. Ser.8, 1971, 242-285.
Bouzek, J. 1990: *Studies of Greek Pottery in the Black Sea Area*, Prague.
Braun, T.F.R .G. 1982: 'The Greeks in Egypt'. In: *The Cambridge Ancient History*, 3^2,3, 36-43.
Braund, D.C. 1995: 'Fish from the Black Sea: classical Byzantium and the Greekness of Trade'. In: Wilkins, J., Harvey, D. and Dobson, M. (eds.), *Food in Antiquity* (Exeter) 162-170.
Burow, J. 1989: *Der Antimenesmaler*, Mainz.
Callipolitis- Feytmans, D. 1965: *Les "Loutéria" Attiques*, Athen.
Callipolitis-Feytmans, D. 1974: *Les plats attiques à figures noires*, Paris.
Cristofani, M. 1981: *Gli Etruschi in Maremma*, Milano
Cook, J.M. 1958/1959: 'Old Smyrna, 1948-51'. *BSA* 53-54, 1-34.
Cook, J.M. 1961: 'The Problems of Classical Ionia'. *Proceedings of the Cambridge Philological Society* 7, 9-18.
Çoşkun, G.: *Daskyleion Siyah Firnisli Attika Seramiği* (unpublizierte Magisterarbeit Ege Universtät İzmir).
CVA Deutschland 38, Kassel, Antikenabteilung der Staatlichen Kunstsammlungen 2 (P. Kranz u. R. Lullies).
CVA USA 25, The J. Paul Getty Museum, Malibu 2 (A.J. Clark).
CVA Russia 1, Pushkin State Museum of Fine Arts (N. Sidorova).
Dandamaev, M.A. 1989: *A political History of the Achaemenid Empire*, Leiden.
Dandamaev, M.A. and Lukonin, V.G. 1989: *The Culture and Social Institutions of Ancient Iran*, Cambridge.
DeVries, K. 1977: 'Attic Pottery in the Achaemenid Empire'. *AJA* 81, 544-548.
DeVries, K. 1997: 'Attic Pottery from Gordion'. In: *APP*, 447-455.
Diehl, E. 1964: *Die Hydria: Formgeschichte und Verwendung im Kult des Altertums*, Mainz.

Dunbabin, T.J. 1962: *Perachora II, The Sanctuaries of Hera Akraia and Limenia*, Oxford.
Ehrhardt, N. 1983: *Milet und seine Kolonien*, Frankfurt a.M.
Figueira, Th. J. 1986: *Aegina-Society and politics*, Nachdruck, Salem, New Hampshire.
Fıratlı, N. 1978: 'New discoveries concerning the first settlement of ancient İstanbul-Byzantion'. In: *X. International Congress in Classical Archaeology, Ankara* (Ankara), 565-574.
Frank, S. 1990: *Attische Kelchkratere. Eine Untersuchung zum Zusammenspiel von Gefäßform und Bemalung*, Frankfurt a.M.
Gans, U. 1991: 'Die Grabung auf dem Zeytintepe'. In: v. Graeve, V., 'Milet 1990'. *IstMitt* 41, 1991, 137-140.
Garland, R. 1985: *The Greek Way of Death*, London.
Gelder, H. van 1900: *Geschichte der Alten Rhodier*, Leiden.
Garnsey, P. 1988: *Famine and Food Supply in the Graeco-Roman World*, Cambridge.
Gill, D. W. J. und Vickers, M. 1989: 'Pots and Kettles'. *RA*, 297-303.
Gill, D. W. J. and Vickers, M. 1990: 'Reflected glory: pottery and precious metal'. *JdI* 105, 1-30.
Graf, D.F. 1994: 'The Persian Road System'. In: Sancisi-Weerdenburg, H., Kuhrt, A. und Cool Root, M. (eds.), *Achaemenid History VIII. Continuity and Change. Proceedings of the last Achaemenid History Workshop April 6-8, 1990 Ann Arbor, Michigan* (Leiden) 167-189.
Güngör, Ü. 1994: *Klazomenai Karantina Adası Sondajı Tabakalanması* (Unpublizierte Magisterarbeit Ege Universität İzmir).
Hannestad, L. 1988: 'The Athenian Potter and the home market'. In: Christiansen, J. and Melander, T. (eds.), *Proceedings of the 3rd Symposium on Ancient Greek and Related Pottery, Copenhagen 1987* (Kopenhagen) 222-229.
Heinrich, H. und Senff, R. 1992: ' Die Grabung auf dem Kalabaktepe' . In: v. Graeve, V., 'Milet 1991'. *IstMitt* 42, 100-104.
Heinz, M. und Senff, R. 1995:' Die Grabung auf dem Zeytintepe'. In: v. Graeve, V., 'Milet 1992-1993'. *AA*, 220-224.
Högemann, P. 1992: *Das alte Vorderasien und die Achämeniden*, Beihefte zum Tübinger Atlas des Vorderen Orients 98, Wiesbaden.
Hornblower, S. 1983: *The Greek World 479-323 B.C.*, London/New York.
Jeffery, L.H. 1964: 'Old Smyrna: Inscriptions on sherds and small objects'. *BSA* 59, 39-49.
Johnston, A.W. 1979: *Trademarks on Greek Vases*, Warminster.
Kaeser, B. 1990: 'Griechische Vasen Trinkgeschirr'. In: *"Schale"*, 186-193.
Karwiese, St. 1995: *Groß ist die Artemis von Ephesos: die*

Geschichte einer der grossen Städte der Antike, Wien.

Kerschner, M. 1995: 'Die Ostterrasse des Kalabaktepe'. In: v. Graeve, 'V., Milet 1992-1993'. *AA* 1995, 214-220.

Kerschner, M. 1999: 'Das Artemisheiligtum auf der Ostterrasse der Kalabaktepe in Milet'. *AA*, 7-51.

Kienast, H.J. 1998: 'Der Niedergang des Tempels des Theodoros'. *AM* 113, 111-131.

Kluiver, J. 1992: 'The 'Tyrrhenian' Group: its origin and the neck-amphorae in the Netherlands and Belgium'. *BABesch* 67, 73-109.

Kluiver, J. 1997: *The 'Tyrrhenian' Group: Athenian Black- Figure Vases from ca. 570/565- 545 B.C.* (Diss. Uni. Amsterdam).

Knibbe, D. und Langmann, G. 1993: *Via Sacra Ephesiaca I, Berichte und Materialien Österreichisches Archäologisches Institut* 3, Wien.

Knibbe, D. 1998: *Ephesus. Geschichte einer bedeutenden antiken Stadt und Portrait einer modernen Grossgrabung* (Frankfurt a.M.)

Koukouli-Chrysanthaki, Ch. 1983: 'ΑΝΑΣΚΦΙΚΕΣ ΕΡΕΥΝΕΣΣΤΗΝ ΑΡΧΑΙ ΤΡΑΓΙΛΟ. ΠΡ ΤΕΣ ΓΕΝΙΚΕΣ ΑΡΧΑΙΟΛΟΓΙΚΕΣ ΙΣΤΟΡΙΚΕΣ ΠΑΡΑ ΤΗΡΗΣΕΙΣ'. *Archaia Makedonia* III, 123-146

Koukouli-Chyrsanthaki, Ch. 1994: 'The Cemeteries of Abdera'. In: de la Geniere, J. (eds.), *Nécropoles et sociétés antiques. Actes du Colloque International du Centre de Recherches Archéologiques de l'Université de Lille III, Lille, 2-3 Décembre 1991*, Cahier du Centre Jean Bérard, 18 (Neapel), 33-77.

Kreuzer, B. Preisamphoren: 'Die Panathenaäischen Preisamphoren aus dem Heraion von Samos: Ein Vorbericht'. In: Bentz, M. und Eschbach, N. (eds.), *Panathenaika, Akten des Kongresses, Giessen 1999* (im Druck).

Kreuzer, B. 1994: 'Überlegungen zum Handel mit bemalter Keramik im 6. Jahrhundert v. Chr. unter besonderer Berücksichtigung des heraion von Samos'. *KLIO* 76, 103 119.

Kurtz, D.C. und Boardman, J. 1985: *Thanatos. Tod und Jenseits bei den Griechen*, Mainz.

Langlotz, E. 1966: *Die Hellenisierung der Küsten des Mittelmeers durch die Stadt Phokaia*, Köln.

Langmann, G. 1967: 'Eine spätarchaische Nekropole unter dem Staatsmarkt zu Ephesos'. In: *Festschrift für Fritz Eichler*. ÖJh Beih. 1 (Wien) 103-123.

Legon, R. P. 1981: *Megara. The Political History of a Greek City-State to 336 B.C.*, Ithaca, NY.

Lenschau, Th. 1913: 'Zur Geschichte Ioniens', *Klio* 13, 175-183

Lioutas, A. 1987: *Attische schwarzfigurige Lekanai und Lekanides*, Beiträge zur Archäologie 18, Würzburg.

Lissarrague, F. 1990a: 'Around the Krater: An Aspect of Banquet Imagery'. In: Murray, O. (eds.), *Sympotica. A symposium on the Symposion* (1990) 196-209.

Lissarrague, F. 1990b: *L'autre guerrier. Archers, peltastes, cavaliers dans l'imagerie attique*, Paris.

Löwe, W. 1996: 'Die Kassler Grabung 1894 in der Nekropoel der Stadt'. In: *SAMOS- die Kasseler Grabung 1894 in der Nekropole der archaischen Stadt von Johannes Boehlau und Edward Habbich,* (Kassel), 24-107.

Luke, J. 1994: 'The Krater, Kratos and the Polis'. *Greece & Rome* 41, 23-32.

Martelli, M. 1985: 'Iuoghi e i prodotti della scambio'. In: Cristofani, M. (eds.), *Civiltà degli Etruschi, Ausstellung Florenz* (Mailand), 175-224.

Meiggs, R. 1972: *The Athenian Empire,* Oxford.

Miller, M.C. 1997: *Athens and Persia in the Fifth Century,* Cambridge.

Möller, D.A. 2000: *Naukratis: Trade in Archaic Greece,* Oxford,

Murray, O. 1988: 'The Ionian Revolt'. In: *The Cambridge Ancient History IV^2* (Cambridge), 461-490.

Müller-Wiener, W. 1983: 'Milet Kazıları', V. Kazı Sonuçları Toplantısı (Ankara), 247-250.

Pagliardi, M.N.1972: ' Sibari'. *Suppl. NSc* 26. Ser.8, 52-143.

Paribeni, E. 1972: 'Un gruppo di frammenti attici a figure nere da Cortona'. *StEtr* 40, 1972, 391-396.

Philipp, H. 1981: 'Archaische Gräber in Ostionien'. *IstMitt* 31, 149-166.

Philippaki, B. 1967: *The Attic Stamnos,* Oxford.

Polat, G. 1988: *Klazomenai 4. Yüzyıl Siyah Firnis Keramiği* (unpublizierte Diplomarbeit, Ege Universität İzmir).

Roberts, S.R. 1978: *The Attic Pyxis,* Chicago.

Roebuck, C. 1950: 'The Grain Trade between Greece and Egypt'. *ClPhil* 45, 236-247.

Roebuck, C. 1951: 'The Organization of Naukratis'. *ClPhil* 46, 212-220.

Roebuck, C. 1959: *Ionian Trade and Colonization,* New York.

Roebuck, C. 1986: 'Chios in the sixth century BC'. In: Boardman, J. and Vaphopoulou-Richardson, C.E., (eds.), *Chios. A Conference at the Homereion in Chios 1984* (Oxford), 81-88.

Roebuck, C. 1988: 'Trade'. In: *The Cambridge Ancient History IV^2,* 446-460.

Rotroff, S.I. and Oakley, J.H. 1992: *Debris from a Public Dining Place in the Athenian Agora,* Hesperia Suppl. 25, Princeton.

Sabbione, C. 1987: 'Matauros'. In: Lattanzi, E., (ed.), *Il museo nazionale di Reggio Calabria* (Rom), 108-114.

Şahin, S. 1983: 'Bir vazo üzerinde arkaik mülkiyet yazıtı, Derippos-şişesi'. In: Akurgal 1983, 113-114.

Salmon, J.B. 1984: *Wealthy Corinth-A History of the City to 338 BC,* Oxford.

Sams, G.K. 1979: 'Imports at Gordion'. *Expedition* 21.4, 6-17.

San Pietro, A. 1991: *La ceramica a figure nere die San Biagio (Metaponto)*, Galatina.

Sarikakis, T.C. 1986: 'Commercial Relations between Chios and other Greek Cities in Antiquity'. In: Boardman, J., Vaphopoulou-Richardson, C.E., (eds.), *Chios. A Conference at the Homereion in Chios 1984* (Oxford), 121-130.

Schaus, G.F. 1992: Archaic imported fine ware from the Acropolis, Mytilene. *Hesperia* 61, 355-395.

Schaus, G.1985: 'The East Greek, Island and Laconian Pottery'. In: White, D., (eds.), *The Extramural Sanctuary of Demeter and Persephone at Cyrene, Libya. Final Reports II*, Philadelphia.

Shear, T.L. Jr. 1993: 'The Persian Destruction of Athens: Evidence fron the Agora Deposits'. *Hesperia* 62, 383-482.

Scheffer, Ch. 1988: 'Workshop and Trade Patterns in Athenian Black-Figure'. In: Christiansen, J.-Melander, T., (eds.), *Proceedings of the 3rd Symposium on Ancient Greek and Related Pottery, Kopenhagen 1987* (Copenhagen), 536-544.

Scheibler, I. 1983: *Griechische Töpferkunst. Herstellung, Handel und Gebrauch der antiken Tongefäße*, München.

Scheibler, I. 1987: 'Bild und Gefäß. Die ikonographische und funktionale Bedeutung der attischen Bildfeldamphoren'. *JdI* 102, 58-118.

Schiering, W. 1979: 'Milet: Eine Erweiterung der Grabung östlich des Athenatempels'. *IstMitt* 29, 77-108.

Schiering, W. 1983: *Die Griechischen Tongefäße. Gestalt, Bestimmung und Formwandel^2*, Berlin.

Schleiffenbaum, H.E. 1991: *Der attische Volutenkrater*, Frankfurt a. M.

Senff, R. 1992: 'Die Grabungen auf dem Zeytintepe'. In: v. Graeve, V., 'Milet 1991'. *IstMitt* 42, 105-108.

Senff, R. 1995: 'Die Grabung am Kalabaktepe'. In: v. Graeve, V., 'Milet 1992-1993'. *AA*, 208-213.

Shefton, B.B. 1994: 'Massalia and Colonization in the North-Western Mediterranean'. In: Tsetskhladze, G.R. und De Angelis, F. (eds.), *The Archaeology of Greek Colonisation. Essays dedicated to Sir John Boardman* (Oxford), 61-86.

Shipley, G. 1987: *A History of Samos 800-188 B.C.*, Oxford.

Simon, C. 1986: *The Archaic Votive Offerings and the Cults of Ionia* (Diss., University of California, Berkeley).

Sparkes, B.A. 1991: *Greek Pottery. An Introduction*, Manchester/New York.

Starr, C.G.1975: 'Greeks and Persians in the fourth century B.C.'. *Iranica Antiqua* 11, 1975, 39-115.

Tiverios, M. 1981: *ΠΡΟΒΛΗΜΑΤΑ ΤΗΣ ΜΕΛΑΝΟΜΟΡΦΗΣ ΑΤΤΙΚΗΣ ΚΕΡΑΜΙΚΗΣ*, Thessaloniki.

Tiverios, M., Manakidou, M. und Tsiafaki, D. 1994: 'ΑΝΑΣΚΦΙΚΕΣ ΕΡΥΝΕΣ ΣΤΟ ΚΑΡΑΜΠΟΥΡΝΑΚΙ ΚΑΤΑ ΤΟ 1994: Ο ΑΡΧΑΙΟΣ ΟΙΚΙΣΜΟΣ'. *AErgoMak* 8, 197-202.

Tölle-Kastenbein, R. 1974: *Samos XIV. Das Kastro Tigani*, Bonn.

Trinkl, E. 1999: 'Fragmente eines attischen Schalenskyphos in Silhouettentechnik aus Ephesos'. *ÖJh* 68 Beibl., 206-219.

Touchefeu-Meynier, O. 1972: 'Un nouveau "phormiskos" à figures noires'. *RA*, 93-102.

Tronchetti, C. 1983: *Ceramica attica a figure nere, Museo Archeologico di Tarquinia*, Rome.

Tsakos, K. 1970: 'ΣΑΜΟΣ. ΑΝΑΣΚΑΦΑΙ'. *ADelt* 25-2,2, 416-418.

Tsakos, K. 1980a: 'ΕΝΑ ΙΕΡΟ ΤΗΣ ΑΡΤΕΜΙΔΟΣ ΣΤΗ ΣΑΜΟ'. *AAA* 13, 305-318.

Tsakos, K. 1980b: 'ΣΑΜΟΣ'. *ADelt* 35, 460-472.

Tsetskhladze, G.R. 1994: 'Greek Penetration of the Black Sea'. In: Tsetskhladze, G.R. and De Angelis, F. (eds.), *The Archaeology of Greek Colonisation. Essays dedicated to Sir John Boardman* (Oxford) 111-135.

Tsetskhladze, G.R. 1998: 'Trade on the Black Sea in the archaic and classical periods: some observations'. In: Parkins, H. and Smith, Ch. (eds.), *Trade, Traders and the Ancient City*, London.

Tuchelt, K. 1988: 'Die Perserzerstörung von Branchidai-Didyma und ihre Folgen- archäologisch betrachtet'. *AA*, 427-438.

Tuna-Nörling, Y. 1997: 'Attic Black-Figure Export to the East: "The 'Tyrrhenian Group' in Ionia". In: *APP* 435-446.

Tuna-Nörling, Y. 1999: 'Hektor's Ransom on a krater from Tekirdağ'. In: Docter, R.F. und Moorman, E.M. (eds.), *Proceedings of the XVth International Congress of Classical Archaeology, Amsterdam, July 12-17, 1998* (Amsterdam), 418-420.

Tuna-Nörling, Y. 2001: 'Polyxena bei Hektors Lösung', *AA* (im Druck).

Utili, F. 1999: *Die archaische Nekropole von Assos*, Asia Minor Studien 31, Bonn.

Vickers, M. 1985: 'Artful crafts: influence of metalwork on Athenian painted pottery'. *JHS*, 108-128.

Vickers, M. and Gill, D. W. J. 1994: *Artful Crafts: Ancient Greek Silverware and Pottery*, Oxford.

Villard, F. 1992: 'La céramique archaique de Marseille'. In: Bats, M., Berucchi, G., Congés, G. and Tréziny, H. (eds.), *Marseille grecque et la Gaule. Actes, Colloque international d'histoire et d'archéology et du ve congrès archéologique de Gaule méridionale, Marseille 1990*. Lattes und Aix-en-Provence, Etudes Massaliètes 3, 163-170.

Voigtländer, W. 1982: 'Funde aus der Insula westlich des Buleuterion in Milet'. *IstMitt* 32, 30-173.

Vokotopoulou, J. 1994: 'Anciennes nécropoles de la Chalcidique'. In: de la Geniere, J. (ed.),

Nécropoles et sociétés antiques. Actes du Colloque International du Centre de Recherches Archéologiques de l'Université de Lille III, Lille, 2-3 Décembre 1991, Cahier du Centre Jean Bérard, 18 (Neapel), 79-98.

Vokotopoulou, J. 1996: 'Cities and sanctuaries of the archaic period in Chalkidike'. *BSA* 91, 1996, 319-328.

v. Graeve, V. 1986: 'Grabung auf dem Kalabaktepe'. In: Müller-Wiener, W., v. Graeve, V., Pfrommer, M. und Pütz, St., 'Milet 1985'. *IstMitt* 36, 37-51.

v. Graeve, V. 1987: 'Grabung auf dem Kalabaktepe'. In: Müller-Wiener, W., v. Graeve, V., Pfrommer, M. und Pütz, St., 'Milet 1986'. *IstMitt* 37, 6-34.

v. Graeve, V. 1988: 'Notgrabung in der archaischen Nekropole von Milet'. In: Müller-Wiener, W. und v. Graeve, V., 'Milet 1987'. *IstMitt* 38, 253-278.

v. Graeve, V. 1990: 'Der Schnitt auf dem Gipfelplateau des Kalabaktepe 1988'. In: v. Graeve, V., 'Milet 1989'. *IstMitt* 40, 39-50.

v. Graeve, V. und R. Senff 1991: 'Die Grabung auf dem Kalabaktepe'. In: v. Graeve, V., 'Milet 1991'. *IstMitt* 41, 100-104.

Waiblinger, A. 1978: 'La Ville Grecque d'Éléonte en Chersonèse de Thrace et sa Nécropole', *CRAI*, 843-857.

Walser, G. 1984: *Hellas und Iran*, Darmstadt.

Walter, H. 1990: *Das griechische Heiligtum, dargestellt am Heraion von Samos*, Stuttgart.

Wiesehöfer, J. 1982: *Beobachtungen zum Handel des Achämenidenreiches*, Münstersche Beiträge zur Antiken Handelsgeschichte 1, Münster.

Yfanditis, K. 1990: *Antike Gefäße. Kataloge der Staatlichen Kunstsammlungen Kassel Nr. 16*, Melsungen.

www.ingramcontent.com/pod-product-compliance
Lightning Source LLC
Chambersburg PA
CBHW041704290426
44108CB00027B/2845